You Never Call!
You Never Write!

"Hello Momma" (or "Phone Call from Momma")—George Jessel's one-sided conversations with his mother—was the entertainer's trademark skit. "Hello Mama, this is George. Isn't it nice to have your own phone? What? Nobody calls you? Even before you had the phone, nobody called you either?" The monologue went on from there, with Jessel embellishing it every time. (Carl Rose)

You Never Call!
You Never Write!

A History of the Jewish Mother

JOYCE ANTLER

OXFORD
UNIVERSITY PRESS
2007

OXFORD

UNIVERSITY PRESS

Oxford University Press, Inc., publishes works that further
Oxford University's objective of excellence
in research, scholarship, and education.

Oxford   New York
Auckland   Cape Town   Dar es Salaam   Hong Kong   Karachi
Kuala Lumpur   Madrid   Melbourne   Mexico City   Nairobi
New Delhi   Shanghai   Taipei   Toronto

With offices in
Argentina   Austria   Brazil   Chile   Czech Republic   France   Greece
Guatemala   Hungary   Italy   Japan   Poland   Portugal   Singapore
South Korea   Switzerland   Thailand   Turkey   Ukraine   Vietnam

Published by Oxford University Press, Inc.
198 Madison Avenue, New York, NY 10016
www.oup.com

Oxford is a registered trademark of Oxford University Press

Library of Congress Cataloging-in-Publication Data
Antler, Joyce.
You never call! you never write! : a history of the Jewish mother / Joyce Antler.
p. cm.
Includes bibliographical references and index.
ISBN 978-0-19-514787-2
1. Jewish women.   2. Mothers.   3. Jewish women—Humor.
4. Mothers—Humor.   5. Jewish women in literature.
6. Mothers in literature.   7. Jewish women in motion pictures.
8. Mothers in motion pictures.   9. Feminist criticism.
10. Stereotypes (Social psychology)   I. Title.
HQ1172.A58 2007
306.874'3089924—dc22   2006036249

1 3 5 7 9 8 6 4 2
Printed in the United States of America
on acid-free paper

To
Rachel and Lauren

and in memory of my mother
and grandmother

The author's mother, Sophie Kessler, ca. 1930.

The author's grandmother, Tillie Sparaga, ca. 1910.

CONTENTS

ACKNOWLEDGMENTS

T HE FIRST INSPIRATION FOR THIS BOOK was my late mother, Sophie Kessler, who modeled my experience of what a loving Jewish mother could be. I am indebted to my niece, Kim Shechtman, whose insights enriched my perceptions of my mother's legacy.

This book has had many other Jewish mothers. I am grateful to them collectively—especially the many historians and other scholars and writers whose work stimulated my thinking—and individually, for there were many wonderful colleagues who intervened in various ways to provide advice, friendship, and, when necessary, even chicken soup. My goal of melding the social history of American Jewish women—how they lived their everyday lives—with the ideas and myths that influenced popular perceptions of them could not have taken root without such camaraderie.

For twenty years, I have been privileged to be part of a wonderful writers' group in Boston that has known this project from its birth, nurtured it in its infancy and early life, and helped me raise it to maturity. I am grateful to its members—Fran Malino, Megan Marshall, Lois Rudnick, Sue Quinn, and Judith Tick—for their friendship and encouragement.

Several colleagues read the manuscript in its totality and provided commentary that improved it in numerous ways. Susan Ware's willingness to share ideas with me was critical. Penina Migdal Glazer and Susan Quinn also provided cogent comments at a crucial stage of the work. For their generosity, knowledge, and helpful critiques, I am grateful as well to Janet Burstein, Patty Margolis, Riv-Ellen Prell, Gail Reimer, Judith Rosenbaum, and Stephen

Whitfield, each of whom took the time and effort to read the entire manuscript and offer sage suggestions.

For insightful advice on specific chapters, I am grateful to Joe Boskin, Phil Brown, Dan Jacobs, Barbara Kirshenblatt-Gimblett, Jayne Guberman, Barbara Haber, Carl Martin, Ted Merwin, Sharon Feiman-Nemser, Sharon Pucker Rivo, Amy Sales, Miriam Slater, Marc Stern, and Lauri Umansky.

I also thank the friends, family, and colleagues who enriched this book with their interest, support, and suggestions, among them Phoebe Becker, Hasia and Steve Diner, Lawrence H. Fuchs, Debbie Heller, Ellie Kellman, Richard Landes, Sonia and David Landes, Erik, Ellyn, and Larry Lerner, Danny Margolis, Ellen and Barry Mintzer, Louie Nemser, Michael Socolow, Roberta Wollons, and my "kitchen-table" comrades: Pam Allara, Erica Harth, Jane Kamensky, Karen Klein, Sarah Lamb, and Sue Lanser. My late cousin Leslie Lerner spent many hours discussing television's representations of Jewish families with me; her enthusiasm energized this project. A special thanks as well to Tom Doherty for title credit (which he shares with Steve Antler).

I am fortunate to enjoy being part of several communities at Brandeis University: the American Studies Department, the Women's and Gender Studies Program, and the Spencer Program for Education Research. I thank each of them for their warm collegiality, their intellectual stimulation, and their encouragement. As usual, I owe a special and huge debt to Angie Simeone for her skilled assistance; thanks also to Cheryl Sweeney and Maayan Zack.

I also have found another special home at the Jewish Women's Archive. My heartfelt thanks to the archive's charismatic director, Gail Reimer, and the dozens of committed board members, staff, and academic council members who share the mission of making the JWA a place where Jewish women's history can "live and grow."

I have benefited enormously from the assistance of a group of remarkable graduate and undergraduate student researchers. Jessica Lepler, Alexis Antracoli, and Denise Holladay D'Amico of the Brandeis history department provided invaluable help with the Rose Laub Coser survey of Jewish mothers; Lynda Yankaskas worked with me on the Weaving Women's Words project of the Jewish Women's Archive. Alexandra Herzog, Rebecca Karp, Rachel Werner, Jodi Ellenbogen, and Sarah Kennedy also offered timely assistance. Hadassah Margolis did invaluable work on the Brandeis University National Women's Committee Mothers Survey and earlier mothers' surveys.

For her contributions to the collection of images for this book, I am deeply grateful to Rachel Berry, Lily Safern Summer Intern of the Hadassah-Brandeis Institute at Brandeis University. Rachel's research played a crucial role in the last stages of the project. Thanks also to the National Center for Jewish Film at Brandeis University for help with film images. In the first stages of this project, I was fortunate enough to have the advice of Andrea Most on early cinema history.

Judy Gold and Wendy Leibman, busy making the rest of us laugh, took the time to talk with me about Jewish mothers and comedy. I am also grateful to Jane Aronson, E. M. Broner, and Joy Rachlin for generously giving me their time and attention.

William Frost and the late Pamela Brumberg of the Lucius N. Littauer Foundation provided critical support that allowed me to undertake survey research. The Women's and Gender Studies Program of Brandeis University and the Hadassah-Brandeis Institute provided funding for research assistance, and I am grateful for their generosity.

I have relied on the assistance of many archivists and librarians at a variety of institutions. I would like to thank the staff of the Brandeis University Library for their help, especially Judy Pinnolis and Karen Adler Abramson; the archivists and staff at the Schlesinger Library of the Radcliffe Institute of Advanced Study; the Henry A. Murray Archive at the Institute for Quantitative Social Science at Harvard University; the Manuscript Division of the Library of Congress; the Special Collections Department of Syracuse University Library; the American Jewish Historical Society, the Leo Baeck Institute, and the YIVO Institute at the Center for Jewish History in New York; and the New York Public Library's Jewish Division.

The members of the Florida Region of the Brandeis University National Women's Committee cheerfully participated in my "Jewish mothers" survey. I owe a huge debt to Amy Sales, who helped me design and evaluate the BUNWC survey, and to Jacqueline Boone James and Janet Zollinger Giele, who also helped in the survey design. Beth Bernstein of BUNWC has been consistently enthusiastic and supportive.

The opportunity to present portions of this work to various audiences improved my ideas immeasurably. These settings include: the Conference on Key Texts in American Jewish Culture at Arizona State University in 2000; the Annual Conferences of the American Studies Association, 2001, 2004; the Florida Region University-on-Wheels programs of the Brandeis University National Women's Committee, 2001; Scholar-in-Residence Lecture at Temple Beth-El, Fall River, Massachusetts, 2001; Keynote Lecture at the Skirball Cultural Center, Los Angeles, California, 2002; Lecture at Temple Israel, Boston, 2003; Conference on Imagining the American Jewish Community, Jewish Theological Seminary, New York, 2004; Lectures to the Modern Jewish Symposium, and the American Studies/Anthropology Department Colloquiums, Brandeis University, 2004; Annual Conference of the Association for Research on Mothering, York University, Toronto, Canada, 2004; Conference on the Jewish Immigrant Experience in America, London, Ontario, University of Western Ontario, 2005; Thirteenth Berkshire Conference on the History of Women, Scripps College, Claremont, California, 2005; Catskills Institute Conference, 2005; Symposium on "The Irish and Jewish Women's Immigrant Experience: Differing Roads to Assimilation," New Center for Arts and Culture,

Boston College, 2005; Symposium on "The Legacy of the Goldbergs," the Center for Jewish History in 2006; Annual Conferences of the Association for Jewish Studies, 2005, 2006.

My agent, Sydelle Kramer, guided this book to the right publisher and was always there to respond to questions and problems with her wise counsel. Elda Rotor believed in this project from the outset and brought it to Oxford University Press, where she was helpful and supportive. After Elda's departure, I benefited from the solicitous care of Cybele Tom, who came to understand and appreciate the world of Jewish mothers and whose skilled readings and trenchant suggestions inform every page. Her dedication to this book has made it a better product in incalculable ways. Thanks also to Joellyn Ausanka for shepherding the manuscript through the production process and to Robin Miura for her excellent copyediting.

Through every moment of travail involved in researching and writing this book, I have been able to rely on the emotional support—and often the illuminating insights—of my two wonderful daughters, Lauren and Rachel. Even though they must have wondered when and if this project would ever end, they were a continuing source of empathy and love. They called, and they wrote—almost daily! And I never had to ask.

My husband, Stephen Antler, can add this book to the list of the thousands of things he has done to support my work over the now nearly forty years we have been together. His sharp intelligence and abiding interest in this subject have sustained me throughout. As our family has often remarked, he is the best "Jewish mother" a father can be.

You Never Call! You Never Write!

Founding members of the improvisational group Second City, Elaine May and Mike Nichols revolutionized American comedy with their brilliant social satire. They performed their "Mother and Son" telephone skit on Broadway in *An Evening with Mike Nichols and Elaine May* (1960). (Photofest)

INTRODUCTION

NE NIGHT IN 1960, comedians Elaine May and Mike Nichols, fresh from Second City in Chicago, wowed a Broadway audience with a sketch about a Jewish mother and her rocket scientist son. "I sat by the phone all day Friday, all day Saturday . . . all day Sunday," the mother, Mrs. Weiss, berates the son. "You never call."

"Mother, I was launching *Vanguard*," the exasperated son protests.

"It's always something!" the mother replies, wringing out still more guilt by adding that she needs to have her nerves "x-rayed" because of all the aggravation he has caused.

"I feel awful," the son responds.

"If I could believe that," the mother declares, "I'd be the happiest mother in the world . . . that's a mother's prayer."[1]

Nichols explained that the sketch came from a call that his own mother made to him: "Hello, Michael, this is your mother; do you remember me?" Nichols immediately discerned potential for a comedy routine and called May, who improvised the skit with him onstage that very night. When his mother saw the act, she identified the character as May's mother, who similarly attributed it to Mrs. Nichols. Nichols confessed, "It was really a big deal for us. Because if you can get a whole audience laughing their ass off at what has made you miserable, you have freed yourself to some extent." For Nichols, mocking his mother was making fun of the "process [of] being Jewish." "We were free at last."[2]

In fact a milder, nicer form of the telephone sketch had already been a part of Jewish comedy nearly half a century before Nichols and May's act, initiated

by George Jessel, who performed "A Phone Call from Mama" on the vaudeville stage as a monologue with just a phone as a prop.[3] Poking fun at his
mother's verbal miscues and mangled language, it was the most popular act of
Jessel's long show business career. In 1925, playing another son of a doting
Jewish mother, Jessel starred on Broadway in the *Jazz Singer*, a landmark play
about an assimilating Jewish son; two years later the play was made into the
first sound film, starring Al Jolson in Jessel's role. In both portrayals, the Jewish
mother is much less intrusive, though no less attached to her son, than the
Nichols and May character.

May and Nichols's "Mother and Son" sketch brilliantly captures the mixture of guilt, dependency, and rebelliousness that came to represent the fault
lines of the Jewish mother-son relationship, a theme that has endured for another half century since Nichols and May.[4] Today, the Jewish mother-son
sketch has been transformed into an edgy routine about interfering mothers
and sassy daughters, performed by such Jewish female comedians as Judy Gold,
Jackie Hoffman, Amy Borkowsky, and Wendy Liebman.

But the specter of the Jewish mother does not stalk only the comedy circuits. Indeed, of all the representations American culture makes of mothers,
that of the "Jewish mother" seems most familiar. Whether drawn as self-
sacrificing or manipulative and demanding, she appears as a colossal figure, her
negative imprint all over the lives of her children. In fiction, films, television,
memoirs, advice books, and even psychoanalytic studies and anthropological
tracts, she is a stock character who provokes our ridicule and our blame. Portrayed by American Jewish writers and performers in the second half of the
twentieth century—beginning with the Nichols and May sketch, stretching
across the 1960s through Bruce Jay Friedman's *A Mother's Kisses*, Dan Greenburg's *How to Be a Jewish Mother*, Philip Roth's notorious *Portnoy's Complaint*,
and on to countless other scenarios in the decades since—the plaintive "you
never call me" became one in a repertoire of techniques in the Jewish mother's
supposed arsenal. The stereotype of the Jewish mother, transmitted through
myriad popular culture outlets and given intellectual credence by scholars
speaking from within academia, became a universally recognized metaphor for
nagging, whining, guilt-producing maternal intrusiveness.

What accounts for the viability of the Jewish mother caricature across time,
across gender, and across genres and disciplines? Why has the Jewish mother
been the figure that so many people love to hate for so long? A chronicle of the
loudest and most infamous blame-laden caricatures that have been portrayed
in American culture and intellectual life, this book investigates the reasons behind the Jewish mother's enduring (un)popularity. Excessive, overprotective,
neurotically anxious, and ever present, the Jewish mother became a scapegoat
for ambivalent and hostile sentiments regarding assimilation in a new society,
changing family dynamics, and shifting gender roles. At times, she also was
an emblem of unstinting love and devotion. This combination of diverse and

malleable characteristics allowed each generation to manipulate the Jewish mother image to suit its particular needs.

ACCORDING TO ONE DESCRIPTION that appeared thirty years ago, the stereotypical Jewish mother

> hovers over her children, preventing them from achieving autonomy by interfering, cajoling, advising, and manipulating. Whether she is actually holding the spoon and urging them to take "just one more bite," or operating through guilt—that most exquisite instrument of remote control—she is seen as ubiquitous and eternal.[5]

In the classic study of immigrant Jews also published in 1976, *World of Our Fathers*, Irving Howe was more brutal: the Jewish mother was a "brassy scourge, with her grating bark or soul-destroying whine, silver-blue hair, and unfocused aggression. . . . Daughters paled, sons fled" at her "groaning, cajoling, intimidating."[6]

Despite the passage of several decades, the Jewish mother described by these authors continues to dominate popular descriptions of Jewish women, although she has shared the stage with the more recent spoiled, shallow, materialistic JAP (Jewish American princess).[7] The Jewish "maternal tyrant," for many, is the destructive American mother in extremis, the ultimate embodiment of overintense, harmful concern.

But does this representation resemble the Jewish mothers we've truly known? What, in fact, is the fit between image and reality, caricature and real character? Paul Mazursky, filmmaker of *Show Me the Magic*, was in therapy for years, trying to overcome the grip of his domineering mother. When his therapist finally met Mrs. Mazursky, the therapist emerged after a few moments, pale and shaking, telling his patient, "It's a wonder you're so healthy"—clearly a case in which reality approximated the fiction.[8] On the other hand, some years ago, I asked Philip Roth when he would be writing the story of his mother. "My mother?" Roth exclaimed with surprise, explaining that his issue had always been with his father.[9] Despite creating the damning Jewish mother character of Sophie Portnoy, Roth seemed to be declaring that his own dear mother was nothing like the caricature; Sophie Portnoy appeared to be mere fiction after all. So, as with all stereotypes, we must ask to what degree does the Jewish mother stereotype miss the complexity and diversity of real Jewish mothers?

I gained a new appreciation for such a question when a colleague told me an anecdote at his retirement dinner a few years ago. Growing up in the Bronx in the 1930s, one day he and his brother went to a baseball game at Yankee Stadium. They heard a commotion in the bleachers and spied their mother vigorously pushing her way through the stands. The embarrassed brothers huddled together, fearing a rebuke. But when their mother reached them she simply thrust forward a large brown paper bag. "Boys," she cried, panting with exertion. "You forgot your lunch!" Though she had never been to the ballpark, she managed to commandeer the superintendent of Yankee Stadium and convince him to let her into the bleachers—with the promise that she would leave as soon as she gave her sons their lunch, which she did.[10]

I had begun to believe that Jewish mothers were no different from other mothers, but listening to my colleague's story I felt uniquely connected to a long line of Jewish mothers. For several years I had gotten up early to make lunch for my daughter Rachel, even when she was a junior and senior in high school. As she would fly out of the house, barely awake and grabbing for her schoolbooks and car keys, I would thrust the brown paper bag upon her. Not only that (I confess), but I would hand her a glass of juice, which she would gulp down, and a piece of toast on a napkin for the car ride. The whole process took ten seconds. When my husband protested that Rachel was old enough to pack her own lunch, I replied what I knew to be true: left to her own devices, she would not take the time to prepare lunch or stand in line for it. I made the lunch to make sure that she ate—because it mattered to me. Food may be an offering of love, as is commonly believed, but to myself and many Jewish mothers before me, food, foremost, is simply a necessity; providing adequate nutrition is a dietary mandate, essential to our children's vitality and a protection from lurking dangers. Anticipating punishment that day more than seventy years ago, my colleague and his brother received only a paper bag full of sandwiches and, with it, a token of their mother's affection, an expression of her confidence in them, and her implicit support of whatever they chose to do. The caricature of the Jewish mother as guilt-tripping, overprotective, and controlling only partially grasps my and my colleague's mother's behavior, ignoring the caring motivation behind our unflappable lunch-making. The core ingredient of this and other Jewish mothers' overbearing care is their deep and abiding concern for their children, which the flat stereotype fails to convey.

Because such strong love both attracts and repels, understandably, it has been the subject of varying and contradictory interpretations. While most offspring sought to free themselves from the Jewish mother's overwhelming devotion by mocking it—in the manner of Nichols and May's comic sketch and many more disparaging portrayals—others appreciated such abundant maternal attention and longed to bask in it. The nostalgic lyrics in "Yiddishe mama" songs and tributes, the benevolent character of radio and television's "Molly Goldberg," the stories of women writers, and the testimonies of mothers themselves all point to a more positive portrait of the Jewish mother. Drawing attention to these lesser-known perspectives, this book opens up a more panoramic view of the lived lives of Jewish mothers.

However, despite these numerous positive threads throughout the history of the Jewish mother, it is the most unflattering aspects of the Jewish mother that have endured and are most familiar. Why? This book argues that humor has been a main culprit. A far-reaching and effective medium, comedy is in large part responsible for making the negative Jewish mother stereotype so pervasive and disproportionately popular.

Drawing on the wellspring of the innovative Jewish comic tradition, Jewish men and women embellished the core tenets of the Jewish mother idea that passed down through Jewish history, religion, sociology, anthropology, and literature, until it became a rapid-fire comic device. American comedians, writers, and performance artists transformed anxieties into humor, giving them, in the words of comedy historian Lawrence J. Epstein, "a shape and a name as well as a way to cope."[11]

> A Jewish girl becomes president and says to her mother, "You've got to come to the inauguration, Mom." The mother says, "All right, I'll go, I'll go. What am I going to wear? It's so cold. Why did you have to become president? What kind of job is that? You'll have nothing but tsuris." But she goes to the inauguration, and as her daughter is being sworn in by the chief justice, the mother turns to the senator next to her and says, "You see that girl up there? Her brother's a doctor."[12]

Stereotype has been central to comedy, particularly the tradition of stand-up that arose in the mid-twentieth century largely as a consequence of the contributions of Jewish Borscht Belt comedians and that continues today everywhere in clubs and on television. In its origins, a joke about the Jewish mother boasting about her "son, the doctor," drew on the enormous pride of the Old World mother that her Americanized son had achieved the immigrant's dream of success. But this joke, contemporary when it was first performed in the 1950s, also carries embedded memories of the Jewish mother's tradition of sacrifice for her beloved son.

> A young man begs his mother for her heart, which his betrothed has demanded as a gift; having torn it out of his mother's proffered breast, he races away with it; and as he stumbles, the heart falls to the ground, and he hears it question protectively, "Did you hurt yourself, my son?"[13]

This folktale, cited in a 1950 article on the Eastern European Jewish family that became part of Margaret Mead and Ruth Benedict's landmark study of immigrant cultures, was itself taken from sources dating back generations; it circulates widely even today. "My son, the doctor" jokes have similarly become folklore, updated as above to reflect the current status of women. While the stereotype of the Jewish mother with bursting heart—from pride or sacrifice— remains frozen in a time warp, the reinvention of a key component of the Jewish mother myth makes this old joke new and funny again.

When such jokes, originally told to Jewish audiences, crossed over to the mainstream, the Jewish mother became a recognizable commodity, the embodiment of the monstrous qualities of all American mothers. The image of a dominating, ridiculously overprotective Jewish mother became ubiquitous, appearing not only in comic routines on stage, screen, and in nightclubs, but on cartoons, greeting cards, stationery, cocktail napkins, posters, tee shirts, wall plaques, coloring books, and board games. "I Survived a Jewish Mother," "Call Your [Jewish] Mother Once in a While," "If You Want to Feel Guilty, Call Your Mother" were among the many variations of the comic Jewish mother theme.[14]

That the Jewish mother became the butt of humor within her own ethnic group is itself unusual. "Why are there no jokes about possessive Scottish mothers or manipulative Polish wives?" asks humor scholar Christie Davies. In his view, Jewish jokes about Jewish wives and mothers simply had no equivalents among other cultures.[15] Yet within a relatively short time, Jewish mother jokes became so notorious that the Jewish mother's miscues came to stand in for those of all mothers. The JAM was "not just the Jewish American mother," writes folklore historian Alan Dundes, "but any American mother ignorant of the possible ill effects of overindulging her children." Although the jokes might be "fantasy," Dundes believes that by couching ideas about the Jewish mother in a joking format, they came to have a significant effect on individuals and society at large.[16]

According to humor historians Joseph Boskin and Joseph Dorinson, the negative sentiments behind many ethnic jokes tend to sanction oppression, conflict, and control.[17] In the case of Jewish mother jokes, the combination of derogatory attitudes toward both Jews and women makes the effect especially pernicious. "What's the difference between the Jewish mother and a vulture?" goes one joke. "The vulture waits until you're dead to eat your heart out." "What's the difference between a rottweiler and a Jewish mother?" asks another. "Eventually, the rottweiler lets go."[18] With cruel caricatures becoming acceptable through endless joke telling, the result has been to heighten the tendency to portray Jewish women as "other." When Jewish mothers' "bowls of chicken soup" become "philters of hemlock," the stereotype cues danger and derision, not mere foolishness, ineptitude, or excess.[19] The yoking of anti-Semitism and misogyny has been responsible for the most vicious Jewish mother humor.

But the problem is not only in how the stereotype presents Jewish women to society, but also in how Jewish women themselves are affected. Real Jewish mothers internalize the negative attributes of the stereotype, judging themselves and others by these traits. For fear of being labeled a "Jewish mother," they may stifle their own "creativity, warmth, caring and expressiveness." In so doing, they become "their own worst attackers."[20] Historian Paula Hyman admits that she was so appalled by thirty years of the Jewish mother stereotype that "the last thing" she wanted to be was a Jewish mother. "Since we don't want to be 'Jewish mothers,'" Hyman writes, "we hold ourselves back from the kind of behavior satirized in the caricature. When we find ourselves, despite our best intentions, behaving 'just like a Jewish mother,' we condemn ourselves for doing so."[21] Thus the stereotype influences mothers' relationships with their children and their self-evaluation as parents.

FAMILIAR REPRESENTATIONS OF THE JEWISH MOTHER, like that expressed in the May and Nichols telephone sketch, may illuminate certain aspects of cultural life regarding women, mothers, and Jews, but the relationship of that image to the lived life of the many varieties of real Jewish women remains unexplored. The stereotype bears no resemblance whatsoever to my own soft-spoken, laid-back, loveable mother, or to her mother, or to millions of other mothers who came before. And the unidimensional portrait may bear even less resemblance to Jewish mothers today, who are a diverse and complex group, with many different child-rearing styles and demographic and religious characteristics. Secular and observant; Jewish-born and Jewish by choice; feminist and traditionalist; heterosexual and gay; single, married, and divorced, contemporary Jewish mothers are among the most highly educated and achieving mothers in the world, yet they are deeply involved with their children. Are they "good mothers"? Sacrificing, demanding, intrusive, overprotective ones? Are there maternal behaviors—such as an emphasis on food, telephoning, or "be carefuls"—that mark them as a distinctive ethnic group? If there are unique Jewish mothering styles today, have these been inherited from ethnic forebears, or is it only the stereotype that links them to the past?

Answering these questions is no simple task. How similar or different Jewish mothers may be from Greek, Italian, Irish, African, Chinese, and other types of American mothers is a question beyond the scope of this investigation. Each culture may be said to have its own images and values concerning motherhood, revealing some degree of similarity to each other as well as vital differences. Within Jewish culture, for example, mothers held great importance. In her role as the "woman of valor," celebrated in Biblical verse praising her familial, communal, and religious undertakings, the Jewish mother assumed primacy in the preservation of the Jewish people. Even when women lacked substantive power, the central connection of motherhood to Jewish peoplehood, symbolized by the Biblical matriarchs' passionate interventions on behalf of the sons who would carry forth the Jewish line, elevated mothers' status. However, because the family is so central to Jewish life, anxieties concerning its well-being have tended to target the mother.[22] Questions about the origin and accuracy of the Jewish mother image are further complicated by the fact that the stereotype has subtly morphed throughout history—each variation embodying the pertinent issues in Jewish culture of the particular time.

One or another form of the Jewish mother image has been present in

American society from the turn of the twentieth century, but the ending of mass emigration in the 1920s served to coalesce the type within American culture. Although both positive and negative images of the Jewish mother existed simultaneously from this time forward, increasingly after World War II she was portrayed as a threatening, intrusive, guilt-inducing "vampire."[23] The Jewish mother emerged out of the war as a unique female type, different from both European representations and earlier American ones. Aggressive and manipulative, living vicariously through her children, especially sons, she was drawn as a "satirical harpy"—domineering, meddling, suffocating.[24] In contrast to the previous generation's appreciation of her toughness, considered to have ensured the family's survival amid the hostile environments of Eastern Europe and immigrant ghettos, now her fierce protectiveness seemed crude and gratuitous.[25]

Jewish sons have given us only one kind of Jewish mother—"the all-engulfing nurturer who devours the very soul with every spoonful of hot chicken soup she gives."[26] Yet their verbal attacks on Jewish mothers may have been only a reflection of what cultural historian Ann Douglas has argued was a "matricidal" impulse in American society. According to Douglas, in the name of modernism and broader horizons, "modern" sons rebuked their mothers' culture.[27] From another viewpoint, psychoanalytic historians find traditional Freudian theories more persuasive in explaining the rampant misogyny of the mid-twentieth century.[28] An ugly "momism," made famous in Philip Wylie's best-selling *Generation of Vipers* (1942), seemed to prefigure the case against passive-aggressive mothers that Jewish sons would make in the postwar period, although seeds of Jewish offspring's discontent had appeared earlier.[29] The new affluence of Jews, inspiring guilt as well as pleasure, was another ingredient in the mix of mother-blaming that now came down on the Jewish mother. Paradoxically held responsible for her offspring's incomplete assimilation as well as for their success in achieving the fruits of American materialism, she served as a convenient scapegoat for postwar Jewish ambivalence toward acculturation.

But it is not only men who demonized mothers. Women, too, harbored rages and resentments against maternal power, although female rebellion against matriarchal figures is complicated by the unique and powerful mother-daughter bond. From the 1960s and 1970s, when feminists questioned motherhood as a destiny for women, to the 1980s and 1990s, when they began to reaffirm, and even celebrate, the mother's family, community, and cultural roles, the subject of motherhood remained as fraught and perplexing from the daughters' vantage point as from the sons'. Jewish-born feminists were at the forefront in articulating this ambivalence. While their stories and memoirs often portray rejecting and aggressive mothers, they also provide many well-rounded, sympathetic portrayals. Jewish mothers as presented by Jewish daughters are often troubled and troubling, but they are rarely the extreme caricatures given to us by men.[30]

Both daughters' and sons' representations of the Jewish mother reveal deep-seated anxieties about Jews' relation to the culture at large and to each other. Like the American-as-apple-pie mother, the Jewish mother became a vessel into which the cultural contradictions of a society grappling with ethnic, gender, class, and racial tensions were poured. The exaggeration of her traits into a caricature of maternal excess offers one gauge with which we can measure Jews' anxieties about their place in American society. As Jews successfully acculturated to mainstream norms, joking about old ways, old values, and Old World characters such as the outsized Jewish mother could help to alleviate the tensions of acculturation and modernization. In the transition to modernity, she became a foil for the self-doubts and insecurities of her children.

The tension of Jews' growing pains within mainstream America is paralleled in a second powerful narrative that fueled the obsession with the Jewish mother. As the continuous appeal of the "you never call!" routine suggests, the conflict between the quest for independence and the lure of dependency extended beyond a single generation and across America's ethnic groups. Reflecting the push and pull between the parent who cannot let go and the child who wants freedom, this narrative expresses the disappointment experienced when parents and children fail to negotiate the boundaries and separations that are a necessary consequence of growth and development.[31] An expression of the power and limitations of motherhood, the Jewish mother image stands in for the more universal experience of the fundamentally fraught, ambivalent, but profound relationships between mothers and their children.

In addition to struggles around issues of cultural modernization and psychological maturation, the contested nature of gender relationships within the Jewish family has contributed to the development of the Jewish mother ideal over time. Congruent to the portrayal of the mother as overbearing and manipulative has been the depiction of the father as ineffectual, weak, and passive. The apparent reversal of the normal balance of power in the Jewish American household helped to promote the construction of the Jewish mother as dominant and controlling. Even though women had authority and power in the East European Jewish family despite their officially subordinate status, role reversal in the American Jewish family seemed extreme. Strong, indomitable, and dangerous, the developing Jewish mother icon was fashioned as a warning against the usurpation of patriarchal authority.

The convergence of these three themes—tensions regarding acculturation and modernization, parent-child struggles over autonomy, and gender role imbalances—has afforded the cultural idea of the Jewish mother a steady, continuous existence with multiple points of connection for audiences. Metamorphosing over successive generations, perpetuated by Jewish women as well as men and by non-Jews as well as Jews, this maternal image emerged as an icon of enduring power. By the 1970s, the image of the Jewish American princess (JAP) had come to share the spotlight with that of the Jewish mother; they continue in tandem to define Jewish women in the popular culture, yet neither idea can be reduced to the monolithic portrayals said to define them. The portrait of the Jewish mother has thus been continually revised and reinvented over nearly a century of American life. Not only writers, artists, and performers, but also psychoanalysts, psychologists, anthropologists, sociologists, and historians shaped the image according to their own beliefs. A powerful ideology of motherhood, constructed through representations drawing from both real and imagined sources, ensured that this creation would become a familiar cultural "type."

Although the Jewish mother idea eventually congealed into a predictable stereotype, the overlapping representations offered by social scientists, psychoanalysts, novelists, filmmakers, comedians, and performers reveal a dynamic cultural legacy. Interrelationships among images, realities, audience, and creators, each responding to and influencing the other, continually extended the breadth and reach of the representations. Flexible and resilient, the Jewish mother image permeated nearly every part of the intellectual, artistic, and media communities. In so doing, it permeated American culture.

Even today, when the conditions that led to the creation of the Jewish mother stereotype have long since disappeared, the idea has been reanimated by a diverse group of contemporary Americans: stand-up comedians (particularly women), writers, and scholars. Such longevity reveals that despite its seeming rigidity, the stereotype incorporates core components that continue to appeal to Americans. While its main outlines remain firm, shifting cultural norms continue to subtly transform the seemingly static stereotype.

Because of its persistence and versatility, the Jewish mother image is in fact the dominant Jewish American stereotype—with a more energetic and longer life than the JAP idea or negative images of Jewish men such as the schlemiel. Examining the history of the Jewish mother image illuminates fantasies, anxieties, and ideals critical to family and the cultural fabric as they changed over time. To understand this image—how it arose, who it influenced, and how it has constantly transformed—is to understand the larger story of Jewish life in America and the changing face of motherhood.

THIS BOOK FOLLOWS THE MAIN MOVEMENTS across the twentieth and twenty-first centuries by which the Jewish mother stereotype tells the American Jewish story: immigration; acculturation; the response to World War II and the Holocaust; the transition to a consumer-oriented postwar suburban society; the triumph of Jewish writers and entertainers in American culture; feminism; and the response by writers, scholars, daughters, sons, and mothers themselves to new currents of women's empowerment and ethnic pride.

Beginning with the rise of the Jewish mother idea during the mid-1920s, I have chosen as my jumping-off point for this book the immigrant generation's determination to succeed. As sung by jazz singers Al Jolson and Sophie Tucker, the Jewish mother was then a source of strength and nurturance, although a contradictory image of the character as selfish, materialistic social climber was already brewing. Later, Gertrude Berg's benevolent character, Molly Goldberg, who dominated American radio and television sitcoms from the late 1920s through the early 1950s, demonstrated that acculturation need not mean abandoning traditional values. Molly was an early example of the new Jewish matriarchy that championed progressive Americanism, simultaneously embodying old-fashioned, *haimishe* (homelike) ideals and modern styles of child-rearing.

By midcentury, as Jews successfully completed their assimilation into mainstream America, the Jewish mother's fierce loyalty to her family, mixed with her pungent desire for its success, fueled the indictment that Jews themselves increasingly made of this indomitable matriarch: that by her overbearing control, she pushed and prodded her offspring to succeed but relegated them to a clinging dependency. Responding to the pressures of postwar adjustment and the traumas of the Holocaust, a new, exaggerated portrait of the Jewish mother developed—backward, crass, and manipulative. The prominence of Jewish authors and performers within American culture helped propel the ugly Jewish mother to mainstream fame.

During the 1960s, the women's liberation movement and ideas about the Jewish mother engaged in a massively formative relationship that influenced the way Jewish mother images were used in subsequent popular culture, scholarship, fiction, and memoirs. Jewish daughters such as Shulamith Firestone, Robin Morgan, and Jane Alpert railed against their own mothers' choices while ultimately elevating motherhood as an ideal. In their essays, novels, and memoirs, they etched new pathways to connect daughters and mothers, and liberated women around the world from stereotyped roles.

Following these women's liberationists were others who used popular culture, literature, and social science to create new images and stories about Jewish motherhood. Jewish-born Roseanne Barr's irreverent "Domestic Goddess" creation, though not specifically Jewish, drew on the strengths of her grandmother, a strongly Jewish-identified Holocaust survivor. In contrast to Roseanne's nonethnic character, those created by Nora Ephron, Barbra Streisand, and Fran Drescher were marked as Jewish, often excessively so. A growing body of memoirists, novelists, and women's studies scholars set out to recover and recast an authentic Jewish mother's story on both the personal and broader historical stages. Whether fictionalized in such works as Wendy Wasserstein's *The Sisters Rosensweig* or Anita Diamant's *The Red Tent*, recalled in the autobiographical testimonies of Holocaust survivors' offspring, or documented in dozens of scholarly studies, these new portraits of historical Jewish mothers emerged as vibrant and compelling. These historically based representations counteracted the negative versions of Jewish motherhood disseminated by entertainment media.

The stories told by Jewish mothers themselves have potential to do important work in changing the public face of the Jewish mother and of motherhood in America. When narrating their own stories, these women talk of meaningful involvement in their children's lives and satisfaction with their roles as citizens and community members. They describe their parenting and that of their own mothers as nurturing, a rejection of the pop culture images that present them and their forebears in solely pejorative ways.

These nurturant, enabling portraits of mothers are the newest additions to the long history of the Jewish mother and attest to the resiliency and adaptability of the image over time. Despite the survival of the familiar negative trope, today, more than ever, writers, comedians, filmmakers, artists, scholars, daughters, and sons are resisting its confines. Even mothers themselves are appropriating the stereotype, using it to bolster their authority and power. For example, once when Alan Dershowitz, the outspoken, media-savvy, law professor and author, was arguing with his mother, she suddenly asked him, "What's the difference between a terrorist and a Jewish mother?" Without pausing, she answered her own question, "With a terrorist, you can sometimes negotiate."[32]

The new meanings of the Jewish mother image are formed by real experiences with actual Jewish mothers such as Mrs. Dershowitz, who refuse to apologize for their toughness. A fuller, more nuanced understanding of the history of the Jewish mother—one of the aims of this book—incorporates the interpretations of such mothers. As contemporary American Jews become more confident and informed about their history, they can confront the distortions that arose from the anxieties of previous generations. This new resistance thus reflects a new stage of the Jewish trajectory in America.

It is likely that transformations in intellectual life as well as in comedy and performance art in the new millennium will continue to affect representations of Jewish mothers. At the same time, new social conditions are altering the experiences of real-life Jewish mothers, who are a much more diverse group in terms of their racial, religious, educational, occupational, and marital backgrounds than their predecessors only a generation ago. In the culture at large, a new model of "intensive" or "anxious" mothering has come to dominate middle-class parenting. With contemporary parenthood increasingly "colored by apprehension," as historian Steven Mintz writes, "all parents are Jewish mothers now."[33] The conclusion of this book explicates the convergence of the new parenting style with cultural ideas about Jewish motherhood.

This convergence may mean that contemporary American mothers, increasingly consumed with modern "intensive" mothering, will come to face the same accusation borne by their Jewish forebears—that they are obsessive, "engulfing, octopus mothers."[34] The experience of Jewish mothers who have lived with the constraints and possibilities of a famous but fundamentally flawed icon created in their likeness can serve as a metaphor—and perhaps, indeed, a behavioral guide—for these mothers. The voices of Jewish mothers and the stories and legends about them, continually reinvented as they do ever-new cultural work, need to be heard.

When the house was full with the sound of children's voices
And the kitchen smelled of roast and dumplings.
You can be sure our house did not lack poverty,
But there was always enough for the children.
She used to voluntarily give us bread from her mouth
And she would have given up her life for her children as well.
Millions of dollars, diamonds, big beautiful houses—
But one thing in the world you get only one of from God:
A yiddishe mama, she makes the world sweet
A yiddishe mama, oh how bitter when she's missing.
You should thank God that you still have her with you—
You don't know how you'll grieve when she passes away.
She would have leaped into fire and water for her children.
Not cherishing her is certainly the greatest sin.
Oh, how lucky and rich is the person who has such a beautiful gift from God:
Just a little old yiddishe mama, my mama.

—*"My Yiddishe Mama," sung by Sophie Tucker,*
(translation of Yiddish version)

1

"MY YIDDISHE MAMA"

The Multiple Faces of the Immigrant Jewish Mother

Fᴿᴏᴍ Bɪʙʟɪᴄᴀʟ ᴛᴀʟᴇs ᴛʜʀᴏᴜɢʜ ᴛʜᴇ ɴᴀʀʀᴀᴛɪᴠᴇs ᴏꜰ ᴇᴀʀʟʏ ᴍᴏᴅᴇʀɴ Eᴜʀᴏᴘᴇ, the image of the Jewish mother in song and story has been that of a strong, determined, family-bound, and loyal matriarch, raising her children, helping to sustain the family economically, and keeping the domestic flame of Judaism alive.[1] Even beyond the Talmudic law that defines a Jew as anyone with a Jewish mother, the continuity of Jewish life depended on the mother's commitment to the spiritual health of her loved ones and to the Jewish community in which she lived. Though mothers lacked legal power and could not participate in public religious worship—a sphere left entirely to Jewish men—their social power in the domestic realm and in the secular, communal world beyond the household was an undeniable fact.[2]

The primary role of Jewish mothers within the Jewish family survived the often chaotic migration to the North American continent. From the earliest known records of colonial America, when Jewish life was often fragile and uncertain, Jewish mothers modeled acceptable behavior for their children, holding fast to their values and using the domestic sphere to transmit them.[3] By the mid-nineteenth century, after a second migration of Jews from Central Europe boosted the Jewish population of the United States to several hundred thousand, the public role of Jewish mothers took on new dimensions, as Jewish women played increasingly visible roles in communal and philanthropic activities in the public realm.[4] Guardians of Jewish values, these idealized "mothers in Israel" were admired for their dedication to the precepts of Jewish religious and moral life and the supreme importance of home and family.[5]

Throughout the massive wave of Jewish immigration from Eastern Europe that brought more than two million Jews to the continent between 1880 and 1920, the Jewish mother remained the emotional "heart of the family," as Irving Howe put it in his memorable account of Jewish immigrant life in New York, *World of Our Fathers*.[6] In the Old Country, the term *mame-loshn* (literally, mother's words), connoting a folksy association with the common people, had in fact become the standard reference for Yiddish literature. At its very core, the definition thus referenced an attachment to women and motherhood that was sentimental and "deferential, if not reverential."[7] While in Eastern Europe, comic figures of Jewish wives (as gossiping shrews, for example) appeared in parables, proverbs, stories, and legends, the new shtetl writers such as I. L. Peretz, Sholem Aleichem, and Mendele Mokher Seforim pointed their satire to the backward mores of men rather than the foibles of mothers.[8] In the United States, before the early twentieth century, fiction created by Jewish writers was meager, so the accounts of Jewish mothers remained "minor."[9] But in the cataclysmic stresses associated with the transition to modernity, both the role and image of Jewish mothers would be radically transformed.

During the 1920s and 1930s, a new and vibrant series of images of Jewish mothers began to circulate in the popular press, fiction, films, music, and memoirs. While historians generally speak of these images as sentimental and endearing, the period in fact bore witness to a vigorous debate among multiple representations of the immigrant Jewish mother. The conflicting images that appeared in these venues afford the Jewish mother a primary place in debates concerning the nature of the Jewish adaptation to modernity.

The 1920s marked an especially important cultural moment in Jewish life in the United States. By that time, the wave of East European immigration that had swept the shores of America since the 1880s had spawned a generation of daughters and sons making their way into a different, more open world than their parents'. Many first-generation parents had moved forward into American society, if not on equal terms as American-born citizens, then surely in ways that allowed them the benefit of expansive social and economic opportunities. The closing of the immigration gates due to the National Origins Act of 1924 made it seem likely that the already settled generation of East European newcomers might well be the last new settlers for a long time to come.

Yet Jews harbored great anxieties about the mainstream American world that beckoned to them. As the first generation of East European immigrants gave way to sons and daughters making their own way in America, stories of generational conflict, lament, and forgiveness occupied a prime space in the Jewish imagination. Increasingly comfortable with American landscapes of opportunity, the second generation cast off the older, anachronistic familial supports—particularly the embrace of mother love—all the while mythologizing it. The pathos, uncertainty, and guilt sons and daughters faced in moving away from their parents—emotionally and physically—had become a familiar theme of Jewish cultural narrative in the early twentieth century. From the popular Yiddish song *"A brivele der mamen"* ("A Letter to Mama") in 1907, to the beloved ballad "My Yiddishe Mama," introduced by Sophie Tucker in 1925, to scores of memoirs, films, and novels, the loving but abandoned Jewish mother was a staple of Jewish art, music, and literature during this period. Because they associated the Jewish mother with home, family, tradition, and religion—the bodily representation of all that was familiar, loved, and therefore missed—Jewish artists and writers invested their "Yiddishe Mamas" with extraordinary energy and sympathy, but often with an obsessive and confining control seen as necessary to the immigrant struggle for survival. The momentous changes in Jewish social norms that accompanied rapid assimilation were fast coalescing into a new and compelling, but problematic, figure: the Americanized "Yiddishe Mama." By the early 1930s, with the nation in the grips of a bitter Depression that heightened familial struggles, these images grew ever more forceful and complex.

My Red-Hot "Yiddishe Mama"

Tucker's poignant ballad "My Yiddishe Mama," offers a prime example of the sentimentalized ghetto mother during this transition period.[10] Along with "Some of These Days," "My Yiddishe Mama" was Tucker's most famous song, introduced into her repertoire after the death of her own mother, Jennie Abuza, in 1925. A mainstay of Hartford's Jewish community and respected for her charitable work, Jennie died when Tucker was crossing the Atlantic, returning from an engagement in London. Tucker was grateful that as she lay dying, her mother had left word to delay the funeral until Tucker arrived. Sophie realized that in suspending her Orthodox beliefs (which called for immediate burial) her "darling yiddishe mama" had demonstrated "how much she loved me and how well she understood my love for her."[11]

Jennie's death proved deeply traumatic for Sophie. In the aftermath of the funeral, Tucker became "paralyzed" while performing at a Jewish Theatrical Guild benefit at the Manhattan Opera House. Led off the stage, she stayed in bed for weeks, her self-confidence gone. "I had a feeling I was done for as a performer," she recalled.[12] But soon after, her long-time songwriter and accompanist, Jack Yellen, together with Lou Pollack, wrote "My Yiddishe Mama" for her, and the effect was cathartic. Tucker sang "My Yiddishe Mama" at the Palace Theater and at the Winter Garden in New York, where "there wasn't a dry eye in the house." After that, she sang it in the United States and throughout Europe, where it was always a "sensational" hit.[13]

"My Yiddishe Mama" drew upon the tradition of ethnic nostalgia songs that had become popular in the early twentieth century.[14] Earlier emigration songs emphasized the intimacy and warmth of the Old World environment and the pain of leaving. *"A brivele der mamen"* was the most maudlin of this group, expressing the plaintive cry of a lonely mother in the pale begging her son, in America for eight years, to write home.[15] As the immigration period receded, the anxiety of separation embedded in the process of emigration focused more than ever on the abandoned mother. Tucker's "Yiddishe Mama" grieved for the loss of community and family embodied in this figure. As a nostalgic celebration of the ghetto mother's nurturance, love, generosity, and forgiveness, the poignancy of "Yiddishe Mama" came from coupling this emotion-laded tribute with the recognition that the child, however grateful to her mother, still had to leave home and would forever be caught between the pull of loneliness and the necessity of independence. The "Yiddishe Mama," as Tucker sang her, existed in a world where parents offered love and protection; but it was a world of the past that was vanishing even as Tucker herself grew up. This plaintive, mournful song perfectly expressed the predicament of second-generation Jews, and its appeal was universal.

But while mainstream audiences appreciated its sentimental motherhood motif, Jewish audiences for whom Tucker performed the song in Yiddish heard a radically different version.[16] Music historian Mark Slobin observes that in English, the song "straddles the fence" musically and linguistically. The singer acknowledges her ethnicity, referring to her humble "East Side tenement," and the descriptor "yiddishe," as well as the song's minor key, creates a slightly exotic aura. But overall, the lyric and style are more Victorian (that is, crossing "trails of time") than ethnic Tin Pan Alley. The singer speaks affectionately of her mother, but in referring to the "quaint old lullabies" of her past and acknowledging that she owes "what I am today" to the mother, this Yiddishe mama seems "irretrievable . . . buried in time," no longer a part of her children's lives—or their achievements.[17]

In Yiddish, however, the song is deeper and more tragic, with many references to Jewish culture and Jewish spiritual values. In this version, the Yiddishe mama's nurturing self-sacrifice is put forth as the emblem of mother-love. "Bent over from great sorrow, with a pure Jewish heart/And cried-out eyes," the mother dreams of "long-gone days" when her offspring were still at home. Despite poverty, "there was always enough for the children" to eat because the Yiddishe mama "used to voluntarily give us bread from her mouth." Her mother-love had no bounds: "She would have given up her life for her children as well . . . she would have leaped into fire and water" for them. The acute emotion of the song couples the mother's sacrifice with the imminence of her death: "Oh how bitter when she's missing . . . you don't know how you'll grieve when she passes away."

Hidden from the non-Jewish world, the deep emotions of the Yiddish version illuminate just how intensely felt were the separations that acculturation demanded. Emphasizing sacrifice and loss, the Yiddish version, symbolic of second-generation tensions, bridges the Yiddish and American worlds through sorrow; in sentimentalizing the Jewish mother, the singer appeased

Jazz singer Sophie Tucker first sang the sentimental "My Yiddishe Mama" in 1925, after her mother's death. Taken the same year, this photo reveals that Tucker's maternal voice coexisted with a more glamorous—and usually more ribald—image. Tucker was known as the "Last of the Red Hot Mamas." (Corbis)

her own guilt at moving on. Yet her ambivalence is deeply felt, especially since the mother remains a still active and timeless presence.[18] The English version, dwelling on the offspring's feelings and acculturation even more than the mother's sacrifices, stretches out less ambiguously to establish an identity acceptable within American culture. Both, however, provide an elegy to a rapidly receding past.

Some thirty years after Tucker introduced "My Yiddishe Mama"—which along with the sexy jazz tune "Some of These Days" became her signature song—she revealed the depth of her attachment to her mother in an interview with Edward R. Murrow on his television show, *Person to Person*. Showing off her new Park Avenue apartment—her first "real home" after years of traveling show business circuits—she brought Murrow and the TV audience to her huge closet, peopled with photographs of dozens of her entertainment friends. Standing guard over its entryway was a large framed picture of her mother, Jennie; and across from that stern-faced photo hung a graceful portrait of the young Sophie, glamorous in a Gainsborough hat and smiling shyly. Not a sorrowful, abandoned, tenement mother, as Sophie sang her in "Yiddishe Mama," the mother who framed Sophie's closet gallery was a formidable presence. Sophie had in fact left home in defiance of her mother, leaving her infant son to be raised by Jennie and Sophie's sister. But Jennie Abuza's model of authority, her strength and nurturance, and her concern for social justice remained a powerful influence on her daughter. Tucker saw her mother's ideals in the work of women of her generation who served "their synagogues, their sisterhoods, their community centers, their settlements" and homes. It was in their image that Tucker liked to call herself "just a Yiddishe Momme [*sic*], begging, pleading and weeping, like Mother Rachel for her children," when in later life she set out to raise money for Israel, children's and women's causes, and other philanthropies. Admiring what she called Jennie's *dreistige* (guts, or courage), Sophie never forgot her mother's example. "I ran away from [the ghetto in Hartford]," Tucker told old friends at a fund-raising speech in that city toward the end of her life. "But I've been running back to it [and] to Mama ever since."[19]

Of course, Sophie herself as mother was a far cry from the sentimental template she herself did so much to create. Because of her unconventional career, she sacrificed her young son, not herself, leaving him behind as she climbed the ladder to show business success. Sophie was not a "nice Jewish girl," nor a "Yiddishe Mama" at all, but rather, as she belted out in her nightclub routines, she was a sexy "Red-Hot Mama," full of desires and appetites, and with a raucous sense of humor.[20] Just as the "real" Jennie Abuza, the mother still hidden in her Park Avenue closet, was more tough-minded, competent, and authoritative than the ballad about her revealed, so did the song conceal how in her own life Sophie had transformed the image of her beloved Jewish mother by her unabashed, brazen sensuality and her rejection of the standard role of mother. Even in the moment of its genesis, the Yiddishe mama thus contained its outlaw opposite.

The "Jazz Singer" with His Jewish "Mammy"

The Jewish mother as sentimental Yiddishe mama was memorably presented in another work that premiered the same year as Tucker's poignant ballad. Opening on Broadway in 1925, Samson Raphaelson's play, *The Jazz Singer*, written first as a short story, was inspired by Al Jolson's life story.[21] Two years later it became the world's first feature film with spoken dialogue. In this landmark film, Jakie Rabinowitz (played by Jolson), the American-born son of Cantor Rabinowitz and his wife, Sara (Eugenie Besserer), wants to pursue a career as a jazz singer rather than as a cantor, the career of generations of his ancestors. Over his father's objections, the young Jakie leaves home to become a performer. Years later, as he is about to debut in his first Broadway revue on the eve of the sacred holiday of Yom Kippur, he receives word that his father is deathly ill and cannot sing Kol Nidre, the holiest chant of the High Holy Day liturgy. If he leaves the show to replace his father, his career will be destroyed. In the film, Jakie, now known as Jack, has it both ways; he sings in the synagogue (and his father dies happy), but he also returns to Broadway. The film ends with Jack performing "Mammy" in blackface to an enthusiastic theater audience, including his adoring mother in the front row.

Much attention has been paid to the father-son conflict at the heart of the story. However, the role of the Jewish mother is central to interpreting the story. It is the mother who sees the importance of letting her child adapt to American ways; she serves as an intermediary between the rejecting father and the assimilating son. "Maybe our boy doesn't want to be a cantor," the mother tells the father. "Our boy doesn't think the way we do." Jack's father is characterized as an Old World patriarch, his ethnicity exaggerated by his profoundly Jewish profession as well as by his stereotypical Old World appearance. Jack's mother, on the other hand, assumes a more universal character. The only overt reference to her Jewishness is her lighting the Sabbath candles, an act traditionally performed by Jewish women. Her appearance is plain and old-fashioned, but she does not wear a wig or cover her hair in the manner of traditional Jewish wives. Emotionally, she also differs dramatically from her husband. While she is loving and caring, Jack's father is stern and bitter; adherence to tradition overwhelms his love for his son.

When Jack first returns home, learning that his mother is there alone, the first conversation he has—the historic first sound in any film—is with his mother. He hugs her and kisses her on the lips, gives her a diamond brooch, and sings to her, promising her a pink dress, a new apartment, and a trip to Coney Island where they will ride the "Shoot-the-Chutes" and the "Dark Mill." "I'll kiss you and hug you," says Jack, "see if I don't." When his mother starts to blush, Jack tells her, "You're getting kittenish." The cantor then comes in, but as Jack says, he has "no word for [his] son." With no interest in the modern world (or modern technology), he utters only one word, "Stop!" which renders the film silent once again. The cantor orders Jack out of the house, which he believes has been defiled with jazz singing. Jack tells him that he hopes "someday you'll understand the same as Mama does." Later, after the father has taken ill, Mama visits her son in his dressing room at the theater to beg him to sing the Kol Nidre in his father's stead. In blackface, Jack sings "Mother of Mine" to her, a pseudo-Irish sentimental song about mother-love written by Jolson for the film:

> Mother, I wandered away,
> breaking your heart.
> Now I'm grown up,
> Mother of mine
> When friends all doubt me,
> I still have you,
> Somehow you're just the same.
> Mother divine,
> With your arms around me,
> I know I'm not to blame[22]

The musical rendition of this sentimental song marks the mother-son relationship as one that is loving and, to many observers, sexual as well.[23] The romanticism of the score whenever Jack meets his mother—including a theme from Tchaikovsky's *Romeo and Juliet* and a lush theme from Brahms—underscores their mutual love. Indeed, his mother's love moves Jack more than the impending death of his father as he weighs the decision of whether to sing in his father's place rather than debut on Broadway. He sees his choice as "having the biggest chance of my life—and breaking my mother's heart." Jack's Gentile girlfriend, Mary, understands that his mother is "reconciled" to Jack's larger future. "Here he belongs," the mother acknowledges. "If God wanted him in His house, He would have kept him there. . . . He's not my boy anymore," Mama says; "he belongs to the world." As Jack sings in his father's place on the Day of Atonement, his mother tearfully looks on from the ladies' gallery.[24] Although the planned end of the film had been the penultimate scene of Jack being visited by the ghost of his father as he is praying, indicating that by relinquishing his Broadway opening night he has made amends for his defiance of the patriarch, the film in fact closes with the Jazz Singer's triumphant performance of "My Mammy" on stage in the presence of his beaming mother. With outstretched arms, in blackface, he declares his love and loyalty to "Mammy."[25]

Commentators disagree about the significance of framing this celebration of the Jewish mother in a blackface image. For many, Jews' impersonation of blacks was deeply problematic. Blackface allowed Jews to transfer their identities from immigrants to American: "in playing black, the Jew becomes white." But in acquiring "exchange value" at the expense of blacks, they rendered the real people behind the mask invisible.[26] For others, blackface expressed Jews' confusion about identity and the "torment" of living in two imagined worlds—Jewish minstrelsy and jazz performance, the inherited past and the beckoning present.[27] But it did not signal racism, exploitation, or contempt.

Still others emphasized the oedipal nature of Jolson's blackface impersonation. It is as a "Jewish Mama's boy" that Jack moves forward, his life passage reflecting not only his own rise, but also "the infantilization of the stereotypical black boy." Moreover, his success as an American comes at the price of his feminization and ultimate emasculation: as a blackfaced son, he weeps and beams, always to please his mother.[28] That the mother-son nexus is the key to the blackface dynamic deserves special comment. Although Jack learns to sing

In the *Jazz Singer* (1927), the first sound film, Jack (Al Jolson) needs the emotional support of his mother (Eugenie Besserer) to become a successful performer. The film concludes with Jack's triumphant blackface performance in which he sings "My Mammy" with love and gratitude for his mother. (Warner Bros./Photofest)

Mammy songs by listening to his cantor father, he sings them to honor his mother.[29] By favoring the son over the husband, contrasting the father's economic failure to the son's success, the mother in fact fans the flame of the oedipal conflict between them.[30]

That Jack is able to Americanize through his mother's love—that he needs her emotional support in order to assimilate—underscores the complexity of the process of acculturation. His mother's understanding allows Jack to become the fully American person he wants to be, to have both Americanness and his Jewishness. Assimilation can be demonstrated in different arenas—the innate, biological sphere of family and the "performed identity" of stage and film.[31] In each, the support of mothers is critical. Fathers are much less helpful; the Old World patriarch in *The Jazz Singer* does not fit into the New World and has to die at the end; it is a "parricide."[32] From its very beginning, then, the sentimentalized but essentially positive Jewish mother image embodies a deep gender discord. The enabling "good" mother, celebrated in song and in the almost erotic nature of the film son's elaborate praise, appears as the polar opposite of the rejecting, old-fashioned, once-powerful father.

Yet the blending of the Jewish mother with the Southern mammy, as Jolson sings to her at the film's conclusion, may signal another interpretation. With fathers effectively removed, the sons—including the Hollywood moguls who made these and other films—are "freed of their ethnic burdens"; with their heartstrings "tangled about Alabamy," not the shtetl or the Lower East Side, they move forward into the New World. But the nurturant, sacrificing Jewish mother may have been as anachronistic as her husband, for as her sons assimilated she became increasingly unnecessary. "Past redemption," "no longer a moral force," the old-time Yiddishe mama would become "a nudge, a yente, a yidene"—a mere caricature—in the next generation.[33]

While the male offspring marginalizes the Jewish mother even as he relies on her to move forward, for the Jewish daughter, represented in Sophie Tucker's lyrics, the process—if not the outcome—was different. Tucker had been one of the earliest Jewish performers to don blackface; from 1906 to 1912, she was known as the "world-renowned Coon Shouter," a singer of "coon," or minstrel, songs originally sung in Negro dialect.[34] On stage, she often lifted a glove to reveal her true color, waving to the crowd "to show I was a *white* girl"; Tucker would also interpolate Yiddish words into her coon songs, announcing her Jewishness as well.[35] In her autobiography, she reveals that she corked up reluctantly, only when a Harlem manager felt she was too "big and ugly" to get a sexy song across. She switched to ballads, torch songs, and ribald comedy, but because she was one of the last coon shouters, the appellation "last of the red hot mamas" stuck to her and perfectly fit the suggestive, self-mocking, sultry lyrics that she performed throughout her long show business career.[36]

Shedding blackface to adopt "My Yiddishe Mama" as the obverse of her "hot" performance personality, Tucker joined ethnic nostalgia with female rebelliousness to create a new, independent, modern stage persona. But the "Jewish mother" icon she transmitted through her famous song, "Yiddishe Mama," was a similar figure to Jolson's "mammy." While her own mother, Jennie, was smart and pragmatic, showing the same flexibility as Sara in *The Jazz Singer*, in the song, as in the first American talkie, the "way out of the ghetto was a one-way street, and those who chose to remain in the old neighborhood were left behind."[37] These Jewish mothers were strong and loving, but more and more, their children saw these traits as hindrances to success rather than aids. The seeds of the overbearing, dominating mother were already planted in these early representations.

"The Kitchen Was Her Life": Remembering the Jewish Mother

Both *The Jazz Singer* and Tucker's "Yiddishe Mama" displaced the real Jewish mothers of the immigrant generation from their living worlds. These mothers seem frozen in time, trapped in a nostalgic Old World habitat where they will forever be weeping and sentimentalized. Jewish fathers appear as even more bloodless; though they may seem forbidding, domineering, and even cruel, they usually do not carry the day. Defeated patriarchs, unable to meet their families' expectations, they, too, seem caught between the world of the past and future.

The destruction of the father's role and status in the face of New World upheavals was overwhelming, its causes economic as well as psychological. With families unable to survive on the father's income (one estimate suggests that less than 20 percent of immigrant families did so), daughters and sons became supplementary breadwinners. Mothers played a vital role by taking in boarders, doing piecework at home, and working in family-owned stores, but their participation in the paid labor force was much less than that of other groups; mirroring the attitude of bourgeois American women in the larger society, Jewish mothers who had often been the economic mainstays of their families in Eastern Europe increasingly thought of paid work as an "embarrassment."[38]

Accompanying the loss of fathers' economic prowess was the erosion of their religious authority.[39] In his study of the changing nature of patriarchy within Jewish families, Lawrence Fuchs explains how difficult it was to balance business success with a life of piety; the latter often went by the wayside as fathers felt the pressure to escape poverty and achieve economic success. While many fathers faithfully attempted to observe Torah practices, in America, "women did not support men who sat and read books."[40]

Mothers assumed increasing authority within the home more than was the case in Europe. "My mother ran the family" was a typical comment in immigrant memoirs.[41] While it is true that mothers, like fathers, were in some ways dependent on their more rapidly Americanizing children—"in America, the children bring up the parents," acclaimed immigrant writer Mary Antin remarked—their loss of authority was never as great as the fathers', whose failure to achieve status and power outside the family diminished their place within it.[42] Bereft of the mainsprings of their identity, many fathers lost their children's respect, especially sons'; in the early years of the century, fathers began to desert their families in disproportionately high numbers—unable and unwilling to shoulder the burdens of family life.[43] Increasingly, they seemed "between two sexes" as well as between two worlds. Writer Kate Simon, who grew up on the Lower East Side of New York, described her friends' unemployed fathers as "emasculate[d]"—"they became quiet, slow-moving old women."[44] In Irving Howe's view, mothers attempted to compensate for the difficulties their husbands experienced in the outside world by creating an "oasis of order" at home, preserving at least a portion of "customary deference" to husbands. But to do this took great strength, "sometimes an excess of strength."[45]

With the father's loss of masculine potency and status, the Jewish mother's power within the family increased to fill the void. The Jewish mother became an object of "sentimental veneration" in Howe's view; the "flow of power" toward her created a "crisis" that twisted the Jewish family "into new shapes." In time, this would lead to a view of the Jewish mother as "smothering," "shrewish," and "insufferable."[46]

These complex and conflicting themes were put forward in many novels, memoirs, dramas, and films of the 1920s and 1930s. One of the most sentimental appearances of the Jewish mother as Yiddishe mama came in Polish-born writer Sholom Asch's *The Mother* (1930), the first of Asch's novels to be translated into English. A paean to the Lower East Side immigrant matriarch, Asch's book celebrated the mother's "majestic and heroic struggle" to hold her family together amid the dislocation and desperation of ghetto life. In Asch's "half-humorous, half-tragic" depiction, the jacket copy proclaimed, the mother's "tenderness and all-embracing love" transcended "all thought of race, religion, civilization and time. She ceases to be the Jewish Mother; she becomes the Mother of all men."[47]

In autobiographical writings, sons remembered mothers with similar nostalgia; as Kathie Friedman-Kasaba observes, they emphasized their mothers' "heroic self-sacrifices and subservience in the name of collective family survival."[48] Who could forget Alfred Kazin's poignant memories of his family's kitchen in *A Walker in the City*, a room dominated "by the nearness of my mother sitting all day long at her sewing machine, by the clacking of the treadle against the linoleum floor"? As Kazin began to understand his mother's "fantastic capacity for labor and her anxious zeal," he realized "it was ourselves she kept stitching together." The centrality of the kitchen to sons' remembrances of immigrant mothers was common. Kazin wrote, "The kitchen gave a special character to our lives; my mother's character," and it illuminated the ways in which in the New World, as in the Old, food remained at the center of existence.[49]

Jewish sons portrayed their mothers not only as providers of food and love, but also as "wielders of enormous power and authority as 'bosses' of their families." In his novel of immigrant life, *Jews without Money*, Michael Gold captured his "funny little East Side mother" as someone who, echoing the lyrics of "Yiddishe Mama," "would have stolen or killed for us. She would have let a railroad train run over her body if it could have helped us. She loved us with all the fierce painful love of a mother-wolf, and scolded us continually like a magpie."[50] Despite the brutal poverty that circumscribed his family's lives, as her son recalled her, Mrs. Gold warded off all material and spiritual enemies by virtue of her indomitable will.

Perhaps the earliest literary depiction of the changing nature of maternal character in the New World appeared in the first great work of American Jewish literature, Abraham Cahan's 1917 novel, *The Rise of David Levinsky*. Considered a classic study of immigration and success, the book recounts the spectacular rise of an impoverished, formerly pious immigrant who becomes a wealthy cloak and suit manufacturer, "the great Levinsky."[51] But accompanying this grand success is the realization of the hollowness of the American achievement myth. Lonely and despairing, Levinsky is unable to find any love that matches the love held for him by the mother who died in the Old Country fighting the Gentiles who had beaten him up.[52] Passionately devout, a leader in her community, and fiercely devoted to her only child, Levinsky's mother formed the model of feminine behavior that the son was unable to erase from his mind despite his prosperity; yet he could not find this ideal in America. As one synagogue-goer whom Levinsky encounters in his travels explains, his own wife had "changed for the worse in America." Instead of "supporting him while he read Talmud," as she used to do at home, she sent him out to business. "He must peddle or be nagged to death." "Alas!" Levinsky's informant tells him, "America is a topsy-turvy country."[53]

Paradoxical memories of pathos and power inhabited the recollections of immigrant daughters as well as sons. However, daughters did not mythologize their mothers' strengths as fully as did sons; sensitivity to the mothers' disempowerment because of their subordinate marital roles tempered daughters' admiration of their mothers' virtues. As Janet Burstein has shown, mothers' submissiveness to male authority led such writers as Mary Antin, Anzia Yezierska, Kate Simon, and Emma Goldman to deny their likeness to their mothers or to revise the maternal strategies they had learned in their mothers' kitchens. While the daughters absorbed their mothers' strengths, the mothers' lack of defiance in the face of fathers' injustices disappointed them.[54]

This was the case in Yezierska's first novel, *Bread Givers*, published to critical acclaim in 1925. The story of an independent-minded young woman who fights her way out of poverty and the patriarchal dictates of her religious, immigrant father, *Bread Givers* paints a sympathetic portrait of the mother, whose hard work and practical business skills help support the family while her husband, living only for God, cannot provide. Cursing the father as a "stone giver" rather than a "bread giver," the mother, accused by her husband of constantly "nagging" because of her worldly concerns about money, nevertheless falls under the sway of his piety and learning. "I'm willing to give up all my earthly needs for the wine of Heaven with you," she tells him.[55] Although she is more flexible and adaptable than the rigid, uncompromising father, ultimately the mother, too, belongs to the Old World. She offers concrete support after the daughter breaks with her hard-hearted father to go her own way, but her failure of constancy leaves the daughter without a viable role model. Her mediation is thus less validating than that of *The Jazz Singer*'s mother.

The presentation of the profoundly maternal, deeply loving mother, Genya Schearl, in Henry Roth's novel *Call It Sleep*, some nine years later, fits a similar pattern. Genya is loving and nurturing, but despite her tender protectiveness of her young son, David, she offers a flawed model of mother-love because of her inability to counter the bullying of her brutal and inadequate husband. Another economic failure who cannot support his family, Albert Schearl lashes out on his son in "electric . . . fury," much as did Henry Roth's own father.[56] Only through the force of his imagination can young David escape the desperation of the ghetto—a world so hostile, wrote Alfred Kazin, "that the hostility begins with his own father." In Kazin's view, the book was the "most profound novel of Jewish life" that he had ever read by an American. According to Irving Howe, it demonstrated, in particular, why the "oedipal romance was peculiarly Jewish, perhaps even a Jewish invention." The "lyrical . . . open sensuality" and "maternal adoration" Howe finds in this work complemented the portrayal of mother-love in *The Jazz Singer*.[57]

"Humoresque" and the Hollywood Films of the 1920s and 1930s

As in literature, early cinematic portrayals of the Jewish family chronicle increasingly problematic conflicts between parents and children and husbands and wives. In general, the Jewish family in early American films is portrayed much like Jack's family in *The Jazz Singer*: mothers are shown as courageous in their embrace of the new while fathers are rigid and impractical. The relationship between mothers and sons is an extremely important issue. Mothers' devotion to sons often contrasts with their lack of respect for fathers, who they see as miserable failures. The daughters that do appear are depicted positively.

According to film historian Sharon Pucker Rivo, the early portrayal of immigrant mothers and daughters as confident, self-reliant, and capable grew out of the "self-assurance and strong character" of the women involved in their portrayal, such as the writers (Fannie Hurst, Frances Marion, and Anzia Yezierska) and the actors (Rosa Rosanova, Mollie Picon, Vera Gordon.)[58] The positive role of the immigrant mother in these early films has also been attributed to the fact that the Jewish Hollywood moguls who produced them doted on their mothers and were "in rebellion against their failed *Luftmen-schen* fathers."[59]

One of the most influential prototypes of the warm-hearted, self-sacrificing immigrant mother came in 1920 with the highly successful silent film *Humoresque*. Developed from a short story by Fannie Hurst with a scenario by renowned screenwriter Frances Marion, the film tells the story of Leon Cantor, a child of the ghetto, who rises to become a great violinist with the encouragement and prayers of his loving mother.[60] Hurst's own feelings about her midwestern, German Jewish mother were much more ambivalent. Simultaneously devoted to her mother and suffocated by her, Hurst feared her mother's "volcanic" rages, yet pronounced undying love for her.[61] In defiance of her mother, who was contemptuous of East European Jews, Hurst married one, then kept her marriage secret for five years until it was revealed by a reporter. *Humoresque*'s paean to mother-love may have salved her guilty conscience at this act of rebellion and deceit.

In the film, the loving Jewish mother dotes completely on her son and displaces the father in her power to shape the son's future. While the father believes she spoils the son and opposes her desire that the son become a musician (why don't you pray "for a business man," the father asks her), the mother holds firm.[62] "A father doesn't understand like a mother," she declares; when Leon achieves success, she gloats that "a mother always can tell what will happen to her children." "Sublimest of all is the faith of the mother," an intertitle declares. With the advent of the World War, the patriotic Leon interrupts his career to enlist in the army; at his leave-taking, his mother insists that the embarrassed soldier sit on her lap while she inappropriately cuddles him. Injured in the war and subsequently unable to play the violin, Leon's spirit is broken, but he eventually recovers.

"God always hears a mother's prayer," his mother intones. "I suppose a papa's prayer has nothing to do with it," the father adds as the film concludes. Film director Frank Borzage acknowledged his own belief that the character of Mama Cantor "represented the most wonderful of all human expressions—the expression of mother love which is the most dramatic, the most inspiring, and the most beautiful of all emotional themes."[63] While the mother in the film is hovering, doting, and infantilizing to a fault, she stands up to her husband and devotes herself to her son's talents and desires. Five years before *The Jazz Singer*, she emotes, without words, her adoration of her offspring.

A less sanctimonious though equally positive portrayal of the Jewish mother appeared in the 1922 silent film *Hungry Hearts*, adapted from an amalgam of Anzia Yezierska's short stories. A Samuel Goldwyn film, *Hungry Hearts* tells the story of a newly arrived immigrant family from Eastern Europe that finds rough going in their new home on the Lower East Side. The father, a Torah scholar with his nose always in the book, is a dismal failure as a pushcart peddler, selling his wares cheaper than he bought them. The mother, played

The silent film *Humoresque* (1920) offered a prototype of the warmhearted, self-sacrificing immigrant mother. It also became a model for the image of an oedipal relationship between Jewish mothers and sons. (Jerome H. Remick & Co.)

magisterially by Yiddish star Rosa Rosanova, is the mainstay of the family, concerned about the practical details of feeding her children but also with helping along her beautiful eldest daughter's budding romance with a young law student who collects their rent. Inspired by the sparkling white kitchen of an upperclass matron for whom she does laundry, this Jewish mother saves money to paint her own kitchen white. When the landlord doubles the rent of the now beautiful apartment, she takes an ax to her kitchen wall in frenzied protest. Her action is driven by the passion and power of a mother's deepest desire—to care for her family and make their lives bearable. Rosanova's eyes, flashing with hurt fury, determination, and rage, express in stark visual terms the fierce protectiveness of a mother who cannot be thwarted and her passionate belief in the American promise of social justice. Capturing a truth about the immigrant Jewish mother that is beyond words, it is an unforgettable moment of silent cinema.

In Yezierska's original story, after the mother is arrested for destroying the landlord's property, the trial judge finds her guilty: in America, after all, a landlord is free to charge whatever the traffic will bear.[64] In Goldwyn's film, the mother triumphs in court, and the landlord, a Jew, is severely reprimanded by the Gentile judge. In the final scene, the family enjoys its second summer in America ensconced in a country home, complete with white picket fence and garden; the daughter has married her beau, now a prosperous lawyer, and the mother, in white apron and carrying a dust mop, is a happy homemaker. Yezierska was horrified that Hollywood had meddled with the script that she had written in "pain and agony," putting in instead a totally false happy ending. "A happy ending!" she wrote in anger. "To my story."[65]

Despite Yezierska's wrath at the mangling of her story, the film presents a dignified portrait of the newly resettled Jewish family, especially the mother and daughter, who are shown to have a close and loving relationship.[66] Moreover, both in the film and Yezierska's story, the mother is portrayed as a figure of courage, strength, and imagination. She is the emotional mainstay of her family, and when justice seems to be lacking, she pursues it. Her husband might be the Torah scholar, but it is the mother's righteous indignation over the abuse of her beautiful kitchen—the almost religious center of Jewish family life—that fulfills the Jewish mandate for moral action.[67]

By the end of the decade, as acculturation proceeded apace and especially after the onset of the Depression, Hollywood's portraits of immigrant Jewish mothers began to shift. Instead of the virtuous, beneficent representation of Yiddishe mamas, directors, writers, and producers offered a more shaded, ambiguous portrait. *Younger Generation*, a 1929 film directed by Frank Capra, is a bitter melodramatic continuation of generational conflict that puts the mother's moral compass under deeper scrutiny. Based on Fannie Hurst's 1925 story, "The Gold in Fish," the film is about the Goldfish family, split apart by the economic rise of older son Morris.[68] Motivated by his mother's ambitions,

Morris has usurped his father's position in the family and turned his parents into obedient children. Morris works his way up from a second-hand store to an antique dealership. His mother supports him in his quest for money and social standing, while neglecting her less ambitious husband, Julius, and her sweet-tempered daughter, Birdie. She calls Morris "my life" and taunts her husband by telling him that "Morris will be a business man like you ain't." Stung, Julius replies, "Money ain't good for nothing, mama—if it don't buy happiness." Morris finally moves the whole family to Park Avenue. Birdie marries a songwriter, of whom Morris disapproves, and leaves home. The father is miserable—he never feels comfortable in the rich surroundings. As the father and mother arrive home carrying packages from a happy visit back to the Lower East Side, they encounter Morris with his society friends in the lobby of their building. Morris denies they are his parents, demanding they use the back stairs. Mother and father both now realize their folly. Julius is taken ill and eventually dies. The mother moves back to the Lower East Side with Birdie and her new family, and Morris is left alone.

The film presents two contrasting representations of Jewish mothers. As Tildie Goldfish, Rosa Rosanova plays a very different character from the one she played in *Hungry Hearts*. She is a social climber herself and initially loves the Park Avenue apartment. While she is more capable than her husband, her economic ambition is viewed as a moral liability. The mother cannot see the ethical implications of her son's upward rise, and she misses entirely the goodness of her daughter. Only in the end does she see the truth, but by this time she is a broken woman. Birdie, the daughter, is a wonderful representation of the next generation. She is good, loyal, and hardworking, but also beautiful, fun, and clever. The birth of her son on the Lower East Side symbolizes the new American Jewish life. In contrast, Morris lives in a tomb of an apartment, as Birdie calls it, and remains unmarried.[69]

The year 1932 saw the release of two films that continued the ambiguous portrayals of Jewish mothers. RKO's *Symphony of Six Million* is another Fannie Hurst melodrama about the dangers of material success. In a plot similar to *Younger Generation*, the family in the film learns the hard way that the ethical core of success—and of the Jewish family itself—is neither money nor status, but the traditional values of care and love.[70] *Heart of New York*, released the same year, is a Mervyn LeRoy film based on the play *Mendel, Inc.* by David Freedman, and it presents an even more compromised Jewish mother. Full of criticism of society and nostalgia for the East Side, the film portrays the mother as so powerful that she insists that her husband, Mendel, give up his patriarchal role. She says to Mendel: "A wife's place is in the house, in the kitchen over the stove. I always wanted to be such a wife. I tried, but you wouldn't let me. From now on I'm the father of the family. If you don't want to go to work, I will." Mendel then has to do the cooking and cleaning, at which he is a miserable failure. As in *Younger Generation*, the father ends up holding the moral high ground while the upwardly mobile and materialistic mother fails to understand the "true spirit" of the Lower East Side.[71]

Given the general absence of cinematic portrayals of Jews over the next three decades, these films are particularly significant. With the implementation of the 1934 Production Code that prohibited negative references to national origins and religion, Hollywood producers censored potentially unfavorable ethnic types from their films.[72] This development only exacerbated the growing tendency of the Hollywood moguls to glorify assimilation at the expense of authentic, full-bodied representations of Jews and other minorities.[73] These films offer the last direct glimpses into the problematic acculturation of Jewish families as seen on screen. For the most part, these films present the experience of assimilation as successful, but nonetheless fraught with the tensions of dislocation and instability.[74] The uprooting and realignment takes its most marked toll not only on relations between parents and children, but also between husbands and wives. The films thrust the Jewish mother into the spotlight because she has the opportunity to influence both relations so powerfully. Embodying conflicting characteristics—both "good" and "bad"—these representations responded to the crises and opportunities of assimilation. Morally suspect or praiseworthy because of her adaptability to the circumstances of immigrant life, the Jewish mother is a figure of contradictory, complex power.

The New Jewish Matriarchy

That the immigrant Jewish mother wielded such influence and power in these films is noteworthy. Social reformers who wanted to help Americanize immigrants claimed that, in reality, immigrant mothers stood guard over backward, dysfunctional households and blocked their families' successful assimilation. Inefficient and static, "immigrant women were very generally years behind the men in Americanization," wrote Frances Kellog, a leading Progressive reformer, in 1916. To such observers, the very notion of an actively Americanized immigrant mother seemed "oxymoronic."[75]

Yet others who worked with Jewish mothers disagreed. "The Jewish mother is a wonderful mother," declared Dr. Royal S. Copeland, New York City's commissioner of health, in 1922. Despite deplorable housing conditions, Jewish babies on the Lower East Side were healthier than those of "Fifth Avenue" mothers because Jewish mothers nursed their own babies and went to milk stations for pure milk for other offspring. According to the director of a clinic in Brownsville who worked with families of different immigrant groups, the Jewish mother was "the most sacrificing mother in the world," knowing no limits where her child's health was concerned. "Continually progressive— eager to learn and grateful for the opportunity of learning," she eagerly sought out the most up-to-date advice from officials, unlike other foreign-born mothers. "The Board of Health is second only to the Almighty in her eyes."[76]

So in the eyes of some, Jewish mothers were thus vindicated as "model mothers," but the majority of reformers, and the public at large, saw her as backward and unrefined—very much like other immigrants.[77] One of the reasons *Humoresque* had created such a stir was the fact that the elevated Jewish mother it portrayed seemed so different than the usual type, even according to Jews themselves. "Our own Jewish mothers must go and see [it]," a critic from the Yiddish paper, *Der Tog*, wrote. "They will discover the fact, that a Jewish mother can be a woman, who does not wipe her nose on her apron, who does not curse and scream until you are deaf, and speaks in moderation and to the point."[78]

The cultural representations of Jewish mothers that appeared in literature and film may have been no more reliable as fact than the mixed characterizations drawn by social reformers.[79] The point is that these varied representations suggest multiple, rather than monolithic, interpretations of the mother's role in a changing world. Literary memoirs, fiction, films, and song romanticized the Jewish mother's piety, hard work, suffering and sacrifice, and her deep affection for her children, especially her sons; at the same time they exaggerated her willfulness and mastery of her household. Consequently she appeared in dual roles—paradoxically materialistic but selfless, backward but modern, lovingly protective and coldly aggressive.

These representations sprang from significant transformations in the social worlds of first-generation immigrants. As previously discussed, new patterns of employment and religious observance removed authority from fathers, creating a "topsy-turvy" world that gave more authority to immigrant Jewish mothers than their European counterparts. That fathers spent more time away from home in business rendered their relationship with children increasingly impersonal; while loving their children, they seemed less able to respond to them emotionally.[80]

In 1932, in a series of lectures presented to the Women's League of the United Synagogue of America (the sisterhood of the Conservative movement), educator Jacob Kohn addressed this transformation. Kohn reflected on the fact that highly civilized societies had left the "patriarchal family" so far behind that the father's influence had shrunk to "comparative insignificance" and was in "danger of disappearing altogether." "In Jewish circles in America, particularly," he told the women, "there are signs of a new matriarchy—that is, signs that the mother of the family is looked upon as more highly privileged and more directly responsible as regards the training of children."[81] The rise of the new Jewish "matriarchy" and the apparent decline of the father's power sprang from universal changes in modern economic life and the particular pressures to acculturate.[82]

Additional changes in Jewish family life in the United States promoted the Jewish mother's dominance at home and, thus, in her cultural image. Because relatively few Jewish mothers participated in the paid workforce, they were able to devote more time to their young children, sustaining them on a daily basis, nurturing them through illnesses and the demands of the new environment. Jewish women breast-fed their babies for longer than was common, and they began to employ contraception earlier and more broadly than other religious groups.[83] While some Jewish immigrant families had as many as five to ten children, the average was smaller, and by the second generation, American Jews had reduced their fertility to usually not more than two children, a significant factor in Jews' impressive social mobility. This movement to smaller families had begun by the 1920s, and it further influenced the portrayal of Jewish mothers as self-sacrificing and devoted, lavishing attention on their children, but also single-mindedly focusing on their families' advances.

Finally, changes in foodways affected the Jewish mother's social roles and cultural representations. In America, wrote one observer, Jewish mothers "went to inordinate trouble to provide their children with the 'best and freshest' food, the best medical care, the warmest clothing—at considerable sacrifice of other needs and wants."[84] "We never had a chance to know what hunger meant," Alfred Kazin recalled of his upbringing in Brownsville. "At home we nibbled all day long as a matter of course," and at dinner time, "great meals" were "rammed down" children's throats:

> Eat! Eat! May you be destroyed if you don't eat! What sin have I committed that God should punish me with you! Eat! What will become of you if you don't eat! Imp of darkness, may you sink ten fathoms into the earth if you don't eat! Eat![85]

While Kazin's portrait may seem extreme, historian Hasia Diner has documented immigrants' "obsession with children's consumption, the belief that food indicated love and ensured health." According to Diner, these attitudes grew out of immigrants' "pre-migration encounter with hunger and America's possibilities." Because of the requirements for *kashrut* (keeping kosher), Jews' concern with obtaining and preparing food had been central to family and collective survival; in America, the new abundance of foodstuffs, coupled with the process of assimilation, altered Jews' relation to food and "divided them among themselves." Aware of these changes, Jewish mothers and grandmothers used food in particular ways—not only to stave off hunger but "to connect Americanizing children to the world of tradition"; they cooked "to sustain life and pass it on." These motives could of course backfire, particularly when children, attempting to assert their independence and their embrace of newer ways, simply refused to eat. As one social worker reported in 1925, the "symbolization of food" among immigrant Jews became a factor in family fights and led to family dysfunction.[86]

The old ways were in fact rapidly growing out of favor. Social reformers increasingly criticized the immigrant diet as "over rich and poorly balanced," as one nutritionist put it in 1928, censuring Jewish mothers for their poor cuisine and crying out for culinary reform.[87] Blamed by reformers and by family members for such backwardness, the Jewish mother did not receive enough credit for her many flexible adaptations in matters of food, health, and other issues of daily existence. Yet the old-fashioned image of Jewish mothers that appeared in these complaints and populated many cultural expressions of the period did not always jibe with the experience of mothers themselves or others who observed them carefully.

"Mothers Who Go to School with Their Children": A Debate

A series of articles appearing in fall 1925 in the short-lived Sunday English-language page of the *Jewish Daily Forward*—the largest Yiddish newspaper in the world—showcases the Jewish mother in the contradictory light that appears in other cultural artifacts of the time. Writing about conflicts between immigrant parents and their "American" children, commentators addressed the new American style of parenting and its effect on Jewish parents. Some wrote about Jewish mothers' deep involvement in their children's lives, especially in school matters. Whether "green" or newly assimilated, these mothers seemed to understand the educational components of success in the new country, and they took action accordingly. Like the popular culture representations, *Forward* accounts paint the Jewish mother's drive in both a negative and positive light. The only area of agreement among correspondents was that the Jewish mother's intense attention to her children was a defining trait of Jewish parenting in the New World.

In an article titled "Mothers Who Go to School with Their Children," Ruth Zuckoff suggested that there were two types of new Jewish mothers, each of whom was deeply committed to her children's lives and their school success. "Practically all Jewish mothers are interested in the school progress of their children," Zuckoff wrote, but they differed in how they showed their interest. Most of them "see that the report cards are regularly brought home for proper inspection, and scold if the marks are not satisfactory." But outside of these concerns, the children are "left alone to make good anyway they can." The "other type" of mother threw herself into everything the children did:

> She knows the names of the teachers and she joins a Parents' Association and takes an active part in the work of such an organization. She frequently visits the teachers, just to know the character of the person who has her children's destinies in charge. At home, this sort of mother watches everything. She studies the children's home work and goes over every example to see that they are right, helps in drilling spelling words, studies the history and geography. But most of all, she wants to know everything that is going on in school—and in the minds of her children.[88]

Given the wide differences in the backgrounds of parents and children, Zuckoff believed Jewish mothers' devotion to their children's school affairs to have been extraordinary. Not only had very few of the immigrant mothers themselves attended school, but they certainly had no acquaintance with the "broadening" kind of education increasingly common in American society: a plethora of extracurricular activities that supplemented traditional academics—"gymnasiums, playgrounds and athletic fields, workshops, kitchens, laboratories, printing shops . . . [s]wimming pools and showers. Huge auditoriums." How much understanding could be possible, Zuckoff asked, between an immigrant mother and a daughter "who had gone through eight years of folk dancing, basket ball playing, foot racing, editing of school papers, acting in the 'Mikado' and then four more years of the same thing in high school, where in addition there are dances, parties and other social life?"[89] While their first impulse might have been to question the newfangled schooling, like it or not, Jewish mothers adapted. "They make up their mind that it is their job to understand their daughters and sons, to know what is in their minds, frequently to interpret them to their father, who often hasn't the time to understand this different kind of education from the system he knew in the old country." In this way, mothers went to school with their children "in spirit" if not in person, thrilling to their successes, and helping them through their failures. Because of the Jewish mother's open attitude, the writer concluded, "there is deeper and better understanding between the two generations."[90]

A much more negative interpretation came from Nathaniel Zalowitz. Writing in the *Forward* a few months after Zuckoff, Zalowitz condemned the Jewish mother's involvement in her children's lives as almost obsessive. "A Jewish mother, especially if European born, lives exclusively for her child," he wrote.[91] "Does little Joey cough at night? Then mother runs pell mell to the 'baby specialist' in the morning! Has Miss Mildred, aged three-and-a-half, bumped her head against a lamp post? Oi vei is mir! Mother must at once take her precious darling to the drug store!"[92] According to Zalowitz, the coddling perpetrated by Jewish parents was unique to the Jewish immigrant population.

> Who ever heard of an Irish janitress paying five dollars a piano lesson for her Margy? Where will you find an Italian peddler sending his Tony to the Ethical Culture School? I have yet to meet the wife of a German mechanic that gives her five year old daughter dancing lessons. Czechs and Swedes, unless they are more than ordinarily well-to-do, don't make college professors of their sons. An American farmer only in rare instances goes out of his way to give his stalwart son a Ph.D. degree.

In an American home, Zalowitz continued, it is the "father and mother who are the most important members of the family; in the Jewish home, Irving and Shirley are the uncrowned King and Queen." "Only Jewish parents do this sort of thing," the author reiterated (although he offers no evidence for that claim). Struggling from morning to night, working their fingers "to the bone," growing old and weak so that their precious son or daughter would become "a lawyer, a dentist, a physician, or a school teacher," these Jewish parents were the "most devoted, self-sacrificing, the most ambitious in the world." At the same time, their children were "horribly selfish, self-centered, arrogant and ungrateful." "Only Jewish children are so disgustingly rude to their old folks, treat them with such indifference," even "contempt."[93]

But Zalowitz's main ire is concentrated on the Jewish mother. In one example, he talks of the immigrant mother making a prominent lawyer of her son, elevating him "to such a height that he must look down upon her as an ignorant and uncouth person." Zalowitz is as certain as was Hurst that the mother's untoward ambition and her extravagance can be blamed for this tragic outcome. "Many a Jewish mother could use the five dollars a week to better advantage than by paying tuition at the 'fancy' dancing school," he writes. "Dancing schools and similar luxuries are all right in their place; but it is nothing less than a shame and an outrage for the wife of a Jewish grocer to waste the precious few dollars in this way."[94]

In his anger at the Jewish mother for her economic and emotional extravagances, Zalowitz parts company with Zuckoff's evocation of an indulgent but effective matriarch who "watches everything" in her children's lives. Other reformers echoed Zalowitz's censure, worried that "the Jewish mother . . . loves the child very much, so that after a time the child begins to control the parent instead of being controlled by her."[95] But both Zalowitz's and Zuckoff's commentaries suggest that by 1925 the idea that the Jewish mother was different from other mothers (whether to positive or negative effect) because of her lavish attention to her "precious darlings" was beginning to coalesce. By the second half of the decade, the case against the Jewish mother for her ambition and her coddling became more prevalent.

"She Is Money Mad": The "Bintel Brief" Column

The *Forward's* own "Bintel Brief"—literally, "bunch" or "bundle" of letters from readers, published with replies from the editor—provides confirmation that the sentimental portrait of the Jewish mother that appeared in "My Yiddishe Mama," *The Jazz Singer*, and other sources had more dubious company.[96] The first such feature in a Jewish newspaper, the "Bintel Brief" was started in 1906 by editor Abraham Cahan in the hope of appealing to "semi-literate" Jewish newcomers, "especially the women," whom Cahan believed could be made to read "simply written accounts of their own affairs, those of their neighbors, and of everything else which was near and familiar."[97] Cahan and subsequent editors preferred to print the letters of married women. "They have the experience of life," one editor explained. "They are more philosophical and they are the sufferers."[98] Into the late 1920s, "American girls" and their Yiddish-speaking mothers devoured the "Bintel Brief." "The American girl asks her mother to read it to her," one editor explained, noting that letters from these "American" youth provided evidence that the reach of the "Bintel Brief" extended into the second generation.[99]

Used by generations of historians as an authentic reflection of immigrant attitudes, the "Bintel Brief" may have been more fictional than at first appears. An analysis of two hundred letters that appeared in the "Bintel Brief" in 1927 by George Wolfe, candidate for a master's degree at New York's Graduate School for Jewish Social Work, cast doubt on the authenticity of the printed correspondence. According to Wolfe, so many changes were made by editors—either by rewriting the text completely or "correcting" it—that the scientific value of the documents was "seriously damaged." Because totally new situations were invented, the result was that much of the printed record was "pure fiction." Its value to research was thus the same as that "attached to a short story."[100]

Wolfe's disclosures suggest caution in interpreting the "Bintel Brief" as a purely documentary source of evidence. Nonetheless, like short stories, novels, films, and other cultural sources, the letters provide important clues as to social beliefs. "Bintel Brief" letters from the first quarter of 1927 disclose a preponderance of family problems—unhappy marriages, separation, desertion, divorce, and parent-child issues.[101] Numerous letters from unhappy husbands and wives indicate a growing unease with family roles that helped propel the Jewish mother to center stage in popular culture.

One pronounced litany of complaints came from husbands who decried their wives' materialism. "She spends more than she ought to," wrote a husband who faulted his wife for refusing to save.[102] "When something is needed for the house she buys the very best," declared another sufferer. "And she is constantly buying things." What made matters worse was that their children considered the letter writer "a schlemiel who can't support his small family."[103] One husband reported that his wife believed that "without money . . . there is no love. Gold is her world."[104] Another husband's brief comment said it all: "She is money mad."[105]

Similar charges came from other relatives and acquaintances. One young letter writer deplored her boyfriend's mother's interference in their relationship. "A physician can exist without love but not without money," the mother told her son, a medical student, who obliged his parent by breaking up with the heartbroken girl.[106] A former rabbinical student who had given up the seminary to become a businessman blamed his mother for preventing him from leaving his unsatisfying commercial career and returning to his former spiritual life.[107]

Wives and mothers often defended themselves from such indictments and offered countercharges. To a shoemaker who reproached his wife for making life miserable for him because he did not make a lot of money, the wife wrote in denying that she was a "spendthrift" and blaming her spouse for being "stuck" in his job and never wanting "to get anywhere."[108] Another told of her family's "hunger and want" because her husband led a "gay life and paid no attention to his business."[109] One wife complained that her husband was "niggardly" and "lords it over her."[110] Another wrote that her husband refused to give her enough for expenses, even though he had money in the bank. "Sometimes I would have to borrow money from neighbors in order to buy bread for the children."[111]

On the other side of the debate, husbands who had gotten ahead in the world occasionally indicted their wives for clinging to old ways. One such spouse admitted that his wife was "frugal and loyal" but resented her stinginess. Refusing to employ servants, walking around the house in a "torn apron," she accepted no luxuries. "Why, pray, should one slave away one's days when one can afford to hire help?" the puzzled correspondent asked the *Forward* editor. Furthermore, the wife wouldn't join a "ladies' society" as was the practice in their nice neighborhood. "Added to all this" was the wife's "piety. She insists on keeping a *kosher* house." "Will anyone advise," concluded the desperate writer, "how to turn a good wife into a bad one?"[112]

While there were other triggers for spousal dissatisfaction reflected in the 1927 *Forward* letters—for example, neglect or abuse, romantic trysts, nagging and cruelty—the dissension wrought by irreconcilable attitudes toward money looms large. Husbands' concern with wives' spending, and on the flip side, wives' dissatisfaction with husbands' failure to provide, reflected a discomfort about the transformation of Jews' class status since the original "Bintel Brief" letters. While 90 percent of the 1927 correspondents were immigrants, approximately half of them had moved up from the working class into the "business class." The more affluent lifestyle available to families who had once experienced the bitter taste of poverty could affect marital partners differently. Amid allegations of frugality or stinginess, husbands and wives grappled with the vexing question of their entitlements to individual happiness versus the responsibility to uphold traditional definitions of family virtue.

The domestic strains revealed in these *Forward* letters suggest how often value conflicts within the Jewish family over issues of upward mobility came to focus on wives' and mothers' seemingly untraditional behavior. In this way, they echo one of the primary narratives of Jewish-themed films and fiction of the era. While mothers in these works were often shown as affectionate and tender, other portrayals emphasized less positive qualities, including the substitution of material for spiritual goals. In the *Forward* letters and in these works, one aspect of the Jewish mother came to reflect the perceived ambitiousness of Jewish families of the time. The Jewish mother appeared on the stage of the new era, not in her "torn apron," grieving her lost children, but, rather, as a "money-mad" gold digger, lamenting her husband's failure and pushing her sons and daughters into a problematic future they would regret.

The preponderance of conflicts around issues of modernity in the *Forward* letters, coupled with the portrayal of similar themes in family melodramas of the period, reveals how deep these concerns ran. The common response was to pillory the Jewish mother for her apparent consumerism and ambitiousness rather than to recognize that these same tendencies evidenced an openness to change and an adaptability that might have served her family extremely well.[113]

The "Jewish Mother" is Born: Odets's *Awake and Sing!*

No work better demonstrated the escalating animosity toward the Jewish mother than Clifford Odets's masterful 1935 drama, *Awake and Sing!*[114] Odets's first full-length play, *Awake and Sing!* introduced the unforgettable Bessie Berger, the character whom some critics have identified as the first full-blown manifestation of the Jewish mother type.[115] As we have seen, several prototypes of the Jewish mother appeared in cultural productions of the 1920s and the early 1930s, and Odets's depiction deepened several of those themes.

Awake and Sing! opened at the Belasco Theater in February of 1935 to enthusiastic reviews.[116] A dark tale that Odets described as a "struggle for life amidst petty conditions," the play chronicles a series of crises that beset the Bergers, a working-class family in New York. The family has struggled for

In Clifford Odets's 1935 play *Awake and Sing!*, Bessie Berger embodies the Jewish mother type as a domineering matriarch who replaces the father as the linchpin of the family. Zoe Wanamaker played Bessie on Broadway in this 2006 revival by the Lincoln Center Theater. (Paul Kolnik)

years with poverty and disappointed aspirations; Bessie, its domineering matriarch, is "constantly arranging and taking care of the family," Odets writes in
the opening notes of the play. As in other 1920s and 1930s texts that comment
on role reversal in the Jewish family, Odets describes Bessie as "not only the
mother . . . but also the father" in the Berger home; her husband, Myron, another economic failure, is "a born follower," in Odets's words, "heartbroken
without being aware of it."[117] His ineffectiveness in life makes him ridiculous
to his grown children—the pregnant Hennie, whom Bessie forces to marry a
man she does not love, and Ralph, an aspiring poet whose romantic dreams
and desire to better himself Bessie thwarts. Bessie's father, Jacob, a Socialist
who lives with the family, hopes to persuade Ralph to join his mission of im-
proving society. But Bessie's yearning for respectability and her materialism
destroy their dreams; after Jacob commits suicide, Hennie, encouraged by
Ralph, decides to abandon her husband and child to seek a better life. Bessie
acts unscrupulously to keep Jacob's insurance money, which he has left to
Ralph.

Undoubtedly the strongest character in the play, Bessie is nagging and manipulative, yet protective of what she sees as her family's best interests. In a line
that has been cited as the core of the author's brutal realism, Odets describes
Bessie as someone who knows "that when one lives in the jungle one must look
out for the wild life." But she does possess positive traits. Highly energetic and
a "shrewd judge" of human nature, she "loves life," Odets wrote, "likes to
laugh, has great resourcefulness and enjoys living from day to day." While interfering and destructive, Bessie's strengths are undeniably considerable, especially her determination to ensure her family's survival. She will "go on forever," one character predicts.[118]

Bessie is less villainous and much less the old-fashioned mama using heavy
Yiddish dialect than the mother Odets wrote into the first draft of the play, titled *I Got the Blues*.[119] In *Awake and Sing!* he makes this mother a full-bodied
emotional figure whose toughness arises from the desperate situation she tries
to maneuver. Bessie is not kind and gentle: she cruelly berates her husband and
father for their failures to provide, and she nags and infantilizes her children.
("You can't even wipe your nose yet!" she tells her twenty-two-year-old son)
and proffers a huge dose of guilt ("He eats out my heart," she says of Ralph.
"When it's too late you'll remember how you sucked away a mother's life"). But
Bessie's manipulations form a compelling part of her character; Odets gives
clues that underneath her tough, embittered exterior there may lie a more
sympathetic persona. "If I didn't worry about the family," she asks her son,
"who would?" Her anxiety for the family is not obsessive, but rather, like the
portraits of the Jewish mother in 1920s and 1930s films and the "Bintel Brief"
letters, extremely pragmatic. And the essence of her pragmatism is the recognition that in the United States, the route to success comes not through the
dreams of idealists, but through concrete material achievement. "Here, with-

out a dollar you don't look the world in the eye. Talk from now to next year—this is life in America."[120]

It is these capitalist yearnings that render Bessie her children's antagonist. Encapsulating the dangerous desires of other Jewish mothers in film and fiction, her embrace of materialism marks her moral decline and is an augur of the seeming irrelevance of traditional Jewish values in confrontation with modern choices. Whatever Bessie's motives, her voicing of capitalist desires situates her as the enemy of freedom and renders the family itself a bourgeois trap. It is not for nothing that Jacob cries out, "Marx said it—abolish such families."[121] Critic Robert Warshow, in an oft-cited commentary on the play, wrote that its brilliance lay in Odets's ability to convey the "master pattern" and "common experience" of American Jews through incisive language and complex characterization; in particular the disruption of the normal pattern by which the "wife was subordinated to the husband and the children to the father," a pattern reversed and manifested "in extreme form" by New York Jews.[122] The tragedy of the play is that despite the necessities that compel their compromises, the Bergers, imbued with a Jewish sensibility that forces them to contemplate their actions, suffer with self-contempt. Full of "bitterness," "suffering and complaining," in Warshow's words, Bessie Berger is a mere carrier of the "sociological truth" conveyed in the play—the family's "loveless intimacy" that reflected the "obverse of the Jewish virtue of family solidarity."[123]

Yet the portrait of the Bergers in *Awake and Sing!* did not wholly stand for Odets's own experience. Throughout his life, the playwright denied any resemblance between Bessie and his own mother, Pearl, to whom he remained deeply attached; Odets's biographer claims that Bessie was based on his father, whom he deeply resented.[124] In fact, Odets's mother seems to resemble the encouraging matriarch of *Humoresque* (who bought her son a violin over his father's objections) more than she did Mrs. Berger: Mrs. Odets gave young Clifford his first typewriter, which his father, preferring to orient the boy to a business career, smashed.[125]

Chronically depressed, Pearl did suffer, but more from the indiscretions of her husband and his dominating control than anything else. There was something "shadowy and romanticized" about Odets's mother, his biographer writes. Many friends and family saw her as a "model of sensitivity, good to a fault, always ready to forgive and forget, putting up with too much."[126] Odets acknowledged that his mother was "extremely subjective and sentimental."[127] He admired her honesty and her ideals—in particular, what Odets's biographer calls her "scorn for middle-class values." But when it came to her emotional demands on her only son, Pearl demonstrated ambivalent attitudes toward material comfort that deepened the playwright's own confusion about success. "The viewpoints of this household are not mine," he wrote after a problematic visit on Mothers' Day, 1932, shortly before he began the draft of *Awake and Sing!* Pearl's desire that her son be "happy"—in Odets's words, by seeing him "successful, having nice things, looking well, so she can be proud of me"—induced anguish and guilt. "Such viewpoints kill me," Odets acknowledged.

> I point out constantly to her that if her happiness depends on mine, as she says it does, that I have never been so happy in all my life as I am now. But no, it goes on as old; she looks at me and is torn between her kind of mother love and an unhappy mild bitterness that I am different from others and not materially rich.[128]

Pearl Odets did die happy, shortly after witnessing the mammoth success of *Awake and Sing!* Odets's grief at her passing is recorded in the journal he kept five years later. "No day or night goes by in which I do not think of my dead mother," Odets confessed. Her influence extended both to inherited physical habits and matters of conscience: "I always turn the picture face down when I do something my mother would not have liked," Odets admitted. So, he acknowledged, "the dear dead mother, peers from behind the face of the living son."[129]

Pearl was not Bessie Berger, to be sure. More likely, the Jewish mother in the play displaces the antagonism that Odets felt for his father, a man who justified "hypocrisy in life" in order "to get someplace in America."[130] To his journal, Odets confided that the "prime split" in his personality was "between a good heart" and a "strong ego." "These two represent in me my mother and father."[131]

Odets was only one of the first in a long line of Jewish writers (mostly male) who would invest their intense struggle between masculine and feminine principles in their literary creations. The Jewish mother "type"—brandished compellingly in *Awake and Sing!*—was thus a psychological construction about gender systems as well as in Warshow's words a "sociological truth" about a "particular stage in the process of [Jewish] acculturation." No longer the sentimental, self-sacrificing, mournful "Yiddishe Mama" of a decade before, or the smiling, well-meaning facilitator represented by Sara Rabinowitz, the Jazz Singer's mother, Odets's Bessie Berger is calculating, cruel, and selfish, representing the most negative qualities of the type that surfaced in the *Forward* letters and the films of the late 1920s and early 1930s. Constructed both from Odets's personal experience, imaginatively stretched and magnified to suit the requirements of proletarian drama, and the profound impact of the Great Depression, this arguably first theatrical Jewish mother would have many successors on the American cultural stage.

The prominence of the Jewish mother in the cultural narratives of the 1920s and 1930s reveals that at its heart, the process of acculturation was deeply gendered. Modernization involved a significant reordering of power relations between parents and children and husbands and wives; in each case, the Jewish mother played a central role in her family's response to the new conditions and in the imaginative renderings of this process. The idea of the Jewish mother, so powerfully evoked in the culture of the period, arose to alleviate, measure, and guide the tensions of adaptation. On the one hand, the cultural evidence embodies an inchoate confidence that Jewish acculturation to New World possibilities could be facilitated and rendered safe by the Jewish mother, who appeared more flexible and capable than her beaten-down husband. On the other hand, these same images bear witness to fears that the mother's very success would irrevocably alter traditional patterns of Jewish life. The "new matriarchy" of Jewish women seemed a threat as well as a cure for the unsettling issues of immigration and acculturation.

MOLLY: Let him go, Jake. Let go. It's not easy for a parent to let go at the right minute . . . Let's both let go.

JAKE: Have we got a choice?

MOLLY: Do we want a choice?

Jake, there comes a time, Jake, when children graduate not only from high school and college but the time comes they get a diploma from parents also. We did our best Jake and we now can only hope that our best was good enough. . . .

I'm satisfied, Jake, and you should be also that we raised a son that can think for himself.

—*The Goldbergs*, "Sammy's Wedding"

2

MOLLY GOLDBERG

"The Prototype of the Jewish Mother" in the Twentieth Century

JUST TWO YEARS AFTER AL JOLSON SANG "MAMMY" in blackface to his beaming Jewish mother, another Jewish mother arrived on the main stage of American entertainment. "Molly Goldberg," the fictional creation of writer-producer-actress Gertrude Berg, debuted in a 1929 radio serial, *The Rise of the Goldbergs*, and made the transition to television in 1949; it was the first family sitcom in each medium. The show ended its run in 1956 but reappeared in two short-lived series, *Mrs. G.* and *Molly Goes to College*, keeping some form of it on the air until 1962.[1] Berg's brilliant creation resolved the contradictions posed by the earlier, bifurcated image of the Jewish mother. Effectively combining the Yiddishe mama's sentimentalized saintliness with the power and energy of her real-life counterparts, Molly Goldberg emerged as a beloved "surrogate mother" to millions of Americans. "Every American is entitled to a Jewish mother," declared film critic J. Hoberman some fifty years after *The Goldbergs* left the air. "And for those who can't have one, there is Molly Goldberg." She was, says Hoberman, "the Jewish mother of us all."[2]

At a time of significant anti-Semitism in the United States, with Jews largely invisible as characters in films, radio, and television, *The Goldbergs* was a cultural phenomenon, effectively representing Jews to a diverse and enthusiastic audience for more than a quarter century.[3] Berg wrote the show's more than ten thousand scripts, starred in it, and produced and directed as well. She was a powerful, pioneering, one-woman "auteur," putting her stamp on every aspect of these productions.[4] Along the way came a touring vaudeville act, a comic strip, syndicated column, cookbook, hit Broadway play, film, and Berg's biography, *Molly and Me*.[5]

The program's Jewishness was a key factor in its huge success. In particular, Berg's conception of Molly as Jewish mother gave the show a distinctive perch from which to view anxieties about social mobility, couching these concerns in the dynamic of family relations. Unlike Clifford Odets or Anzia Yezierska, who portrayed the generational conflict wrought by Americanization as a "war to the knife," Berg allowed the good-natured, astute Molly to resolve contentious social and family issues; she vanquished family dysfunction from popular notions of Jewish family life almost single-handedly.[6] Molly proved that immigrant mothers did not have to be left behind as Jews moved forward, nor would they pollute Judaic values with materialistic concerns. With mothers like Molly reliably steering the course, immigrants and other working-class citizens could make it in America. In fact, because they successfully modernized in spite of their difference—that is, their ethnicity—the Goldbergs, the popular representation of the Jewish American family in the American mind, became inscribed as consummate Americans—*the* American family par excellence.

Molly as Jewish Mother: Universality, Authenticity, Modernity

Ordinary people of all backgrounds identified with Molly, Berg's biographer Glenn D. ("Pete") Smith believes, "because she took their 'everyday' problems—money, politics, health, marriage, children and war—and made them her own."[7] Proof of this came in fan mail from all kinds of Americans— "farmers' wives, Quaker women, lumberjacks, art connoisseurs, physicians, teachers, sailors, and chauffeurs"—even one Mother Superior who wrote to Berg to ask for scripts she missed when her convent gave up the show for Lent.[8] Many people noted the ecumenical appeal of the show: "We like the democratic and friendly feeling they have for Jew, Gentile, and Catholic," wrote an Oklahoma City woman to Berg in 1933. "'Molly' is a beautiful character, an example for all wives and mothers . . . we cannot imagine any portrayal of family life more perfect." According to one commentator, writing a year later:

> "The Rise of the Goldbergs" became much more than an entertaining and popular sketch. It developed into the most valuable means of building inter-religious and inter-racial good will. The universality of its appeal and its refined and restrained sympathy won for it a huge Christian audience that had never before listened in on a Jewish program. Hundreds of Christian clergymen have assured Mrs. Berg that she does more than a thousand sermons to promote Christian-Jewish goodwill and amity.[9]

Although some Jews chafed at characterizations and language that they thought were too Jewish—especially Molly's malapropisms or her Uncle David with his heavy accent—the vast majority of Jews were pleased at the show's portrayal of Jewish life. "This series has done more to *set us Jews right* with the 'goyim' than all the sermons ever preached by the Rabbis," wrote one Jewish educator.[10] Clergy loved the show. One Orthodox rabbi advised listeners to tune in at four o'clock on Friday, before *Shabbes* started, "so when *The Goldbergs* come on," they could listen "without breaking the law."[11]

Berg did not want the show to appear excessively Jewish or partisan. "I don't bring up anything that will bother people," she once told an interviewer.

> Unions, politics, fund-raising, Zionism, socialism, inter-group relations, I don't stress them. And, after all, aren't all such things secondary to daily family living? The Goldbergs are not defensive about their Jewishness, or especially aware of it. . . . I keep things average. I don't want to lose friends.[12]

While she avoided politics, Berg was interested in more than entertainment. In her view, popular culture was a medium through which she could educate the public about issues of social concern, while portraying more positive images of Jewish family life than those expressed in vaudeville, which she found degrading. Considering Montague Glass stories and the dialect humor of 1920s cartoonist Milton Gross to be vulgar, Berg gave the show a softer but distinct immigrant voice with Yiddish-toned inflections and "Mollypropisms."[13] Despite her disclaimer, Berg aired issues of special importance to Jews, minorities, and the working class. For example, in the fall 1949 television season, Berg broadcast both "The Rent Strike," about a greedy landlord who raises rents (Molly solves the problem by baking him a birthday cake), and "Molly's Hat," which discussed European relatives who survived the Holocaust.[14] Neither show took on these charged issues frontally, yet the very mention of struggles with capitalism or the European war on prime-time television comedy was uncommon.

Berg fully understood that in order to win her audience, she needed to center the show not on particular themes, but on the common occurrences of everyday life—the dramatic events experienced by any family, no matter its background. For Berg, "surface differences" only emphasized "how alike most people are underneath." She prided herself that her show had found a "common denominator."[15] By shaping a benign but complex maternal character, and using that character to constructively enter into the affairs and problems of neighbors, friends, and assorted relatives, she managed to keep the show universal in message and supremely entertaining, but also relevant and educational.

While the show depicted many arenas of daily life, child-rearing was a central concern. But this aspect of Berg's vision has escaped attention, perhaps because so many plotlines had the characters busy with other escapades.[16] Yet parenting was a major part of *The Goldbergs*' dramatic mis-en-scène; throughout her career, in fact, Berg took the opportunity to educate parents both as Molly and in her own voice. In so doing, she created a very different image of the Jewish mother than those circulating around her. In 1934, she began "Mama-talks," a column syndicated in Jewish newspapers and written over her own signature, which advised Jewish mothers about child-rearing. The following year Berg created a pilot series for her broad public audience, also called *Mama-talks*, the name she gave to a neighborhood mothers' club on the show. Though the mothers' club show and the newspaper series were short-lived, *The Goldbergs* promulgated modern attitudes about parenting throughout its long run, suggesting in many episodes that even though Molly may have appeared as an instinctive mother, truly enlightened parenting was a matter of learning and psychology. In these beliefs, the show bore witness to the change in parenting standards of second-generation Jews, a by-product of acculturation and modernization. Berg hoped to transmit these new beliefs through the medium of popular culture.

The "Mamatalks" columns and the *Goldberg* shows reveal a porousness between reality and fiction that characterized Gertrude/Molly throughout her long career. Berg's son, Cherney, who wrote and coproduced some of the later television shows with Gertrude, grew up thinking that he "had two mothers": he felt that Molly was the "ideal" mother that Gertrude, the busy professional, might have been had she not pursued her career. But Molly was "not a portrayal, not a stereotype," Cherney told an interviewer. "It's an inflection. . . . She's reflecting what she knew."[17] To instill such a correspondence, Berg cleverly marketed herself as Molly, signing autographs in Molly's name, and publishing a cookbook and magazine articles as Molly. Any differences between the character and the actress-writer were masked. "If you take a consensus," commented Berg's friend Leonard Spielglass in a eulogy, "she finally turned out to be Molly Berg—an amalgam of her own name and the character she had played for so long."[18]

Berg's distinctive melding of modernity with the character's quaintness contributed to the perception of the show's authenticity. On the one side stands Molly's language and appearance, her concern with food and family. On the other is Molly's forward-looking philosophy. Language identified Molly and the Goldbergs as old-fashioned Jews, members of a minority whose speech marked them as outsiders. In the radio years, Molly's speech was heavily Yiddish-accented, but it was Molly's clever malapropisms—"Come sit on the table, dinner is ready. . . . I'll spill you in the soup. . . . You'll swallow a cup, darling? . . . Throw an eye into the ice-box and give me an accounting"—that provided the show's humor.[19] Molly's appearance—her dark, shapeless,

The Rise of the Goldbergs, a pioneering radio, and later television, sitcom, offered a positive view of the rising middle-class Jewish family. Gertrude Berg created "Molly Goldberg"—the "prototype" of the Jewish mother for over a quarter of a century—as a supremely maternal character who used the mother's role to enter into the affairs of her children, assorted relatives, friends, and neighbors. (Special Collections, Syracuse University Library)

unadorned dresses, often covered by a checkered apron; her plain hairstyle, pulled back in a bun; and her very ample girth—exaggerated her old-fashioned, *haimishe* (homelike) authenticity. The camera usually shot Molly surrounded by family members, often in her dining room or kitchen, intensifying her association with domesticity; serving and preparing food for her family was basic to the real Jewish mother. Molly's signature greeting to her neighbor from her tenement window—"Yoo hoo! Mrs. Blooooom!"—became a national catchphrase that further situated the Jewish mother in her characteristic milieu.[20] Selling her sponsors' products (first Pepsodent toothpaste, then vitamins and Sanka coffee) through the open window capitalized on the trust she established with viewers as a housewife and *baleboste* (excellent homemaker).

In spite of her association with immigrant language, food, dress, and her tenement home, Berg established Molly as a woman of remarkably modern sensibilities. With her keen insight, flexible understanding of human nature, and desires for betterment for herself and her family, she was in many ways much more "American" than her rapidly Americanizing businessman husband, Jake, with his patriarchal, traditional beliefs. Molly's psychological astuteness, her "mixing-in" and willingness to take risks and break rules, proved crucial to her family's upward mobility. Molly may have been her husband's superior in practical wisdom, but there was no war between them; the Goldbergs' world was not so "topsy-turvy" that women overpowered weak-spirited men pathetically lost amid the complexities of American life. Jake and the Goldberg children were definitely on the way up the social ladder; Molly was there to guide and temper their advance by providing a moral compass. "Kind-hearted," "humane," "gentle," "gracious," "sympathetic," and "tender" were words typically used in advertisements about the show, and such descriptions bear witness to the fact that Molly Goldberg was not a "dominating" character, although she maneuvered (some said manipulated) other characters to convince them of the right ways. With her benevolent wisdom, her calm problem solving in the face of the challenges of everyday life, and her elevation of moral values over financial gain, she was not much like her Depression Era counterpart, Bessie Berger. Yet both Jewish mothers stood as shrewd, strong guardians of their families.[21]

A Model Family and Molly, the Quintessential Jewish Mother

Molly and Jake; their son, Sammy; daughter, Rosalie; and Molly's Uncle David are the core members of the Goldberg family. The character of Molly was drawn in part from Berg's mother, Dinah, and from her maternal grandmother, Czerna, as well as from several guests who stayed at the family's summer hotel in the Catskill Mountains. Berg, born Tillie Edelstein, was the only child of second-generation Americans whose parents had immigrated to America from Eastern Europe. Both families prospered in the New World, the fathers becoming owners of their own businesses; Berg was especially influenced by her grandfather Mordecai Edelstein, a fervently patriotic new American who encouraged her dreams and ambitions. His son, Gertrude's father, Jake, went to work for a relative and soon became a successful restaurateur. In 1906, when Gertrude was seven, he bought a hotel in Fleischmann's, New York (the Fleischmann's Manor Hotel), where the family spent every summer, Jake managing the business, Dinah the kitchen, and Gertrude the bookkeeping. In the winter they returned to Harlem, then an up-and-coming community where many second-generation Jews had found comfortable, affordable housing. Although Gertrude attended public school in Harlem and later took some courses at Columbia University without matriculating, her most important education came during the summers, when she wrote skits to amuse Fleischmann guests. Gradually she developed a character named Maltke Talnitzky, a fiftyish woman embroiled in disputes with a two-timing, no-good husband. By the time Gertrude had married Lewis Berg, a young engineer whom she met at the hotel, and given birth to two children, Maltke had become Molly, a younger, more self-assured woman with a more cooperative husband, a less foreign-sounding name, and two children, a girl and a boy, like Berg's children, Harriet and Cherney.[22]

Encouraged by her husband, Berg sought an outlet for her writing; she sent some of her short stories to popular magazines but received repeated rejections. Then in 1929, at the start of the Depression, with her husband out of work after the Louisiana sugar refinery that employed him burned to the ground, she decided to try her luck in the new medium of radio. Her first attempt to sell a script led to station YMCA's hiring her for a Consolidated Edison commercial for Christmas pinwheel cookies, which Berg had to read in Yiddish. Although she spoke Yiddish, she neither read nor wrote it, and her husband had to write it out phonetically. More surprising to Berg was the act of advertising "a Christmas cookie in Yiddish for a public utility in America"; she would learn that the combination of Jewish ethnic symbols and the mainstream values of Christian America was a recipe for media success.[23]

A year later Berg sold a script about two five-and-dime-store workers, *Effie and Laurie*, to CBS radio, but the show was canceled after one performance. Next came the pilot for *The Rise of the Goldbergs*, which NBC radio took on nervously, since it showcased a Jewish family. The show debuted on November 20, 1929, just one month into the Depression. NBC knew it had a hit three weeks later when Berg, suffering from laryngitis, missed one performance and eleven thousand irate letters from listeners poured in, wanting to know where they could find *The Goldbergs*. When Pepsodent signed on as sponsor two years later, it tested the show's popularity by asking viewers to write in if they wanted the show to continue. According to Berg, more than a million and a half fans responded, swamping the network.[24] Radio, the glue that held the nation together during the tough times of the Depression, was a perfect vehicle for Berg's narratives about a family's struggles with everyday problems of survival. While her early scripts had been rejected because they seemed too "lifelike," now the show's realism struck an obvious chord with listeners.[25]

Berg developed her scripts "from real life," with the cast of the show "living them" for the audience: her microphone was like a "telephone" through which she could talk about "real" characters.[26] Ideas came from her family, visits to friends' homes, dance halls, restaurants, club meetings, and frequent scouting trips to the Lower East Side.[27] Situations were portrayed "as naturally as if they were pages out of a family diary." In her quest for authenticity Berg occasionally recruited housewives, street vendors, delivery men, and shopkeepers to play their on-air counterparts. Although she did not cook at home, she "prepared" or served food on the show that came from her studio kitchen—"borscht a la

Goldberg," roast chicken; sometimes she even rolled dough as she made *kre-plachs* on the air.[28] Berg felt that her success came from "portraying only what I actually have seen and heard," providing a "concise picturization" of viewers' lives. The most "vital essential" praise was "Why, you'd think she'd been listening in at our house!"[29]

And viewers believed that the television Molly Goldberg was also authentic. When she was shown on TV in a hospital scene, they called the station to find out how she was doing. "Whenever there's a quarrelsome scene in the Goldberg's household," one columnist wrote, "our blood pressure goes up in the same way as it does when there's a family tiff."[30] Compared with characters in other comedies who existed in "comic strip world," another writer observed, "if you opened the phone book to G you could actually call Mrs. Goldberg for a friendly chat. She's *that* real."[31]

How realistic was Molly? Writing in 1951, novelist Charles Angoff praised *The Goldbergs* for its representation of "virtually the whole panorama of middle-class Jewish-American life. . . . I have never heard anyone who knows Jewish life say that 'The Goldbergs' are not true to life." Angoff concluded that "Molly Goldberg, indeed, is so basically true a character that I sometimes think she may become an enduring name in the national literature. She is the prototype of the Jewish mother during the past twenty-five years."[32] In *Commentary* five years later, Morris Freedman likened the show to a "documentary."[33]

Despite the show's verisimilitude, it did not portray the full range of immigrant life. "Allow me to ask whether in Jewish families nothing ever goes wrong," wrote in a fan from Detroit in 1934. "Is it always 'Papa darling' and 'Mama darling?' . . . No wrangling, no quibbling?"[34] Jewish family life could certainly be more problematic. Growing up in an immigrant family in the 1930s, historian Ruth Gay recalled that the ceaseless work of her mother and friends was "humiliating," causing them to grow "irritable, shapeless, and neglected."[35] These "secrets" of family life were the biggest surprise that confronted Neil and Ruth Cowan when they conducted interviews with first-generation immigrants for their book, *Our Parents' Lives*. The Cowans were told tragic stories—about mental illness, suicides, the hidden pain of separation and divorce—rarely exposed to public scrutiny.[36] Despite its vaunted realism, *The Goldbergs* did not probe such dark narratives (including those in Berg's own family); troubling issues, when raised, were resolved in comfortable fashion by the conclusion of each episode or in the following one. The show in fact set the "model of acceptability" that characterized every future family series. As a "chronicler and salesman of American family life," the family sitcom emerged as a "consensual, benevolent repository for all things good."[37]

This positive tone helped *The Goldbergs* locate its broad audience. Especially during the Depression, the general premise of the series—the story of an American Jewish family seeking to rise in the "new" world of America despite desperate economic conditions—fit the exigencies of the time and the dream of American life, not only for Jews but for all aspiring Americans.[38] The show's characteristic optimism sprang from the successful acculturation of Berg's own family. Family members modeled the show's main characters—from Molly, to Jake, a suit manufacturer perpetually seeking new business opportunities and always at war with his partner, Mendel (Berg's own father was named Jake and his father was a cloak-and-suiter); to Molly's "American" children Rosalie and Sammy, whose exploits resembled those of her own daughter and son.

To Berg, the show's characters expressed the view of "first-generation Americans who were trying to make sense out of growing up in one world, America, but coming from another, the European world of their parents. They were being pulled by the new and held back by the old."[39] Molly could change with the times. She was much more forward-looking than Uncle David, whose Old World outlook served as a foil for Molly, yet she also could reject modernity, represented by her children's demands or her husband's business schemes, if it meant compromising basic values.

The philosophical difference between Molly and Jake formed the core of the show's dramatic conflict. While Jake wanted the children to have everything money can buy, Molly wanted them to "have everything money can't buy."[40] In an interview with Edward R. Murrow on *Person to Person*, Berg fondly recalled the first radio script she wrote for *The Goldbergs*. In that episode, Jake, then a dress-cutter in a garment factory, tells Molly of his grand idea—to start his own business. Molly, who has anticipated just such an eventuality, gives him money she has secretly put away to finance this dream. "Molly, darling," says Jake, "some day we'll be eating off of golden plates." Molly responds, "Jake, darling, will it be any better?"[41]

According to Berg, the transmission of values in a way that blended the best of tradition and modernity proceeded through the female line. In her autobiography, she recalls her grandmother Czerna Goldstein's hard work on behalf of the family and the warmth of her Shabbat observances; she understands that this religiously devout ancestor, an Old World immigrant who prospered in the New, could straddle both worlds. So, too, does Berg's mother, Dinah Edelstein, the other template for Molly. Despite her traditional role as homemaker, Berg saw Dinah as a remarkable "modern woman." Drawing on these women, Berg created Molly as an individual "who lived in the world of today but kept many of the values of yesterday. She could change with the times . . . but she had some basic ideas that she learned long ago and wanted to pass on to her children."[42]

Molly's husband, Jake, is an imposing masculine figure, a businessman with many of the hopes and anxieties experienced by Jewish working-class men who struggled to make it into the middle class. Jake is a composite of three entrepreneurs—Berg's grandfather, her father, and her husband, Lew—and bears many of their qualities: stubbornness, "streaking" (or flash-in-the pan

anger), a narrow-minded sense of correctness, and impetuosity. Played on radio by James R. Waters and in the show's first two years on television by noted
stage actor Philip Loeb and later by Robert L. Harris, Jake emerges as stern
and often discontent, yet with an underlying softness—he is the face of the
second-generation Jewish male. While Jake is the breadwinner, Molly plays an
important role in the Goldbergs' advance, saving Jake's factory from bankruptcy
by conjuring up the idea of half-size dresses and providing other sound advice.
Her business acumen reflects that of many Jewish mothers who partnered with
their husbands in family businesses or otherwise participated in their families'
financial lives.

The children, Sammy (portrayed by Everett Sloane and Alfred Ryder on
radio and Larry Robinson on television) and Rosalie (Roslyn Silber, radio, and
Arlene McQuade, television), grew up before the audience's eyes; the Americanization of the family is most perfectly realized in their transformation from
children to young adults. In 1955, in response to the network's demand and
against Berg's wishes, the Goldbergs moved from the Bronx to the suburb of
Haverville (from the tenements of the "have-nots" to the "Village of the
Haves?" asked one television critic).[43] Sammy has gotten married and gone to
war, but never mind; he is reinvented as a young engineering student. Rosalie,
busy with proms, dating, and studying, prepares to go to college. The desires
and activities of these normal offspring provided *The Goldbergs* with rich dramatic opportunities to expose conflicts between the parents' more traditional
beliefs and changing American lifestyles, including suburbanization.

The inclusion of Molly's Uncle David transforms the Goldbergs into the
extended family typical of many Jewish families of the time. David (played
brilliantly by Menasha Skulnick on radio and Eli Mintz on television) calls
himself an "also," but he is totally integrated within the family. Like Molly, he
is a homebody; his heavy accent and intonation pairs him with Molly as her ally
and sometimes foil. With his manners, walk, and speech, he is almost effemi-
nate, compared with Jake and Sammy.[44] This, too, positions him as Molly's soul
mate.

Gertrude Berg, of course, was not Molly Goldberg. Rather, she was a sophisticated, modern intellectual and a pioneering writer, actor, and producer, at
a time when few women held leadership roles in media. Far from the stay-at-
home wife and mother whom Molly represented, Berg had been bored and unhappy after the birth of her children; she found an outlet in writing that helped
cure her malaise. That Berg owned the rights to *The Goldbergs* in perpetuity is
a unique example of the power she came to wield in the entertainment world.[45]

Berg was not only removed from Molly in terms of career, but also by way
of ethnic and religious background. Berg did not observe Jewish holidays as
Molly did (the Bergs celebrated Christmas with a four-and-a-half-foot Christmas tree and bundles of presents) and never lived in a tenement. The Bergs in
fact owned a Park Avenue apartment and a twelve-room weekend home in

Westchester—comfortable but unpretentious, Berg felt, although she did employ a cook and a butler.[46] "Raised with elegance," in her daughter-in-law's words, Berg had impeccable taste, collected modern art, and loved to shop for designer clothes—Molly's housedress and apron were not her raiments of choice.[47] But she understood instinctively that she had to suppress the differences between Molly and herself in order to gain the audience's trust and make her character believable. She did this deliberately and consistently, often mentioning that she spent more time each day as Molly than as herself.

In many ways, it was precisely the performative aspect of Molly as matriarch that was authentic, despite the dissonance between Berg and her character. Berg grew up in a family that "performed" for its customers, providing service and pleasure; she was an integral component of the family's summer resort environment that combined public appearances with private life. The show's plots, furthermore, derived from marital and child-rearing relationships and the entanglements of the larger family circle that she experienced. Critic Gilbert Seldes suggested that it was Berg's performance and directorial skills that created her authenticity. Berg possessed "the capacity to entrance, to absorb us," according to Seldes, "until we reach the point of total belief"; her theatrical instinct prevented her from ever "going wrong." Berg never played to the audience or camera but instinctively "to and with the other people in the dramatic situation. By doing this she made them play to her." In this way, she created "tight relationships" between characters that were "exactly right" for television.[48]

Perhaps the most significant difference between Gertrude and Molly lay in Berg's relationship to her mother, Dinah. Berg had an older brother, Charles, who died of diphtheria at the age of seven, when Berg was about three or four. The death weighed heavily on Dinah, who became deeply possessive of her surviving daughter. She "hovered," recalled Berg's daughter, Harriet, picking Gertrude up from school even when she was sixteen or seventeen years old. Understanding her suffering, Berg tried to provide comfort. But Dinah had a nervous breakdown not long after Gertrude's marriage and had to be hospitalized at Bellevue. This removal was so painful to Gertrude that she could not see her; Gertrude's husband and son visited and cared for Dinah until her death in the early 1940s.[49] The idealized character of Molly, the benign mother at the center of a close family circle, can be read as a cathartic response to the pain of her own separation from her mother and the latter's mental illness.

This shocking development in Gertrude's life led to her determination not to tie the reins to her own children so tightly. Harriet resented the fact that her mother seemed to push her away as a child, sending her to summer camp when she preferred to stay home; no doubt Berg's busy production schedule played as much a role in this as her child-rearing beliefs. Berg was a workaholic who got up at 5 or 6 a.m. to do her writing and was not to be disturbed. She

Gertrude Berg not only starred in *The Goldbergs* but produced the show and wrote its more than 10,000 scripts. At a time when women were rare figures behind the camera, she pioneered the role of "auteur" and media executive. (Cherney Berg)

was the "hub" of her household—the "center of everyone's life. She would have been a terrible mother if she hadn't had a career," in Harriet's opinion. Berg grew more controlling during her daughter's adolescence, leading to a "tug of war" between them. As Harriet matured, the two became much closer.[50]

Berg's maternal role did not stop with her family but extended to the cast of her show as well, whom she treated with a winning combination of warmth and tough-mindedness. Some of the actors who started out on *The Goldbergs* and who went on to greater fame—among them John Garfield, Van Heflin, Richard Widmark, Marjorie Main, Joan Tetzel, Shirley Booth, Anne Bancroft, and Arnold Stang—commented on Berg's "general motherliness." "She seemed to know about things which were happening to me almost before I knew them myself," Stang recalled. "Things I thought nobody knew about myself were always popping up from the pages of the script!" But as a perfectionist Berg ran the show "with an iron fist," Stang added; she was "very tyrannical," although "affectionate."[51] Berg cracked the whip over herself as well. "I am like the mamma in a large family," she insisted, setting the example for others by her own hard work.[52]

On the air, Berg was a quintessential Jewish mother, who not only parents her own children and assorted relatives, but also the entire neighborhood. "All the people in this house are like one big family," she tells the new landlord of her Bronx Tremont Avenue apartment in the 1949 rent strike episode.[53] To Molly, to be a Jewish mother meant helping others—or "mixing-in." Said Berg: Molly was "constantly bringing people together, forcing them to realize what their role in life must be. In a sense, she transfigures and saves each character."[54] Berg developed such skills at the family hotel, where as a teenager she learned to "trouble shoot" and soothe cranky guests by listening, keeping "calm and sympathetic," adding an "amusing anecdote or homely philosophy" from her grandmother.[55]

Jake's opposition to Molly's constant "mixing," which he sees as meddlesome interference, is a key series theme. To Molly, however, "not mixing, is not fixing."[56] "You have to help people help themselves," she declares.[57] Mixing is part of her faith in the overriding importance of love, which in earlier shows is closely connected to her religious beliefs. In the Goldbergs' 1943 Yom Kippur radio show, young Paul, Uncle David's grandson, asks Molly if it's a sin not to love your parents. She replies that "it's a sin not to love the whole world. . . . You must love and obey God, but you have to love and obey Him by loving your neighbor." A neighbor, she continues, is "someone who lives with you in this world," anywhere.[58]

Mixing-in solves the problems that occur continually in Molly's world, whether they stem from economic causes or from personal failings. Molly frequently poked fun at the excesses of Freudian psychology, but her mixing-in, based on her knowledge and love of people, was inherently psychological. Many episodes specifically mentioned psychology—Berg herself took a great interest in Freud. In "Dreams" (1955), Rosalie tells the family that if Molly ever went to college she should major in psychology because she loves people. "She could have been a professor," Jake replies, unkindly. "It's wrong to love people?" Molly asks.[59]

Molly's intuitive psychological approach is a far cry from Jake's rule-based logical problem solving. Typically, Molly persuades Jake to let her intervene "in mine fashion" to deal with a presenting issue. Jake usually agrees, albeit reluctantly, but he is contemptuous of Molly's psychologizing. In "The Boyfriends" (1955), when Jake disapproves of Rosalie's dating a divorced man, he bellows at Molly that "this time I'm speaking as the father of the house, and I will not be stopped. There's a point when psychology stops and the parent begins."[60] However, whenever Jake tries to put his foot down, his intervention inevitably fails. In "Rosie the Actress" (1955), Jake tries to prevent Rosalie from choosing acting school rather than going to college. Molly tells Jake they have to resign themselves to what Rosie wants, but Jake is adamant, insisting, again, that he will "put [his] foot down." But Molly tells Jake, "hands off," advice she heard at the PTA and that had come from "child psychologists." As Molly repeats to Jake, "Children are like horses. If you start pulling the reins too tight, you break their spirit." To do that to Rosie would be wrong.[61]

Typically Molly does not trot out her authority with her children; she is more likely to help them reach a decision she prefers by "psychology." In a radio episode, when Rosalie is also dating a man of whom her parents disapprove, Molly draws back, leaving the ultimate choice—and risk—to her daughter. "Maybe years full of accumulated experience is as bad as no experience," she tells Jake. "Experience makes cowards," she adds, "that's why they say, 'young with courage.' . . . Maybe to look twice means to lose your chance, and maybe its better where I hesitate Rosalie rushes in, maybe it's better, who knows?" Molly does not believe in rules for their own sake. "There are some rules like a rubber band," she tells Jake in "The Girl Scouts." "They can be stretched."[62]

Molly's flexible approach almost always wins the day in contrast to Jake's authoritarianism. Based on understanding and empathy, it is the essence of Molly as Jewish matriarch. Though meddlesome and often a nuisance, Molly accepts her own foibles as well as those of others. She may scheme, but it is as a *fixerke* (meddler) who combines "head and heart, what is one without the other."[63]

"Mamatalks": Berg's Philosophy of Child-Rearing

Molly Goldberg's ideas about parenting were unusual, given the influence of Watsonian behaviorism—the belief that children's behavior could be controlled, especially through conditioned emotional reflexes. But they matched perfectly with those expressed by Berg in her syndicated column, "Mamatalks," which appeared in Jewish newspapers in 1934 and 1935.[64] Touching on such topics as stay-at-home mothers, the empty-nest syndrome, gifted children, and war and peace, Berg's columns revealed progressive, child-centered views that gave primacy to the child's needs while affirming the mother's role in her children's lives and society at large. The columns belie the more manipulative qualities of Molly, and perhaps her relationship to her own children, for in the newspaper pieces Berg passionately argues for improved understanding of children's—especially adolescents'—rebelliousness and urges greater independence for them.

A column on privacy was typical. Berg argued that mothers must learn to respect their children's privacy, since a child's mind was his own; parents of adolescents needed to be especially careful not to intrude on their children. "The important thing for us mothers to remember," Berg wrote, "is that every human being is not only entitled to make his own mistakes, but much more likely to learn from them than from the experience of others." While her intention was not to promote giving children free rein to do what they wished, she insisted that "the reins must be loose." "The best attitude for a mother to adopt," she wrote, "is one of judicious neglect."[65]

Berg's ideal mother respected her child's integrity and sought to promote his or her independence. A child needed her mother's companionship, but even young children could resent parents when they pushed themselves on their off-spring. Parents—especially mothers—needed to guard against giving up too much of their own pursuits to spend time with children, who often preferred to be left alone. "Parental over-emphasis on intimate companionship with the younger generation may rob them of that independence of spirit which should be nurtured in all children," Berg warned. "It is the function of parents to bring up their children to a full and independent life of their own." To promote such independence, a "full understanding and a spirit of cooperation" needed to be created between parent and child. Such a spirit would obviate the need for punishments, which Berg believed should be "reduced to a minimum or abolished altogether." In their place, in the manner of Molly Goldberg, she called for "utmost delicacy and tact."[66]

Love was the ingredient that bound child and parents. In this respect, Berg's advice was at the opposite end of the spectrum from the rigid ideas of psychologist John B. Watson, who advised mothers to restrain their own feel-ings in caring for their children. ("When you are tempted to pet your child," he wrote in a notorious passage, "remember that mother love is a dangerous in-strument.")[67] For Gertrude Berg, in contrast, mother-love was the glue of so-ciety. She might have agreed that women's place was first and foremost in the home, but she saw that home as extending to a wider community and coun-seled mothers to devote time to interests outside their household routines.[68] A progressive Democrat in her own political leanings, Berg was particularly con-cerned with issues of militarism. In 1935, she wrote in her column that "it is the particular duty of mothers to make war impossible" by teaching children to understand the "sordid profit-seeking" that lay behind the "glamour" of uni-forms and the adventures of battle.[69] War could not be effectively abolished, she had written the previous year, until mothers took a role in destroying "every toy pistol" with which their children played.[70]

The liberal content of Berg's columns is far more in tune with the child-rearing principles of progressive educators than that of conventional behavior-ists. In many ways, Berg anticipates the experts' turn to more child-centered approaches based on maternal affection by the late 1930s and early 1940s.[71] Dr. Benjamin Spock's child-rearing advice reflected similar ideals, although Spock's first book, written in 1946, focused more on "improper mother love" than on the full power of mothers' love and their social responsibilities. Though one of Spock's primary goals was to promote the child's "self-realization," he of-ten couched his advice in terms that heightened, rather than alleviated, mothers' anxieties.[72]

Shortly after she stopped writing the "Mamatalks" columns, Berg intro-duced a six-month sequence of *Goldberg* shows also called *Mamatalks*. Run-ning from January–July 1936, when *The Goldbergs* were off the air, these episodes, developed for a possible *Goldbergs* spin-off, centered on a neighbor-hood forum of mothers that Molly organized to help them try "to understand the material we are trying to mould."[73] Each week mothers would focus on a child-rearing question that shed light on the complicated relationships of mod-ern parents and their children. When one resistant mother observes that "her mother and her grandmother didn't have to go to meetings to learn how to raise their children," Molly replies that "we are living in a changing world."[74] In that world, it was necessary to learn what "a mother [must] know in order to be a success."[75] "We can't go forwards looking backwards," says Molly. "Even Lot's wife turned into a bag of salt. Everything is different today than it was a generation ago."[76]

"Instead of taking formulas that are handed down to us," Molly tells the mothers, "we have to teach ourselves to use our own judgment with our chil-dren." "What is it exactly that these child experts and modern parents are trying to do and bring about?" asks a mother. Molly answers: "Only trying to under-stand their children as well as love them." No longer the object of social workers or their own coreligionist "friendly visitors," the mothers of Tremont Avenue—albeit tentatively—join the parent education movement.[77] The moth-ers were helped by a local schoolteacher, Miss McLoughlin, whose advice Molly often communicated to the neighborhood meetings. A representative of the professional middle class, Miss McLoughlin's ideas presumably gave the moth-ers the extra authority they needed to change their behaviors.

Each show discussed several different child-rearing queries raised by mothers. In one episode, a mother asks why her daughter is so moody. Molly replied that adults also "get cranky, gloomy, moody"; the solution was to dis-cover "what brings on the mood, and then try to avoid it." In Molly's view, the best thing was not to intervene: "rest is what they need . . . and silence is the best thing for frazzling nerves."[78] Another question aired on the show was the effect of heredity versus environment. Molly framed the issue in a home-spun way:

> We know that we can't make roast turkey out of cutlets, but we also know that if we cook the cutlets the right way, they can be delicious. [A]nd if we cook them the wrong way, nobody can eat them and they have to be thrown away. So, from the same material, we can either make something worth while or we can ruin it.

In the same way, she added, "Child training teaches us that, while we can-not make a swan out of a goose, we can make the gooseling into a better goose or a poorer goose by the treatment we give it."[79]

The *Mamatalks* episodes highlight Berg's child-centered philosophy. In an episode in March 1936, Jake wants Sammy to join them on a trip away from home, while Molly is willing to let Sammy stay home and make his own decisions.

"He's old enough to plan and judge for himself," Molly insists.[80] When Miss McLoughlin visits the mothers' club, a mother wonders why her husband calls her "a bad mother" even though she sacrifices everything for her family. Miss McLoughlin responds that the bad parent is one who doesn't appreciate democracy in family life, not allowing the children the freedom they need. She and Molly agree that "a new type of education" was needed to help parents improve their parenting behavior. "The movement of parent education," Miss McLoughlin explained, "was the most hopeful sign in American life."[81] When the *Mamatalks* mothers club was revived briefly on the air in 1945, the neighborhood mothers seemed more confident, less in need of advice from educators. "If you ask me, maybe the college professors can come and learn a lot from us," one of them observes.[82]

The concerns of the *Mamatalks* shows appear throughout *The Goldbergs* series. In the 1949 episode "Rosie's Composition," Molly wonders whether she is a "bad mother because her mothering extends beyond her own children to a wider community of friends and neighbors."[83] Her self-criticism is stimulated by the fact that twelve-year-old Rosalie has written an essay for a school assignment that she and Jake fear will criticize them, as other students have criticized their parents—the mothers for being "overprotective," the fathers "domineering." "Not for nothing did the teachers give the subject 'my family,'" Molly remarks. "To know the family is to know the child. It's the background and the foreground." Jake has the most anxiety, fearing that he has not been a "good father" because of his outside responsibilities.

> Did I ever sit and read to her like other parents do? Did I ever take her to the park or the zoo or the botanical gardens or the planetarium? Shouldn't a man of my age be able to control his temper? . . . What right do I have to bring my business worries over the threshold? Shouldn't the child be protected from the storm of the world?

Molly indicates that she knows her faults as Jake knows his: "If I'm mixing, I'll try not to mix."

She and Jake decide to become "models of parenthood" so that Rosie will write a more favorable composition. Jake vows not to raise his voice above a whisper. Molly tells David to stop her if he hears her "give one yoohoo." "Now," she says, "for my family and only for mine family." Molly then stops talking to her neighbors. To make a "good point" for her daughter's composition, she also tells the bewildered Rosalie that she doesn't have to practice the piano anymore: "Neither papa nor mama want you to do anything unless you feel the natural urge. Only do anything that you yourself want to do." Jake insists that Rosalie sit on his knee and tries to read to her—including *Peter Rabbit*. He then suggests that they stroll to the botanical gardens or the planetarium. "We'll look at the celestial spheres, we'll discuss current events . . . it's time that you and I became really acquainted, not just father and daughter."

Rosalie, of course, does not like her parents' changed behavior. In a new composition, she criticizes Molly for her lack of "proper community spirit" and admonishes Jake for failing to understand "that there is a generation" between him and his children; "being a pal" was not being a parent. Jake and Molly are hurt and angry; their dialogue reveals definitions of "good" and "bad" parenting that fit the deeply gendered roles of aspiring middle-class families at the time.

JAKE: Failures, absolutely failures, that's what we are.
MOLLY: To be overprotective is not good. To be domineering is also not good, so what's good? How could a person conduct himself to know what it is to be a perfect mother, how?
JAKE: Perhaps you should have found out long before your daughter's twelfth birthday.
MOLLY: So it's my fault already?
JAKE: A mother should be the kernel and the pivot of the family.
MOLLY: Oh and a father should also be a kernel.
JAKE: I cannot be a kernel and a provider at the same time. . . .
MOLLY: . . . You're the father that's your responsibility. I'm the mother that's my responsibility.

Once again Jake accuses Molly of not being a good mother, because of her mixing. "Jake," she explains, "my mixing is not just mixing; my mixing is interest in people, not in gossip." He tells her in turn that "my hollering is because I love my family and I want to do for them . . . beyond my power and strength and that's why I holler."

In the end, Rosalie agrees with this assessment. She reads them her first composition, the one she turned in, and which she decides is the most truthful. "My family . . . is different," she had written. "They live every minute of their lives for each other but not only for themselves. My mother knows the neighborhood like she knows the inside . . . of her own house. That is because she loves people and people love her." As for her father's terrible temper, it was "kind as a kiss." Rosalie also praises brother Sammy and Uncle David. "I know my family loves me no matter what they say or do. . . . And my mother knows I love her. And my mother loves my father and my father loves my mother."

"Rosie's Composition" reveals insecurities increasingly commonplace to ethnic and working-class as well as middle-class families in the postwar period. Besieged by experts, parents—and especially mothers—had begun to feel much less confident about their roles. In an interview two years later, Berg scolded authorities who blamed mothers for everything from the atom bomb to the high cost of living. "These pseudo-experts are responsible for taking a good deal of natural warmth from family relations," she charged; because of so many "so-called authorities," mothers feared to assert themselves and create opportunities for family warmth and interdependence—now children's independence was being realized by default.[84]

After the Goldbergs moved to the bland suburban Haverville, where their ethnicity initially defined them as outsiders, Berg continued to espouse a child-rearing philosophy that combined benevolent meddling with respect for her children's independence.[85] "More and more, I see that it's not a matter of right and wrong but of different generations and a progress in viewpoints," Molly explained as she talked about the family's move to suburbia. "Rosie wears purple nail polish, Sammy is studying engineering instead of law . . . live and let live."[86] Her philosophy was simply "leave them alone to make their own mistakes, use the word 'yes' more than 'no,' let them grow up." As she told Uncle David when she and Jake prepared for a Florida vacation without the children: "It's my opinion, David, that every mother should leave her nest once and again and the young ones try their wings. How long can you keep your children in an incubator protected with absorbent cotton?"[87]

This message appeared frequently in the suburban episodes. In a 1954 show, Jake feels that "the whole fabric of existence" has come apart when Sammy's fiancée's parents urge him to quit college and work in the family's shoe store. Understanding that Sammy wants to get married and has his own plans, Molly urges Jake to "let him go." "It's not easy for a parent to let go at the right minute," she comments, but "there comes a time when children graduate not only from high school and college but the time comes when they get a diploma from parents also. We did our best . . . and now we can only hope that our best was good enough." In the show's coda, as Berg leans out the window to sell Sanka, she reaffirms the importance of letting go.

> There comes a day when the birds are big enough to leave the nest to fly on their own wings. The wings should only be fine and strong. With all our experience, can we tell our own children how to live their lives? It takes a long time to convalesce from youth and take good helpful advice.[88]

As Jewish mother, Molly Goldberg exhibited progressive leanings in regard to a wide range of women's social roles as well as parenting. But early in the course of her career, she learned that she could not stray too far beyond audience expectations. In 1935, when the radio *Goldbergs* was at its peak popularity, Berg persuaded the network to allow her to broadcast another show she was writing, *The House of Glass*, which depicted the behind-the-scenes working of a Catskills hotel run by the Glasses: Barney, the mild-mannered titular resort manager, and Bessie, his imperious wife who commanded the hotel as her fiefdom, henpecking her husband at every turn. "Mine stemp of approval is

essential," Bessie harangues her husband in Molly's familiar Yiddish intona-
tions. "Leave the managerial end of it to me." While Berg claimed there was
no difference between Molly and Bessie—each "represented women throughout the world"—audiences did not accept the show's premise: that a bossy,
dominating wife could be funny. Wrote *Variety* in its review: "It is no longer
the kindly, Jewish mother and housewife, but a cold, matter of fact business
woman whose major concern is the success of her summer resort." The series
was cancelled after a single season, and Berg went back to the familiar, friend-
lier, Molly.[89]

Molly's Revolt

Even after decades of playing Molly as the kindhearted anchor of her family,
Berg was able to imbue her character with aspects of the power and efficiency
that defined the vanquished Bessie Glass. By the 1950s, after the Goldbergs
had become middle-class suburbanites, Berg created numerous episodes that
enlarged and sometimes challenged traditional gender norms. Because food
played such a large role in the repertoire of the Jewish mother's family management, these shows often related to Molly's cooking skills. In "Molly's Fish"
(1955), Molly fails to duplicate her famous "fish ball" recipe for a national supermarket chain because she cannot commodify the ingredients. Molly learns
that "a mother is not a corporation; she cooks best where they need her
most."[90] Her resistance to commodification is also revealed in "Reach for the
Moon," which similarly implicates domesticity as a strategy of resistance to the
forces transforming American life. This episode finds the Goldberg family
watching a popular television quiz show, *Reach for the Moon*. Uncle David suggests that Molly should appear on the show ("What category?" asks Jake. "Mixing and mingling?"), and the family encourages her to apply, since they are
looking for "ordinary people," and to choose cooking as her category. Jake is
contemptuous. "Your mother cooks by instinct," he tells Rosalie; "she doesn't
know what she is doing."

Molly applies to the show, and becomes a contestant, choosing "gastro-
nomics." Her first question, worth $200, is an easy one, for any Eastern Euro-
pean Jew, that is: "What is borscht?" she is asked. She replies that "it's made out
of beets and you can also make it with cabbages." She decides not to take the
$200, but to try to double it, and is asked a question about dumplings. And so
on—Molly answers five questions and wins $5,000. She has a week to decide
whether to take that amount or to go for $10,000 in the next episode. Although
Molly promises Jake she will let him make the decision—he wants her to quit
and take the money—she spends the week haunted by visions of relatives and
neighbors in distress whom she could help out with higher earnings. Against
Jake's wishes, Molly decides to risk her winnings but can't answer a question
about the caloric count of certain foods. She can cook calories but can't count

them. The "food expert" goes home without cash, but with a fur coat she will sell to help relatives and friends.

As in "Molly's Fish," food is a part of the instinctual jurisdiction of Jewish mothers; ingredients or calories cannot be measured or counted and made into commodities. What matters to Molly is not the idea of spending money on consumer goods (as in other episodes), but in *tikkun olam*—helping others in need, a task pulled from the Jewish mother's repertoire. The episodes reveal that Molly has desires beyond her household—to become a "corporation" and produce her "fish balls," and to be a television contestant—to use her skills publicly. Still, Molly resists the blurring of the line between "Jewish mama and corporate huckster," as Vincent Brook has said; the line he suggests grew out of the consumerism embodied in Molly's product testimonials for sponsors.[91]

Molly does embody the wife and mother's role, but in these and other late shows, she reveals her attraction to alternative paths, or at least insists that she, and nobody else, will determine the parameters of her domesticity. In "Milk Farm," another show about food, Jake sends her to a reducing farm because he thinks she is too fat ("it's only your health I'm worrying about," he insists). But Molly finds the reduced calorie diet and sauerkraut juice unbearable. Pretending she needs to have dental work done in town, she brings back salami, pickles, and other contraband and is expelled for being a "corrupting influence." "You're a compulsive eater," Jake charges; "you can't help yourself." Molly refuses his definition, angrily shouting that she is a "human being, like you."[92] Molly's physical presence, old-fashioned and overweight, at least belongs to her; she will not give it up to become sleek and suburban. As in "Molly's Fish" and "Reach for the Moon," she accepts the Jewish mother's expertise in and love for food as natural, empowering, and a key to authentic personal identity and family life.

"Dreams" is the episode that most explicitly challenges mothers' traditional roles in a manner foreshadowing Betty Friedan's startling exposé that came eight years later and is credited with jump-starting the women's liberation movement.[93] When Mrs. Van Ness, a nosy Haverville neighbor, starts interpreting Molly's dreams and those of other neighbors, Molly is shocked to learn that "most of the women of our neighborhood need therapy. They don't realize how unhappy they are."[94] In reaction, the women begin to change their lives. Molly asks Jake's permission to have Ruby, the maid, come twice a week (the Goldbergs have moved far from their Bronx poverty!) and insists that Uncle David do the cooking so that she can join the executive committee of the PTA. She is thrilled at her new importance and comes home, excited, every night after midnight. But Molly is troubled when she dreams that she sucks her husband and children into the vacuum cleaner bag when she is cleaning, a dream that Mrs. Van Ness interprets as a death wish for her marriage. All comes out well in the end when Jake and David give Mrs. Van Ness her comeuppance and Molly returns to her usual role. Nonetheless, even though "patriarchy has been restored," in Vincent Brook's view, Molly and her friends have participated in a "feminist revolt" that exposes, rather than legitimates, the "fault lines" of suburban, middle-class life.[95]

The Last Years of *The Goldbergs*

For a period of more than twenty-five years, from the start of the radio show to the concluding episodes of the television sitcom, *The Goldbergs* was a media hit, successfully expressing cultural ideals about America and of Jews. Yet in some ways, particularly because of Gertrude Berg's ideas about mothering—of her own children, her neighbors, and the community—the program also stood in advance of them. Within her Jewish family, Molly was a mediating force, aiding her offspring's transition to modern culture. In her belief that children had to make their own decisions, she expressed a new, more progressive, democratic view of family relationships, one unlike earlier immigrant models. Molly Goldberg understands instinctively that in the world her children will inhabit in the future, a patriarchal model will no longer work. She sees her children as individuals who belong to themselves; they are not objects to be controlled or possessed by the family. This—and not the authoritarianism represented by Jake's old ways—is truly "modern" and "progressive."

Through the 1930s and into the 1950s, when presumably "father knew best," Molly Goldberg presented a model of an American mother—and a decidedly Jewish one—who was impressively authoritative and self-aware. At a time when TV sitcoms had largely become "Cold War comedies of reassurance," isolated from the politics and problems of the larger society, *The Goldbergs* offered viewers a novel message about gender roles and parenting. The series may have portrayed the family as a sea of domestic tranquility—a "suburban middle landscape"—as did such shows as *Leave It To Beaver*, *Father Knows Best*, *The Adventures of Ozzie and Harriet*, *The Donna Reed Show*, *I Remember Mama*, and *Make Room for Daddy/The Danny Thomas Show*, but Berg permitted the strains and tensions of contemporary family issues to emerge behind the veneer of family togetherness.[96] The audience's quarter-of-a-century acquaintance with the Goldbergs provided a cushion whereby Berg could experiment with new ideas. In command of her own repertoire of maternal wisdom, Berg/Goldberg steered her family's adjustment to the special challenges of modern American life, while demonstrating for the television audience that conflict could be easily contained if "normal" family values were followed.

The concluding episodes of *The Goldbergs* found the family newly middle class, suburban, and significantly de-Judaized. Not even "gefilte fish" could be said aloud on air—in an ethnically sensitive television climate, the preferred title became "Molly's Fish." Were *The Goldbergs* turning into *Mother Knows Best*, a consequence of the show's loss of its once-vibrant ethnic and working-class identity?[97] In fact, *The Goldbergs* had always been *Mother Knows Best*, with Berg demonstrating over the course of nearly three decades the special wisdom of the Jewish mother; even when the show's Jewish content decreased, Molly's ethnicity itself was easily recognized and vital to her persona. The success of *The Goldbergs* on radio and television influenced studios to introduce other ethnic families into their programming at a time when televised ethnicity was considered taboo. The beloved *I Remember Mama*, starring Peggy Wood as the benevolent Norwegian immigrant mother, was by some accounts a by-product of *The Goldbergs'* popularity.[98]

It was not the show's muted ethnic identity, nor its mother-centric narrative, nor the problem of moving a tenement-based series to the alien suburbs, that ultimately did the program in. In 1950, the same year that Gertrude Berg won an Emmy for Best Actress for her portrayal of Molly Goldberg, *The Goldbergs* became unhappily involved in Cold War politics when Philip Loeb, who played the role of Jake in 1949–50, was identified in *Red Channels* as a Communist; Loeb denied the allegation. The network and sponsors pressured Berg to fire Loeb, but she held firm as long as she could, trying to protect his job at the risk of her own reputation; at least one conservative watchdog group listed her as a "Communist fellow-traveler."[99] Berg managed to keep Loeb on the show for two more seasons, but the sponsors, and then CBS, dropped the show

Philip Loeb played Molly Goldberg's husband, Jake, in the 1951 Paramount film *Molly*. After Loeb was blacklisted, Berg was forced to fire him from her TV show, *The Goldbergs*. Loeb committed suicide in 1955. (Paramount Pictures Corporation)

despite the fact that it was the seventh-highest-rated program on the air and highly profitable. NBC briefly picked it up, without Loeb, and then the independent Dumont Network ran it for a few months. In 1955, unable to find work, Loeb committed suicide. *The Goldbergs* limped along briefly but went off the air in 1956.

But Gertrude Berg had left an important public legacy. In the 1930s and 1940s, she used the new medium of radio to create stories of family life centered on a working-class, Jewish family that came to stand in for more universal aspirations.[100] Using her formidable talents as writer, actress, and producer, Berg created Molly Goldberg as the prototype of the Jewish immigrant who was at the same time an all-American mother. A woman of insight, intuition, and firm moral reasoning, Molly grew with the times, becoming a sounding board for new ideas. While supporting acculturation, she maintained the family's ethical compass, responding to the temptations of capitalism by asserting the Jewish mother's sound values; in her wake, the shady materialism associated with other Jewish mother representations was nearly forgotten. When the show moved to television, the strong shaping role of the Jewish mother remained central, a stark contrast to the chorus of antimaternalism welling up in the psychiatric and behavioral professions, as well as in literary and popular culture.[101] Incarnated as Molly Goldberg rather than Bessie Berger, the Jewish mother remained a consistent force for righteous behavior.

In its decades as a hit show, *The Goldbergs* enshrined positive maternal values as the centerpiece of a vibrant family and community. As critic George Lipsitz has noted, memory as expressed in nostalgic shows such as *The Goldbergs* or *I Remember Mama* enables us to "see beyond our own experience . . . modeling an alternate past" through which "family and ethnicity can be sources of affirmation and connection to others." This can happen when the "core tensions" of a program "exude the truths of lived experience and memory."[102] Even in its radio beginnings, *The Goldbergs* had functioned as a repository for ethnic memories as the determined immigrant family endeavored to move beyond its class origins. By the 1950s, Jews looking back on their trajectory into mainstream, middle-class America could pride themselves on the accomplishments of the Goldbergs as they basked in what Vincent Brook calls "kosher nostalgia."[103] The mythical power of the American dream was realized in the ascendancy of both Berg and her alter ego as effective, wise, and competent—though totally different—Jewish mothers.

A "modern" "yesterday woman," manipulative but kindhearted, open to change and new understandings, Molly Goldberg became the "quintessential" Jewish mother of the first half of the twentieth century.[104] She was, according to some television historians, "one of the most empowered images ever" of a Jewish woman on prime-time television.[105] Yet just as the Molly Goldberg image was born amid competing Depression-era messages about gold-digging Jewish women that it came to supplant, another set of negative representations followed, this time from social and behavioral scientists. In spite of Berg's great success as a media figure, her positive characterizations would find tough competition from these new experts.

What have you done, what are you going to do, are you warm enough, put on another muffler, have you had enough to eat, look take just a little of this good soup.

—Mark Zborowski and Elizabeth Herzog on the "shtetl mother,"
Life Is with People: The Culture of the Shtetl

3

MARGARET MEAD
AND RUTH BENEDICT

Social Science Uncovers the Jewish "Family Plot"

IN JULY 1942, WRITER PHILIP WYLIE PUBLISHED *GENERATION OF VIPERS*, a wide-ranging critique of American materialism.[1] It was the book's tenth chapter on "momism" that attracted the most attention, catapulting the book and author into lasting national fame. Depicting the middle-aged, middle-class American mother as a destructive and sinister tyrant who stifled, dominated, and manipulated her family—especially sons—and the entire nation, Wylie's Mom was an economic parasite and cultural menace. Pathological and tyrannical, she pillaged men's money, their right to vote, and raped the men, "not sexually, unfortunately, but morally."[2]

Wylie's ingeniously coined "momism" critique picked up on a slew of attacks against the American mother in the late 1930s and early 1940s fomented by critics across the political spectrum. Under Wylie's and these other writers' unforgiving gaze, Mom became the scapegoat for a host of perceived national deficiencies. No longer celebrated as in the past for her moral rectitude and organizational savvy, Mom was now castigated as frivolous and dependent—yet despotic. Sentimental maternalism—exhibited in garish Mother's Day celebrations, maudlin lyrics, and other "commercial ballyhoo"—came in for similar skewering.[3]

Wylie's critique was part of a broader assault against the maternalist tradition that since the 1920s had centered blame for all manner of American failure on the body of the mother. In the wartime context and especially amid the tensions of postwar domestic readjustment, this critique became increasingly powerful. However paradoxically, in view of the pervasive postwar message of domestic fulfillment conveyed by popular culture, the demystification of motherhood proceeded apace in the late 1940s and early 1950s. According to some observers, the widespread adoption of Wylie's momism critique led to the decisive repudiation of the iconic middle-aged mother in the Cold War era.[4]

No part of the assault on "momism" was specifically addressed to Jewish mothers, but the core notion of a powerful mother who held her children, especially sons, in her indomitable grasp, forever trapping them in a clinging dependency, ran parallel to the postwar critique of the Jewish mother. Blossoming in the fiction, films, and stand-up comedy of the Cold War era, the Jewish mother critique drew on much of the same psychoanalytic and sociological tenets that had stirred Wylie's analysis. But Jewish momism was different in many respects from the rampant mother-blaming of the 1940s and 1950s. Deriving less from an analysis of the deficiencies of contemporary social life caused by maternal wrongdoing than from the depiction of so-called unchangeable patterns of the Jewish family, Jewish momism was drawn more sharply and more ominously than the general critique.

Just as Molly Goldberg was settling into her suburban home, offering entertainment to millions, a counterportrait of Jewish motherhood developed by behavioral and social scientists was forming. In large part due to their critiques, including the work of a cross-cultural research team directed by anthropologists Ruth Benedict and Margaret Mead, the fully benevolent image of Gertrude Berg's Jewish mother prototype would begin to wane. In the late 1940s, the Mead-Benedict group identified a veritable "stereotype" of the Jewish mother, which it promulgated in several publications, including the pioneering study *Life Is with People: The Jewish Little-Town of Eastern Europe*, by Mark Zborowski and Elizabeth Herzog, published in 1952.[5] The study became an "enduring landmark" in American anthropology, continually cited as an "authoritative account of East European Jewish culture."[6] In the view of anthropologist Barbara Kirshenblatt-Gimblett, *Life Is with People* (*LIWP*) represented a "turning point in the relationship of American Jews to their East European Jewish past," allowing Jews to take pride in the distinctiveness of their heritage and to celebrate, in Margaret Mead's words, "the affirmative joy in being Jewish" after the tragedy of the Holocaust.[7] Although the book has been criticized for its nostalgic, unrealistic, positivist tone, its portrait of a "nagging, whining" Jewish mother slipped under the radar and went unchallenged. Mead had hoped that the project would "refute or . . . illuminate current stereotypes" about Jews and contribute to the postwar effort to reclaim and honor the Jewish past.[8] Although *LIWP* accomplished this latter goal, the image of the Jewish mother disseminated by the book and related articles did not so much break stereotypes as entrench them.

"One of the Best Documented Undertakings
in the History of American Anthropology"

Benedict and Mead, the nation's two leading female anthropologists, were un-likely sources of the developing postwar paradigm of the ugly Jewish mother. The two were among the first to look at human development in cross-cultural perspective, emphasizing the cultural specificity of gender roles, sexuality, and child-rearing. Their pioneering work in probing the complex meanings of sex-ual and gender difference and their own sexual nonconformity (each had het-erosexual and homosexual relationships, including a one-time relationship with each other) earned them an early reputation as feminist "scholars, activists, and sexual rebels."[9] But here, more than two decades before the publication of *Portnoy's Complaint*, they directed a massive study of "cultures at a distance" that introduced a narrow, single-themed portrait of the nagging, intrusive Jew-ish mother into the American cultural vocabulary. Despite the rich promise of their innovative research project, they faltered in describing a Jewish mother beyond the stereotype.

Mead and Benedict's study pioneered a new way of examining civilized nations—or "high cultures"—as opposed to the simple primitive tribes that were the usual subjects of anthropological analysis. In attempting to create a model of comparative research that integrated scientific and humanistic ap-proaches, however, they were only partially successful. While the anthropo-logical community ultimately rejected many of their project's findings, their study of Jewish culture, considered its "most visible, durable and successful" outcome, produced a portrait of Jewish family that has had a remarkably long-lasting shelf life. More than fifty years after their publication, these reports continue to be regularly cited as sources for interpreting Jewish history.[10]

Benedict and Mead's work on "culture at a distance" took shape during World War II, when both women consulted to the government on morale-building and the use of social science methods to explore international prob-lems.[11] In 1941, Benedict; Mead; Mead's husband, Gregory Bateson; and other colleagues founded the Council for Intercultural Relations (later known as the Institute for Intercultural Studies), to explore "national cultures." The council began the first studies of national character with investigations of German and Austrian cultures based on informants living in the United States.[12] In 1943, Benedict joined the Office of War Information; under its auspices she pre-pared reports on several European and Asian cultures. By interviewing immi-grants in the United States and studying child-rearing approaches, literature, films, radio broadcasts, and official documents, Benedict fostered new ways of studying complex contemporary societies inaccessible to direct research.[13] Her influential work, *The Chrysanthemum and the* Sword (1946), a study of Japanese culture based on her wartime research, became the prime exemplar of the "culture at a distance" model, revolutionizing the field of applied anthropology.[14] These works established the methodology for Mead and Benedict's joint research on Jewish culture.

Immediately after World War II, the Office of Naval Research (ONR) developed a plan to utilize funds already appropriated for warfare to create the conditions for lasting peace. A member of the ONR's committee on research, Benedict was asked to submit a proposal. When she told colleagues that she knew where to obtain $100,000 for the study of "culture at a distance" in highly literate societies, "none of us believed her," Mead recalled; "it seemed like an extravagant sum."[15] In a proposal titled "Cultural Study of American Minorities of Foreign Origins," Benedict argued that through the comparative study of national character, the aggressive and belligerent characteristics that caused World War II might be better understood, and thus eliminated. Originally, she included six cultures: pre-Soviet Great Russian, Czech, Polish, French, Syrian, and Chinese.[16] But Benedict had become aware of Eastern European Jewish culture through her wartime research, and she developed an interest in distinguishing between types of European cultures as represented by Jews.[17] Benedict and Mead decided to include a study of Jews in each of the European cultures in which they were interested—for example, "Czech Jews, Russian Jews, Polish Jews."[18] But after the team began their research, they quickly discovered that "Eastern European Jews had in fact a living culture," no matter which country they inhabited, and they amended their plans to include Jews as a separate area of study.[19]

Administered through Columbia University, the Research in Contemporary Cultures Project (RCC) ran from 1947 through 1951, at a cost of a quarter of a million dollars, and involved 120 participants representing 16 nationalities and 14 different disciplines.[20] Benedict, project director and convener of the Czech group, remained its driving intellectual force. Mead, coconvener of the Russian group, member of the French group, research director, and director of the general seminar, supplied much of its day-to-day energy. After Benedict's untimely death from a heart attack in 1948, her bereaved colleague assumed its directorship.[21]

Much about the RCC was distinctive. This was the first time that relatively large groups of individuals from different backgrounds, rather than a single individual or small teams, joined research teams with the intention of illuminating cross-cultural patterns; Mead and Benedict believed that in this way, the research group mirrored the "diversity of a living society." The range of methods used was also distinctive: in Mead's words, "interviews, interpersonal accounts of situations, films, projective tests, written materials, historical documents, descriptive accounts of material culture, etc." were all viable sources.[22]

Another unusual factor was that each of the RCC area groups included members of the cultures being studied.[23] To develop the optimum degree of cross-cultural comparison, no one on the project held a fixed position; most played at least two roles and worked on two cultures. Thus each individual cultural seminar (or "research group") was diversified in discipline, nationality, and skills. Though it had a convener who was a senior anthropologist, all participants were full members with equal status, volunteers and paid workers alike; all members, including the office staff, attended bimonthly general seminars where research groups' reports were presented.[24] According to Mead, this would facilitate research comparisons between groups. Extensive, mostly verbatim, notes were kept, making the RCC "one of the best documented undertakings in the history of American anthropology."[25]

Finally, the project was organized in a way that was "equally holistic and human," as Mead and her colleague Rhoda Métraux described it. It did not demand a "strict accounting for hours," gave people time off "to deal with personal crises without question," and expected that "some workers will sleep until ten in the morning." In the opinion of Benedict biographer Margaret Caffrey, the project's nonhierarchical, "circular" structure, and its commitment to taking into account each person's special abilities, made it an early model of a "feminist" think tank.[26]

After several years of meetings, interviews, and ancillary research, the RCC completed its investigations.[27] More than fifty publications were produced, the major one being *The Study of Culture at a Distance*, a compilation of the project's interdisciplinary methods, edited by Mead and Métraux. The publications that resulted from the work of the Jewish group included *Life Is with People*; "Hypotheses Concerning the Eastern European Jewish Family," an article coauthored by Ruth Landes and Zborowski; and Martha Wolfenstein's "Two Types of Jewish Mothers."[28] According to Mead, Zborowski, a Russian-born Jew who studied anthropology at the Sorbonne before he fled Paris in 1941, was "the crucial person" on the Jewish team because he combined "the living experience of shtetl culture" along with a background in history and anthropology.[29] Herzog was a professional writer with a social science background; Zborowski's other collaborator, Ruth Landes, the principal author of their joint article, was an iconoclastic anthropologist who had studied with Benedict and was an RCC interviewer.[30] Wolfenstein was a psychoanalyst, and Métraux an anthropologist who became Mead's partner in much of her later work; Métraux moved in with Mead in 1955, but their private relationship (like Benedict's and Mead's earlier one) was long concealed.[31]

Mead assigned Zborowski the task of writing a "unified book" in which Jewish readers could recognize themselves and their parents and that would also appeal to a general audience. She urged the American Jewish Committee (AJC) to fund it in the interest of developing "counterpropaganda" to repudiate

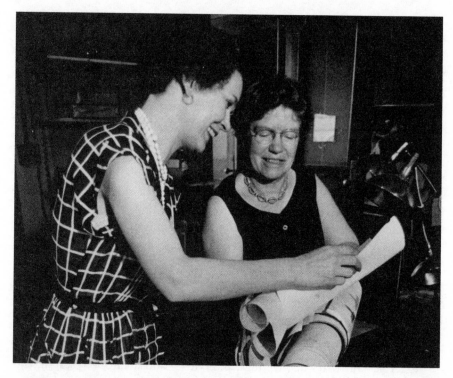

Anthropologists Margaret Mead and Rhoda Métraux collaborated on the postwar study of contemporary cultures that popularized a European Jewish mother "type." One result of the project was their influential 1953 volume *The Study of Culture at a Distance*. Here Mead and Métraux are shown examining children's drawings of Sputnik in 1958. (Courtesy of the Library of Congress)

anti-Semitism and help integrate Jews into American life. She argued that the project would help instill "positive attitudes towards the traditional Eastern European Jewish culture" and thereby serve "indirectly to refute or to illuminate current stereotypes about the Jew." Because these purposes matched the AJC goals of postwar "domestic defense," the AJC agreed to fund the "*shtetl* study," as it called the project.[32]

Within two years of the release of *Life Is with People* in 1952, allegations surfaced about Zborowski's role as an agent of the Soviet police and his participation in the death of Trotsky's son and others. The AJC distanced itself from the project, but Mead remained loyal to Zborowski. Although he was not tried on any charges, Zborowski admitted to perjury relating to his testimony in other spy trials and went to prison.[33] Nonetheless, the book was well received. In this time of Cold War angst, Zborowski's doings were not so much covered up as deemed irrelevant by those who wished to dissociate themselves from the ugly red-baiting of the era.[34]

The book succeeded not because of or despite its political undercurrents, but because it read "like a novel or a script of a film."[35] Most importantly, it presented an easily digestible and definitive portrait of a familiar culture receding into the past. Not only nostalgia, but also the very fact of its ability to paint this "culture at a distance" in bold brush strokes while incorporating material from a vast range of sources, created *LIWP*'s distinctive quality. It is largely for this reason that *Life Is with People* emerged as authoritative.[36] While Mead's introduction to the book heralded the study's "objectivity," her insistence on incorporating researchers' subjective experience into RCC findings may have been responsible for the portrait of the unacculturated, romantic "shtetl" culture it produced. In Zborowski's case, he possessed a subjective "insider" view that insulated him from problematic areas of his own life from which he wasn't able to distance himself.[37] The "shtetl" that emerged in *Life Is with People* was more of a state of mind, as Zborowski described it, than a physical space with a unique material and historical reality. In fact, the team did not set out to study shtetl-born Jews, as it conducted interviews in the United States with 128 individuals who had been born in a range of European Jewish communities from big cities to villages. Only as they approached the writing of the book did researchers extrapolate cultural patterns that they identified with traditional Jewish core culture, which were then attributed to what they considered the prototypical Jewish community—the "shtetl."[38]

That the view of Jewish life in *Life Is with People* is monolithic rather than heterogeneous is undeniable. The same is the case with Landes and Zborowski's "Hypotheses Concerning the Jewish Family" and Wolfenstein's "Two Types of Jewish Mothers," each of which, like *LIWP*, was cited by social scientists for decades following their publication.[39] When we turn to the portraits of family life, sex roles, and child-rearing in these publications, we see further evidence of this quality: relations between family members are presented as time-honored verities, historical truths that characterize Jewish culture as a whole and brook no competing interpretations. Unintentionally reifying "stereotypes" that Benedict and Mead sought "indirectly to refute," as Mead had promised the AJC, these studies supported rather than challenged the standard popular conception of Jewish women.

Although meeting records show a give-and-take between researchers, the official public report expressed none of the hesitations, contradictions, and complexities that characterized the actual research. Instead, RCC authors offered a unidimensional portrait that focused narrowly on the "shtetl" Jewish family. At its center was a "negative nagging, whining and malingering" Jewish mother, a powerful though "loving despot" who ruled her family with "solicitude, sacrifice and suffering."[40] How did this innovative research study, designed and managed by two of the most creative social scientists in the country—in collaboration with many female colleagues—come to what was, in the end, a predictably "stereotypical" conclusion?

"Did You Hurt Yourself My Son?": The Jewish Mother Stereotype

"Certainly there is a stereotype of the Jewish family," Elizabeth Herzog acknowledged to Mead at one meeting of the Jewish research group. But she worried that they had not yet discussed "what basis of that stereotype rested in fact." Two years into the group's research, Herzog still felt the question had not been satisfactorily answered. She wanted to probe this issue, and especially to explore the role of the mother—"if it is a mother cult" and "what the facts of the matter are."[41] Without proper investigation into the matter, in *Life Is with People*, Herzog and Zborowski nevertheless presented a definitive formulation: "The stereotype of the 'Yiddishe mammeh,' familiar in many lands, has firm roots in the shtetl," the authors declared. What they referred to as stereotypical was the Yiddishe mammeh's love: "No matter what you do, no matter what happens, she will love you always." Though the mother may have had "odd and sometimes irritating ways of showing it," the belief in her love was "strong and unshakable."[42]

A second aspect of the stereotype was that maternal love was rooted in "boundless suffering." The ideal shtetl mother, "toiling constantly for her family, is the eternal fountain of sacrifice, lamentation, and renewed effort. When misfortune strikes she cries out with tears and with protests, but her efforts never flag." Suffering was in turn connected with worrying, which was viewed not as an indulgence, "but as an expression of affection and almost a duty. If you worry actively enough, something may come of it." Thus the intensity of worry, because it showed the extent of identification, was the mark of love. "Even before anything happens, a good mother worries about it and there is magic in her worry."[43] "What have you done, what are you going to do, are you warm enough, put on another muffler, have you had enough to eat, look take just a little of this good soup."[44]

In addition to "unremitting solicitude about every aspect of her child's welfare," the Jewish mother's love, Zborowski and Herzog argued, was especially manifested in "constant and solicitous overfeeding." Associated with the "tangibles of existence," the mother prepared and served the family's food. Because offering food meant offering her love, she offered food constantly. "When her food is refused it is as if her love were rejected." As a consequence, refusing to eat became a method by which children, or the parents themselves, could coerce other family members. Rejection of the mother's food was "intolerable," causing "acute anxiety."[45]

The stereotypical elements of Jewish mothering cited in *Life Is with People*—love, suffering, worrying, and food—had been influenced by the innovative gender analysis developed by Ruth Landes in the article she had written with Zborowski. From her extensive fieldwork in North American and Brazilian indigenous cultures, Landes had developed a dynamic model of culture that highlighted internal differences based on gender, sexuality, class, and race.[46] Landes now brought this focus to bear on the polarized sex roles of the shtetl. Viewing women as representing emotion and men spirituality, the "dichotomy between the intellectual burdens" charged to men and the "earthy opportunities charged to women" seemed formative and total. On the one side stood learning—"the monopoly of men"; on the other stood "food as a social control"—"the monopoly of women." Defining "social functions in terms of sex" meant that men were responsible for "almost all values and ideals and honorific activities" while women dominated the private life of the family.[47]

Though the wife came to serve as "the actual head of the household," responsible for its "Jewish way of life," the shtetl's male culture made wives officially subordinate and inferior.[48] This vulnerability, expressed through constant suffering, "concern and . . . criticism," became a powerful weapon by which women could regulate their households and control the future. "The Jewish mother of our informants is known for nagging, quarreling, worrying and hypochondria," Landes and Zborowski wrote. "By her conduct the woman manipulates her traditionally subordinate status to win some advantages." In the authors' view, the Jewish mother's domination of the household went beyond family structure, beyond law and custom, to penetrate the very core of Jewish identity: it represented the very ethos of the people.[49] In a word, the Jewish mother could no more prevent her suffering, worrying, and nagging than she could halt her breathing—it was in her nature to do so.

For an anthropologist wary of generalizing from experiential research, Landes's quick conclusions are striking and puzzling. Landes's biographer, Sally Cole, notes that Landes's work highlighted themes of "diversity" and "contradiction," often putting her at odds with Benedict's "patterns of culture," as well as with Mead's and Bateson's views of cultural "ethos."[50] But in the case of her Jewish study, Landes's findings only confirmed these theories of "general culture."

Perhaps it was her direct participation in a study shaped by Mead and Benedict that caused Landes to alter her standard approach; she may have been influenced as well by the congruence of her own family patterns to those she observed in her Jewish informants. Landes did not like her mother, whom she described as domineering and controlling: "My fear of marriage and childbirth is all tied up with my rejection of my mother. She was so cold, cruel and small, filled my young life so with terror that I rejected anything that would put me in her role—and there lay all my destructiveness."[51] These factors, combined with the information gathered by the RCC team, led Landes to formulate hypotheses about the Jewish family apparently so deeply etched in Jewish character that she theorized them as fundamental and unchanging, reflecting the "ethos" and shared "sentiment" of the Jewish people. This ethos had two distinct parts: an acute gender analysis recognizing differences between the sexes; and the mother's pattern of "suffering," which reduced her temperament to a single flat note.

Yet Landes and Zborowski observe that the mother's conduct was "understood, tolerated, loved," and in retrospect, "idealized." " 'She kills herself,' people say of a good mother, in order to bring up her children," they quoted from one memoir.[52] The Jewish mother's "constancy, her boundless sacrifice," and her love for her brood were celebrated in folk songs and stories.[53] Landes and Zborowski cited one folk tale that has lived on until the present day and is often cited as typical of the Jewish mother:

> A young man begs his mother for her heart, which his betrothed has demanded as a gift; having torn it out of his mother's proffered breast, he races away with it; and as he stumbles, the heart falls to the ground, and he hears it question protectively, "Did you hurt yourself, my son?"[54]

Worrying, adoring, and devoted, the Jewish mother presented by Landes and her colleagues fit a normative cultural pattern that allowed little room for diversity. Suffering and self-sacrificing, she "nags at all members of the family."[55] Such were the strategies of the Jewish mother.

The Jewish "Family Plot": A "Perfect Fit" between Ideals and Behavior

Because it concerned the East European background of Jews, *Life Is with People* and the Landes and Zborowski article omitted discussions of how the Jewish family fared in America. But in their article Landes and Zborowski expressed surprise at the continuity of traditional Jewish ideals and behavior in the United States.[56] This finding contradicted the premise apparent in an outline that Benedict had made for a proposed "field study of American Jewish family life," which posited considerable conflict between the "ancestral culture" and the "American norm."[57] The team speculated that the unexpected perseverance of customs lay in the fact that so much of Jewish life was based on observance of ideal codes of behavior that had guided Jews over the centuries. Mead went so far as to assert that the ways in which Jews embodied cultural patterns reflected a "perfect fit." But did the "perfect fit" still apply when cultural customs were disrupted by immigration?[58]

Martha Wolfenstein's article and the research group minutes suggest that the team believed that the force of traditional cultural patterns overwhelmed pressures to assimilate. According to Wolfenstein, American Jewish mothers who retained the psychological focus of East European child-rearing created dysfunctional American families. She called them "shtetl mothers," thus branding the apparently backward ethos of the shtetl on immigrant mothers. Separated from her very young son at an early age, the shtetl mother in Europe never saw him move beyond the nursery stage. Fixated in the "earliest infantile phase," the son was helpless and "terribly vulnerable, a baby incapable of taking care of himself, who would perish without her constant vigilance. At the same time the baby appears as terribly strong, capable of killing the mother." "A righteous figure, capable of damning or giving absolution," this mother was "a suffering person, being incessantly wounded and killed and deriving her major unacknowledged emotional gratification in this masochistic way."[59] Suffering, indeed, was the major motive of the mother's life; with deep emotion and dramatic cadence, she dwelled on the failures of her children and the grief they caused her.

For Wolfenstein, the mother's maladaptation stemmed from several causes, structural and psychological: first was the early—and wrenching—departure of the son from the mother's care to attend *cheder* (religious school); secondly, the premium placed on male piety and study relegated sexual pleasure to secondary status, so that the "sexually unsatisfied" mother unnaturally harked back to childbirth, "the great genital experience," and the child's earliest years. Finally, while Jewish men may have had similar "sado-masochistic motives," these were elaborated in highly ritualistic ways—they accepted their suffering from God. But with women excluded from this realm, their sufferings were expressed in "free flowing emotional relations with the children."[60]

Fixated on the child's helpless infancy, the "shtetl" mother and son became a "symbiotic pair, with their fates inseparably intertwined."[61] Her ceaseless worries, especially in the United States, could create deep conflict, as in the example of a mother who constantly warned her adolescent son that he was "in danger of catching cold from not buttoning his jacket or not wearing his scarf or sleeping with the windows open," only to have her son just as frequently fly into a rage, yelling "that he is not a baby." In America, "reality factors" that influenced European anxieties, like the infant mortality rate, no longer applied. Neither were young boys routinely "thrust out" of the family, "snatched" from their mothers, to go to cheder at age three. American Jewish mothers who adapted to the new conditions created more functional families than did the maladaptive shtetl mother:

> Th[is] American Jewish mother . . . sees her child mainly as an independent being, who should stop as quickly as possible being babyish and proceed to acquire skills. A different aspect of the growing child is emphasized, that having to do with learning, and the child is not seen as fragile.[62]

Wolfenstein based her theory on only two mothers whom she had treated at the Child Guidance Institute of the Jewish Board of Guardians in New York City for about two years, although she supplemented this evidence with research on Eastern European culture, observations of "American and Jewish mothers," American non-Jewish families, "and American child-training literature." Her small case sample did not prevent her from concluding that the contrasting maternal patterns she saw represented generic types of Jewish mothers—one, Eastern European ("shtetl"); the other, American. That the children of the "shtetl mother" whom Wolfenstein treated were in fact American-born and raised in different conditions than the Old World mattered little. Wolfenstein explained that although she had immigrated to the United States, the shtetl mother learned mothering from her own European Jewish mother, and there-fore the Jewish mother type lived on. The "American" mother broke with shtetl parenting patterns and was less melodramatic, authoritarian, and suffer-ing. Wolfenstein thus provided one answer to the question Benedict had posed in her "Field Study" guide: "how the transition from the Eastern European Jewish to the American Jewish family is achieved."[63]

The Jewish study group and general seminar further explored the issue of differences between European Jewish and American Jewish mothers. Mead be-lieved that a primary difference arose because of the fact that the "high ideal of the shtetl"—the husband studying and the wife supporting him—was "antipa-thetic" to Americans. Herzog still pressed the researchers to analyze the East European "mama cult"—the dominance of mothers—which she considered anal-ogous to "American momism." But Mead disagreed sharply, and she also called Herzog to task about using the word "cult," which she argued more correctly labeled purely religious affiliations. To the contrary, Mead believed that rela-tionships "between, mother, father, son, daughter" were the key to Jewish family life. This she called not "cult" but "plot." The "family plot" of Jewish life—which Mead defined as "the basic interfamilial relation in a culture which gives you the idea of the whole culture"—had to be seen among its dynamic interfamily relationships.[64]

Mead considered one of the key elements in the Jewish family plot to be its "irrevocableness." "In the Jewish community you can leave but unless you leave absolutely and completely you're really completely in," she told the seminar. "Consider the precariousness of the American family . . . it's too dangerous to quarrel with your parents." But for Jews, dissolving kinship ties was impossible. "They're just there forever," Mead believed. You could shriek or scream at any of your relatives, "but they will be right there when you're thru [sic]."

> The Jewish girls called their family everything under the sun; the Gentile girls spoke very highly of the members of their family, said they were very nice, we never fight, etc. But the Jewish girls said they wanted to live at home and the Gen-tile girls wanted to go to California.[65]

Even after conversion, Zborowski observed, you could never erase the Jewishness in a Jew.

Despite strong family ties and the pervasive ideal of *shalom bais* (family harmony, or balance), Mead believed that Jewish family life was a "game of chaos," without much privacy but with "enormous zest." The Jewish family existed in a state of "dynamic equilibrium" that never calmed down. "There was a preference for a hell of a lot going on at one time," Mead thought, not anger, but tension.[66] Love was not expressed openly, but through quarreling. "Use words like intensity, enjoyment of emotion," she advised the staff in describing the Jewish home.[67]

Distinct parenting styles were another key element in the Jewish "family plot." Jewish parents possessed a "unique love" for their children. So important was the relationship between parents and children that it was *the* crucial family tie, more primary than husband-wife. Every Jew was expected to become a parent; and every parent was expected to *makhn fun kinder mentschen* (to make children into responsible adults). Parenting meant joy, but also sorrow. As *naches fu kinder* (prideful pleasure from one's childrens' accomplishments) was the epitome of joy, *tsores fun kinder* (troubles from children) was likewise responsible for almost any illness.[68] As automatic as the inculcation of values was *derekh erets*: a child's responsibility to behave respectfully toward adults, especially one's parents. "Parents are assumed to know their business. The children are expected to accept instruction and discipline, and whether they understand just why is unimportant."[69] Parental authority was absolute. Parents could vent their rage at disobedient children freely, with punishment often taking a corporal form, from the mother's "quick slap" to the father's "premeditated strap." Though mothers often applied discipline, formally the father, as head of the household, administered actual physical punishments.[70]

On one level mothers and fathers worked as a "complementary" unit, reflected in the colloquial Yiddish term for parents, *tateh-mammeh* (father-mother). This hyphenated concept did not imply "equation," but rather reflected that parents functioned as a "dualistic entity in which the component factors are complementary." According to one team member's report, the father was a "remote," passive guide, while the mother was warm and protective to her children, although a "nag" to her husband.[71] Because mothers had the greatest responsibility for child-rearing, family ties were closest to the mother's family, even to the "entire ignorance" of the father's relatives.[72] "Every time I talk about my family, I say we're going to mother's," one researcher noted. "Everybody I know says it's my mother's house."[73]

The dynamic relationships between mother and son and father and daughter, even more than the bond between husband and wife, was another distinctive characteristic; indeed, it formed the "institutional universe" of Jewish family life.[74] "We have found the involvements between mother and son to be so far-reaching and intense as to approximate a kind of adoration," Landes and Zborowski wrote. Because of the mother's "great concentration of loving, admiring attention" on her son, she created an "interacting libidinal universe" that would last throughout the son's lifetime. "To no one else will he ever be so desirable and important, nowhere else will he receive the indulgences shown a helpless child. If the son does not know this," the authors concluded, "the mother and the whole tradition so inform him."[75]

Daughters enjoyed warm bonds with fathers in contrast to the sons' "remote" ones. But daughters' relations with mothers were marked by conflict, manifested in the Jewish mother's "negativism" toward her daughter and her determination to keep her "in her place." "While she nags at all members of the family," Landes and Zborowski wrote, "she nags at her daughter in a consistently hostile manner." For example, the Jewish mother refused to teach her daughter cooking or any other domestic skills. "Keep out of my kitchen! This is *my* kitchen," she railed.[76] Mead pointed out that in an Italian kitchen, on the other hand, there would be three generations over the pot. The peculiar characteristics of "shtetl" society were to blame for this situation. The "interchangeability of any individual's role" in that society created a "threat of replaceability" that afflicted the Jewish mother with "anxiety and tension." The "monotonous theme in her nagging is her articulated anticipatory refusal to be supplanted in any capacity by her daughter."[77]

For all of the opprobrium directed at those who fashioned American "momism," in some ways the American mom seemed more psychologically sound than the Jewish mother. "American momism has much less of the masochistic element in it," Mead told the seminar. Says the American mother: "Go out, be a success, and prove I'm a success. Do it because you love mother. . . . Show you're the best boy." The Jewish mother: "Look what I suffered for you, look what you did to me. You owe this to me." The Jewish mother is the woman who bore you, the American mother fed you vitamins. Continues Mead: "The model Jewish mother is the womb; the American mother is when her son is college president and sends an automobile to get her. The model is not the unborn or newly born child, but a *grown* son."[78]

The Jewish mother as "womb" babies her son "until she dies," in Zborowski's words, echoing Wolfenstein, because she must part with him when he leaves to study at cheder at a tender age. The consequence of being "thrust out" from the "safe, enfolding warmth of the feminine world" was that the son lived forever in perpetual babyhood.[79]

Erik Erikson: The Jewish Mother as "Destroyed Torso"

The Europeanized American Jewish mother whom Wolfenstein described deeply influenced Mead's views, and also those of her protégé Erik Erikson, who would become one of the nation's innovative and influential psychoanalysts. Erikson's contribution to the group's final product was especially substantial, but its importance has been ignored until now. Erikson had come under the influence of Mead, who introduced him to Benedict, a decade earlier, when all three participated in Columbia University seminars dealing with culture and personality. Critical of Freud, Mead had been particularly impressed with Erikson's focus on bodily zones, while Erikson had become increasingly dependent on Mead and Benedict's ideas around the social and cultural matrices of personality; Benedict's ideas about social "configurations" particularly resonated with Erikson's developing work on childhood. During and immediately after World War II, when Mead and Benedict were deeply involved in national character studies through such groups as the Committee for National Morale and the Council for Intercultural Relations, they recruited Erikson into a variety of policy-oriented psychological seminars. Mead involved him in projects dealing with German character and German war prisoners, while Benedict commissioned him to study children of foreign backgrounds in the United States. Both projects were compatible with Erikson's interest in how social and historic conditions affected personality development.[80]

It was during this period that Erikson sketched out his thinking on the subjects of Jews and mothers, though he did not join the two issues. In a 1942 essay on Hitler, Erikson commented on the nature of Jewish identity, which he expanded in his landmark work, *Childhood and Society* in 1950, distinguishing between the "religiously dogmatic, culturally reactionary Jew" and those Jews for whom "cultural multiplicity" and relativism had become absolutes.[81] He wrote about "Moms" in his section on American identity, historicizing the phenomenon of "momism" by which blaming mothers had become a "manifest literary sport."[82] Erikson derided mother-blaming for its "moralistic punitiveness"; "Mom's" composite image was a "stereotyped caricature," he complained, a "classical" psychiatric syndrome of "neurotic conflict."[83]

Erikson's "free associations" on the Jewish mother, presented privately to Mead and Benedict on March 4, 1948, four months before Erikson wrote his outline for the "Moms" section, were quite a different matter, no doubt related to problems involving his own Jewish identity. A response to the RCC's Jewish research data presented to him orally by Ruth Benedict, Erikson's stream of consciousness, taken down by Mead as he spoke, depicts the Jewish mother in strongly negative terms:

> Enormous oral dependency. Jerusalem, the destroyed temple; Jewish mother constantly complains, "I am old. I am destroyed." Nagging is not the right word. It is filled by a whining sound. The mother acts like a destroyed torso, "My guts are falling out," "My breasts are sagging because you bit me." Jewish child is a child who because of the underdevelopment of locomotion seeks eroginous[*sic*]-zone stimulation as a search for peace. Note emphasis on anorexia nervosa and obesity.[84]

Whining and complaining, the Jewish mother—"a destroyed torso"—is immediately linked to a historical circumstance, the destruction of the Jewish

temple, but her physical, biological reality and the effect it has on the inadequate location of her offspring, is given primacy. Erikson continues his associations by focusing on the mother as an introjected object, part of the Melanie
Klein psychoanalytic view of the "bad" mother: "The Melanie Klein system is
really a Jewish system. Badness of the introjected object; you swallow something and it turns into poison within you. Melanie Klein stuff only comes up in
very deteriorated patients and in Jews." The negativity with which Erikson
paints the Jewish mother is here definitively linked to the Kleinian system ob-
servable only in one other category: "deteriorated patients." Erikson adds that
the "Jewish neurotic" assumes that the "consolation for every trouble in the
world is food." With Jewish mothers, the connection is "physical intimacy—
food—delicatessen." And further:

> The Jewish mother doesn't let her babies go. She shows her breast all through the
> child's life while the father covers his penis early; wouldn't even uncover it in the
> countryside because God might see it. The child only has to refuse food and
> mother is back again. . . . introjected mother turns into a poison.[85]

For Erikson, then, not only is the Jewish mother the "introverted," "bad"
object, negatively focusing the child's attention on food and creating oral dependency; she also weakens the father in the eyes of the child. The father's
weakness matches the child's underdeveloped locomotion.

> As mother offers the scared child the sight of the breast and significant intimacy as
> a way out, much clear feeling of incestuous feeling of mother (not genitals.) Inces-
> tuous intimacy turns into psychological intimacy. She offers this at time the child
> reacts with *loathing* (because kept so aware) because provocative outer mother
> turns into a loathed object. Introjected mother turns into a poison.

When Mead asks why the mother is introjected, Erikson responds that it is
a term of analysis for "what hurts you," what is "foreign" to you. Specifically in
regard to Jewish mothers, said Erikson, "If you have no country, the individual
mother has to be your country."[86]

After his private meeting with Mead and Benedict, Erikson lectured to the
RCC general seminar. In this talk, Erikson expanded his free associations of
the previous day to explain that his Jewish cases fit better with his psychoanalytic theories than other cases but that references to Jews could be associated
with Western civilization more broadly, just as Chinese examples referred to
Eastern civilization. He asserted that Jewish data showed "a lot of emphasis on
oral incorporation: food, the stomach, elimination, the skin surfaces to be
shown, exhibited, touched."[87]

Erikson's discourse on the Jewish mother, even in the privacy of his discussion with his old friends, did not touch on his relationship to his own mother,
Karla Abrahamsen. An unwed mother who came from a prominent Jewish

family in Copenhagen, Karla later married Theodor Homburger, a respectable Jewish physician whom Erik, then only three years old, never accepted as his natural father. Erikson's childhood was spent learning to negotiate borders—between Judaism and Christianity, between his mother, stepfather, and biological father, whose identity his mother never disclosed to him; because of this, although he invented his own surname, the identity issues in his own life went unresolved. Erikson's daughter, Sue Erikson Bloland, believed that her father suffered immensely from having been "betrayed by his own mother," who in keeping painful secrets from him prevented him from coping with his enormous loss. According to Bloland, Erikson never acknowledged the depth of his anger toward this narcissistic woman.[88] Erikson once confided to Anna Freud that his mother was "an admirable woman, but of a very penetrating personality, hard on a son."[89]

Whether or not Erikson's views on the Jewish mother's powerful "introverted" presence in the lives of her dependent children and the seeming marginality of the father can be traced at least in part to his own biography, his musings on the Jewish mother were apparently taken at face value by Mead and her team. Mead told the working group, "Both Erikson and Martha, working separately, think that the mother's body is intensified in importance because of the lack of one's own soil, and the mother's body becomes motherland. Ruined breast, ruined temple; they go together symbolically."[90] Here Mead conflated Erikson's views with those that Martha Wolfenstein elaborated in "Two Types of Jewish Mothers." Both interpreters believed that the breast was important because of the notion that it symbolized the lack of a Jewish homeland. Wolfenstein also focused on children's aggression against mothers being tied up with the "milk-meat taboo"; in Jewish culture, she speculated, the characteristic relationships between the mother's "indulgence, deprivation, and withholding" may have derived from the infant's tendencies to bite the maternal breast coupled with the "equally intense interference with such tendencies" because of the prohibition against eating meat with milk.[91] In Wolfenstein's speculation, biology meets religion, resulting in a tense relationship between the Jewish mother and her child over food:

> The child imposes on himself in a spiteful way a taboo against eating solid food which is expressed in refusing the food mother cooks for him. The mother then develops anxiety about whether she can get the child to eat. A favored and most severe punishment of Jewish mothers is refusing to talk to the child. The mother seems to parallel the child's closed mouth policy in the child's case, not taking in food; in the mother's case, not giving out words. (This seems to be one of many interrelations between what goes into the child's mouth and what comes out of the parent's mouth. . . .)[92]

Mead related material about babies' biting mothers' breasts to Melanie Klein's ideas about negative introjection. Despite the milk-meat taboo, she felt that the Jewish mother could be "masochistic." Zborowski agreed that the "Jewish woman certainly suffers from her husband and baby."[93]

Although at the outset of the RCC project Mead had explained that its goal was to study immigrant societies within the "entire context" of knowledge in diverse fields rather than to narrowly focus on "oedipal fantasies," "castration fears," and other psychological markers, through such insights the psychoanalytic perspectives of Erickson and Wolfenstein held sway.[94]

The "Real Point" of the Jewish Mother—Not Only "Nagging," But "Unconditional Love"

Seminar notes suggest evidence pointing to different attributes of the Jewish mother than the stereotype the researchers recognized. Beth Herzog observed that as well as "negative nagging, whining and malingering," "there are some positive things"; the problem lay in finding the "phrases for warmth." The group understood Herzog's point and appreciated the idea that the Jewish mother possessed more complimentary characteristics. For Mead, these were that "she feeds you, she worries about you . . . she loves you 'even if.'" For Landes and Herzog, nagging about health and safety—"It's cold outside, put on your rubbers, wear your scarf"—were a welcome reflection of the mother's attention, as was the fact that "you could always go to mother." The difficulty arose in conceptualizing the "many assumptions" they held about the Jewish mother. Herzog urged them to find a way: "We might present the rest [of] the picture of mama, not only nagging."[95]

Indeed, some members of the team questioned the concept of "nagging" itself: if nagging were considered as "continuous querying and expostulation," could it not be seen as "a form of love-making, of giving attention to the cherished one and demanding attention from the loved one in return"?[96] Herzog summarized: "After all there are undoubtedly many positive values"; "there is a cohesiveness, there is an affirmative feeling, and in not having it unbalances the picture." To incorporate such attributes in their portrait of the Jewish mother would allow the team to create a fuller picture and "see the wood for the trees."[97]

Shortly before her death, Ruth Benedict herself took note of the positive qualities of the Jewish mother in a report on child-rearing patterns among RCC area groups. She pointed out that while Russian mothers swaddled to protect babies from destroying themselves (since they saw infants as potentially violent) and Polish mothers swaddled to "harden" vulnerable babies through suffering, Jewish mothers stressed "warmth and comfort."

> The pillowed warmth of his swaddling period apparently becomes a prototype of what home represents, an image which he will have plenty of opportunity to

contrast with the world outside, the world of the goy. . . . She is starting the baby in a way of life where there is a lack of guilt and aggression in being the active partner in all complementary relationships and security in being the passive partner.[98]

Mead did not disagree with the thrust of Benedict's observations, but she believed that "a confusing number of contradictions" exist whenever a "single practice" like swaddling was followed cross-culturally.[99] As she tried to understand "the real point" about the Jewish mother in response to Herzog's probing, she turned to her own experience.

American mother's love is conditional. Jewish mother's love is unconditional. American mother loves you *if* you do—Her love for everybody is conditional. The Jewish mother loves you *even* if. I always tell a story on myself. I was walking Cathy through Washington Square Park in her carriage when she was a baby, seeing all those fat babies and I said, "Sugar, if you ever look like that I won't forgive you."

For Mead, despite masochism, there was still "unconditional love of the [Jewish] mother. She scolds and nags, has fits when you do things to her, but anywhere else she's still your mother."[100] Zborowski and Herzog also addressed the Jewish mother's love for her children. Her affection was so "taken for granted," they argue, that to question it caused bafflement: "She loved us, so how could she be angry even if we did hurt her?" Parents' love for children was "unconditional," the authors declared, "but perhaps 'unbreakable' would be more accurate."[101] Natalie Joffe made a related point. "I wish to state emphatically and categorically," Joffe reported, "that it is impossible for a Jewish mother to accept the fact that a mother may not love her child." Joffe observed that "even relatively sophisticated, second-generation mothers, who have read widely in child development and other psychoanalytically oriented literature," believed that if their children showed hostility, it was because they took out their feelings on those with whom they felt most secure. The mothers could in no way imagine that children's hostile behavior could be a response to hostile feelings on their own part.[102]

After several years of gathering material, the RCC had amassed reams of data about the Jewish family, much of it pointing in different directions. While this material was "extremely elaborate," it was "scattered" and contradictory.[103] How could the group reconcile both positive and negative notions of the Jewish mother and build a coherent portrait? How could the investigators see through the trees to find the forest?

To construct what it hoped would be a coherent portrait, the team turned to supplementary sources—folktales and songs, fiction, plays, and especially films. "This is how the movies came in," Landes explained to Mead. Faced with puzzling data, team members decided to go to the movies together—they saw Yiddish films. "It was extraordinary how it seemed to focus our thinking," Landes reported.[104] Most Yiddish films of the time emphasized the close emotional bonds of the Jewish family, but also the deep sense of suffering and sacrifice, especially on the mother's part, often highlighting the ingratitude of children toward parents and the former's gradual recognition of the parents' goodness and wisdom.[105] In the article on the Jewish family for which she was the lead writer, Landes referred to several films, including *Bar Mitzvah* (*Bar Mitsve*, 1935); *Long Is the Road* (*Lang Iz der Veg*, 1948); and *The Eternal Song*, better known as "A Letter to Mother" (*A Brivele der Mamen*, 1939), each of them Polish-made films that depicted the Jewish mother's essentially tragic attachment for her son. Perhaps it was these films that led Mead to tell Landes: "These movies that you saw were given you by God. They were just the ones you needed for your work."[106]

Benedict helped pioneer the use of film as anthropological data in *Chrysanthemum and the Sword*, and Mead contributed to a book on the subject that Wolfenstein edited in 1950. In Wolfenstein's view, film was more culturally significant than a single work of art "because it is group produced and made for the taste of the many." "We do not regard movies as being true or false representations of life," Wolfenstein told the general seminar, "but rather as phantasy material containing residual material which does not come out in life."[107] Providing clues to cultural patterns, the content analysis of film was a valuable—indeed, a scientific—method of inquiry.

But what is the fit between film—especially Yiddish film—and real life? As an anthropologist colleague later admonished, the actual significance of fiction films to the study of culture needed to be determined by a careful study of film images "in relation to the film makers, their audiences, and to other information about their subject matter."[108] To properly apply film to the study of culture, it was necessary to provide a "thick description" that put "social events, behaviors, and processes" in their wider contexts.[109]

An understanding of Yiddish film in such specific terms would have aided RCC work. Film historian J. Hoberman notes that Yiddish films are "a site where historical and cultural forces converged to find often nightmarish representation." "Born mid-earthquake," amid the destruction of East European communities, the films, he believed, reflected the "profound uneasiness" of Jews caught in this frightening transition. Because Yiddish films expressed these anxieties through "family melodrama," Yiddish film must therefore be seen as "an extended family quarrel." "Inherently unstable," "self-contradictory," and full of "discrepancies," there is a "stark, aggressively unmodulated quality to their tear-jerking," Hoberman explains, a theatricalization of the "representation of loss" experienced by Jewish communities.[110]

In fact, the films that Landes cites in her article exemplify the characteristics that Hoberman discussed. *Bar Mitsve* tells the story of a widower (Boris Thomashefsky) who returns to the Old Country for his son's bar mitzvah with his fiancée; his wife, presumed dead after she was lost at sea in the voyage to America, appears at the ceremony, exposing the fiancée as a gold digger after her son gives his bar mitzvah speech—a paean to his mother's virtue. "The word to describe *Bar Mitsve* is *shund*," Hoberman asserts, "a term of contempt indicating literary or theatrical 'trash' and denoting variously an inept mishmash, a vulgar display, a mass-produced trifle, or a piece of mental claptrap." In his view, *Bar Mitsve* was an "exploitation film" that drew upon "the most hackneyed clichés of the Yiddish stage."[111]

Lang Iz der Veg, produced in Munich after World War II with performers from the Munich Yiddish Art Theater, also uses conventions of the Yiddish *shund* film.[112] One of the first fiction films to represent the Holocaust and the displaced persons camps after the war, it offers a compelling account of Jewish tragedy. But Landes and Zborowski's account focused exclusively on the mother-son nexus: "mother and son, separated by Nazi occupation of Warsaw, seek each other in concentration camps, etc., until he locates her in state of breakdown in hospital; her acceptance of her husband's murder by Nazis contrasts with her agonized search for her son."[113]

The third film that Landes mentioned, *A Brivele der Mamen*, is "arguably the most artful and shameless of Yiddish weepies."[114] The last Yiddish film to be produced in Warsaw before World War II, it tells the story of a Jewish mother holding her family together in Eastern Europe after her husband immigrates to the United States. Taking its title from the well-known turn-of-the-century lament of a mother left behind after her child journeys to America, *A Brivele der Mamen* offers actress Lucy German as the long-suffering mother who witnesses bitter poverty and emotional distress, the breakup of the family, and the deaths of her husband, daughter, and one son, who dies in battle during the World War. "His last word was 'Mother,'" she learns, shortly after peace is declared. "He died like a hero." At the end of the film, the mother, now in the United States, is reunited with another long-lost son as she lies dying after being run over at the moment she recognizes him as he sings his father's composition, "Memories of My Old House." The film is "an endurance test to determine the amount of *tsores* one mother can endure," says Hoberman.[115]

Landes and the RCC team largely missed the opportunity for a new perspective offered by Yiddish cinema. Had they evaluated less sentimental dramas—for example, *Mirele Efros*, made in America in 1939 and considered the "Jewish Queen Lear," the story of a competent, strong-willed, and highly ethical widow in conflict with her narcissistic daughter-in-law—they might have reached different conclusions. Instead, the films that the teams relied on became further evidence of the complex "plot" of Jewish family life—especially the intense "libidinal" relationship between mother and son. "There is no

Margaret Mead and Ruth Benedict's influential postwar research project used *A Letter to Mother* (1939) as evidence of the "ethos" of the Jewish family. The last Yiddish film produced in Warsaw before World War II, it tells the story of a Jewish mother's lament for her missing child. (Courtesy of The National Center for Jewish Film at Brandeis University)

avoidance between mother and son," Landes and Zborowski wrote, "except that intercourse is forbidden. Mother is the embodiment of warmth, intimacy, food, unconditional love, security, practical reality," yet her "high feeling," her "concern and her criticism," insured that the mother-son relationship would not go smoothly. Mother-son "adoration" and deep maternal suffering, along with "male-status superiority," "female-status inferiority," and "nagging, whining and hypochondria" became characteristic traits of the Jewish matriarch.[116]

Thanks to these film insights, the seemingly contradictory evidence gleaned from interviews and other sources took on new "clarity" for the group. The Jewish family "ethos" and the leading character in the drama, the Jewish mother, could now be described according to a defined, confirmed, pattern.

As the RCC was completing its work, Mead addressed the general problem of validating hypotheses developed through national character studies. In her view, testing the "intra-cultural" and "intra-psychic fit" to assure that the large patterns held was essential to establish vital proofs. "Any discrepancy within the material should immediately demand a revision of the . . . hypothesis," she explained. "Each discrepancy or contradiction means that the whole pattern is not understood."[117] But it is unclear whether the RCC's Jewish team addressed such contradictions. In the RCC's published reports, there is no hint of any discrepancy—whether the idiosyncracies of the interview process, the give-and-take that went into interpreting responses, the clues given by swaddling, "unconditional" love, or any of the other tangled findings that both Benedict and Mead had recognized as part of the patterns of Eastern European Jewish life. Instead, the Jewish mother emerges according to a one-note pattern: she is the nag—an "eternal fountain of sacrifice, lamentation."[118]

The decisions the RCC made regarding which aspects of the studies to publish—and in which formats—may have covered over discrepant findings. Because the "shtetl" book—written to appeal to a general audience—focused attention on the "rich but vanished past" of East European Jewish life, the often conflicting evidence of contemporary witnesses inevitably caused distortion. In the case of framing a portrait from materials that came from a variety of respondents—those from towns and cities as well as villages—patterns discerned by researchers became overgeneralized and frozen in time. This was especially true of the image of the Jewish mother as nagging, whining, and forever suffering. The RCC simply could not find an effective way of presenting the full nuanced picture that their research had in fact gathered.

The main components of the Jewish family plot drew on the psychoanalytic theories of Erikson and Wolfenstein, the memories of Zborowski and team members, and interviews and related data, including evidence from film narratives. Although none of this material was collected from sources within Eastern Europe, the findings were said to directly represent European Jewish "shtetl" types that were then seen as timeless, since they carried over into the New World present. Thus contemporary cultural practices were seen as forming personality that continued over the generations.[119] Given Jews' especially strict adherence to religious law and customs compared to other immigrant groups, the relation of Jewish customs to personality showed, in Mead's view, an even more "perfect fit" than those of other cultures.

But the immutable patterns of culture in *Life Is with People*, Landes and Zborowski's "Hypotheses about the Eastern European Jewish Family," and Wolfenstein's "Two Types of Jewish Mothers" fail Mead's vital proof test. As Kirshenblatt-Gimblett observes, the RCC team omitted signs of "modernization, enlightenment, Westernization, urbanization, secularization, industrialization, assimilation, nationalism, and political mobilization" because it focused on the "core culture" of the "unacculturated" shtetl.[120] As a result, Eastern European Jewry appears remarkably untouched by change; a "perfect"—but in reality, an artificial—"fit" between ideal "type" and recurring behavior, one which squelches jarring contradictions.

Landes and Zborowski's remark on the "surprise" they felt at recognizing the "perseverance" of European modes in the United States—"even in the third generation" and despite "shifts of emphasis"—points to the irony of the RCC's conclusions, particularly regarding Jewish families.[121] As an outcome of their wartime experience, both Mead and Benedict had become especially interested in how cultures changed—indeed, Benedict's original field guide for the Jewish study focused on questions of acculturation. Nonetheless, for the reasons described above, the team's Jewish work came to emphasize the indelible rather than changing factors in national cultural life. "Shtetl Jews themselves expect perseverance," Landes and Zborowski explained; "in orthodox religious circles" any changes in family life were decried.

"Who Do You Love More Than Anyone Else In the World?"

In fact, an unpublished child study of Jewish parents and children conducted as part of the RCC investigation by the Jewish research team's Naomi Chaitman did show significant changes in Jewish parenting patterns in the New World, pointing to a very different set of characteristics of Jewish mothers than the ones described in *Life Is with People* and the other RCC articles. The mothers Chaitman interviewed in New York and Montreal—all of whom had been born in Eastern Europe and had emigrated as young children—demonstrated modern, flexible, and pragmatic child-rearing attitudes; they resembled the progressive East European "Molly Goldberg" prototype more than they did the "nagging" RCC shtetl mother.

Like the mothers Ruth Zuckoff praised in the *Jewish Daily Forward* in the 1920s, these mothers took a keen interest in their children's success. "After an interview with a child, the parents quietly asked me what I thought of the children," Chaitman reported, "did it answer all the questions well, and [did I think] the child was clever or not. And very often the mother would come to me with problems that they had with the child, or general questions about what I thought [was] modern child rearing."[122] One mother told Chaitman that if she had given her a copy of the questions the night before, she was sure that she could answer them far better because she had a copy of Gesell (the child-rearing expert) and could look up all the answers.

Although the children interviewed by Chaitman described a "good mother" as "one who *doesn't* spoil her child," or "who *doesn't* give them everything," the interviews revealed that Jewish parents did provide many material advantages, and much encouragement for academic and social success. "You couldn't walk into their apartment building without hearing screeches of violins, pianos and a collection of other musical instruments," Chaitman noted. "Everybody took music lessons, whether they wanted them or not. And if the child showed any talent, it was immediately taken out of school, given a private tutor and forced to practice 8 hours a day." Parents devoted themselves to their children's advancement: they "actually lowered their own status so that their children will appreciate the education as well as the material things with which they were being showered." But the children did not consider parents to be nagging or unduly interventive, and defended their mothers against any criticism. When Chaitman posed the question: " 'Whom do you love more than anyone else in the world?' every single child answered: 'My mother.' "[123]

Chaitman's informants generally considered themselves to be "modern" parents who believed that they were bringing up their children much better than did their own parents. Because of language and cultural barriers, they felt that they had spent their own childhoods torn between two worlds; they were ashamed of their immigrant parents and did not believe their parents could understand them. As parents themselves, they used modern methods of psychology and hygiene and, whether correctly or not, they believed they could understand their own children. They rejected the automatic rendering of *derekh erets*—the "blind obedience and respect" that they had to bestow on their parents; in contrast, they wanted to earn their children's respect rather than commanding it. As one subject explained:

> If you apply yourself to understand your child, with the proper upbringing it can be molded into almost anything you desire. Whereas to their parents, if the children didn't turn out just right, it was because they had sinned and God was punishing them. The constant saying was, "What did I do to deserve such a child?"[124]

A far cry from the nagging, whining, malingering Jewish mother drawn by Erikson, Wolfenstein, Landes, Zborowski, and Herzog, this Jewish mother seems open to the world around her. Although she imposed high behavioral standards for home and school, her children accepted her guidelines as clear and fair. Her greatest success lay in her child's achieving beyond her own status; her greatest failure was to so entice the child with easy material rewards that she interfered with its ability to internalize the drive for success. Having assumed the position of supreme familial authority that had been shared, at least nominally, in Eastern Europe, the mother wielded her power assertively, using it to impart strongly held values.

This report from the RCC's Jewish child study suggests a sharp break between European and first-generation immigrant child-rearing patterns and those of the emerging second generation. For these New World parents, the religious rectitude of the past, founded in a strict Orthodox God and the age-old rules of Judaism, no longer structured parent-child relations. Chaitman's interviews reveal that Jewish parents were modern Americans who treated their children according to psychological authorities such as Arnold Gesell. But despite the fact that Chaitman conducted her research for the RCC, it was never published. Only the "shtetl" findings publicly represented Jewish parenting.

The RCC's research has enjoyed particular prominence among RCC pub-lications. Many anthropologists rejected other RCC national character studies because of methodological limitations; lacking fieldwork in the countries stud-ied, the RCC's approach seemed subjective and intuitive.[125] Negative attention focused especially on Geoffrey Gorer's swaddling hypothesis. While critics mocked Gorer's focus on swaddling as a causal determinant of Russian national character by labeling it "diaperology," Benedict's work on swaddling escaped such bromides.[126]

To some anthropologists, the problem with the RCC findings recalled broad issues associated with the "cultural patterns" approach. In the scien-tific climate of the era, the project's use of sweeping characterizations, value-laden terms, and generalizations across cultures and national boundaries implied a lack of objectivity and precision.[127] Although *Life Is with People* gar-nered some criticisms, for the most part, readers accepted its concrete, realis-tic observations as fact. Yet the book and related articles blurred distinctions between patterns of folk culture and the precise sociological moment being explicated.

Nonetheless the stereotyped portrait of the Jewish family that emerged from the RCC study contained more than a grain of commonly recognized truth—for example, the close bonds of the Jewish family, the centrality of children, the Jewish mother's attentiveness. But the research has endured not because its accounts seemed familiar, but because of its claim to scientific va-lidity, which imbued the work with a seemingly authoritative and reliable voice across generations.

Yet this claim cannot stand. Pioneering in so many ways, the RCC Jewish study remains flawed in its methodology and its static, unitary perspectives. As Jenna Joselit has noted of Wolfenstein's article, this research "mistook a spe-cific cultural moment for millennial tradition." The result was that researchers came to define the "emotionally extravagant and overprotective Jewish mother as a timeless cultural *type*, enshrining her within the American popular imagi-nation."[128] *Life Is with People* and Landes and Zborowski's "Hypothesis about the Eastern European Jewish Family" committed the same errors.

Although the Jewish mother who emerged from the RCC project was drawn as much from impressionistic and anecdotal sources as from purely "ob-jective" ones, bolstered by the Mead-Benedict team's credentials and authority, she grew into a cultural figure of enormous power, no longer a folktale depic-tion, but a real scientific type. In this manner, social and behavioral scientists were drawn into the cauldron of forces naming American Jewish mothers as negative forces in their children's lives.

With the aid of this material, a new notion of the Jewish mother began to solidify. Different from earlier, bifurcated portraits that focused on the "good" mother's loving support of her children or her economic opportunism, the postwar Jewish mother paradigm emphasized "nagging" and other negative psychological traits that defined her attachment to her offspring as dysfunctional. Crossing the boundaries of appropriate domestic power, this Jewish mother displaced her husband and nagged her children excessively. The cultural construction that emerged in this new recycling would have lasting influence.

Q. What did the Jewish mother bank teller say to her customer?
A. You never write, you never call, you only come to see me when you need money.

Q. How many Jewish mothers does it take to screw in a light bulb?
A. Never mind, I'll just sit here in the dark.

Q. What did the waiter ask the group of dining Jewish mothers?
A. "Is anything all right?"

A woman takes her son to the doctor. At the end of the appointment the doctor calls the mother into his office and says, "Mrs. Goldstein, I'm afraid that your son Barry has an Oedipus complex." To which Mrs. Goldstein replies, "Oedipus, Shmedipus, just as long as he loves his mother."

—Jokes from the Borscht Belt

4

FROM MARJORIE MORNINGSTAR TO JENNIE GROSSINGER

The Suburbs, the Catskills, and the Jewish Mother Joke

IN HIS 1955 BEST-SELLING NOVEL, *MARJORIE MORNINGSTAR*, Herman Wouk tells the romantic story of a beautiful Jewish girl who falls in love with a dashing theatrical director whom she eventually rejects for a more mature relationship and a fulfilling, if conventional, marriage. The story "made me wish I was Jewish," Linda Ronstadt recalled. Many readers saw Marjorie as "an American Everygirl who happens to be Jewish," as a *Time* magazine cover story that year described the fictional heroine.[1] Three years later, the film version of the novel, starring Natalie Wood as the eighteen-year-old Marjorie and Gene Kelly as her bohemian lover, Noel Airman, presented this apparently universal account of the agonies of young love in brilliant Technicolor.

Yet there was much about the original work that marked it as uniquely Jewish. Marjorie Morningstar, née Morgenstern, is the daughter of Eastern European immigrants who, as the story opens in 1933, have just moved from the Bronx to a spacious apartment on Central Park West. Marjorie, enrolled in Hunter College, is the first Morgenstern to receive a college education, and much is made of her aspirations to move beyond the bourgeois trappings of her upwardly mobile Jewish family. Despite her desire to amount to something "important," even "distinguished," Marjorie winds up two decades later living not as the actress "Morningstar" but as the wife of a stolid lawyer and mother of four children. As a regular synagogue-goer and a leader in Jewish community organizations in the suburb of Mamaroneck, she is even more Jewishly identified and observant than her mother, Rose Morgenstern; she is the "personification of female suburban middle-class existence," but with a Jewish slant. Marjorie has in fact transformed into "Shirley"—Noel Airman's derogatory term for "the respectable girl, the mother of the next generation, all tricked out to appear gay and girlish and carefree, but with a terrible threatening solid dullness jutting through." In fact, she seems to have *become* her mother— "coarsened, wrinkled, fattened, with the deceiving bloom of girlhood all stripped away, showing naked the grim horrid respectable determined *dullness*."[2]

In this emblematic text of the mid-1950s, the Jewish mother emerged in a new caricature that would echo in dozens of portraits of the next decades: "Oh God, Marjorie," Noel Airman cries out, "the dullness of the mothers! Smug self-righteousness mixed with climbing eagerness, and a district attorney's inquisitive suspicion."[3] Manifest in both Marjorie Morgenstern Schwartz and her mother, Rose, the Jewish mother type had moved beyond her association with the tensions of the first stage of Jewish immigrant acculturation. Now she would stand in not only for Jews' conflict over the values of materialism versus Old World piety, but for a newer version of their ambivalence about joining the American middle class—reflected in ongoing debates about suburbanization, the conflicting demands of leisure and work, and changing child-rearing styles.

The Jewish mother's experience encapsulated these changing lifestyles. From the self-enclosed European shtetl, described unforgettably in *Life Is with People*, to the immigrant ghettos of the New World, Jews were moving on. Though they still remained an urban people, in the two decades after the war, about a third of American Jews—even the fictional Goldberg family—had left the city for the suburbs, the new "middle-class Shangri-La[s]." In the 1950s, the suburban Jewish population more than doubled, with Jews suburbanizing at a rate almost four times that of non-Jews. For Marjorie Morningstar and thousands like her, the new communities were a "symbol of Utopia"—a "sign of success, prestige, money, power and security."[4] In little more than one generation, Jews had triumphantly moved from "shtetl to suburb," as one sociologist famously remarked.[5]

Yet the new residents often found themselves isolated in the new communities without conventional supports. Fitting in with non-Jewish neighbors who typically wanted little social contact with them, melding new styles of conspicuous consumption with traditional values, and, for women especially, finding friendship and community posed formidable challenges. Because role definitions were more fluid in communities that lacked the tight definition of the older, generally Orthodox, urban areas of the first settlements, women discovered new opportunities in the suburbs. But there were also new anxieties. Old norms no longer fit, but new ones were not yet established. Many Jewish mothers rose to the occasion, becoming, in one rabbi's words, "the modern matriarch[s] of suburbia."[6] Much as Molly Goldberg settled into TV's Haverville in the mid-1950s and built a new community, these mothers also adapted to their environments, creating a new model of Jewish motherhood that revised older images. Marjorie Morningstar, younger and more typical of the married sub-urban lifestyle, provided an even better mass media model than Molly of the changing Jewish mother.

In addition to the suburbs, the Borscht Belt resorts of upstate New York also led second-generation Jews to reflect on their new circumstances. Here, too, women became new matriarchs, both as hoteliers and as clients (with hus-bands often weekend-only visitors). The spawning ground of hundreds of comics, many of whom would go on to mass media fame, the Catskills region of New York offered another setting that provoked Jews to examine their rela-tionship to consumption, modernity, and changing family patterns. With sharp and sometimes brutal humor, the new comedians mocked the Jewish mother—a convenient symbol of the distance they had traveled, literally and figuratively, between their old homes and the new possibilities before them. In the relative freedom of the Catskills, guests and entertainers lived out their fantasies and pleasures in novel ways. Yet the break with the past was rough and extreme. In the developing postwar struggle between tradition and modernity, the Jewish mother would occupy a pivotal place.

The "Sex Gap" in Suburbia

Why would men who some twenty years earlier had idealized Jewish mothers for their strength in the community and their dedication to their families "turn around" in the 1950s and give the world some of its most "misogynistic" im-ages of "smothering and emasculating mothers?" asks Karen Brodkin in her 1998 book, *How Jews Became White Folks*.[7] As we have seen, both women and men had in fact been deeply ambivalent about Jewish mothers decades earlier, resulting in many conflicted and often negative images of Jewish mothers. Brodkin's book highlights a new aspect of Jewish men's ambivalence regarding their mothers, an ambivalence that in Brodkin's words revolved around the "promise and the reality of patriarchal domesticity, upon which so much of 1950s white masculinity depended." Jewish mothers in the 1950s, and again in the 1960s, became the "first victims" of the Jewish sons who sought to free themselves from Jewishness "in order to possess the fruits of the mainstream." Confronting the hollowness of their own materialism, they projected blame onto their mothers and, later, their wives: Jewish women became the "lightning rod for the electricity of Jewish men's ambivalence."[8]

To understand exactly how the Jewish encounter with suburbia created such negative characterizations of Jewish women, particularly the Jewish mother, we must first ask why tensions of suburban lifestyle fell so frequently and squarely upon their shoulders. It turns out, in fact, that the literary and dramatic representations of Jewish sons about their mothers often differed from the postwar accounts of scholars, professionals, and activists. There was a gender inequity—or "sex gap"—in the values and activities of Jewish suburbia, according to Marshall Sklare (the dean of Jewish sociologists) and Joseph Greenblum, writing in the 1960s.[9] But it came out disproportionately in the Jewish mother's *favor*. At the same time, observers noted a remarkable change in the power dynamics of Jewish suburban families, one that tended to solidify the role reversals that had taken place in urban settings. This perceived transformation fueled the new images of Jewish mothers.

The story of the postwar Jewish suburban experience was first told by Rabbi Albert Gordon in his 1959 account, *Jews of Suburbia*.[10] Gordon, who had previously assisted with the founding of such congregations as Levittown, Long Island—the granddaddy of suburban communities—and St. Louis Park, Minnesota, spent the 1950s serving Temple Emanuel of Newton, Massachusetts, a prominent suburb of metropolitan Boston, where he came to understand the fundamental changes that the suburban lifestyle had wrought in Jewish mores. American Jews, predominantly the children of immigrants, were among the groups most affected by the suburban migration, agreed Oscar Handlin, the preeminent historian of American immigration, who wrote the foreword to Gordon's book. Handlin noted that while for much of the twentieth century populations who wanted to escape contact with minorities ordinarily fled from cities, now, with the Jewish out-migration of the 1950s, minorities themselves led the trek out of urban centers. For Jews in particular, the suburban style of life symbolized the success of Americanization and of Jews' acceptance into American culture.[11]

Gordon's description of Jewish suburbia was based on data from hundreds of Jews in eighty-nine communities, plus information from rabbis and lay leaders. Out of this mix came a striking finding about the transformation of Jewish family life in the suburbs. Gordon asserted that while the father was the head of the household according to Jewish tradition, in America, with wives assuming the preponderant responsibility for child-rearing, including the moral training of children, there was a "far greater degree of equality between husband and wife than is generally assumed." By virtue of her increased duties and responsibilities within the family in its new surroundings, the new Jewish wife had become "the modern matriarch of Jewish suburbia. Her ideas, opinions and values clearly dominate."[12]

Just as commentators in the 1920s and 1930s had discussed a new matriarchy of Jewish women who gained power in the place of absent fathers, Gordon noted that in the postwar generation, the Jewish mother similarly gained status because of her husband's default; so completely engrossed in business affairs was the absentee Jewish father that he neglected spiritual and cultural matters that had once been his province. Arising to fill this vacuum, the "new 'matriarchate'" assumed a position of "executive leadership" in her home; it was she who chose her children's schools and determined the family's organizational and social affiliations, including the extent of religious observance, a matter that a generation ago, in Gordon's opinion, had been the direct responsibility of the Jewish husband.[13] As one youth told Gordon: "I really don't talk to Dad about my problems in school or about my friends, because I know that it is really Mother who knows what is going on with us kids. . . . She really runs the family."[14]

The suburban Jewish mother played a vital and growing role in her synagogue and in the larger community as well. Indeed, said Gordon, "no synagogue in America could function well these days if it were not for the women who help to blueprint the program, agitate for its adoption and support it with their devoted efforts."[15] Yet he was not convinced that the Jewish mother's prominence in temple affairs was all to the good, since her Jewish knowledge lagged behind men's. Still he acknowledged that the Jewish woman's "realism, devotion, and concern" could override her current backwardness about the details of Jewish texts and ritual practice. Moreover, the rabbi admitted that the Jewish mother's desire for acquiring Jewish education seemed to know no bounds. While Jewish husbands did not read very much, their wives "read the 'best sellers,' particularly those with Jewish themes, and belong to book clubs and lending libraries. Study classes sponsored by temples and by organizations like Hadassah . . . and the Council of Jewish Women attract thousands of female Jewish suburbanites throughout the country."[16] Rabbis and Hebrew educators were reporting "the zeal of these young Jewish suburbanite matrons as they turn to serious study of the Hebrew language, Jewish history, Jewish ritual and ceremonies, the Bible, and even theology."[17] "Something quite remarkable is happening to the Jewish woman in the suburbs and, through her, to her husband," Gordon concluded.

> Never in all my years of my rabbinical career have I seen such concern for factual knowledge about Judaism and the Jews. Mothers seem anxious to know as much about Judaism as do their young daughters, who are attending Hebrew schools in greater numbers than ever before. They have all been much impressed by the State of Israel and its accomplishments. Whatever it is that impels them, I must pay my tribute to them. It is they, even more than their husbands, who are re-establishing today's Jews as "the People of the Book."[18]

Gordon also commented on the Jewish mother's penchant for community activism, reflected in her membership in such Jewish organizations as "Hadassah, the Women's Zionist Organization, Pioneer Women, Mizrachi, Women's Auxiliary of a hospital, O.R.T., or the Women's Division of Brandeis University, Federations or Jewish philanthropies" as well as secular organizations such as "the League of Women Voters, the PTA (usually more than one) . . . the Garden Club . . . the Cub Scouts and the Brownies . . . the March of Dimes, Community Fund, Salvation Army, Muscular Dystrophy and/or any other organization that requires support. She is indeed the modern prototype of the 'woman of valor,'" Gordon asserted, and the success of these organizations was due in no small part to her participation and leadership.[19]

In their study of the Jews of a midwestern metropolis they dubbed "Lakeville" a few years later, Marshall Sklare and Joseph Greenblum agreed that the differential response of men and women to organizational life was one of the outstanding features of "Jewish identity on the suburban frontier," the title of their book on the subject. Like Gordon, Sklare and Greenblum found the greater involvement of women in Jewish and communal organizational life to be so pronounced that they argued that "traditional sex roles have been . . . upset." Nothing less than a "sex gap" existed in suburbia, with Jewish women deeply involved in multiple organizations and Jewish men involved in comparatively few.[20] Sklare and Greenblum also believed that the prominence of women in Jewish community life contrasted with historical gender roles in the Jewish community, when Jewish men undertook the major roles in fundraising and other communal functions.

Sklare and Greenblum, however, rejected Gordon's explanation that Jewish men were too overwhelmed with business pursuits to devote time and attention to communal responsibilities. They believed that Jewish men did participate in leisure activities, but these were "personal, non-philanthropic, and intended for amusement," orientations that they viewed as foreign to traditional Jewish culture. Jewish women, on the other hand, chose a more meaningful involvement. While their husbands selected "expressive" organizations that appealed to more private interests, Jewish women joined "instrumental" organizations that aimed to "affect the lives of others"; they were attracted to organizations with "concrete and tangible" goals rather than those that stressed "conviviality." Overall, women's "greater organizational seriousness" provided evidence of a pronounced "change in sex roles." According to traditional norms, Sklare and Greenblum concluded, "males are the more serious sex—the sex whose horizon is not limited to the frivolous. . . . But in Lakeville we find that it is the woman more than the man who desires transcendence."[21] Sharing similar maternal motivations with the fictional Molly Goldberg, the Jewish mothers of suburbia harnessed neighborly "meddling" to more organized and far-reaching aims.

Sklare and Greenblum and Gordon thus portrayed the Jewish mother in suburbia not as "dull," "smug," and "self-righteous"—in the manner of Wouk's "Shirley"—but as an alert, competent, and active participant in the lives of her family and community. She fit the profile precisely of the "intelligent Jewish woman" whom the Women's League—the Sisterhood of the Conservative movement, the largest Jewish denomination in suburbia—called upon to make her home a center of "inspired Jewish living."[22] After its founding in 1918, the league had focused on Americanizing immigrant masses in tenement neighborhoods; now it replaced the earlier concern with the admonition to suburban Jewish mothers to Judaize themselves, their families, and neighborhoods.[23] Beautifying her home with Jewish objects, creating a program of Jewish study and reading, guiding her children's learning and contributing to and leading the groups with which she was affiliated, this intelligent Jewish woman would naturally become a "better mother and a better member of the community."[24] Her job was to create the Jewish personality of her home—its "spiritual" as well as "social" character. "Food for the stomach is an inadequate diet without food for the mind and soul," the Sisterhood guide instructed, and the Jewish mother was therefore to "prepare both types of nourishment for her family."[25]

There was an obvious difference between these portraits and those the critics of suburbia painted, which accused the Jewish mother's lifestyle of overwhelming materialism and social conformity. Irving Howe was merely one of many observers who contrasted the spiritual "vulgarity" of the suburbs with the lively political passions of the ghetto.[26] The Jewish community of suburbia "has traded its soul and creativity for the power of consumption," commented another unhappy observer in a typically derisive comment.[27] But according to Gordon and Sklare and Greenblum, Jewish women's interests and activities, so radically different than their husbands, transformed the empty sterility of the suburban environment into something much more positive. A contemporary scholar studying Jewish women in the postwar suburbs has reached a similar conclusion. "Like their foremothers," Aleisa Fishman writes, "Jewish women in suburbia continued to negotiate the competing concerns of traditional Judaism and American modernity." They played a crucial role in their families' adjustment to suburban life and made conscious choices to "create a lifestyle and a community that incorporated new postwar trends" and enhance Jewish identity. Through their power as consumers, they "created, shaped, and sustained synagogues, Jewish businesses, and social and charitable organizations."[28]

Yet the transformation of power embodied in the new patterns of suburban life pointed to new fault lines of gender relations that intensified wife- and mother-blame. Less influential in suburban synagogues and community organizations than before, men may have projected their anger at losing their dominance onto women, just as the earlier generation of immigrant men blamed women for their loss of power. Even though men may have experienced greater difficulty in adjusting to the new boundaries and lifestyles, women were portrayed as the neurotic, excessive ones. A second consequence of the suburban transformation that put women at fault for standing in for absent men had to do with child-rearing. Wanting their families to assimilate but unable to provide daily support, men placed their women on a pedestal where they had to dress and act the part of suburban matrons. But at the same time, men criticized their wives for playing by the new rules.

The Jewish mother's great attentiveness to her children, intensified by the move to suburbia and the absence of her husband, became a key factor in the not always positive reconstruction of the Jewish mother's image in the 1950s. According to a survey conducted by Gladys Rothbell, the negative comic stereotype of the Jewish mother was created during this decade. Rothbell found that while there were very few jokes about Jewish mothers in the 1920s and

1930s—and those that existed were generally positive—Jewish mother jokes proliferated in the 1950s and grew more negative. Among the most prevalent themes of these new jokes were "overprotection" and "boasting about children."[29] While the immigrant Jewish mother had been recognized for her ambition and competitiveness on behalf of her offspring, it was the "economically secure, suburban wife," devoting even greater attention to her children and displacing all her aspirations onto them—"bombarding them with verbal stimulation from an early age and thus laying the groundwork for their later educational development"—who stimulated the stereotype of the "'overprotective, self-martyring,' guilt-inducing Jewish mother."[30] The suburban mother's anxieties spurred her child to achieve, but they also induced guilt, a key theme in the emerging comic stereotype. Marjorie Morningstar—the ambitious young woman who becomes a suburban mother—was not herself a joke, but women like Marjorie might have been templates for this new style of Jewish humor.

"You Are Your Mother": Marjorie Morningstar Becomes "Shirley"

It is unclear what Wouk himself thought of Marjorie's apotheosis as a suburban matron. The screenplay of *Marjorie Morningstar* concentrates on the years of Marjorie's development from adolescence to womanhood, concluding at the moment Marjorie ends her passionate affair with the dilettantish Noel Airman—that is, before she marries and begins her run-of-the-mill life of suburban comfort.[31] Yet even in the film, Marjorie's incipient revolt from the moral code of her conventional parents, and her subsequent recognition that she should always listen to her mother's advice, lies at the heart of the drama. Some critics were disturbed that Wouk might have regarded his "Shirley" as a genuine heroine.[32] Wouk acknowledged that Marjorie became "just another wife and mother"—but with a family and a husband she loves. He refused to comment on whether the book's ending was happy, just that it was "truthful."[33]

And as we have seen from Gordon and Sklare and Greenblum's investigations, the novel's conclusion may not have been far from the truth, at least for Lakeville and Newton, Massachusetts. Not yet forty, Marjorie is depicted in this scene as a "sweet-natured placid gray mama" active in the town's Jewish organizations, president of the women's branch of the local community chest, attentive to her children, and religiously observant. Now a contented suburbanite, she is a different kind of Jewish mother than Rose, the immigrant parvenu. Marjorie respects her mother but admits they are two "cats in the sack," fighting all the time, no doubt because as Marjorie admits later on, her mother usually turns out to be right. (It was amazing, thought Marjorie, how her mother could "crash to the heart of a matter.")[34] Rose *is* an interfering mother: she openly listens to Marjorie's telephone conversations; manipulates her dates and spies on her; Rose "pushed, pushed, pushed all the time."[35] Yet Rose has

At this Passover seder in the 1958 film version of Herman Wouk's novel *Marjorie Morningstar*, Marjorie's lover (Noel Airman), joins Marjorie (Natalie Wood) and her mother, Rose Morgenstern (Claire Trevor). Taunted by Noel that "you are your mother," Marjorie eventually abandons her romantic dreams and becomes a suburban housewife, a "Shirley." (MoMA Film Stills Archive)

Marjorie's best interests at heart; while her husband worries about finances, Rose insists that the Morgensterns move to Manhattan so that Marjorie can meet a better class of men. Yet she tells her husband that Marjorie "gets what she wants, not what we pick. That's the right way."[36] Rose similarly acknowledges Marjorie's acting ambitions and does not override them. Even the men in the novel recognize Rose's authenticity: Noel says that she is "perfect," with a "Shakespearean exactness and intensity of character," and Milton, Marjorie's husband, admits that although she would give him trouble, "she's all there."[37]

Interfering, manipulative, materialistic, protective—traits that became the emblem of the Jewish mother—apply very well to Rose, who lives through her children in a way that the suburban Marjorie, deeply engaged in the life of her community, may not have done. Marjorie may have become an "authoritative parent," but that is not the sum total of who she is.[38] The two women in this fashion represent two generations' accommodation to Jewish success: Marjorie may have become "Shirley," but as a second-generation suburban mother, more comfortable in her place than her anxious mother seemed in hers, she is not necessarily Rose.

"Oedipus, Shmedipus, Just as Long as He Loves His Mother": The Catskills and the Birth of the Jewish Mother Joke

Not for nothing did Herman Wouk locate his love story in the Catskills resort of South Wind, the charming summer colony where Noel Airman spun his romantic fantasies as summer theater director. According to Phil Brown, president of the Catskills Institute, Jews "created in the Catskills a cultural location that symbolized their transformation into Americans."[39] Catskill vacationers were primarily East European immigrants and their families who found the entertainment, food, outdoor sports, and release from the grind of everyday routine just about perfect. Perhaps the biggest hotel of the group of fabulous resorts, Grossinger's, was considered literally "*Gan* Eden"—a heaven on earth, a paradise where American Jews could bask in the glory and honor of their new status.[40]

One of the special delights of the area was its vibrant expression of Jewish culture. Music, theater, and humor were everywhere. The area spawned dozens of first-rate Jewish comedians—among them Danny Kaye, Jack Carter, Henny Youngman, Alan King, Sid Caesar, Sam Levenson, Buddy Hackett, Carl Reiner, Myron Cohen, Jan Murray, George Burns, Red Buttons—even the American Jewish genre of stand-up comedy itself.[41] But another offspring was the particular variety of Jewish satire that focused on woman-bashing. The Jewish mother/wife, in particular, was a staple of the Catskill comedy circuit. Its legacy would be to propel the Jewish wife and mother into the mainstream of American comedy; and once she arrived, she never left.

Why was it that the Jewish mother "found herself center stage" in the Catskills?[42] Phil Brown suggests that the Catskills were a place where "Jews could become Americanized while preserving much of their Jewishness."[43] Humor was a perfect route to this process. Cultural historians note that by the 1930s and 1940s, the "comic Jew"—like other representations of Jewishness—had largely disappeared from films, theater, and other media. Because of the "de-Semitization" of American culture in this period, Jewish performers practiced American-style comedy in which Jewishness was communicated through gestures, allusions, accents, and inflections that non-Jews had difficulty recognizing. Jewish humor thus became a "secret language, a silent wink to fellow Jews."[44]

The Catskills, however, offered an almost total Jewish environment that provided a "haven" from the trend toward de-Semitization.[45] Many hundreds of Jewish performers got their start at the big mountain resorts, where they often began as *tummlers*, or social directors, their job to provide diversions for hotel guests through the day and evening.[46] Tummlers created their own acts, drawing on vaudeville roots and plagiarizing the jokes of other comics, so that material was truly held in common. (Mama Berle, the mother of one of the Catskill comic kings who would become Mr. Television himself—Milton Berle, "the thief of bad gags"—was notorious for sitting night after night at Grossinger's and copying down jokes; Berle's stealing of material itself became one of the comic's best-known routines.)[47] For the tummlers, the Catskills served as an "intermediary station" as they moved from vaudeville to Broadway, film, radio, and television.[48] The unique style that the tummlers developed, like that of comedians who were solo performers, was predicated on the fact that their audiences came from similar backgrounds and shared common experiences. The Jewishness of this environment, extending from the extravagant ten-course dinners to the headliners with their riot of staccato one-line gags, was an absolute given.

Jewish mother jokes arose out of this "insider" milieu in which topics that touched a chord with vacationing Jews could be raised as together audiences breathed out a collective sigh of release. Lacking delicacy and subtlety, just like the heavy kosher-style foods patrons ingested in the area's extravagant resorts, the jokes recognized that despite all the changes in American Jews' lives, the bedrock family virtues—no matter how exaggerated and extreme in their presentation—remained firmly embedded in the Jewish middle class. This legion of new Jewish mother jokes appeared as old wine in new bottles, expressing at midcentury the continuing concerns of Americanizing Jews—modernity versus tradition, assimilation versus heritage, autonomy versus dependency.[49]

Despite the enormity of many Catskills resorts—particularly Grossinger's and its arch rival, the Concord—the best-loved hotels exuded an air of intimacy. Phil Brown emphasizes the village-like atmosphere of the resorts; "the Catskills was a magical place to form communities and friendships," he reports.[50] The hotels' Jewish ambience was a significant part of this intimate tone; at Grossinger's, Friday night religious services were mobbed, and there was no smoking from Friday sunset to Saturday sunset.[51] The solicitousness and efficiency of Catskill hoteliers, especially the women, proved critical in establishing the homelike atmosphere of the Borscht Belt resorts; especially in the smaller and more typical Catskill hotels, which were even more family oriented than the large, opulent resorts, female proprietors predominated.[52]

Jennie Grossinger, a legendary hostess, was one of many women who ran Catskills hotels. Every guest felt a special bond with Jennie, often claiming to be her personal friend (in the 1950s, Grossinger's served more than one hundred thousand guests annually). While Jennie's husband came out only on Saturday night to greet the guests, "Jennie was there every night. She always moved around the dining room talking to people, and when she got old and sick, she sat at the entrance to welcome her guests."[53] Singer Eddie Fisher, one of the great entertainers to be discovered at Grossinger's, recalled that he knew right away that Jennie was a "great lady. She treated me like a son, and I behaved like a son, and my mother didn't mind. My mother always used to say, 'I live for my children.' Jennie lived for her children, but she went beyond—her guests were her children." Fisher even married Debbie Reynolds in a grand ceremony at Grossinger's in 1955 because Jennie, and her daughter Elaine, were his "family."[54] Fisher was one of the special guests on an episode of Ralph Edwards's television show, *This Is Your Life*, devoted to Jennie Grossinger, in December 1954. Another of the surprise guests was baseball player Jackie Robinson, one of the many celebrities who liked to vacation at the hotel. In the 1950s, Robinson and other African Americans were not welcomed at many of the finer hotels, in the North as well as South. But "when we went to Grossinger's," Robinson said in his testimonial, "it was like going home."[55]

Grossinger's was more than a resort, wrote Morris Freedman in a two-part piece in *Commentary*—it was "a way of life."[56] Indeed, Grossinger's was to resort hotels as "Bergdorf Goodman is to department stories, Cadillac to cars, mink to furs, and Tiffany to jewelers," but only "roughly." Sometimes called "Waldorf in the Catskills," the Catskills resort went beyond that elegant Manhattan institution in its opulent facilities and *haimishe* services: "a strictly kosher cuisine, a full-time hostess to introduce unattached guests to one another, an Olympic swimming pool, an airport, a ski slope, or champion prize-fighters training on the premises."[57] (The matchmaker, by the way, was none other than Karla Grossinger, Jennie's cousin, a Jewish mother herself who allegedly spoke thirteen languages and had a Ph.D. in philosophy.)[58]

Freedman presented Grossinger's as an "enormous horn of superabundant plenty," a place of "utter tranquillity and fulfillment," where every "tenuous inclination is at once luxuriously catered to."[59] Yet to this visitor as well there was a sense of "common proprietorship" for which Jennie was responsible. She gave the resort its "tone," "dignity and hospitality," its essence as a community and a family. In Freedman's view, Jennie "produced the impression that she saw each of us as a special guest of the Grossinger family, and that it was her pleasure to have us visit her private establishment."[60] The peculiar bond between guests and hotel owners and staff drew upon the sense of lavish comfort—physical as well as emotional—that Jennie Grossinger encouraged. Among Grossinger's guests, the "awareness of material success" was both "un-self-conscious and outspoken." "People were constantly being evaluated in terms of what they had," Freedman explained in a revealing portrait:

> Announcements were made about how much money was being spent daily in the beauty parlor or barber shop. Many of the women had dyed hair, either in shades of silver blue, or in very light blonde, depending on their ages. One dinnertime a woman with a diamond ring about as wide as a dime and as thick as a pencil stopped to talk with one of my neighbors. The others at once began speculating in low voices about the size of the diamond. Then, unhesitatingly, someone asked her about it, and she answered just as unhesitatingly that it was seventeen and a half carats. When she had gone, one woman remarked that it was really not so big.[61]

Considering the background of Grossinger's guests—men and women whose wealth was of their own making, in the garment industry, as fur and diamond merchants, with no bankers or industrialists among them—Freedman did not find their attitudes surprising or offensive. As only the self-made could, these visitors knew the importance of worldly goods; once they got their preliminary probings of wealth and success out of the way, they were "more ready than most to engage one another on less material questions."[62]

The positing and acceptance of excess, in maternal as well as material behavior, became an ingredient of the hotel's effusive and welcoming style. Not surprisingly, food itself—and the excesses of the Jewish mother around feeding her offspring—was a key component of the 1950s comic mix. One joke had Jewish mobster Louis (Lepke) Buchalter, shot by police and desperately clawing at the doors of his mother's apartment. "Mama!" he cries as she opens the door. She looks out, horrified at his appearance: "Eat first, Lepke. Talk later."[63]

In an appearance on *The Ed Sullivan Show* in the 1950s, a showcase for many of the Catskills comics, Jack Carter—considered by many observers to be the quintessential representative of the breed—told several Jewish mother jokes that focused on typical issues of overfeeding and silent, henpecked husbands. "It all starts when we're little kids," Carter began. "The mothers start with the spoon barrage. They trap you in the crib or the high chair and they go, 'a spoon for Daddy, a spoon for mommy [drum roll] one for Uncle Sam, one for President Eisenhower.' No wonder everyone is blown up, we're eating for the whole country."[64]

There was more:

> Isn't it true whenever you go to your mother's she has food ready? It's murder. You can never catch her short. She has 80 courses already. And she's always running and up on her feet, and then they stand behind you like an umpire. "How's the chicken liver?" "Fine." "It needs salt, pepper; you don't like it?"

And more: "My mother has what I call warning food. Everything is 'watch out.' She puts down the soup, 'Watch out; it's hot.' 'Put it down Ma, I'm 37, I'm not an idiot. I know if it's hot.'"

Carter's routine ended with the father as well as the son rendered ineffective by the mother's hovering: "And is he going to get it after I leave. Look how she dragged this poor soul in. This man hasn't said a word in 40 years."[65]

Many components of the Jewish mother jokes that flourished in the following decades are to be found in these Catskill prototypes. Similarly emblematic were jokes at the expense of the Jewish wife, the trademark of comedian Henny Youngman. The next generation of female antagonist to the Jewish mother, the wife represented another target of the gender wars, but jokes about her focused on egregious marital disappointments, especially the wife's appearance, and, like the Jewish mother, her coarse habits and controlling nature. "I haven't talked to my wife in three days," quipped Youngman in his typical "Take my wife, *please*!" routine. "I didn't want to interrupt her." Another

Youngman favorite emphasized the wife's ugliness. "My wife went to the beauty shop and got a mud pack. For two days she looked nice. Then the mud pack wore off."[66] In recounting how she bombed at the Catskills in her early years as a stand-up, Joan Rivers cites this Youngman joke as an example of the misogynistic humor Borscht Belt audiences came to expect.[67] Carried over easily to other middle-class female targets, such misogynistic humor would find an appreciative audience outside the resort community.

According to Riv-Ellen Prell, Jewish mother jokes embodied three main characteristics: the Jewish mother's excess, seen in her insatiable demands for love and obedience; her arsenal of guilt, aimed at her son's inevitable failure to please; and her simplicity and foolishness.[68] Guilt was a special trademark. As Alan King, another Catskills stand-up, told it:

> A man calls his mother in Florida. "Mom, how are you?" "Not too good," says the mother. "I've been very weak." The son says, "Why are you so weak?" She says, "Because I haven't eaten in thirty-eight days." The man says, "That's terrible. Why haven't you eaten in thirty-eight days?" The mother answers, "Because I didn't want my mouth to be filled with food if you should call."[69]

Mike Nichols and Elaine May wove this same joke into their routine, and it was used as a plot device on a 2006 episode of the TV drama *Studio 60 on the Sunset Strip*.

Jewish comedians focused special attention on the Jewish mother's "excessive and dangerous nurturance." Such overprotection "held back her sons," who failed to move on to adulthood.[70] Yet while the jokes expressed resentment at the mothers' penchant for smothering, at the same time, they may be seen to ridicule the comics' own need of nurturance. In effect, the comics acknowledge this need while at the same time distancing themselves from it. Told in the safety and comfort of the ethnically homogeneous Borscht Belt, the jokes, while full of pique and irony, were private.

In referring to the power of the mothers' influence over their sons, comedians also spoke to the fact that sons knew they were watched over in a profound—if confining—way. Their jokes gave recognition to the bonds between mothers and sons yet announced that the sons were, in fact, moving on. By attributing foolishness, guilt-making, and other excessive powers to mothers, the sons, in a contrary way, acknowledged their mothers' strength. Humor provided an excessive and perverse empowerment.

Catskills historian Samantha Goldstein believes that Jewish mother jokes arose because of the gender gap between male comedians and the largely female audiences they played to. With husbands joining their wives and children only on weekends, comics developed their "insult humor" based on the resort life and the familial environs they knew best. According to Goldstein, insult humor is an acknowledgment of "presence and significance." While the jokes the Catskills comedians told were "masculine to a parodic extreme," they acknowledged women's influence and power in the lives of their families.[71]

Esther Romeyn and Jack Kugelmass offer still another reason for Jewish mother jokes. Borscht Belt audiences were notoriously tough, they point out; performing before them was a certain "trial by fire," and failure to amuse could be "damning." Quick-witted but desperate, the comics' strategy was to turn the humor on themselves and their families; when it worked, it quickly caught the attention of restless and overstuffed listeners. Mostly the comedians' style was "hyperactive" and, in Romeyn and Kugelmass's words, "shpritzing"—it deliberately "played upon the self-consciousness of its audiences, who had gained a foothold in American culture but remained very much aware of how close they still were to their 'lowly' past."[72]

Another intriguing explanation comes from psychiatrist Samuel Janus's 1980 study of Jewish comedians. Of Janus's sample of 76 (71 of them male), 92 percent came from struggling, low-income families, whose values and lifestyles—"frugality, worry, guilt, caution, and passivity"—the comedians associated with being Jewish and which they emphatically rejected as an "inborn albatross about their necks." "Mother hangup; Jewish guilt; Oedipal problems," "be careful; don't get hurt" and "study hard; be smarter; be a doctor or lawyer" all found their way into jokes so that humor became a form of "ritual exorcism": comedians identified with the ethnic traits but rejected them. Janus felt that Jewish audiences also distanced themselves from the stereotypes by laughing at them: "Some Jews may be like that, but not me." But Janus did not go nearly far enough, says Gladys Rothbell. By casting Jewish women as "deviants, manipulative, materialistic, crass, nouveau-riche, primitive, loud"—Jews of the "worst kind"—Jewish comedians transformed the Jewish mother into the "quintessential 'other' for modern Jewish comedy in America."[73]

While these comics freely used stereotypes, as opposed to the satire and outrage that became the hallmark of the next generation of Jewish stand-ups, the Catskills comics and the wider group of comedians that Janus surveyed did not offer comedy as acute social commentary. To the contrary, the Borscht Belt comedians suffused their quick-witted humor with nostalgia as well as insult. In his history of the Catskills' summer world, Stefan Kanfer writes that by the 1950s, thousands of Jews had already graduated from the resorts' hotels as employees and guests; these alumni provided the core audience of the new comedy that left the resorts and played on Broadway in shows such as *Wish You Were Here*, in novels and films such as *Marjorie Morningstar*, and, especially, on the new medium of television with such must-watch 1950s programs as *The Ed Sullivan Show* and *Your Show of Shows*. The latter show starred Sid Caesar, a former Catskills comic, and employed a writing team that included many Catskill alumni—Mel Brooks, Carl Reiner, and Woody Allen among them.

For the Jewish audience that delighted over the antics of these comics, the world had been transformed; for them, says Kanfer, "the Old Country no longer signified Eastern Europe or the Lower East Side. It meant the Catskills." Whatever the comics said, on stage or in the other new mediums, "was suffused with nostalgia."[74] This was the world as it was, and which they, as a private, exclusive, members-only party, could recognize and delight in. The barbs about the Jewish mother's overfeeding, her guilt-producing anxieties, and her strangeness, simplicity, and her nagging must be seen in this light. Of course they contained their own kernel of truth, and the recognition with which audiences greeted the many jokes about the Jewish mothers' excesses testified to the symmetry of Catskills-style humor with the audiences' own family histories.

This could be true for women as well as men. As historian Ruth Gay recalled her own response, even Jewish daughters—"all the Ruthies and Rosies and Myrnas"—told Jewish mother jokes. By making fun of mothers, they were signaling that they were gradually "moving out of emotional reach" of their immigrant parents, but also that they feared being "drawn back into the old vortex."[75] Freezing the Jewish mother as a caricature in time was one way to deny their likeness to her and move on.

But history it was—not necessarily, and not usually, written in the vital present tense. Kanfer notes that by the 1960s, the younger generation was already impatient with the old-style "mother jokes," much preferring the hip satire of comics such as Lenny Bruce. For example, one of Bruce's few mother jokes referred to his mother's pleading, as he got into a taxi with some girls in the Catskills, to "make sure my son gets some."[76] A very different kind of Jewish mother, to be sure.

As a delayed response to previous periods of modernization, comedy anchored people in the past and elusive present. It is an imaginative form that draws on history and tradition even as it endeavors to be up-to-date. Combining the verities that are ensconced in lore and ritual with a cutting-edge sensibility, the most talented comics made use of a particular culture's "rules of meaning," says Mark Shechner.[77] But the formations that linger in the comedian's grab bag may not be current. "Because family and culture" provide these perceptions, "they are tenacious; they resist easy uprooting, and one may find in them anachronistic remnants of past time and conditions."[78] Jewish mother jokes may have been out-of-date even as they were born.

The Jewish mother had not passed into oblivion by the 1950s. But, to be sure, she was changing.

Jennie Grossinger and the New Art of Jewish Cooking

One ironic indication of generational transformation is demonstrated by the passing on of the Grossinger inheritance; Jennie evoked a very different style of Jewish mother than her own mother, Malka. Malka and Selig Grossinger had immigrated from Galicia, where Jennie was born in 1892. They settled on the Lower East Side and opened a restaurant, but the business failed, in large part, it was said, because of Malka's overgenerosity. In school but for a few years, Jennie left to help support the family as a button maker. In 1914, the Grossingers purchased the farm in the Catskills for $450, where they hoped to raise crops. Finding the soil too poor for this purpose, they took in boarders and Mom (Malka) Grossinger was back in the kitchen; Jennie served as chambermaid, bookkeeper, and hostess. After three years, the family bought a hotel on a hill in nearby Liberty, New York, and Grossinger's was born.

Mom Grossinger continued to demonstrate her famous generosity in the kitchen, where her recipes and ample portions made visitors extremely content. Working long hours, sometimes Mom would sleep sitting on the stairs so she would not miss cooking breakfast for the guests. By this time, Jennie had married her cousin Harry Grossinger, who gradually built the resort to its extravagant physical proportions while Jennie concentrated on the guests' emotional comfort. With all the changes, as Morris Freedman reported, "'Mom' Grossinger retained her old-fashioned, Old World ways":

> She spent a great deal of time in the kitchen, gossiping with employees, and forever slicing prunes and keeping a suspicious eye out for violations of *kashruth*. A gentle and kindly woman, she was upset by the establishment of the fighters' training camp and accepted it only after she had been charmed by Barney Ross, the first occupant and an Orthodox Jewish boy; it was at her insistence, however, that the camp was kept so far away from the main area. A photograph in the canteen shows her wearing a kerchief, long coat, dark hose, and high-buttoned shoes while shaking hands limply with an immaculately dressed Governor Dewey.[79]

Jennie's largesse was not similarly exhibited in the kitchen, but rather in her guest caretaking. Neither was she dowdy or "high-buttoned" like Malka. Jennie more than lived up to the myth created about her as great hostess and modern woman. A lively conversationalist, she was interested in everything around her. When Morris Freedman visited her in 1954, she was a trim, blond woman, looking much younger than her late fifties. "I was impressed," Freedman reported, "captivated possibly, by a graciousness that approached elegance, and by an embracing, glowing femininity that covered over and made unimportant her obviously sharp business sense. Her manner was a mixture of the humble and confident."[80] Freedman and other visitors commented on Jennie's keen intelligence, her interest in books and learning. She had many tutors, her friends reported, a rabbi who taught her Hebrew texts, an instructor for dance, and others for different kinds of learning, and she hired the best available instructors for her daughter, Elaine, and son, Paul. Jennie had wanted to introduce cultural activities onto the Grossinger's agenda, inviting important American writers and intellectuals to the resort, but her husband was uninterested: "He builds, and he buys food," Jennie remarked, "and of course, that's very important." As for her, she preferred "learning and art. . . . I wish I could read every book I ever see and learn to write short stories."[81]

Jennie's hunger for learning, and especially Jewish learning, resembled that of so many Jewish suburban matrons who filled her hotel and those of other Borscht Belt establishments to overflowing. Jennie belonged to dozens of Jewish organizations, and she made them feel welcome at Grossinger's: Hadassah was one of many Jewish groups to hold its regular meetings there. Self-educated, a community activist deeply dedicated to Jewish causes and to Israel, raising millions of dollars on its behalf, Jennie took pride in her femininity and in her modern maternalism. But she was different from her mom, Malka, whose recipes she had inherited from her own mother in Galicia—and which both Jennie and Malka took pride in serving at Grossinger's, "where epicures can eat the finest in Jewish cooking."[82] The home-flavored recipes in Jennie's 1958 cookbook, *The Art of Jewish Cooking*, based on Malka's cooking, included a typical one for "fillet of pickled herring" that called upon the housewife to "select large fat herrings, with superior flavor and tenderness," and to "soak them in water for three days changing the water daily."[83] In Levittown, Hewlett, Woodmere, Great Neck, Mamaroneck, New Rochelle, Newton, and hundreds of new suburbs all over the United States, it is doubtful that all the new Jewish mamas found the time to soak their herrings in the traditional manner. More likely, they were out taking classes at the synagogue, selling and buying Judaica at the local gift shop, organizing rallies and meetings, buying their kosher items (if, in fact, they still kept kosher) in jars and frozen packages, and learning to cook from Jennie Grossinger and Molly Goldberg, whose own 1955 cookbook included many recipes with shtetl roots that she needed to explain to curious readers. Molly's cookbook posted no fewer than three recipes for herring (fried, pickled, and herring salad), as well as several for borscht and pike, and a cabbage soup that her mother made to last for three days (with and without meat and bones).[84]

The idea that Jewish women may have needed help in the kitchen because they did not cook very well remained a "heretical view," as union organizer Harry Gersh confessed in a 1947 *Commentary* article. "Ma's cooking is enshrined in Jewish tradition, as well as in American folklore," he wrote. "Thousands of pretty pictures in magazine ads, subways and billboards had taught me that motherhood was a higher cooking diploma than a *ruban bleu*." But his own immigrant mother's cooking was flavorless and indigestible. Moreover, she was not "the only Jewish mother who couldn't cook. Joe's mother wasn't any better and Irving's was definitely worse."[85] His detractions provoked a spirited reaction. "You remain a prisoner of your infantilism," one letter writer responded. "We proclaim to the world that we have returned to Ma's cooking. . . . Just take a stroll down Broadway and gaze at the menu in Lindy's."[86]

As this comment acknowledged, the Jewish mother's traditional cooking—which, like their old neighborhoods, many second-generation Jews had preferred to leave behind—began to enjoy a renaissance in Jewish-style restaurants, cookbooks, and new food products. With the packaging of the most famous product from Jennie Grossinger's kitchen—her tasty rye bread—the image of Jewish mother as cook and baker reached a vast new audience. Although by the 1950s Jennie neither supervised nor worked alongside the 175 workers who were needed to prepare Grossinger's meals, the hotel's rye bread had her personal signature. In 1954 the family sold the right to produce and sell "Jennie's" bread to the General Baking Company of Brooklyn, a national company. With her smiling face on every mass-produced wrapper, exuding warmth and domestic cheer, Jennie became the Jewish mother personified, the "Jewish Betty Crocker." Images of the two women side-by-side bear a remarkable resemblance: in plain dark dresses with starched white collars, both are tightly coiffed, with polite but firmly reassuring smiles.[87] Betty Crocker, who once polled second to Eleanor Roosevelt as the most famous woman in America, was in fact a made-up personality whose image kept changing with the times; her most recent makeover came in 1955, a few years after the publication of the first Betty Crocker cookbook.[88] Her look-alike was, of course, authentic, even if the "rye-bread" Jennie Grossinger, constructed as idealized Jewish matriarch of the 1950s, bore greater resemblance to Malka's domestic persona than to her daughter's. Notwithstanding Jennie's impressive business acumen, like that of many other Catskill women hoteliers, in the public mind she was primarily defined by her place in the kitchen.

Grossinger's rye bread enjoyed a remarkable shelf life, even after Jennie's death, as customers continued to buy the rye with the guarantee that it was "hearth-baked" according to the "authentic formula from the kitchen of Jennie Grossinger."[89] In this way, Jennie's traditional "*haimishe* hospitality" became outsourced and trademarked, like the rye itself, never growing stale. "She always stressed the freshness," her daughter remarked, and the "authentic" mass-produced bread was in fact served at Grossinger's own tables (though all other breads the hotel served were home-baked).[90]

Jennie Grossinger's cookbook, too, focused on fresh, homey recipes like "great-grandmother and grandma" used to make.[91] Stressing homemade ingredients, the cookbook resisted the postwar trend toward standardized, processed foods, even as it simultaneously associated Jewish cuisine with increasingly popular international and luxury food. Bantam Books, which published *The Art of Jewish Cooking* in the 1960s, bridged the seeming contradiction between the unfamiliar and exotic by selling the cookbook in a six-book set that included *The Art of French Cooking, The Art of Italian Cooking*, and *The Complete Book of Oriental Cooking*. Jennie's son, Paul, in his introduction to the cookbook, suggested that Jewish cooking was by its very nature "thoroughly international . . . a Melting Pot": due to the "Dispersion," Jewish kettles had "simmered in every country of the world." Thus Jewish cooking could simultaneously be "worldly and sophisticated" and " 'home' style."[92]

What most distinguished Jewish cuisine, however, was the care and attention not of fancy chefs, but the Jewish mother herself. According to Paul

Legendary Catskills hotelier Jennie Grossinger lived for her children; and her guests were also her children. The image of the Jewish mother as cook, baker, and maternal feeder reached a vast new audience with the packaging of the most famous product from Jennie Grossinger's 1950s kitchen: her tasty rye bread.

Grossinger: "French cuisine may be famous for its Escoffier. Italian for its Alfredo. But Jewish cooking, well, for generations and generations, way back to Sarah, Rebecca, and Rachel, the master chef has always been the mistress of the particular tent: Mom."[93] The long-time association of the Jewish mother with food, in the words of Jennie's own son, was thus given the stamp of Biblical authenticity.

Through recipes, cookbooks, and special Jewish foods such as Grossinger's rye, the Jewish mother as a benevolent, traditional "type" was preserved, mass-produced, and exported to a broad public in the 1950s. Enshrining the Jewish mother as maternal feeder became a critical part of the reconstruction of Jewish motherhood during the decade, one that connected to Jewish roots that were firmly planted—as was Molly Goldberg—in "kosher nostalgia."[94] In the constructions of Jewish women themselves, this image was notably positive, nurturant, and supportive, rising above the hostility expressed in the often vicious jokes told about them.

The other notable Borscht Belt export, Jewish wife and mother jokes, as well as 1950s fiction and film images of Jewish women such as Marjorie and Rose Morgenstern, proved equally significant in preserving the Jewish mother as a living memory. By remembering their mothers, writers and comedians called forth the entire body of tradition and folklore with which they identified, but often with nostalgia-tinged ridicule and hostility. Second-generation Jews could laugh at what they saw as the Jewish mother's backwardness—her excessive pride, her overbearing manner, and her deep attachment to her children. Not even the Jewish mother's cooking skills escaped the comedians' barbs. Buddy Hackett's jokes about his mother's bad cooking typified the lot. One was his famous quip that his "fire" went out after he joined the army—no more heartburn from his mother's cooking. And another Hackett joke: "My mother had two menu choices. Take it or leave it." More cruelly, Zero Mostel joked that kosher cooking had killed more Jews than Hitler.[95] However essential Paul Grossinger believed the Jewish mother had been to the creation of Jewish cuisine, she was mere grist for other sons' one-liners. As the narrative of Jews was transformed in midcentury America, so, too, was the comic treatment of them. In their jokes, comedians proclaimed their independence from the past, yet the very fact of such Jewish-based routines acknowledged common bonds and a shared heritage with ancestors whose old-style behavior the comics bashed. Even the most brusque and brutal Catskills-style Jewish comedy helped to manage change and contain the tensions it created.

Such theme-centered humor left another legacy. With the Catskills considered the birthplace of modern stand-up comedy—indeed, the "symbolic location of American humor"—Jewish wife-and-mother jokes became a staple of modern American comedy.[96]

Underlying all techniques of Jewish Motherhood is the ability to plant, cultivate, and harvest guilt. Control guilt and you control the child. . . .

The Jewish Mother's cardinal rule:
Let your child hear you sigh every day; if you don't know what he's done to make you suffer, *he* will.

—Dan Greenburg, *How to Be a Jewish Mother:*
A Very Lovely Training Manual

5

"AMERICAN MOTHER OF THE YEAR" VERSUS MONSTER MOTHERS

Will the Real Sophie Portnoy Please Stand Up?

I T IS SAID THAT GOD COULDN'T BE EVERYWHERE, so he created mothers." So wrote a friend in May 1959 congratulating Judge Jennie Loitman Barron on her selection as American Mother of the Year by the American Mothers Committee, a national organization.[1] Barron's selection as this veritable "Mrs. America of 1959" was widely heralded in the Jewish community. A leader in numerous Jewish organizations, including Hadassah and the Women's Division of the American Jewish Congress, Barron proudly identified herself as a Jew; half a dozen years earlier, in fact, she had been awarded the title of "Jewish Mother of the Year." "I know that it is sometimes unfashionable among intellectuals to praise America," wrote one rabbi from Pittsburgh, "but I cannot help feeling that it is [a] wonderful evidence of the essential soundness of our American life that the child of immigrants can be held up as a nationwide example of motherly nobility."[2]

Judge Barron's award symbolized not only Jewish mothers' "nobility," but also their extraordinary mobility in American life. Barron's achievements as lawyer and judge—certainly unusual for any woman at the time—were especially noteworthy given her ethnic background and the fact that she prioritized her family responsibilities as well as her career. As "Mother of America," Barron was cited for the extraordinary quality of mothering she brought to the courtroom and community as well as her family. To Abram Sachar, president of Brandeis University, Barron embodied the quintessential union of "public service and family devotion"; seamlessly melding these worlds, she used motherhood as a "counselor's staff and never a protective crutch."[3]

The year of Barron's award marked another symbolic event in the story of the Jewish mother in America: the publication of Philip Roth's debut novella, *Goodbye, Columbus*. The decade that followed saw the release of three additional works that decisively entrenched the image of the overprotective, stay-at-home Jewish mother—not the enabling, successful career mother—in the American consciousness: Bruce Jay Friedman's *A Mother's Kisses* and, especially, Dan Greenburg's *How to Be A Jewish Mother* and Roth's *Portnoy's Complaint*. The Jewish mothers in these best sellers had more in common with Borscht Belt routines than the smiling image of Jennie Grossinger or the real-life story of Jennie Barron. Through their considerable talents, these Jewish male writers turned the Jewish mother from a mere lighthearted joke into a veritable "comic monster," extending the overpossessive persona to the literary realm, while entertainers also continued to turn the screws in their comedy routines. All through the 1950s and 1960s, the male voice sounded loudest, universalizing stories of Jewish angst and achievement amid the crucible of family life. The triumph of the Jewish literary voice in American letters reintroduced the Jewish mother as an unforgettable, but almost wholly negative, character.

"The Mother of America"

In some ways, Jennie Loitman Barron fit the parameters of the earthy, old-fashioned "Jewish mother" type as it was being broadcast from the Borscht Belt resorts and to the wider world in the late 1950s. But the model of motherhood that she demonstrated in decades of public and private life points to a more complex set of characteristics. Barron's life history and those of other real Jewish mothers complicates the portrait of the postwar Jewish mother that emerged from the behavioral and social sciences, fiction, film, and comedy. Judge Barron deeply respected motherhood and explicitly acknowledged its influence on her own career. In exhibiting a different kind of Jewish motherhood, Barron revealed a competing vision of Jewish motherhood that challenged the rapidly ascending literary and media myth.

The daughter of Eastern European immigrants who came to Boston's West End from Russia in 1887, Jennie Loitman Barron grew up as a dutiful Jewish daughter, one of four sisters. Her father, Morris, became an insurance salesman, and her mother, Fannie, remained at home. Both parents urged their daughters to get as much education as they could. Jennie remembered one piece of advice in particular: "Money isn't important," Fannie used to tell her daughters; "it can be lost or stolen. Learning is the thing that enriches your spirit—and that, no one can take from you."[4] Her daughters must have listened well, since two became lawyers and one a doctor; all married. But their educational success did not come easy. Graduating from grammar school as class valedictorian, Jennie had to work in a shoe factory after school to help make ends meet. By age fifteen, she had completed high school and was on her way to Boston University. Again she paid her way, selling Shakespeare door-to-door and teaching Americanization classes at night school. Nonetheless she managed to complete the four-year course in three years, then went on to law school at Boston University, where as one of only five women out of three hundred students, she excelled and graduated in two rather than the expected three years.

At college, Jennie had started an equal suffrage league and became its president. Women's rights would remain a formative issue for Jennie after she married fellow law student Samuel Barron, a distant cousin, in 1918. Sam accompanied her when she stood on soapboxes on street corners to urge passers-by to support votes for women; often he had to protect her from hecklers. Throughout their long marriage, Sam was a devoted husband who supported Jennie's career achievements and never minded putting himself in the background. In their first years together, the Barrons opened a joint law practice. Whenever Jennie became pregnant, Sam built a framework of boxes in front of his wife to block her from clients' view, since in the twenties and thirties a pregnant lawyer was unacceptable. But business matters were never hidden from the couple's three daughters, who would clamor to hear stories from the office every night at the dinner table.[5] Two of their daughters became lawyers themselves; indeed, to fill a vacancy at "Barron and Barron" after her mother was appointed to the bench as district court judge, Joy Rachlin joined the family firm. In Joy's view, her mother's absorbing career was never an issue for her children. "If any of us needed some advice, help, or just wanted to think out loud," Joy recalled, their parents "were always there for us. The fact that [Jennie] had a full-time career, and then some, would never compete with us. We had the sense we came ahead of everything else and every one, in a very loving sense. We always felt that we were first, not in the way of putting down other people or matters."[6]

Barron made motherhood a key issue not only in her life, but also in numerous policy and legal matters. By the early 1920s, she had become president of the Massachusetts Association of Women Lawyers and played a leading role in introducing a bill to allow women to serve as jurors in the state. Barron argued that women should be allowed to serve on juries precisely because they were mothers and because their "mother instinct" was needed in the "big troubled nursery of the world." In rearing their children, mothers constantly acted as jurors in fact; as a class, they had a "keener consciousness of the human side" of questions than men and were natural "respecter[s] of laws and champions of equality and justice." As to the question, "who would look after the baby?" Barron had a ready response. "The 'babies' of many women are school teachers, clerks, doctors, and in our stores and factories," she wrote. "These babies probably would not miss mother's care more than usual." As for mothers of young babies, they could be exempted.[7]

When Barron decided to run for election to the Boston School Committee in 1925, many of her friends and colleagues advised against it; no mothers had ever served on the committee, and as a mother *and* a Jew, they warned, her candidacy would be particularly risky. But Barron accepted the challenge and with the slogan "Put a Mother on the School Committee," she ran a feisty campaign, polling more than seventy thousand votes, more than the mayor received, and easily won a place on the committee.

Barron used her identity and experience as a mother in her court cases as well. One characteristic story was about a defendant who pleaded guilty to assault and battery on his wife because his dinner wasn't ready when he got home one evening. Rather than send him to jail for giving his wife a black eye, Judge Barron ordered the unrepentant husband to take his wife out to dinner once a week, with a probation officer babysitting. The problem disappeared, and the family lived happily, crediting the judge's innovative solution.

Barron believed that the "family is the essence of our civilization" and that it was important that public policy and the courts emphasize the responsibilities of parenting. But she made it clear that the well-being of the family unit was a joint venture in which fathers had to participate: "It takes fathers to make good mothers," she declared.[8] That was the case in her own life, and she always credited Samuel Barron, who left the practice of law to become a banker, with helping her achieve many "firsts." Accepting the award for American Mother of the Year, she paid tribute to Sam's devotion and his active role as father and husband.

The Barrons prided themselves on their close family life. In the early years of their marriage, they lived in the same building as Jennie's parents. When their own three daughters grew up and married, all the families would have Shabbat dinner together every week; Barron employed a housekeeper to help with the dinner. Family seders were of course de rigueur, and Jennie and Sam built a special horseshoe table so that the whole family (eventually up to fifty people) could fit around it. The Barrons also provided a recreation room for the grandchildren, with every kind of electric train and a huge walk-in toy closet, with groups of toys labeled according to age groups. Jennie boasted that she spoke to each of her daughters, and sometimes with as many as five of her grandchildren, every day. Several grandchildren slept over every Friday night.[9]

Did her children find the closeness that gave Jennie such pleasure burdensome? Joy claims that she was not bothered by Jennie's intense presence, laughing as she recalled the instructions Jennie sent to her when, as a teenager, she was off traveling in Europe: "Be sure to eat a bit of chocolate or lifesaver or chew gum while on train or bus and *ask* for *water* which you pay for. . . . If the room assigned to you is not good, don't hesitate to pay more and try to get a better accommodation with more air or bath etc. . . . Take your vitamins daily. Drink frequently. If you have to stand for any length of time, move around for circulation. . . . If you perspire much, perhaps you should get salt tablets, and take them occasionally if you feel weak."[10] Family members had a "mutually passionate affection for each other," Joy Rachlin insists; her mother's involvement in her children's lives was never seen as interference.[11]

Jennie didn't give up the family togetherness that sustained her when in February 1959 she moved on from the district court to become the first woman to serve on the Superior Court of Massachusetts. Three months later she was selected as the "American Mother of the Year." Judge Barron made a point always to be available for her children and grandchildren; Friday nights found her making chicken soup, as usual, as she waited for her family to arrive for Shabbat.[12] In a television discussion with Rabbi Roland Gittelsohn of Temple Israel in Boston in 1958, twenty years after her appointment as the first full-time female judge in the state, Barron explained that there was no conflict between being a wife and mother and a judge. To the contrary, she insisted, her career had made her a better wife and mother, while her experience in those roles had given her special opportunities, and a particular wisdom, in legal cases.[13] Combining both led to "broader vistas" and a better appreciation of human values.[14]

Judge Jennie Loitman Barron, shown with her daughters and grandchildren at the Massachusetts State House in February 1959, after taking the oath of office as the first female Justice of the Massachusetts Superior Court. Three months later, the American Mothers Committee selected her to be "American Mother of the Year." (Courtesy of the Schlesinger Library, Radcliffe Institute, Harvard University)

Barron related her own experience in these dual roles to the legacy of her own mother, Fannie Loitman, and also to the Biblical matriarchs. That three of her mother's four daughters had "received and followed professional training . . . could not have been possible unless my mother had occupied a major position of value and worth in my home," she told Gittelsohn, indicating the value, not the secondary status, of Jewish mothers within the tradition. Similarly, the role of the Biblical mothers' in their families was active and positive—Rebecca comforted Isaac for the death of his mother, she pointed out, and even though Sarah is not mentioned in connection with the attempted sacrifice of Isaac, surely she "sustained and strengthened Abraham in this crisis."[15] Furthermore, it was time, Barron believed, for women to serve as rabbis, the one profession in which they had not yet trained but which, like law, teaching, and so many others, their experience as mothers could only enrich.

At the end of the 1950s, then, more than a decade before Jewish feminists took up the issues of women's apparent inferiority in Judaism and their potential to become full-fledged clergy, Jennie Loitman Barron used the mantle of her acknowledged superiority as an "American Mother" to create awareness of Jewish mothers' talents and abilities. "Mrs. America of 1959"—a "Jewish mother" par excellence—successfully blended the Jewish and American elements in her maternal identity, just as she joined the professional and family aspects of her dual responsibilities with apparent ease. In her own mind, she was merely carrying on a tradition that started with Sarah and Rebecca and extended to her own immigrant mother.

While Barron's celebrity and the extent of her judicial influence distinguished her from the ordinary Jewish mother, her real-life example recalls other mothers who found satisfaction in combining their family activities with volunteer or professional commitments in similar arenas. Several Jewish women's groups directed their attention to problems of Jewish family policy and communal life, both in the national and international arena. While maintaining local study groups and domestic charity work, Hadassah, the Women's Zionist Organization established by Henrietta Szold and colleagues, pioneered education and welfare work in Palestine to fulfill its founding mission, "the healing of the daughter of my people (*aruchat bat-ami*)."[16] The National Council of Jewish Women (NCJW) expanded on the immigrant aid work that had been a cornerstone of its founding mission to develop a unique service for Jewish refugee families that it carried on through wartime and the postwar period. Hadassah, NCJW, and other Jewish women's groups skillfully used the rhetoric and strategies of maternalism to legitimate their ventures at home and abroad. In the cause of aiding impoverished, suffering mothers and daughters, these Jewish mothers intervened in practical, political, and policy matters.[17] Although social scientists and cultural observers typically represented the Jewish mother in relation to her domestic life, in community work of this nature, this new matriarch reached out and affected the world.

In synagogue sisterhoods, too, Jewish women built on the historic and Biblical roles of Jewish mothers to establish educational and community programs. In the late 1950s and early 1960s, for example, the Women's Branch of the Union of Orthodox Jewish Congregations of America developed a guide for Jewish girls' clubs honoring Jewish mothers, organized Jewish Mother's Day programs, and provided contemporary and historical materials about mothers. One of these was a children's play, "Our Jewish Mothers' Hall of Fame" by writer Elma Ehrlich Levinger. "Jewish history isn't very interesting," exclaims a Jewish child in the script. "Why don't they tell about something except their mean old kings; why don't they let the women do something?" "We should never forget the Jewish mothers," says another, trying to recall the names and deeds of the matriarchs, coming up in addition with Beruria, a wise woman and scholar who appeared in Talmudic literature, and American poet Emma Lazarus. They conclude that a proper Jewish Mothers' Hall of Fame must include their own Jewish mothers, whose centrality to the continuity of Jewish life was often overlooked.[18] Through such programs, the women of the Orthodox sisterhood hoped to convey the essence of Judaism to girls of the next generation. The Jewish Welfare Board similarly published a booklet suggesting ways to celebrate Jewish mothers' contributions to Jewish history.[19] Sisterhoods of other denominations, and even radical, secular groups such as the Emma Lazarus Federation of Jewish Women, conveyed similar messages.[20] Like the work of Hadassah and NCJW and leaders such as Jennie Loitman Barron, such early reminders of Jewish mothers' importance in Jewish tradition provided a glimmer of possibilities for constructing new, more positive portrayals of Jewish mothers.

Grace Paley and Tillie Olsen: Writing about "Woman Who Is Mother"

Female writers also enlarged the spectrum of Jewish mother types in postwar American society with fresh portrayals of female characters. For Grace Paley and Tillie Olsen, two important literary voices first heard in the 1950s, motherhood was a central artistic concern. The innovative portraits they created in their fiction drew from the milieus they knew best—the worlds that their immigrant mothers had inhabited and their own more modern environments as immigrant daughters. Just how absorbing the subject of motherhood was to these writers is revealed by the fact that fully twenty-two of the forty-five stories in Paley's three fiction anthologies have motherhood as a central subject; eight others include it as a major issue, while almost all of Olsen's short stories and her novel, *Yonnondio*, also emphasize the experience of mothering.[21]

Grace Paley was the daughter of Jewish parents who emigrated from the Ukraine, where they were active in the socialist movement; in the United States, her mother, Manya Goodside, worked several jobs to make Paley's father, Isaac, "strong enough and educated enough so he could finally earn enough to take care of us all." (He became a successful doctor.) Born in the Bronx in 1922, with two teenage older siblings, Grace grew up preferring her "humorous . . . brilliant . . . sophisticated" father, but she and her siblings knew that her mother was at the heart of the family.[22] "The excitement was with the men . . . with the boys in the street and with the men in their talk, man's talk," but the women's "*bobbeh* meisehs" and "gossip" in fact concerned "the real things . . . what actually happened in life."[23] The women in her extended family, and the many friends who constantly visited her mother, provided models that she would use later in her fiction. Many of the characters she wrote about came from this milieu; identifiably Jewish, they reveal the generational and gender conflicts that often arise between immigrants and their more modern descendants. While Paley does not probe the religious aspects of Judaism, her stories portray the moral dilemmas of contemporary Jews and, most poignantly, of women and mothers.[24]

Paley began writing after what she termed "that long period of very masculine writing which followed the Second World War." Though she admired the work of such writers as Saul Bellow and Philip Roth, she knew "it wasn't written for me at all . . . there were no women in it."[25] Though at first Paley worried that perhaps her subject was "trivial," she became increasingly confident that the lives of the "bunch of women" who interested her—PTA women and ordinary mothers—were "important" because of "how strong they were."[26]

It is through Paley's women characters that the link between individual daily life and the larger historical process is articulated. Her leading protagonist, Faith Darwin, is a divorced wife and mother deeply involved in raising her children, devoted to her neighbors and her friends, and committed to her urban environment. Over the course of Paley's first book and later collections, Faith moves out from the shackled insecurity of her domestic role to become a committed social activist and aspiring writer. Her bonds to her family and friends are matched by a larger social and artistic vision rooted in the female world. As Faith matures, she accepts the burden of social responsibility inherited from her Jewish ancestors, if not their darker visions. To be truly American, Faith learns, is not merely a matter of unflinching optimism, but of commitment to others. Indeed, Paley's characters are rarely defined separately from communities; because of such ties, they can both invent themselves anew as they express their needs and desires and connect themselves to others.[27]

Paley's portrait of Faith and of her female friends was deeply affected by the 1950s culture of motherhood: "the PTA and the park, her children's needs and their environment, became the sources of her art and her politics."[28] But for Paley, as for Jennie Loitman Barron, motherhood extended beyond the personal to a kind of "mothering-in-the-world"—the "global need for taking care."[29] Mothering became a "mode, a metaphor" for a kind of "caring, nurturant, healing" radically opposed to the violence and coercion of patriarchy, but also differing from the typical self-denying, sacrificial aspects of traditional motherhood.[30] In many stories, Paley portrays quintessential maternal dilemmas—the conflicting desires and pleasures of parents and children, the inevitability of separation and struggle. Her stories are an attempt to convey the complexity of motherhood, including the ambivalent feelings.

The pain, ambiguity, and joys of motherhood are similarly refracted in Olsen's stories of the 1950s, which are marked by their profound concern with mothers and by their linguistic and stylistic inventiveness—both of which are developed with a characteristically Jewish sensibility. A "compound of Jewish, working class, immigrant, poor and female," Olsen was born in 1912 to Russian Socialist immigrants in Omaha, where she grew up "alienated and marginalized." After dropping out of high school to work, she became involved with the Young Communist League (YCL). Through this background she imbibed a keen class consciousness, a connection to radical tradition, and a strong sense of *yiddishkeit* (Jewish morality and values), which she claimed lay at the root of her beliefs.[31]

At the age of nineteen, Olsen began to write her first novel, *Yonnondio*. After giving birth to a daughter that year, then three more daughters after she married a YCL comrade, Jack Olsen, several years later, she put her writing on hold to help support the family through a variety of dead-end jobs, including tie presser, housemaid, ice cream packer, and book clerk. She remained an activist while raising her children and working her day jobs but was most involved in the next decade in organizations relating to child care and education, including the Parent Teacher Association.[32] By the mid-1950s, when Olsen resumed her creative writing, it was as an "artist who had lived her life as a woman."[33]

"I Stand Here Ironing," one of the stories in her *Tell Me a Riddle* collection, presents a compelling portrait of a mother and her "thin, dark and foreign-looking" daughter. Though she has little control over her own and her daughter's lives because she has to work outside the home, the mother in the story hopes that her daughter will be able to determine her own future despite the disadvantages of her background. She wanted her daughter to be "more than this dress on the ironing board, helpless before the iron."[34]

The title story, "Tell Me a Riddle" is marked by Olsen's skillful use of the rhythms and locutions of Yiddish speech and her exploration of Jewish secular humanism.[35] Though Eva, the central character of the story, is an atheist, she reaches back through her past to recover what she considers to be the spiritual essence of Judaism—its messianic mission and its concern for a wider humanity. On her deathbed Eva recalls the hopes and dreams of her revolutionary youth in czarist Russia, when as a socialist orator and organizer, she talked not of family but beyond, of "humankind." In this moment of epiphany she also solves the riddle of her family life. As she recapitulates the zeal and commitment of her girlhood, the anger she has felt at sacrificing her own identity to her family's demands dissipates. Beyond mothers' anger and their first necessary

steps toward independence, Olsen hints, lies a realm of interconnection, caring, and forgiveness.

Joining self-assertion with independence, Olsen's vision is a strongly feminist one. When women live only through their families, she suggests, they are
denied their own individuality and any possibility for a larger connection to
humankind. As Olsen herself recognizes, at its core this vision is also a Jewish
one, drawn from her Jewish socialist background. "What is Yiddish in me,"
Olsen has remarked, "is inextricable from what is woman in me, from woman
who is mother." The mothers at the core of her best stories are drawn from her
own experience, but also from that of her mother, Ida Lerner. Keenly sympathetic to the deprivations that limited her mother's existence, she nevertheless
admired her enormously:

> If you [could see] my mother's handwriting, [in] one of the few letters she ever
> wrote me . . . she could not spell, she could scarcely express herself, she did not
> have written language. Yet she was one of the most eloquent and one of the most
> brilliant . . . human beings I've ever known . . . some of whom have a lot of stand-
> ing in the world.[36]

Though she "had no worldly goods to leave," Ida Lerner nevertheless provided her daughter, in Olsen's words, with "an inexhaustible legacy . . . a heritage
of summoning resources to make—out of song, food, warmth, expressions of
human love—courage, hope, resistance, belief; this vision of universality, before
the lessenings, harms, divisions of the world are visited upon it."[37]

And so the experiences of these radical Jewish mothers—Ida Lerner and
her daughter, Tillie Olsen, and Grace Paley and her immigrant mother and
friends—entered the literary canon. Amidst the din created by Jewish male
writers, they would not have the "Loudest Voice," to use the title of a Grace
Paley story published in her 1959 debut collection, *The Little Disturbances of
Man*. Yet the positive models of Jewish matriarchs created during these midcentury years would have a continuing influence.[38]

Roth, Greenburg, and Friedman: The "Coming of Age of the Jewish Mother"

Beginning with Roth's *Goodbye, Columbus*, it was the Jewish male writers' vision
that more prominently framed the portrayal of the Jewish family in the public
mind. *Goodbye, Columbus* won its twenty-six-year-old author the National Book
Award, and according to critic Sandy Pinsker, forever changed the ground
rules for writing about American Jewish life. If, as Bernard Malamud insisted,
"All men are Jews!" according to Roth, "all Jews were also men" and the male
character's sexual and psychological drives, rather than his status and identity

as a Jew, came to occupy the novelist's primary imagination.[39] No matter how strongly and unforgettably Roth's female characters are drawn, men receive the lion's share of this writer's attention and the Rothian world remains that of patriarchy—usually patriarchy manqué.

Women—especially Jewish mothers and spoiled Jewish daughters— became particular objects of satire in the Rothian universe. Alfred Kazin once wrote scornfully of Roth that he could write of Jews only as hysterics, ultimately blaming all their problems on "My Jewish Mother."[40] This tendency, which reaches its apotheosis in *Portnoy's Complaint*, is foreshadowed in the female characters of *Goodbye, Columbus*. The novella chronicles the summer romance of twenty-three-year-old Newark-born and -bred Neil Klugman and Brenda Patimkin, a delicious beauty from Short Hills, a nearby affluent suburb, but it is as much about the conflicts between the lovers' two different classes—lower-middle versus upper-middle—and two different ways of life— urban versus suburban—as it is about the couple's passionate affair.[41] As few other fictional works have been able to do as precisely, the contradictory worlds of the Klugmans and Patimkins perfectly capture the "Jewish moment of suburbanization of American life."[42]

The upwardly mobile Patimkins show off their prosperity conspicuously. Visiting the household for a long week to stay with his lover, Neil is struck with the cornucopia of fruits that tumble from the Patimkins' refrigerator— "greengage plums, black plums, red plums, apricots, nectarines, peaches, long horns of grapes, black, yellow, red, and cherries, cherries flowing out of boxes and staining everything scarlet . . . melons—cantaloupes and honeydews— and . . . half of a huge watermelon." The reader can't help but compare this lavish display with the penny-pinching of Neil's Aunt Gladys, with whom Neil boards while his parents are off taking a cure in Arizona—Aunt Gladys complains bitterly that Neil is wasting the carrots she has put in front of him and eating only the peas! A true mother substitute, Aunt Gladys also worries that Neil has enough clean underwear for his visit.[43]

In spite of the Patimkins' new wealth, demonstrated by the relaxed idleness of Brenda, who suns herself at the country club while Neil works downtown in the public library, Brenda's hardworking father continues to commute to Newark, where his plumbing supply business is located. Wealth has taken the Patimkins far beyond the cramped lifestyle of struggling first-generation urban Jews, but they have not replaced the core values of the immigrant world with ones that Neil can respect. Brenda, a student at Radcliffe, an elite women's school that accepts few Jews, has her nose done, the better to enter the Americanized world of wealth and power. Neither she nor her nice but dim brother Ron exhibit positive work orientations or any interest in their studies. Why bother when Brenda can wheedle anything she wants from her adoring father? Even her mother criticizes her for being "lazy." "You ought to earn some money and buy your own clothes," Mrs. Patimkin yells at her. "Good God, Mother, Daddy could live off the stocks alone," an exasperated Brenda retorts.[44] Brenda and her mother's habitual quarrels are one expression of the disturbing lack of connection at the heart of this newly rich but spiritually empty family.

Even beyond his mocking of the good-hearted but ineffectual paterfamilias, Roth skewers Mrs. Patimkin for her superficiality. In one memorable scene, Roth—through his alter ego, Neil—rakes her over the coals for her mindless Hadassah list-making and superficial interest in synagogue matters. Hypocritically, Mrs. Patimkin is serious about Neil's Jewishness, wanting to know what temple he goes to and whether he is "orthodox or conservative." Trying to think of a response to convince her that he was not an infidel, Neil blurts out: "Do you know Martin Buber's work?" Mrs. Patimkin responds with her own question: "Is he orthodox or conservative?" When told that he was a philosopher, Mrs. Patimkin asks if he is *"reformed."*[45]

In the end, after Brenda's mother confronts her with the diaphragm she finds in Brenda's drawer, Brenda chooses to side with her mother—and the values of suburban propriety over those of freedom and nonconformity that her affair with Neil presumably represents. Like Marjorie Morningstar and mother Rose, Brenda will imitate the "Shirley" in her mother, sacrificing the authenticity of her own person and the possibilities for full self-expression. To Neil, the materialist vision that Brenda and her Jewish mother represent are simultaneously tantalizing and frightening. At the conclusion, Brenda leaves Neil, but he feels some relief that he has not won her after all, becoming a commodity, like the vacuous Patimkin family, in the bargain.[46]

However much the Jewish mother and her suburban daughter became the objects of literary ridicule in the 1950s, it was the pairing of the Jewish mother and her nervously antagonistic son the following decade that was a watershed in Jewish literature. According to critics, the 1960s marked the literary "coming of age of the Jewish mother."[47] With her overbearing presence and darkly comic personality, the Jewish mother not so subtly pushed the Jewish father into a subordinate role, dominating fictional representations of the Jewish family as never before. But even as she became the "nerve center" of the Jewish novel, the Jewish mother would share the spotlight with one other essential family member—her clingingly dependent, neurotic, but deeply ambivalent son, with whom she was locked into a grueling and emotional battle of self-assertion.[48]

As talented Jewish male writers translated the bare bones of stand-up routines into instant best sellers, the ethnically distinct comic caricature of the Jewish mother became a widespread source of fun, universally recognized. Just as a previous generation had also projected their own anxieties onto her, so these 1960s writers rebelled against the Jewish mother's bourgeois materialism and suffocating concern. In so doing, Jewish men were able to "amuse the world at large while exorcizing [their] private ghosts."[49] Blaming their Jewish mothers, they assuaged guilt about their own success and estrangement from their roots.

As the decade opened, the battle between mothers and sons was presented in deliciously ironic form on the Broadway stage by Mike Nichols and Elaine May. Part of their sold-out Broadway show, which became a best-selling record, was their famous "Mother and Son" skit, which had a pushy Mrs. Weiss telephoning her rocket-scientist son, Arthur, to complain that he never calls. "I'm sure that all the other scientists have mothers," Mrs. Weiss starts out. "I'm sure they all have time to call their mothers." The son, who has just launched the nation's first spaceship, is at first chilly and distracted but quickly becomes concerned when his mother tells him that she is sick because of "nerves." Even Mrs. Weiss's doctor turns pale when he learns that a son was "too busy to pick up the phone and call his mother." Mrs. Weiss admits that she is a "nagging mother" but explains to Arthur that he is her "baby, the only baby I got . . . I can't help it." "Is it so hard to pick up a phone?" she asks, her voice at once hard and demanding. "I promise," replies the now truly cowed scientist: "If mommy's happy, then he's happy . . . nanny noony noony." Arthur has once again become his mother's little boy.[50]

The comedy duo's brilliant sketch was followed in the 1960s by several sharply satirical works about Jewish mothers and sons. Bruce Jay Friedman's novel *A Mother's Kisses*, published in 1964, was one of the first of this new genre; preceding *Portnoy's Complaint* by half a decade, its portrayal of an obsessive, guilt-producing mother enjoyed a respectable commercial success. Like several 1960s parodies of Jewish mother-son relationships, the story draws on many of the humorous elements of the Nichols and May sketch, but to darker effect.

A Mother's Kisses is set in Bensonhurst, Brooklyn, shortly after World War II, and in a nameless community in the Midwest, where, thanks to Joseph's mother, he has been admitted to the Kansas Land Grant Agricultural College, a ridiculously uninformed choice; "Joseph's mother" not only brings him to the school but to his chagrin, spends several months there sharing his hotel room. With her "hennaed hair and mammoth breasts," always ready to "stocking-knot and perfume-flash" her targets, "Joseph's mother" uses what she considers to be her considerable sex appeal to get what she wants. Joseph's mild-mannered father, described as a "helpless imbecile" by his wife, is hardly present—happy simply to stay out of the way.

"Joseph's mother" has a healthy but madly inaccurate sense of her abilities to smooth Joseph's way in the world. "Well, your mother's here," she would say to Joseph. "And already she's got the place in stitches."[51] She boasted to him of her smartness, her sacrifices, and her courage. "Someday you'll see it written on a monument," she tells Joseph. "Who knows how to treat a son?" she would ask, and he would reply, automatically, "You do."[52]

But Joseph knows his mother is wildly inappropriate. On the first day of class at Kansas Land Grant, he is horrified to see a familiar sweater passed down the aisle—and then he sees his mother. "He ran outside without anything on," she shouts to the class, "and you could die from the weather." Nor does she apologize for embarrassing him: "What can I do? I'm one of those crazy mothers."[53] The kisses she gives Joseph—"wide, and gurgling" with "some suck to them"—are also unhealthy. As Joseph received them, "he felt as though a large, freshly exposed, open-meloned internal organ had washed against his face. She pinched him often, too, saying, 'Ooooooch, that child. I could die. My life.'"[54] Frequently she has to tell strangers that Joseph is her son, "not my lover."[55] What strides could his anger make against the force of such oedipal love?

Finally, Joseph convinces her to leave. The novel ends with his mother boarding a train home; as the train pulls out of the station, Joseph jumps on and off it, wracked with doubt, till finally it reaches the end of the platform. "I never enjoyed one second with you," he yells after her, but he is shouting to the wind.[56] Despite her departure, Joseph will undoubtedly remain trapped in their ambiguous relationship.

The full-blown comic possibilities of that entrapment are realized in the two works that, along with *A Mother's Kisses*, formed the composite triptych of

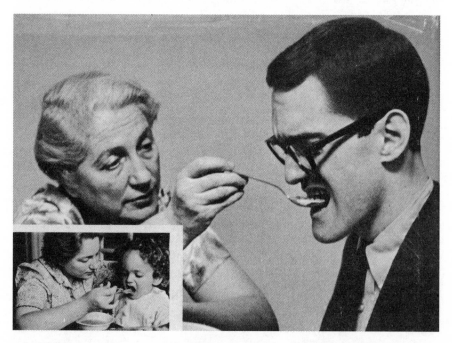

The back cover of the original hardcover edition of *How to Be a Jewish Mother* showed Mrs. Greenburg spoon-feeding Dan as a child and again in 1964, when the author was twenty-eight. (Courtesy of Dan Greenburg)

the Jewish mother that emerged by the end of the 1960s.[57] Dan Greenburg's *How to Be a Jewish Mother*, published in 1964 and since selling more than three million copies in fifteen editions, established the Jewish mother as a nationally and internationally recognized stereotype.[58] Roth's *Portnoy's Complaint*, which appeared four years later, evoked "new whines out of the old bottles," as the *New York Times* reviewer put it, and established, according to another writer the following year, "the caricature to end all caricatures of the Jewish mother."[59]

Greenburg's slim volume, written in large bold print and accompanied by cartoon line drawings, offered eight chapters, or lessons, on "How to Be a Jewish Mother"; an additional chapter gave instructions on becoming a Jewish grandmother. The back cover of the first edition showed Mrs. Greenburg spoon-feeding Dan as a child and again when the author was twenty-eight. "He is still unmarried," the back-copy read, "and does not know how to stand up straight or eat properly."[60]

Greenburg's guide cleverly encapsulated the archetypal Jewish mother's stratagems for ensuring that her children remained dependent. The main technique was the cultivation of guilt. "Control guilt," Greenburg's guide instructs, and "you control the child."[61] To "mak[e] guilt work" Greenburg offered "the

"Proper Form for Administering the Second Helping," from Dan Greenburg's *How to Be a Jewish Mother*, which established the Jewish Mother as a nationally and internationally recognized stereotype. Its "Basic Techniques of Jewish Motherhood" included guilt, suffering, and the techniques of first and second helpings. (Courtesy of Dan Greenburg)

Jewish mother's cardinal rule": the child must hear his mother sigh every day. This was part of the all-important "Technique of Basic Suffering" that Greenburg promised could be mastered by learning the list of "Basic Sacrifices to Make for Your Child."

As might be expected, food was critical in establishing the Jewish mother's control. Greenburg's "guide to food distribution" included a core philosophy— "the Jewish mother abhors an empty mouth"—and many practical hints ("bread with everything"; "how to administer the third helping"). Similarly there were techniques for "relaxation"; "thrift"; "education"; "sex and marriage"; and "children leaving home": "How many miles away should you allow your child to move?" the Jewish Mother asks. The answer: "DISTANCE = M.P.H. X LAMBCHOP DEFROSTING TIME."[62] If her son did move out, the Jewish mother should visit as soon as possible, bringing food ("he probably does not know where to buy any in a strange city and is starving. Tell him how thin he looks"), a warm sweater, a pair of gloves, a hat, and earmuffs.[63]

Behind the surface humor of this "training manual" stood a key aspect of the mother-child relationship that was not so funny: the Jewish mother and her offspring were on a psychological collision course, with the mother striving to outwit her children by any means possible to keep them forever childlike. "Remember," says Greenburg's expert Jewish mother, "the child is an unformed, emotionally unstable, ignorant creature. To make him feel secure, you must continually remind him of the things which you are denying yourself on his account, especially when others are present."[64] In this war of wills, the odds of victory lay with the mother since by using guilt as the basis of her battle tactics, she could overwhelm her opponent—her child—with relative ease. The child could never win, a fact made clear by one of the most popular jokes to appear in Greenburg's book, where it is offered as a "practice drill": "Give your son Marvin two sportshirts as a present," the Jewish mother explains. "The first time he wears one of them, look at him sadly and say in your Basic Tone of Voice: 'The other one you didn't like?' "[65]

The "exposé" of the Jewish mother's parenting strategies was marketed to a wide public with the claim that *any* mother could be a Jewish mother. The Jewish mother wasn't different from other mothers, the jacket copy exclaimed, she just happened to possess more of the qualities described than other mothers. In fact, it read, "You don't have to be either Jewish or a mother to be a Jewish Mother. An Irish waitress or an Italian barber could also be a Jewish Mother."[66] Despite this disclaimer, some real Jewish women objected to the book's caricatures. Leah Greenburg, the author's own mother, though unable to refuse her son an endorsement on the book's cover, was privately "flabbergasted" at the book's success—when she first read it, she wondered "who would buy it." Though she concedes that the book has some "funny things in it," she wondered "where he got these things," adding, "It's amazing how a person's imagination can work."[67] Mrs. Greenburg disputed the notion that only Jewish mothers were overprotective, citing the example of an Irish mother whose son married a Greek girl, whom the mother-in-law called every day "to find out if her son had his oatmeal or if he is drinking his milk."[68]

However much the author—and his mother—denied the verisimilitude of the Jewish mother caricature, the portrait was fostered by the rhythm, cadence, and syntax of the speech reproduced on the very successful LP record produced in 1965, with the familiar voice of Gertrude Berg playing the Jewish mother. With sentences that "twist and turn like a snake," one critic wrote, the Jewish mother spoke in a Yiddish-inflected English that reminded readers and listeners of the Old World, or at least of the "Yinglish" ghetto.[69] No matter that the real Gertrude Berg and her first-generation character, Molly Goldberg, did not fit the guilt-producing character. With a familiar voice projecting Greenburg's Jewish mother prototype, listeners easily forgot the more modern and progressive mothers they already knew. Greenburg's *How to Be a Jewish Mother* was a huge hit, effectively stamping an old-fashioned and manipulative face on the public's conception of the Jewish mother.

But nobody spun the comic Jewish mother as well as Philip Roth in *Portnoy's Complaint*, Roth's simultaneously celebrated and reviled breakthrough novel. In his hands—and those of his sexually obsessive character, Alexander Portnoy, a thirty-three-year old assistant commissioner for the City of New York Commission on Human Opportunity—the domineering, obsessive, nagging Jewish mother achieved her apotheosis. The shock value of the novel, which put its hero on the psychoanalyst's couch telling the story of his mother-blaming and sexual addictions—especially masturbation—in a relentless psychiatric monologue, guaranteed that it would catapult Roth to enormous critical and public attention.

With *Portnoy's Complaint*, Roth demonstrated his abilities as a skillful narrator steeped in the traditions of Jewish humor. Indeed, Roth grew up admiring many Jewish comics, considering himself a disciple of Henny Youngman.[70] Perhaps it is no accident that *Portnoy's Complaint* imitates the voice of the comic Catskills genius whose fame relied on his unique insult humor.

That comedy is the author's intent in *Portnoy's Complaint* was confirmed in Roth's response to those critics who chafed at what they saw as the book's unfair portrayal of Jewish life. In a biting rebuke to critic Diana Trilling, Roth acknowledged that his view of life was imbedded in the book's "parody, burlesque, slapstick, ridicule, insult, invective, lampoon, wisecrack, in nonsense, in levity, in *play*—in, that is, the methods and devices of Comedy."[71] Roth believed that if properly understood the comic voice did not stand in opposition to the larger contexts of realism, but in fact acted almost as an anthropological lens. "The mimicry, reporting, kibbutzing, disputation, satire, and legendizing, from which we drew so much sustenance," Roth explained, were "something like the folk narrative of a tribe passing from one stage of human development to the next."[72]

The narrative that Roth paints in comic terms highlights the disabling conflict he experiences between "American" desires and Jewish conscience, one which resonated with many second-generation Jews. In *Portnoy* as in *Goodbye Columbus*, the original cause of this impasse is the family. Like Bruce Jay Friedman's Joseph, Alexander Portnoy is trapped between his yearning for freedom—represented in his obsessive sexual rebelliousness—and his deep ties to his mother. In Roth's words, the "Jewish son railing against the seductive mother" expresses both rage and a powerful sense of loss and nostalgia for the "American family myth" of closeness.[73] That the book exposed, in Roth's words, "the brutality of feeling, brutality of attitude, brutality of anger" deep within the Jewish family was what was "shocking, not masturbation per se"; it was "writing about masturbation in a domestic Jewish situation that was taboo."[74] Roth's discovery of the psychoanalytic narrative gave him permission to write freely about sex in ways that rarely had been attempted; the framework of the psychoanalytic session opened up his "verbal floodgates" and led back to the family.[75]

But it was not Roth's own family that the author was describing. "The more I stuck to the actual and the strictly autobiographical," he has said, "the less resonant and revealing the narrative became."[76] To grapple with his true subject— "the argument between the Abel and Cain of my own respectable middle-class background, the Jewboy and the nice Jewish boy"—Roth had to invent an upstairs family whom he called the Portnoys. Only loosely modeled on his own family in combination with those of several Newark neighbors, the portrait of the Portnoys was most tellingly informed by stories written by three graduate students in a University of Iowa writing workshop. As Roth describes their contributions, the three students wrote stories about a Jewish childhood in which a Jewish boy was

> watched at bedtime, at study time, and especially at mealtime. Who he is watched by is his mother. The father we rarely see, and between him and the boy there seems to be little more than a nodding acquaintance. The old man is either working or sleeping or across the table, silently stowing it away. Still there is a great deal of warmth in these families—especially when compared to the Gentile . . . family—and almost all of it is generated by the mother. . . . [But] the fire that warms can also burn and asphyxiate: what the hero envies the Gentile boy is his parents' *indifference*, and largely it would seem, because of the opportunities it affords him for sexual adventure. . . .

Concludes Roth: "Here then was the folktale—transmitted to me by my students as an authentic bit of American-Jewish mythology—that began as my sense of who these Portnoys might be . . . or become."[77] Roth has repeatedly referred to *Portnoy*'s origins in "legend" and "folklore."[78]

Nonetheless, certain dynamics in Roth's own family provided the emotional backdrop of the novel. Because of a financial crisis his father suffered at the time Roth was entering high school, Roth believed that his behavior as an adolescent had to be squeaky clean "to allow paternal power to weigh what it *should.*" Trying not to disappoint his father, whom he admired for his stubborn determination, or his mother, he repressed all "rebellious and heretical inclinations." In this way, the family became a "coercive force." Portnoy, too, fights against the "burden of respectability" that his parents bequeath him but also "the burden of transgression"; he wants to be relieved of the guilt that his defiance and rage cause him.[79] In the novel, it is not the father, but Sophie Portnoy who is most responsible for Portnoy's obsessions. Because of her constant interference, Portnoy rebels against his family's values—including Jewish dietary laws and sexual propriety. In his search for liberation, the adolescent Alexander takes refuge in masturbation, graphically detailed. Later his sexual exploits focus on Gentile women; sex with them will allow him to "discover America": "America is a *shikse* nestling under your arm whispering love love love love love!" Portnoy exclaims.[80] After affairs with "The Monkey" from West Virginia, "The Pumpkin" from the Midwest, "The Pilgrim" from New England, and a failed tryst in Israel with Naomi—"The Jewish Pumpkin" whom he sees as a "mother substitute"—finally lead him to seek professional help, the book begins, and ends, with his mother.

As a young boy, Portnoy believed that his mother "could accomplish anything"; whether getting peaches to hang suspended in jello or scrubbing the house with utmost determination, Sophie filled the Portnoy home with an "electric . . . vitality," singing with "health and joy, of heedlessness and self-sufficiency."[81] Laughing at his jokes, praising his intellect, she seduces Alex with her attention and physical intimacy; to the young Alex, the world seemed "rich with passion . . . dense with possibility."[82] But because everything about Alex interests his mother, from his eating habits to his bowel movements, he is under constant scrutiny from her "loving, devouring gaze":

> What radar on that woman! The energy on her! The thoroughness! For mistakes she checked my sums: for holes, my socks; for dirt, my nails, my neck, every seam and crease of my body. She even dredges the furthest recesses of my ears by pouring cold peroxide into my head. . . . [W]here health and cleanliness are concerned, germs and bodily secretions, she will not spare herself and sacrifice others. . . . Devotion is just in her blood.[83]

Behind Sophie's maternal overpossessiveness is her Jewishness; Roth makes clear that Sophie is not entirely idiosyncratic, but is, in fact, representative of an ethnic type. "Vying with twenty other Jewish women to be the patron saint of self-sacrifice," Sophie and her cohort of Jewish mothers, with their "watch-its" and "be-carefuls," made their sons "morbid and hysterical and weak"; in short, they "crippled" them. Behind it all was guilt: "Call, Alex. Visit, Alex . . . Alex, to pick up a phone is such a simple thing—how much longer will we be around to bother you anyway?" Recognizing that his mother's telephone plea was a comic routine (in fact very much like Nichols and May's a decade earlier), Alex tells his shrink, "I'm living in the middle of a Jewish joke! I am the son in the Jewish joke—*only it ain't no joke.*"[84]

The joke, however, is more on the mother than the son. Both father and mother are "outstanding producers and packagers of guilt in our time," says Alex, yet it is Sophie who becomes the figure of incredible power and "ubiquity."[85] "If my father had only been my mother!" Portnoy laments. "And my mother my father!"[86] In this "patriarchal vacuum," maternal overprotectiveness goes well beyond gentle persuasion or crafty manipulation—it is war to the knife. Quite literally, when the young Alexander will not eat his food, his mother points a bread knife at his heart. The chilling image of Sophie standing over her little boy with a knife calls up the castrating perversity that Roth puts at the center of this reductive portrayal of a Jewish mother.

For all his railing against his mother, however, Portnoy remains deeply attached to her. Portnoy's complaint is that despite his deep desire to break the taboos that have repressed him, he cannot escape his Jewish conscience; no matter how much he wants to put "the id back in the Yid," he cannot enjoy his badness. Alexander blames Sophie, whose approbation he continues to struggle to achieve, for this life-long neurosis. As the agent of Jewish tradition, it is as mother that she stifles Alexander's growth, especially his sexuality, making it impossible for him to misbehave. "WE CAN'T TAKE ANY MORE!" Alex protests. "BECAUSE YOU FUCKING JEWISH MOTHERS ARE JUST TOO FUCKING MUCH TO BEAR!"[87]

Roth's novel received massive critical comment, both hyperbolic praise and derogatory criticism. While some critics deemed *Portnoy's Complaint* a brilliantly rendered comedy of the absurd, a "major event in publication history," "the American novel of the sixties"—even "an American masterwork in the tradition of *Huckleberry Finn*"—others vilified Roth for writing a revolting, vulgar, obscene, self-hating work. Roth's Portnoy, wrote Gershom Scholem in *Haaretz*, was a "loathsome figure whom the anti-Semites have conjured in their imagination"; he was the "most disagreeable bastard who ever lived," fumed Marya Mannes.[88] Within the Jewish community, debates raged from "magazines to pulpits" and were almost as "feverish as sales of the novel."[89]

Roth had expected as much. Shortly before the novel was published, he took his parents to lunch to warn them that there would be an onslaught of publicity and that reporters might contact them. He urged them not to talk if they did not want to. Only after his mother died did he learn from his father that after the couple left the restaurant, his mother burst into tears. "He has delusions of grandeur," she cried to Roth's father, worrying about her son's feelings rather than her own. "I can't bear how hurt he's going to be when this doesn't happen." And although she thought her son deluded in this instance, Mrs. Roth had great faith in her son, even when rabbis charged him with anti-Semitism. As Roth tells it: "My mother did ask me . . . 'Philip, are you anti-Semitic?' And I said, 'Ma, what do you think?' 'No!' I said, 'Ok, you got it.'" Dutiful son, loving mother—Roth would later comment that *Portnoy's Complaint* contained "genuine lyric interludes" and, despite evidence to the contrary, was "a love song to the mother."[90]

Roth in fact never indicated that his own mother was as much a "devourer" as "nurturer," as was Sophie Portnoy. In *Patrimony*, his nonfiction memoir about his father's illness and death, the author provides one of his few descriptions of the real Bess Roth: "One of those devoted daughters of Jewish immigrants who raised housekeeping in America to a great art," she had established "a first-class domestic management and mothering company." Opposed to Bess Roth's "nurturing domesticity" and "wizardly proficiency" was Herman Roth's "obsessive stubbornness." His was the "more difficult personality, far less seductive and less malleable."[91] Sophie, says one Roth scholar, is "more Borsht-Belt fantasy than actual person."[92]

But because these debates deeply ingrained the book onto the public consciousness, Roth's larger-than-life fictional mother and her troubled son became part of a widespread conversation about Jewish identity and Jewish values, the pull of assimilation, the meaning of "goodness" in a secular world. Perfectly expressing the anxieties of Jews seeking material success and cultural acceptance—their fears about being excluded from the dominant society as well as their concerns about the costs of inclusion—*Portnoy's Complaint* was a cultural event whose social effect may have even outstripped its considerable literary merit. A crucial ingredient in this phenomenon was the misogynist message that coded unacceptable behavior as female rather than Jewish. Roth, like other contemporary male novelists, projected onto the Jewish mother the negative features of "Otherness—Old World backwardness, loudness, vulgarity, clannishness, ignorance, and materialism . . . ."[93]

Only an occasional observer found positive elements in Sophie's characterization. But they are worth noting. Writing in 1970, for example, psychologist Matthew Besdine emphasized that while Sophie's exaggerated "Jocasta-style" mothering caused Alex's many hang-ups, she deserves credit for "the extraordinary development of his talents and gifts." According to Besdine, "the intensity, quantity and quality of Sophie's deep interest in her son developed the positive aspects of his intellectual and creative abilities."[94] Other critics have noted that when Sophie Portnoy leaves the narrative, the writing seems to lose its comic force. Whether wielding her glinty knife or merely probing the crevices of her son's body, his bureau drawers, or of his mind and conscience, Sophie stands at the epicenter of the novel.[95]

Of course it is the *son's* complaint that is the real story of this book. Says Alex:

The idea that seems to generate and inform her works is that she is some sort of daredevil who goes exuberantly out into life in search of the new and the thrilling, only to be slapped down for her pioneering spirit. She actually seems to think of herself as a woman at the very frontiers of experience, some doomed dazzling combination of Marie Curie, Anna Karenina, and Amelia Earhart.[96]

If Sophie could have spoken to us directly, as Molly Goldberg did to her television audience, leaning out of her tenement window, what "frontiers of experience," what desires and disappointments might she have claimed?

While Sophie Portnoy could not address the accusations against her, many of her real-life counterparts did just that. When queried by *New York Times* reporter Judy Klemesrud shortly after the book's appearance, they had their own complaints. "Jewish mothers have had it," Klemesrud reported. "They are sick and tired of being portrayed as nagging, overprotective shrews." Almost all denied that they came anywhere near being like Mrs. Portnoy, though some grudgingly admitted they had friends like her. "If she does exist, I think that what she has for her children is a total love," commented the wife of New York Senator Jacob Javits. Norman Mailer's mother replied that she was indulgent and permissive with her son because he was so gifted—"we never interrupted Norman when he was doing anything." Leonard Bernstein's mother revealed that she "encouraged" but never "pestered" her son ("we had to do some nagging to get him away from the piano so he could eat"). Bess Myerson, who in 1945 had become the first Jewish "Miss America," was so angry that she predicted a "Jewish mother's [*sic*] backlash": "With all these attacks on them, Jewish mothers are going to stop calling their sons to find out how they feel, stop asking them to visit, and stop taking their grandchildren on weekends. They might even start writing books about their children."

A discordant note came from the only two males cited in the article. Comedian Shelley Berman quipped that the Jewish mother "possesses an omniscience that is pressed only after you make a mistake. . . . Like if you fall down the stairs, she'll say, 'You see?'" A more serious condemnation came from psychologist Sanford Sherman of the Jewish Family Service in New York. "We get a tremendous number of people who come in here complaining about their mothers," he declared. The problem was the mother's "inability to let her children go, to let them do their own thing. And also because she keeps reminding them of the 'debt' they owe to her." But the mother of the president of the Waldbaum's supermarket chain countered that "psychiatrists were often as much to blame as mothers" since they were the ones who labeled ordinary problems as pathological. In Klemesrud's article, the battle lines seemed drawn: a comedian and psychologist in alliance with a literary lion, all lining up against very real Jewish mothers.[97]

"You Do Not Have to Be Jewish to Be
a Jewish Mother, But It Helps"

Together with the works of male and female writers, these readers' comments reveal that two opposing discourses about the Jewish mother had developed by the end of the 1960s. Exaggerating comic stereotypes, male writers emphasized aspects of the Jewish mother's personality that tended to stifle development. In women's creations, the Jewish mother incorporated her parenting into a varied repertoire of aspirations and frustrations. Her mothering could serve as a launching pad for her offspring and for wider nurturing in the world, or she could find herself exasperated and vulnerable, hemmed in herself by the responsibilities of keeping her children safe.

Although based on techniques of satire and burlesque, the comic mode in which male writers wrote the Jewish mother's story crossed over the narrative borders of humor into what Roth himself disparaged as "sociological realism." For example, Portnoy complains to his doctor that all the Jewish joking going on was terrible because it was at the expense of the victim, people like himself. Whereas for the Catskills comics, in-group humor provided respite from anxiety brought about by Jews' midcentury successes, for Roth's Portnoy, the "Jewish joke" was misplaced and way out of line: "It *hoits*, you know, there is *pain* involved . . . that's the part Sam Levenson leaves *out*! Sure, they sit in the casino at the Concord, the women in their minks and the men in their phosphorescent suits, and boy do they laugh, laugh, laugh and laugh—'Help, help, my son the doctor is drowning!'—ha, ha *ha*, ha ha *ha*, only what about the *pain* Myron Cohen! What about the guy who is actually drowning! Actually sinking beneath an ocean of parental relentlessness!"[98]

But "parental relentlessness" could be interpreted less darkly. Two years before *Portnoy's Complaint*, sociologist Zena Smith Blau took issue with the negative portrayal of the Jewish mother popularized in books by Greenburg and others, arguing as Besdine did that if Jewish mothers were blamed for their children's psychological problems, they should also get credit for their strengths.[99] While Blau provided no evidence to support her observations, in writing from her own background as a second-generation daughter of an immigrant mother who had known many "Yiddishe Mamehs," she claimed the truth of her own experience.

In Blau's view, while it was true that Jewish mothers perceived the child as a "fragile creature" who needed to be nurtured and protected throughout infancy and even adolescence, the mother's determination to provide the best for her children led to the child's astonishing intellectual and social achievements. As scholars have verified, her high standards and ambitions for his future achievements was a significant factor in the educational attainment of second-generation Jews.[100]

That the Jewish mother accomplished this feat by denying the child's declaration of independence until relatively late in his or her life thus served as an effective maternal strategy. Early independence could result in conformity and mediocrity, Blau notes, while later maturation fostered "autonomy and excellence."[101] "We lost a good many skirmishes with our mothers," Blau concludes, "but we ultimately won the war."[102]

Ultimately, it was the male invective that overwhelmed the more complex portrayals by female observers, determining how the Jewish mother would be remembered for years to come. Adding to the weight of the literary sons' pronouncements was the negative testimony of the psychiatric community. Unlike psychologist Matthew Besdine, most of these professionals condemned the Jewish mother's pathology. Typical of the venom that could inhabit such accounts was a 1963 article by Dr. Alexander Grinstein in the prestigious *Psychoanalytic Review*. Grinstein charged immigrant Jewish mothers—"rather harsh, primitive, loud, aggressive women who did not fit in well with the American way of life"—with reproducing their own "infantile" characteristics in their second-generation daughters, now mothers themselves; he called them "dolls."[103]

Ultimately, even feminists accepted and disseminated medicalized notions of the Jewish mother. In 1970, in a much-discussed article in the journal *Transaction* titled "Portnoy's Mother's Complaint," sociologist Pauline Bart reported on her empirical research with middle-aged women, Jewish and non-Jewish, who had been hospitalized for depression. Bart's interviews led her to conclude that "you do not have to be Jewish to be a Jewish mother, but it helps." Jewish patients were "overprotective, conventional martyrs" who saw the world differently than non-Jewish patients. As opposed to the latter, who said they wanted their children to be independent, the Jewish mothers attributed their illnesses to their children, complaining when they didn't call every day or that they did not see them often enough. These mothers "overidentified" with their children, "obtaining narcissistic gratification from them." They viewed their children as "simultaneously *helpless* without the mother's directives and *powerful*—able to kill the mother with 'aggravation.' "[104] Far from the work-and-family model utilized by Jennie Loitman Barron or the activities of mothers who volunteered for Jewish or secular organizations, none of these Jewish mothers mentioned any accomplishment outside of being "a good mother."

Bart argues that the Jewish mothers' "extreme nurturant" patterns were demonstrated by their reactions to her, a stranger. One gave her unsolicited advice on whether she should remarry, another forced her to eat candy ("Don't say no to me!"); the non-Jewish mothers were "more restrained." Jewish mothers' language also indicated guilt, suffering, and martyrdom. "My children have taken and drained me," one reported to Bart. In a sentence completion test, this respondent filled in the blank after the words, "I suffer" with "from my children." These kinds of evidence led Bart to diagnose these women with a syndrome familiar to Martha Wolfenstein's "Two Types of Jewish Mothers," if not to the wholly negative traits suggested by Grinstein.

But Bart is a self-described "radical feminist," and she views her study as a feminist analysis of the issues raised in *Portnoy's Complaint*, proudly reporting that Tillie Olsen called it "the first pro-mother piece in the Women's Movement." A mark of Bart's distance from male voices is her belief that mothers' "pride in the children and concern for their well-being" needed to be acknowledged, not ridiculed.[105]

Bart's article became a reference point for feminist ideas about Jewish mothers—even though, in fact, her subjects had been clinically depressed patients, not ordinary mothers. The conversation about Jewish mothers would take a very different direction in the 1970s as the voices of a new generation of radical Jewish daughters replaced those of sons and provided another angle of vision for literary humor and mother-blaming psychological and sociological reports. Although these theorists and activists also faulted mothers for their personal and social limitations, this generation of young Jewish feminists would shift the critique of Jewish motherhood into new and potentially revolutionary territory.

" 'Matrophobia' " . . . is the fear not of one's mother or of motherhood but of *becoming one's mother*. Thousands of daughters see their mothers as having taught a compromise and self-hatred they are struggling to win free of, the one through whom the restrictions and degradations of a female existence were perforce transmitted.

—Adrienne Rich, *Of Woman Born: Motherhood as Experience and Institution*

6

THE MOTHER AND
THE MOVEMENT

Feminism Constructs the Jewish Mother

THE GENERATION OF AMERICAN JEWISH DAUGHTERS WHO CAME OF AGE IN THE 1960s have a formative place in American history. Trailblazers and pioneers, putting themselves on the line in the civil rights movement or advocating for social change as feminists, they transgressed traditional gender norms and protested against inequalities. In so doing, they helped to change the course of American history.

While many of the young women in these movements used lessons learned from their families as they fought prejudice and patriarchy, others rejected their mothers' lifestyles and prescriptions for "good" behavior. For many of these women, the Jewish mother stereotype was alive and well—and part of the problem.

When Carol Ruth Silver told her mother she was going south on an early freedom ride, her mother sobbed: "Oy, my heart, my heart . . . You're going to kill me." "Mother, this is what you taught me to do, and this is what you taught me to be," Silver replied. "If I don't do it, then I will not be true to all that you have taught me."[1]

At a training session to prepare for the 1964 Mississippi Freedom Summer Project, Irene Strelitz waited "every night, in complete fear and anguish" to see her mother on the TV screen, begging her to return.

> She had sent me a telegram signed with my brother's name saying that she had had a heart attack and I must come home immediately (none of which was true). Telephone calls, with her screaming, threatening, crying until I hung up, came every day.

Long vituperative letters came from her for me. After the phone calls I would disappear into the ladies' room, and cry out the engulfing rage and accumulated frustration. When I recovered, I desperately threw cold water on my face as it was rather well advertised that there were psychiatrists around looking for people showing signs of breaking down and who thus should be weeded out before they got to Mississippi. *Mississippi had nothing over a Jewish mother.*[2]

Later in the 1960s, as the second-wave feminist movement began in earnest, several of its most influential leaders created their own briefs against overinvolved, guilt-inducing Jewish mothers. But because they did not write specifically as Jewish women, nor identify their mothers as Jewish, their diatribes have not been associated with "Jewish-mother" bashing. Yet the resentments these women harbored against their mothers bear much in common with 1960s male expressions. Their memoirs and other writings attest to the fact that for at least some Jewish daughters, the power and often negative influence of the Jewish mother was real.

Disproportionately represented in the movement, these women helped to shape its theory and practice, creating many key texts of radical feminism and voicing their discontent in the process. Feminism in turn provided them the occasion to develop more positive ideas of Jewish mothering.

According to Adrienne Rich, the "cathexis between mother and daughter—essential, distorted, misused" was "the great unwritten story." In her groundbreaking 1976 book, *Of Woman Born*, she attempted to explain the troubled ambivalence of that relationship, which she felt embodied both the "deepest mutuality and the most painful estrangement."[3] The puzzling contradictions of motherhood received deep and painful scrutiny from daughters. Although less of a "mocking campaign" than the ruthless caricatures of the Jewish literary sons, Jewish feminists' interrogations of motherhood were nonetheless deeply felt protests.[4] Their anger—and the search for connections and understanding that followed—helped chart the direction of the evolving women's movement, transforming the Jewish community as well.

Amid the turmoil of the sixties, Jewish mothers received little comfort from these activist daughters, who saw their own mothers as negative role models. In interviews, memoirs, and fiction, the daughters worried they might become as unhappy, frustrated, and controlling as their own mothers.[5] In this respect, they resembled Betty Friedan, who admitted that she wrote her landmark book, *The Feminine Mystique*, in order to distance herself from her mother.

Friedan blamed her mother, Miriam Goldstein, for "dominating the family," for being "hypocritical" and selfish.[6] Editor of the women's page at her hometown newspaper, Friedan's mother gave up her work when she married and regretted it for the rest of her life. Because of her unhappiness, she lived through her children, especially Betty, and sniped at her husband. "Discontented, running the Sunday School one year, Hadassah the next, the Community Chest, talking about 'writing,' though she wouldn't or didn't do it, taking up . . . fads," Friedan's mother was a terrible role model. "When I still used to say prayers, even as a child, after the 'now I lay me down to sleep' and the Schema Yisrael—I would pray for a 'boy to like me best' and *work* of my own to do' when I grew up. I did not want to be discontented like my mother was."

In contrast, Bella Abzug, like Friedan also born in 1920, created a different relationship with her mother, Esther Savitsky. Becoming the family breadwinner after the death of her husband when Bella was just thirteen, Esther was a positive model of female achievement who nurtured Bella's talents and ambitions. She supported Bella's enrollment at Hunter College in Manhattan, where she commuted every day from the Bronx, armed with a liverwurst sandwich made by her mother "to keep up your strength."[7] After graduating from Hunter in 1942, Abzug wondered whether she should quit a boring job in the defense industry, which she had taken "because . . . it was important to fight the Nazis"; her mother encouraged her to go to law school, despite the objections of everyone else. Following her mother's advice, Abzug applied to Harvard Law School but was "outraged" when they told her they didn't accept women. Again she went to her mother for support. "In those days we didn't have a woman's movement," she recalled, "so you turned to your mother." Always her biggest fan, Bella's mother wondered in later years why the Vietnam War proved so difficult to end, since her "Bella was against it." She eventually became a civil liberties and civil rights lawyer, founding Women's Strike for Peace and became one of the nation's most outspoken and effective opponents of the Vietnam War. Abzug won her first campaign for election to the House of Representatives on an antiwar platform. Elected twice more, she often thanked her mother for her successes. Abzug did not view her mother's involvement in her life as pushy or interfering. She liked to think, however, that because of second-wave feminism, her own two daughters could come to her and find both categories in the same place, "the mother and the movement."[8]

It was Friedan's negative perception of her mother, rather than Abzug's respectful admiration of hers, that provided the driving force of the liberation movement that younger feminists put in motion by the end of the 1960s. Young Jewish women's relationships with their own Jewish mothers served as one factor in the mix of causes that generated the energy of women's liberation. Alternatively resentful of their mothers' domination of their lives or disappointed in their weaknesses, these women scornfully rejected both their mothers' authority and their compromises and sought other models. By the early 1970s, as the women's movement spread like wildfire across the country, the Jewish mother was already firmly ensconced in the American mind as the prototypical overbearing mother, and it was she whom the youth of America, Jewish or not, sought to get out from under.

Radical Feminists and the Attack on Motherhood

The discourse around motherhood reflected a broad concern among feminists with the choices their mothers made. Rejecting their mothers' lifestyles, most of these rebel daughters sought alternative pathways.[9] "The women's liberation movement . . . intervened between our mothers and ourselves," Wini Breines wrote. "We rejected as models the families in which we had grown up."[10]

In her study of second-wave feminism, Ruth Rosen asserts that in the 1950s daughters blamed the feminine mystique—the rigid belief system that prescribed domesticity as women's exclusive sphere—for the "deep and stagnant well of frustration and sorrow" that underlay their mothers' lives, despite appearances to the contrary.[11] Naomi Weisstein, a theorist and early movement activist, explained that as the daughter of a politically radical mother who gave up her career as a concert pianist to raise her family, she vowed "that I would never get married and that I would never have kids. I was sure it ruined her life."[12] "No one wanted to be a discontented mother living through someone else," writer Anne Roiphe recalled.

> "My son the doctor" became a nasty joke. . . . All my friends were complaining about their own mothers, how pathetic their lives were, how they hovered, how they wasted their time dusting the furniture, how boring, how they had limited their daughters while encouraging their sons. Everyone had a version of the bitter tale to tell. Sometimes it seemed as if we were engaged in an Olympic competition to decide whose mother was absolutely the worst.[13]

"We were set against each other," radical feminist Andrea Dworkin agreed, "every mother Clymtemnestra, every daughter Electra. I did not want to be her. I wanted to be Miller, or Mailer, or Rimbaud . . . a hero."[14]

For writer Alix Kates Shulman, it was the sense of her mother's "circumscribed possibilities and thwarted ambitions, however unacknowledged," that sent her "reeling headlong into the movement"; to avoid her mother's fate, she vowed to remain "forever childless." When she changed her mind and had a child on the eve of her thirtieth birthday—then considered "the last safe moment to begin a family"—she was startled by the reaction of friends.[15] Shulman discovered that being a mother was "reactionary," "an embarrassment." "From the minute my children were born, I felt excluded from the human race. . . . Though I loved mothering, I thought my life was over"; being a mother in the women's movement (she was a member of the New York Radical Feminists) was akin to being "some kind of Martian." Shulman felt that at any moment she could be kicked out, which she knew was extraordinary, "because I couldn't have been. And yet, whenever the question of spies came up, I would think they must mean me because I was married and had children."[16]

Erica Jong, poet and novelist, author of the groundbreaking *Fear of Flying*, published in 1973, found herself similarly isolated as a mother. "At one festival, women 'hooted and booed' as Jong read poems about motherhood, though many of them had children in their arms," she recalled. "At the time I was devastated. The criticism by women hurt far more than criticism by men." Later, Jong wrote about her sympathy for the many mothers involved with organized feminism who had encountered "the same kind of painful rejection I had experienced."[17] For movement mothers of sons, feminists' rejection of mothering hit hardest. Activist Robin Morgan, who would play a central role in constructing the movement's key ideas about women and motherhood, was often trashed for being a wife and mother. "I had a male child and kept him," she recalled. "I couldn't figure out whether I was supposed to put him in a garbage can or what I was supposed to do, but I felt guilty about that too."[18] Phyllis Chesler, another feminist who would address the subject of mothering in her writing, at first chose to keep her motherhood "in the closet" when among "revolutionary activis[t] friends." When once she brought her young son to a benefit, a feminist accused her of parading her "biological narcissism all over the place." "Psychologically, we had committed matricide," Chesler notes.[19]

Both as daughters and as mothers, Jewish feminists struggled with the ambivalence of the mother-daughter relationship. Among other writings, Shulamith Firestone's *Dialectic of Sex*, Robin Morgan's *Sisterhood Is Powerful*, Jane Alpert's "Mother Right," and Jane Lazarre's *The Mother Knot* grew out of these personal agonies to become some of the most influential feminist treatises of the women's liberation movement. In coming to terms with their private experience of motherhood, these Jewish women became agents of change for the politics of their generation.

Shulamith Firestone: The Rejection of Biological Motherhood

Especially notable in the early feminist assault against motherhood was Shulamith Firestone's 1970 *The Dialetic of Sex*, an influential but controversial theory that attacked the very notion of biological motherhood and sought to replace it with engineered reproduction.[20] In 1967, Firestone was a twenty-two-year old student of drawing and painting at the Art Institute of Chicago when she became involved in the nascent women's liberation movement. With Jo Freeman, she organized Westside, the city's first women's liberation group, after the National Conference of New Politics denied women activists an opportunity to discuss their resolution about the situation of women in the Left.[21] Firestone and Freeman's Westside group lasted only through the spring, but by the time it dissolved, consciousness-raising groups had mushroomed across the country. *The Voice of the Women's Liberation Movement*, the newsletter of the Westside group, gave the burgeoning movement its name.[22]

Firestone grew up in an Orthodox Jewish home in Cleveland, Ohio, but like several sisters and brothers, rebelled against her parents' strict adherence to Jewish law and the narrowness of her upbringing. Judgmental and absolutist, the Firestone parents showed little compassion for their children's strivings. Later, Firestone's attack in her book on the nuclear family shocked her parents and even her siblings.

It was through the total rejection of motherhood that Firestone sought to free women from the "tyranny of their biology."[23] Arguing in *The Dialectic of Sex* that the family obstructed human happiness, Firestone turned her greatest ire on childbirth and child-rearing, both of which led to the "maintaining of power relations, forced internalization of family traditions," and women's dependency.[24] In the "cybernetic socialism" that she hoped would replace existing social relationships, "childbearing could be taken over by technology" (essentially, test tube reproduction—a radical strategy in 1970), and child-rearing would be diffused to the whole society, "to men and other children as well as women."[25] Firestone not only called for nonbiological reproduction, but also urged a replacement of the nuclear family with new options for more humane households, which included single people and large groups living together and raising children. With the "blood tie of the mother to the child" severed, "a paradise on earth" would be created anew. The alternative was "our own suicide . . . the creation of a hell on earth, followed by oblivion."[26]

Her father called her manifesto the "joke book of the century." According to her sister Miriam Tirzah, now a rabbi, their father never realized how much his own patriarchal behavior shaped Shulamith's feminism. Mrs. Firestone was no less rigid—sitting shiva for Tirzah when she married a non-Jew and threatening suicide when her children moved away from strict observance—but she took great pride, nonetheless, at the success of Shulamith's book.[27]

Firestone's tract created a firestorm in the women's movement, with many applauding her vision but others severely critical of her rejection of motherhood, which even most radical feminists felt went too far. For Firestone, the biological fact of pregnancy would always result in oppression; no cultural changes could alter this profound cause of their subjection. While most women's liberationists were suspicious of technology, Firestone embraced it for providing the opportunity for profound social transformation.

The Dialectic of Sex became feminism's most famous "demon text." It was one of the books "demonized, apologized for, endlessly quoted out of context" to prove that radical feminism in the early seventies was "strangely blind."[28] Although Firestone's book was the starting point for discussions of feminism's mistakes about motherhood, some disagreed that *The Dialectic of Sex* was a "mother-hating book." Ann Snitow argues that Firestone wanted to "'smash patriarchy', not mothers," and insists that her analysis should be seen as rhetorical and utopian, not instrumental.[29] But time has not dimmed Firestone's reputation as feminism's most extreme antifamily critic. She went out on a limb in imagining a nonsexist world where women would be free to follow the dictates of their hearts and brains. Her place in history is as a radical feminist who despised pregnancy and the private burden of child-rearing. Firestone not only blamed biological mothers; she hoped they would be eliminated. Her views reflected her discomfort with the narrow strictures of her own family; ironically, Firestone's work is criticized for a similar rigidity.

Robin Morgan and Jane Alpert: "Sisterhood Is Powerful" and "Mother Right"

In place of motherhood, radical feminists offered sisterhood. A metaphor for friendship and mutual relations between women, sisterhood freed women from the necessities of pregnancy, childbirth, and lactation. In the 1970s, feminist critic Marianne Hirsch points out, "the prototypical feminist voice was, to a large degree, the voice of the daughter attempting to separate from an overly connected or rejecting mother, in order to bond with her sisters in a relationship of mutual nurturance and support among women."[30] Sisters were better mothers, radical feminists believed, at once providing greater nurturance and greater autonomy while avoiding the harms of maternal power. In their "daughter-centric" texts, women's liberationists objectified and "othered" the mother figure, in effect banishing feminists who were mothers to the "mother-closet."[31]

"Sisterhood is powerful," the title of a landmark anthology edited by Robin Morgan in 1970, became the paradigm for these rebel daughters. Morgan's widely read essay, "Goodbye to All That," published that same year, decried the destructive effects of male-dominated politics and urged feminists to band together to seize power and "make the Revolution."[32] An eclectic collection of essays by different writers, *Sisterhood Is Powerful* exemplified the grassroots nature of radical feminism and its commitment to fundamental change. In her introduction, Morgan called her companions to arms: "You begin to see how all-pervasive a thing is sexism," she wrote. "Once started, the realization is impossible to stop, and it packs a daily wallop. To deny that you are oppressed is to collaborate in your oppression. To collaborate in your oppression is a way of denying that you're oppressed—particularly when the price of refusing to collaborate is execution."[33]

Unlike Shulamith Firestone, Morgan's espousal of total sisterhood was

Blake
and Robin at
her home in
Manhattan

In the early days of the women's liberation movement, feminist activist and theorist Robin Morgan, shown here with her son, Blake, was "trashed" for being a wife and mother. She recalled: "I had a male child and kept him. . . . I couldn't figure out whether I was supposed to put him in a garbage can or what I was supposed to do, but I felt guilty about that too." (Courtesy of Robin Morgan)

rooted in the female body and its ties to nature.[34] But Morgan's account of her unhappy relationship with her own Jewish mother—described in her memoir, *Saturday's Child* (named after the youth in the Mother Goose rhyme who had to work for a living)—reveals that the feminist problem with motherhood was deeply personal. Robin's father abandoned the family when she was an infant, and Robin grew up as the daughter of a controlling single mother, Faith Teitelbaum Morgan. Robin was modeling by age two; at four she had her own radio show; in 1950, at seven, she achieved fame by playing the younger daughter, Dagmar, in the homespun drama *I Remember Mama*, starring Peggy Wood, on the new medium of television.

The worrying, suffering, controlling Faith Morgan—"Vibrant, some-times offensive," sometimes radiating "electrifying energy"—emerges as the "enemy" with whom Robin had "a lifelong contest of wills."[35] In her teen years, the conflict intensified, as the mother and daughter fought over Robin's acting career (Robin defied her mother by ending it); college (her mother re-fused to let her go); and dating. But although the boys in her life came and went, the "greatest passion" of Robin's adolescence, "the one boiling and erupting with love, possession, hatred, rage, and obsession, the one that trivial-ized whatever I felt for anyone else—was with *her*."[36] Faith was incapable of moderation, and her domination was total. "It's as if Faith has no notion of her power over me. She can whine and she can thunder. She can crack me like an eggshell so that I splatter out with pity for me." Saying no to her was impossi-ble, because "she established herself as the epicenter of your child's universe, as . . . your first and basic preoccupation, as the beloved for whom you would nurse a lifelong passion, staggering under its burden, sometimes of bitterness or fear but mostly of merciless love."[37]

Morgan's portrait bears close resemblance to the grasping, omnipotent Jewish matriarch portrayed most often by Jewish men. However, despite her rage at her mother, Robin empathized with her, understanding the connections that bound them. In one adolescent dream, she sees her mother crying:

> She already was riddled with stakes—a pincushion, a female Saint Sebastian. There wasn't one inch of room for me to hurt her more. So I gave up and tried to embrace her instead. But as I pressed myself against her, my embrace drove the stakes deeper into her. Then the stakes turned double-edged, so I was also impaling myself. She and I both screamed at the same time, and I woke up with my heart banging.[38]

Here Robin's pain is her mother's pain; they both feel life's piercing. But although Robin attempts to reach her mother, a real connection is impossible; if she gets too close, both will be impaled. Unaware as to how patriarchy has caused their common suffering, they remain divided as its victims.

In her autobiography, Robin attempts to forgive her mother. Unlike male writers, she believed her mother "never meant to harm," she explains; "she never destroyed outright." Robin declares that she loved her "hurt and hurt-ful" mother "as strongly as a daughter could love a mother."[39] She insists that she is grateful "for the intense warmth, the intense heat even, with which her love radiated," despite its extremity.[40] For her mother, the relationship to her daughter seemed simple. "She's given me her entire life, she expects only love in return. Who could be so warped as to deny her that? She only did what she thought was best for me. That's also a truth."[41]

This sentiment was put to the test when, barely twenty-one, Robin mar-ried poet Kenneth Pitchford; her mother opposed the marriage, and the two did not speak for several years. Even in her misery Robin believed that she would "survive my mother's hurt and horror" and "never stop a barrage of love toward her . . . I will watch her always and be there when she needs me."[42] Her ability to forgive distinguishes her from many of the most prominent male writers who tended to see their oppressive Jewish mothers only from the outside, and who did not often ask the question that she poses: "Why does running away from [the mother's] tyranny also mean running away from her love?"[43]

Married, still painfully split from her mother, Morgan left her television celebrity behind as she struggled as a budding writer and social activist. A powerful voice in second-wave feminism, she participated in several consciousness-raising groups—New York Radical Women, WITCH (Women's International Terrorist Conspiracy from Hell), and Redstockings—and helped launch the protest of the Miss America Pageant in 1968 at Atlantic City, the event that spawned the stereotype of feminists as "bra-burners." One of the founders and later editor-in-chief of *Ms. Magazine*, in the 1980s she was instrumental in creating the international feminist movement.

Morgan acknowledges that in some respects, her leadership in the movement was an anguished plea for her own mother's love:

> A lifetime of fleeing her, being caught by her, escaping her, reclaiming her; supporting her emotionally, financially, and physically; organizing her liberation, dancing and singing or speechifying and organizing hundreds of thousands of women who were her and never her, all to win her love.[44]

As she continued to struggle with her relationship with her mother, Morgan's own mothering of her young son, Blake, caused her deep anxiety. She found herself feeling guilty for "not being there every single second" for her son, husband, and for the feminist movement.

Yet gradually her anguished cry about the ambivalence of mothering became a paean to motherhood in its most idyllic form. As Morgan came to understand the positive force of motherhood as an ideal—"mutual love and sensuality," "*inter*dependence," "vigilance and sensitivity to unspoken need; true nurturance"—which she believed was present in ancient societies, she was shocked to realize that "to live in such a culture would mean that I could feel about every single thing—male and female, child and adult, human and animal and plant—the way I feel about Blake."[45] This understanding reverberated back to her personal life, and she grew closer to her "beloved, exasperating, guilt-producing family," even to her dominating mother. Matriarchal love—in the ideal form she experienced as mother, not daughter—stood at the root of feminist transformation; of this her own life bore witness. "Of such stuff are made changes in world consciousness—sometimes called revolutions."[46]

But even with her newfound accommodation to her mother's failings, Robin knew she could not rely on her for support. More than anyone else, the Jewish feminist leader Bella Abzug provided this encouragement; Robin called

Abzug her "second mother" as well as political mentor.[47] Morgan herself provided nurturance to another second-wave Jewish-born feminist, the self-styled political revolutionary Jane Alpert, who similarly sparked the feminist movement to turn its attention toward mothers.

Five years younger than Morgan, Alpert came of age in New York, the daughter of middle-class Jewish parents from whom she was deeply alienated. A militant leftist who went underground after she fled her sentencing hearings in 1970 for conspiracy to bomb corporate buildings in Manhattan, Alpert was the former lover of Sam Melville, who died in the 1971 riots at Attica, where he had been imprisoned for his role in the bombings. A year after the publication of "Mother Right," Alpert surrendered to the FBI.

During Alpert's years in hiding, Robin Morgan helped her break with the male-dominated radical left and gave her an "ideology I could live by"— feminism.[48] Morgan had been deeply influenced by Shulamith Firestone, as was Alpert. Alpert recalled: "I bought a copy of Shulamith Firestone's *Dialectic of Sex* which Robin had told me had helped convert her away from working at *Rat* . . . several of her passages struck me with particular force."[49] Yet Alpert, like Morgan, would develop a new vision "diametrically opposed" to Firestone's view of motherhood.[50]

Alpert championed women's collective power as the route to liberation, but she offered a novel theory of empowerment in her manifesto, "Mother Right," that went beyond Morgan's insights into matriarchy. Still in hiding, Alpert had taken a cover job in Denver working for Temple Beth Jacob; as she was formulating her ideas for "Mother Right," she became interested in the "intricacies of Talmudic law," talking about these and her new feminist ideas with the temple's sympathetic rabbis. When she completed the final draft, she sent it to feminist papers, including *Off Our Backs*, which published it, but the biggest coup was the manifesto's appearance in the August 1973 issue of *Ms.*, the new feminist magazine. The article, though anonymous, with an introduction by Gloria Steinem, attracted widespread attention. Morgan extravagantly predicted that its influence would outlast *Das Kapital*.[51]

"Mother Right" was an articulate statement about Alpert's transformation from a male-identified woman to a feminist who believed that the "*biological difference between the sexes*" was of "*immense significance*" (italics hers). Taking issue with Firestone's denunciation of biology, she argued that "*female biology is the basis of women's powers*."[52]

Centering feminist attention on a "mystified spiritualized vision of motherhood," she brought together the disparate strands of "feminist essentialism, universalism and spiritualism" to promise a new vision of feminist community. In their roles as mothers, instigating a "new matriarchy," women could act as the "vanguard" of the revolution that could end their oppression and reshape society in the image of the new "matriarchal family." The uprising of women, she insisted, must be an "*affirmation of the power of female consciousness, of the Mother*."[53]

The irony was that at the time she wrote her manifesto, Alpert had been deeply estranged from her own mother, whom she blamed for much of her childhood unhappiness. Alpert's gifted mother graduated from high school at fourteen and from Hunter College at eighteen. After her marriage and Jane's birth, her mother suffered injuries in a car accident that caused Jane's younger brother to be born with serious birth deformities. With her mother's attention focused on her brother, Alpert spent most of her time with her father, whom she adored. Deeply Jewish-identified, the Alperts helped to build the synagogue in Wantagh, the Long Island community where Jane went to kindergarten and first grade; her father was temple vice president and her mother a Sunday school teacher. But the family left this comfortable suburban haven, moving to New Jersey and then to rural Pennsylvania, where her father took a new job; there, and later in New York City, Alpert grew up as an "outsider," with no friends. After her father's business failed, he experienced a nervous breakdown. Her mother took charge of the family, selling encyclopedias to support them. Although her father eventually recovered, Alpert never forgave her mother for her treatment of her father during his illness. "If only he had left her and taken me with him! I would have helped him without ever inflicting the humiliation on him that my mother did."[54] Alpert was convinced her mother hated her, and she hated her mother in return.

Like Firestone and Morgan, Alpert rejected her mother's values and found her power over her to be constricting and oppressive. All three feminists saw their mothers' strength and will as negative forces. For each, rage against the mother was an important ingredient in the mix of motives that led to radical activism, and then feminism. For Alpert, however, and to some extent for Morgan, feminism led eventually to a reconciliation with her mother. When she became a feminist, Alpert attempted to get along better with her mother, even taking sides with her against her beloved father. When her mother expressed support for female construction workers, Alpert felt a new "surge of empathy and love" for her. Their time together, when her mother came to visit her when in hiding, was "the happiest I could remember having with her."[55]

Her celebration of the power of women's bodies, women's culture, and women's maternal roles initially caused dissent within the women's movement. In time, Alpert came to question her advocacy of matriarchy as "wrongheaded or at least naive." But the ideas she had boldly placed on the feminist agenda had already become a leading theme within cultural feminism.[56]

Alix Kates Shulman, Jane Lazarre, and Phyllis Chesler: Joining the Mother and the Movement

Struggling to find role models, second-wave feminists had to pioneer ways to reconcile their ambitions to become independent women within traditional

social structures. For those who were mothers, the task could be especially difficult. In the women's movement, motherhood remained an "explosive divide,"
as Alix Kates Shulman put it. With the birth of her two children, born in 1961
and 1963, Shulman's whole life changed. Feminists pitied her for her new responsibilities, and she felt excluded, "humiliated and vulnerable." But surprisingly, she found that in her own life, motherhood and feminism "were integrated
from the start," with motherhood providing new opportunities for personal
and professional development.[57]

Shulman began to write books for her children and organized a pioneering
group investigating sexism in children's literature: "Feminists on Children's
Media." Moving on from short stories and children's books, Shulman published her highly successful first novel, *Memoirs of an Ex-Prom Queen* in 1972.
Being able to write at home while being a "full-time, hands-on mother" was a
great gift to her children, she thought, ensuring them of "both my maternal
presence and the model of my passionate engagement," even if the children
later admitted that they saw her disciplined work habits and high standards as
"hard to live up to." At the same time, because her work and her parenting
were joined, Shulman never experienced any internal conflict "between the
movement and motherhood."

> Feminism healed my conflicts. Once I joined the movement I never again felt I had
> to sacrifice anything or choose between being a mom and having my own indepen-
> dent life. . . . In fact, it was as a mother that I most deeply engaged with feminism.
> I spoke up for mothers, defended mothers. To the young women in my group I was
> that rarity, a genuine mother-housewife, who could speak of motherhood not from
> theory but from experience.[58]

Shulman's success in combining motherhood with feminism may have resulted from the fact that her mother, Dorothy Davis Kates, provided her with
a "magnified sense of possibility" unusual to young women at that time. A college graduate with bohemian and artistic interests, Dorothy Kates was an en-
terprising woman who had an important job as a designer of history projects
for the Works Progress Administration (WPA) in Cleveland during the Depression. After she left the WPA, Kates led an active life as three-time president of the Federation of Jewish Women of Greater Cleveland and a board
member for many other organizations. Nonetheless, Shulman came to define
Dorothy by her "maternal sacrifice, smearing her worldly accomplishments,"
her status reduced to the "dependent role of *housewife*" after she left the workforce. As a role model, Dorothy's legacy was deeply ambivalent.[59]

Memoirs of an Ex-Prom Queen, hailed as one of the first novels to expose
the cultural and sexual contradictions of the 1950s, became an immediate feminist classic, selling more than a million copies.[60] It traces the life of Sasha, a
middle-class Jewish girl from Ohio who escapes her conventional upbringing
by moving to Greenwich Village, much like Shulman herself. After several

romantic escapades, Sasha marries and has children, but her quest for intellectual fulfillment remains unsatisfied. Sasha becomes a "perfectionist" mother, though her husband laments the loss of his carefree bride. Six years later, Shulman published *Burning Questions*, a fictional memoir of a feminist rebel, Zane IndiAnna, modeled on Shulman's journey from a respectable Midwest childhood to the antics of bohemian life in Greenwich Village. Zane's marriage and the birth of her three children transform her into "something else entirely . . . A Unit; a schedule; a family."[61]

Creating novels about "the centrality of the mother-child relationship," in Shulman's words, was a singular achievement for a radical feminist.[62] Yet Shulman's transformation into a feminist mother came at the cost of a painful divorce, and also meant neglecting her own mother. "Effectively banishing" her mother Dorothy from her life, Shulman failed to acknowledge her ties to her— ties that "had once been so tight that to honor them, or even acknowledge them, was to risk being hobbled by them." "To have my life," Shulman admits, "I had to leave them." Only at the end of her parents' lives did she return to Cleveland Heights to care for them. In so doing, Shulman at last expiated her "nagging guilt."[63]

Thus Shulman's passionate motherhood, which she artfully combined with her feminist career, excluded a fully present, loving relationship with her mother, despite her respect for Dorothy's qualities and the gift of her support and nurturance. Her ambiguous feelings about her Jewish mother reflected those of many other feminists as they sought to blaze new paths that would free them from the narrow social roles that restricted their mothers' lives.

By the mid- and late 1970s, as more feminists became mothers, a new genre of feminist writing on motherhood took shape. Key texts of this genre were penned by Jewish women: Jane Lazarre's *The Mother Knot*, published in 1976, and Phyllis Chesler's *With Child*, published three years later, fruitfully brought the authors' personal experiences to bear on the issue of joining motherhood and the feminist movement.[64] According to Lauri Umansky, Lazarre's book was the "preeminent example" of the new genre of feminist writing about motherhood: "thinking through the body," Lazarre's vivid account of pregnancy, lactation, and child care, revealed fluid and conflicting emotions as she endeavored to live up to her image of the "good mother."[65] Lazarre wrote in order to break the taboo of silence about motherhood—the experience of isolation; the loss of self; the "miserable body"—yet she wound up validating motherhood as she connected to her child and her new role.[66] Though she did not have to overcome the influence of a pushy Jewish mother as she learned her maternal role, her mother nonetheless occupied a huge place in her psyche:

> My mother had died when I was seven. For many years I lived primarily to search for her. I would pretend to find her in every new woman I met. I imagined her to

be hiding behind walls, on the other side of mirrors, within my favorite photographs of her. But I never quite convinced myself that she had returned to me. For a while I tried secretly being her. But that only made the confusion worse. I ended up, during my teen-age years, holding on to reality by my fingernails, unsure whether I wanted to be her, the price of which was the loss of myself, or to be myself without her.[67]

In her early twenties, Lazarre determined to free herself of her mother; she no longer thought about her every moment of her life. But when she became pregnant, her mother returned to her in dreams, appearing so vividly that Lazarre saw precise details about her mother that she had long ago forgotten. Her mother most often came as a "wise priestess offering love and encouragement," but once she visited as a witch, warning about things that lay ahead.[68] Only at this moment, with Lazarre about to become a mother herself, could she recover the mother she had lost long ago.

Another example of radical feminists' turn to motherhood is provided by Phyllis Chesler's 1979 *With Child*, a book that Robin Morgan believed would make all mothers weep with "tears of rage, love, ambivalence, laughter—and

Phyllis Chesler explored the issues of joining motherhood and feminism in her book *With Child* (1979). She described becoming a mother as a rite of passage that both "humbled and empowered" her. (Courtesy of Phyllis Chesler)

recognition."[69] Published seven years after Chesler's *Women and Madness*, a key text of the early women's liberation movement, *With Child* provides a diary of Chesler's pregnancy and the first year of her son Ariel's life. "Before I became a mother," Chesler wrote, "my ego knew no bounds." But giving birth to Ariel, whose father was an Israeli who later walked out on them, led her from "detachment to attachment," making her "kinder and infinitely more vulnerable to cruelty." Becoming a mother was a rite of passage that both "humbled and empowered" her.[70]

Chesler acknowledged that "like most women," she had yearned for her mother's love and approval and in its absence sought a child—"as if only a child could meet a grown woman's longing for union and intimacy." In choosing motherhood at age thirty-seven, she satisfied "a Jewish daughter's obligation to become a Jewish mother."[71] In so doing, she was one of the first feminists to make a connection not only to her biological mother, but also to Jewish tradition.

Shulman's, Lazarre's, and Chesler's accounts were emblematic of the feminist turn to motherhood in this period as many daughters themselves became mothers. Despite the stark fears that radical feminists had once expressed about motherhood, by the mid- and late 1970s, their immediate experiences of the role proved essentially positive. As mothers themselves, they sought to recover the relationships to their mothers—metaphorical, historical, and familial—that had been covered over by patriarchy.

Adrienne Rich, "Matrophobia," and Psychological Theories of Motherhood

"The loss of the daughter to the mother, the mother to the daughter, is the essential female tragedy," Adrienne Rich wrote in *Of Woman Born*, published the same year as Lazarre's *The Mother Knot*.[72] Minimized and trivialized by patriarchy, the mother-daughter relationship became a source of the "most painful estrangement." Because daughters could not respect mothers in a "society which degrades them," they could not respect themselves. In this manner, the mothers' victimization was carried over to daughters.[73] To empower daughters as well as mothers, motherhood had to be set free from its bonds. Rich made a clear distinction between mothers as *persons* and the *institution* of motherhood, trying to understand rather than blame mothers for their socially determined shortcomings.[74] Adding to the work of Morgan, Alpert, and others, she reconceptualized feminism in strongly maternalist terms.

In the late 1970s and early 1980s, the feminist gaze was increasingly directed to questions of motherhood as psychoanalysts and psychologists examined different types of mothers in order to develop new understandings of the experience and influence of mothering. Dorothy Dinnerstein focused on the "bad mother" who overwhelmed the infant with her power. In her view, maternal omnipotence during infancy and a "mother-dominated childhood" led men to project the "bad mother" throughout their lifetimes, planting the seeds of a controlling misogyny and the will to destroy the hateful aspects of femininity represented in both nature and culture. While Dinnerstein highlighted male discontent, the mother she depicted was an all-powerful figure against whom even female children needed to rebel. As the "earliest and profoundest prototype of absolute power," the mother was a "boundless, all-embracing presence" upon whom both men and women could project their "core ambivalence" about human life. Despite her lack of real power in the world, the mother thus became a scapegoat for all people.[75]

Nancy Chodorow also acknowledged the infant's overly enmeshed relationship with her mother, but she portrayed a "good mother" whose instinctual attraction to her baby created a unique bond between mothers and daughters, leading to the reproduction of mothering into subsequent generations. Because they were mothered by women, daughters grew up "with the relational capacity and needs, and psychological definition of self-in-relationship, which commits them to mothering." Men, because they also were mothered by women, did not.[76] Chodorow decried the social imbalances that resulted from unequal parenting, calling for men and women to share child care responsibilities in order to break the "mothering" cycle, a solution that Dinnerstein also urged.

The new motherhood-focused feminist psychology developed by Dinnerstein and Chodorow had an enormous impact on feminist theory and practice in the 1980s and beyond. Although many of these theorists were Jewish, their work did not examine ethnically specific motherhood.[77] How much their portrayal of infantile experience dominated by powerful mothers was affected by their own family relationships remains an open question. But it is noteworthy that these theorists, like most second-wave Jewish feminists, did not publicly identify with their Jewish mothers—and rarely as Jews at all.

"Had we come to feminism as daughters, to Judaism as mothers, or vice versa?" asked feminist literary critic Susan Gubar. "Why had we waited so long to attend to our backgrounds? Had we been ashamed of being Jewish? Were we afraid of exposing ourselves as Jews?"[78] Only much later did Gubar begin to understand that Jewish experience "profoundly shaped the evolution of feminist thinking in our time" and to appreciate the "strength and success of female immigrants—mothers and grandmothers." While feminists had "documented the influence of Civil rights on the women's liberation movement, we never understood the impact of our own past. Despite the antagonisms between Judaism and the women's movement, Jewish history furnished a leavening for the second wave of American feminism."[79]

Though Gubar did not attribute the failure of Jewish feminists to claim their heritage as having been caused by "matrophobia"—Adrienne Rich's term for the fear of *becoming one's mother*—matrophobia offers one reason why Jewish feminists shied away from appreciating the significance of their background to their feminist beliefs. According to Rich, matrophobia was a "womanly splitting of the self, in the desire to become purged once and for all of our mothers' bondage, to become individuated and free." The mother stood for "the victim in ourselves, the unfree woman, the martyr."[80]

Because of the crucial role Jewish mothers had played in the shtetl and ghetto, Rich suspected that matrophobia was a "late-arrival strain" for Jewish daughters; in earlier periods, they apparently admired their mothers. But when the Jewish mother lost her active role in society and became a mere caricature of "overinvolvement . . . martyrdom . . . possessive control . . . chronic worry over her children," matrophobia set in. Jewish daughters were "left with all the panic, guilt, ambivalence, and self-hatred of the women from whom they came and the woman they may become."[81] "Where a mother is hated to the point of matrophobia," Rich observes, "there may also be a pull toward her, a dread that if one relaxes ones's guard one will identify with her completely." Rich's anger at her own (non-Jewish) mother dissolved into grief and "anger *for* her" when she considered her Jewish father's "impossible expectations" and "hatred of all that he could not control"; nevertheless her empathy always doubled back into renewed anger at her mother's victimhood. Unless daughters understood this "double vision," Rich thought, they would never understand themselves.[82]

In the years following the pioneering works of Firestone, Morgan, Lazarre, Chesler, Shulman, Dinnerstein, Chodorow, Rich, and others, feminists increasingly attempted to understand motherhood rather than to reject their mothers and demean the experience of motherhood. Later in her life, even Betty Friedan recognized that the myth of controlling, aggressive mothers—especially Jewish mothers—was dangerous to women's self-esteem. This feminist icon, her consciousness raised about negative stereotypes and now Jewishly identified, wanted to reclaim the image of the strong Jewish mother, now only a "dirty joke," with "chicken soup as her symbol." Friedan declared: "I hereby affirm my own right as a Jewish American woman feminist to make chicken soup, even though I sometimes take it out of a can."[83]

Other attempts at understanding came from literature. Erica Jong became one of the new generation of feminists who deliberately crafted an alternative to the Jewish mother stereotypes of "my son the novelist." In *Fear of Flying*, the "sexual manifesto" of the women's liberation movement, Jong created a portrait of a Jewish mother who was "a bohemian, a rebel against convention," a woman who instills in her offspring "artistic confidence and psychological self-sufficiency" rather than guilt.[84] This intriguing character provided a refreshing alternative to prevailing images of the Jewish mother.

Slowly but perceptibly, as leading Jewish women writers, theorists, and activists acknowledged the beginnings of a Jewish feminist awareness, Jewish women began to identify, and then to embrace, their connection to Jewish mothers. Their strivings would eventually stimulate a new outpouring of Jewish mother images different from all that came before.

DARLENE: I said I'm sorry; what do you want me to do, jump off a bridge?
ROSEANNE: Yes, and take your brother and sister with you.

(Kids leave for school)
ROSEANNE: Quick they're gone, change the locks.

BECKY: Alright, I'll just look like a freak, that's all.
DARLENE: What's new?
BECKY: Shut up!
ROSEANNE: This is why some animals eat their young.

—*Roseanne* (TV program), "Life and Stuff"

7

ROSEANNE AND *THE NANNY*

The Jewish Mother as Postmodern Spectacle

THE NEW INSIGHTS DEVELOPED THROUGH FEMINISTS' LIVES AND WORK inevitably shared center stage with mass media portrayals of mothers; it would take another decade before a feminist perspective on motherhood penetrated prime-time popular culture. One vehicle for this radical reworking of media images was the Jewish-born "sarcastic redneck hausfrau," Roseanne Barr, whose popular sitcom, *Roseanne*, premiering in the late 1980s, challenged depictions of such benevolent *balebostes* as Molly Goldberg as well as more negative monster mothers.[1]

Roseanne portrayed a crude, boisterous, but nonethnic mother, drawn from the actress's own experience and her real-life role models, especially her Jewish grandmother, a Holocaust survivor. As opposed to Roseanne's largely positive portrayal of motherhood, Jewish-identified screen mothers more often than not embodied extremely negative traits. These overlapping and clashing models established the conundrum of representing Jewish mothers in recent times. On one hand, they were rendered invisible by being folded into more generic models of American mothers. On the other hand, when shown explicitly as Jewish, they exhibit the stock features of manipulation, overprotection, and narcissism. As a result, ethnically identified Jewish screen mothers have come to stand for the outlandish traits of the domineering, universal mother-at-large.

Although novels about Jewish mothers in the 1970s also blamed mothers for being weak, submissive, or malevolent, it was through film and television that the "whining," "nagging," overbearing Jewish mother reigned over the public imagination.[2] Despite the considerable achievements of feminist theorists in trying to understand the experience of motherhood, the Jewish mother remained a target and an easy source of laughs.

In the late 1960s and throughout the 1970s, a new scapegoat for Jewish humor arose: the Jewish American Princess, or JAP. A representation of Jews' recent affluence, the stereotype is a mirror image of the Jewish mother—while the latter exaggerated her maternal nurturing, JAPs "required everything and give nothing. If housekeeping, cooking and overstuffing her children were the Jewish mother's metier, then the JAP's withholding qualities [were hers]."[3] The JAP became a dominant image just at a time when Jews' access to American society was greater than ever. Higher rates of educational and professional success along with expanding rates of intermarriage and, especially, new wealth led to renewed questions about Jewish identity, and these doubts were projected onto Jewish women. A backlash against feminism played a role as well.

Throughout the 1970s and 1980s, both the JAP and Jewish mother images were mass-marketed in joke books, greeting cards, posters, tee shirts, and especially through broadcast media. But eventually a vigorous campaign of protests against the JAP stereotype led by *Lilith* magazine and Jewish feminists cut off many of these outlets. The JAP stereotype faded from film, commented *Ms.* founder Letty Cottin Pogrebin in 1991, "not because it's gone from the culture," but "because we've done such a good job consciousness-raising."[4] Lacking a similar lobby, the Jewish mother stereotype remained in vogue in film and other commercial markets.

"The Biggest Jewish Mother Joke in Cinema History"

The 1970s began with several important Hollywood films that highlighted the negative Jewish mother image, especially mother-son relationships. One of the first was *Where's Poppa?* (1970), directed by Catskills alumnus Carl Reiner, a film which, according to cinema historian Lester Friedman, presented "the most unsavory portrait of a Jewish mother in the history of the Jewish-American cinema."[5] The film's depiction of the aged and senile Mrs. Hocheiser provoked such a hostile reaction that at one showing in Florida a good part of the audience walked out.[6] Played by Ruth Gordon, Mrs. Hocheiser humiliates her son Gordon (George Segal) at every turn: she tells him she prefers his brother because "he's got a pecker this big"; she pulls off his pants and bites his buttocks when he brings home a shiksa girlfriend. The *New York Times* aptly called the film a comedy for "post-Oedipal America."[7] When the girlfriend tells Gordon she cannot compete with his mother, the son unceremoniously deposits his mother in a dreaded nursing home and runs off with the girlfriend. There are no redeeming graces in this depiction of a horrific Jewish mother.

If the print version of *Portnoy's Complaint* created waves, the maliciousness of the screen portrait of Sophie Portnoy, played by Lee Grant in Ernest

Lehman's 1972 film, stirred up new controversy. Reviewing it in *The New York Times*, Fred Hechinger excoriated the film as an "unfunny, vulgar, anti-Jewish joke," and outraged viewers complained to the Anti-Defamation League. As in the novel, the film presents Portnoy's point of view, blaming his neurosis on the guilt produced by his nagging mother. Yet while the novel makes clear that the characters' images are a "figment of a deliberately distorted and distorting imagination" (specifically, Alex Portnoy), the visual medium does not provide this context. Even the director later agreed that the film was anti-Semitic.[8] It was surely misogynistic as well.

The Jewish mother in Paul Mazursky's 1976 semiautobiographical film, *Next Stop, Greenwich Village*, is overbearing and possessive, but not quite the monster that Sophie Portnoy represents. Shelley Winters plays Mrs. Lapinsky, the overinvolved mother of Larry (Lenny Baker), a wannabe-actor who struggles to achieve his independence from her and his passive father. Set in Brooklyn in the early 1950s, the film opens with Larry packing his suitcase as he prepares to leave his Brooklyn home for a new apartment in Greenwich Village. With his mother screaming that he is "deserting" the family, Larry storms out,

The intrusive Sophie Portnoy in the 1972 film version of Philip Roth's novel *Portnoy's Complaint* had few redeeming features; neither did the film. (Lee Grant plays the nagging mother; Richard Benjamin, the unhappy son.) (Warner Bros.)

Larry Lapinsky (Lenny Baker) feels guilty when he leaves home and his over-possessive mother, played by Shelley Winters, in Paul Mazursky's 1976 semiautobiographical film, *Next Stop, Greenwich Village*. (20th Century Fox)

refusing to take the yarmulke he has found in his dresser. On the subway, he puts on a beret, but arriving at his new home, he admits to himself that he has not left behind his Jewish conscience. "Oh boy, am I guilty," he laments. It is not long before Mrs. Lapinsky arrives with challah, lox and bagels, chicken, a roasting pot, and clean underwear. She and Larry's father make regular visits; crashing one rent party, Mama dances seductively with guests, to Larry's great embarrassment. Several dream sequences couple Larry's anger at this over-bearing mother with his dependence on her: in one oedipal fantasy, he grabs her, bends her over, and kisses her on the lips. When Larry finally lands a job in

Hollywood, his mother offers her blessings, and some apple strudel to eat on the train. Larry recognizes his mother's misguided love—"I'm not angry any more," he tells his father. "I'm crazy, not angry." The director acknowledged his own feelings about his mother: "The silver cord tremendously overdone is bad. But no cord is worse."[9]

In 1989, two decades after the publication of the novel *Portnoy's Complaint*, a film by another second-generation son—Woody Allen's *Oedipus Wrecks* (the title gives away the story)—further cemented the Jewish monster mother notion in the public mind. Considered one of Allen's better works, the forty-five-minute film introduced what has been called "the biggest Jewish mother joke in cinema history."[10]

Oedipus Wrecks was perhaps more affectionate in its depiction of an overbearing Jewish mother than many other screen portrayals of these decades, but Allen's portrayal of a nagging mom who constantly intruded into her son's life—at his workplace, therapy sessions, and even his romantic trysts—was memorable for the extreme exaggeration of the Jewish mother's foibles. In the film, Sheldon Mills, a mild-mannered attorney played by Allen, admits to his psychiatrist that he wishes that his busybody mother would disappear. Sheldon gets his wish, thanks to a magic show at which his mother is chosen as a volunteer; for a brief moment, Sheldon is motherless and happy. But suddenly, Mrs. Millstein's inflated torso and head appears on high, hovering closely, and humiliating Sheldon from beyond the Manhattan skyline. Up in the clouds, looking somehow like a cross "between the Wizard of Oz and My Yiddishe Mama," she looks down on Sheldon's every moment, gossiping about him to the entire city.[11]

With her unforgettable whining voice (that of actress Mae Questel, who played the original Betty Boop and Olive Oyl), Mrs. Millstein constantly pesters her son; Sheldon must hire an occultist (Julie Kavner) to rid himself of his mother's apparition. Replacing Sheldon's shiksa fiancée (Mia Farrow), whom his mother did not accept, the occultist turns out to understand Mrs. Millstein perfectly and to be a better match for Sheldon. The film is an authentic Allen satire, and it hits the bull's-eye with its humorous depiction of this interfering Jewish mother. She is the epitome of the nag, and despite her obvious affection for her son, the Allen character cannot be blamed if he takes to draconian means to escape her reach.

In Allen's view, which according to interviews and a film documentary is derived from his view of his own mother, the Jewish son's matrophobia has its causes. Not least of these may be the fear that too great an attachment to dominating mothers calls the sons' masculinity into question. In *Oedipus Wrecks*, just as Sheldon tries to eradicate his Jewishness (his "otherness") by changing his name, he must also abolish his mother, and his oedipal link to her, to eradicate any suspicion of effeminacy.[12]

After *Oedipus Wrecks*, where could cinema take the image of the Jewish mother? With their satirical, sensationalist portraits, Reiner, Mazursky, and

With *Oedipus Wrecks* (1989), Woody Allen took the notion of the Jewish monster mother to new heights. When Sheldon Mills wishes for his busybody mother to disappear, her inflated head and torso appear on the Manhattan skyline; she can now gossip about him to the entire city. (Touchstone Pictures)

Allen had in effect painted the Jewish mother into a corner from which it would be hard to exit. The film portraits of the 1970s and 1980s set the mold for representations of the Jewish mother for years to come—and they would be plentiful, as well, on the television screen. But following the original Borscht Belt routines and the 1960s comic treatments of the Jewish mother, these images seemed largely strained and derivative. It was left to an upcoming generation of female comics, writers, and interpreters to freshly reimagine the Jewish mother in contemporary times.

Roseanne's "Domestic Goddess": "Actually a Jewish Mother"

The outrageous, outspoken Roseanne, in her television sitcom of the same name, ventured beyond the masculine terrain of stand-up to create a new context for satire that was openly and broadly feminist. *Roseanne*, the TV show about a working-class housewife and mother named Roseanne Conner, debuted in October 1988. By the end of its second season, it had knocked *The Cosby Show* out of its first-place rating. That same year, while Woody Allen's fake Jewish mother was levitating over Manhattan, Roseanne reached the heights of her own stardom, making more magazine covers than anyone in history.[13] From 1988 to 1993, *Roseanne* was consistently one of the three highest-rated television shows; it was canceled in 1997, but not before the show had won four Emmys, three Golden Globes, six People's Choice Awards, one Peabody, and the Eleanor Roosevelt Award, among many other honors. Not bad for a Jewish girl from Salt Lake City who went into comedy to change men's and women's thinking and, immodestly, to change the world. Roseanne invented "funny womanness," in her words, as a "vehicle for rebellion."[14] Because of her upbringing by a mother and, especially, a father who loved comic performances, Roseanne identified comedy as a Jewish tradition, a kind of "midrash." But she considered the Jewish humor that filled the airwaves of her childhood an insult to women.[15] Deliberately, self-consciously, and with an overt political agenda, she went about creating an alternative that proved to be enormously influential.

As a show about working-class families that was honest and unsentimental, *Roseanne* changed the ways viewers regarded sitcom families and their relationship to the world. "Roseanne turned the pain of poverty into comedy," wrote TV critic David Plotz. The show "exposed the absurdities of family life [and] gave life and warmth to the ugly, the fat, and the poor; it was social criticism of the best sort," just as Roseanne had intended—"a tonic to the *Family Ties/The Cosby Show* pablum of the Reagan-Bush years."[16] Mocking middle-class ideals and social pretentiousness of all sorts, the show gave attention to controversial issues seldom discussed on mainstream television, among them homosexuality, child abuse, domestic violence, mental illness, alcoholism, and teenage sexuality.

The show was also a tonic to predecessors such as *The Honeymooners* and *All in the Family* that privileged the male point of view: *Roseanne* was the first blue-collar sitcom to put women at the center of the family. The undisputed ruler in her household, Roseanne was both breadwinner and moral guide; she was also sarcastic, uncouth, and "unruly," a true "anti-June Cleaver."[17] Where did the character originate? Roseanne has said that Roseanne Conner combined elements of fantasy with her own experience; in a recent interview, she acknowledged that the colorful character—which she liked to call her white trash "Domestic Goddess" persona—was "actually a Jewish mother."[18] Given the Jewish influences in Roseanne's childhood and adolescence and the significance of feminism to her later life, the claim bears consideration, despite the fact that Roseanne Conner had no specific ethnicity and was never portrayed Jewishly.

Roseanne Barr, the daughter of Jerry Barr, a salesman and factory worker, and housewife Helen Davis Barr, was born in Salt Lake City in 1952; she grew up there, as she writes in the first line of her autobiography, "amongst Mormons as a Jewish girl."[19] Roseanne's beloved Bobbe Mary, her mother's mother, had immigrated to the United States from Lithuania before World War I, leaving behind eight siblings, all of whom were killed in the Holocaust. Bobbe

Mary, an aspiring musical performer, settled first in Kansas, then followed her music teacher to Salt Lake City, where she married Benjamin Barr, a recent immigrant from Austria-Hungary. Bobbe Mary helped Ben run a kosher butcher shop selling meat to Jewish families in Utah and neighboring states. Later the shop became a full grocery store; eventually the couple bought an apartment house that Mary managed after her husband's death. Roseanne grew up knowing her Bobbe Mary as a "woman of independent means," a strong, assertive, and positive role model.[20]

Roseanne "adored" Bobbe Mary; going over to her house—"for tea, refuge, conversation, warmth, a game of gin rummy"—was the "most wonderful experience in the world." Food associations were positive and plentiful: Bobbe Mary smelled soothingly like "bread and pickles," and she always asked her favorite grandchild "what did I want to eat: bagels with chicken fat and salt, or challah with chicken fat and salt, or chicken soup with chicken fat and salt," thereby encouraging Roseanne to believe that she was the "center of all creation."[21] Roseanne's younger sister, Geraldine, believed that her sibling's close relationship with their grandmother was fostered by their common enthusiasm for the stage. Bobbe Mary encouraged the young child's performances—she was always prancing before a mirror, singing into a pretend microphone—and Roseanne, nicknamed "Sarah Bernhardt" by her family, was in turn inspired by her grandmother's love of the Yiddish theater.

But Bobbe Mary's influence upon her eldest grandchild extended beyond their shared theatrical passions and their love of food and games. Roseanne saw Bobbe Mary as a beacon of honesty and courage. "I loved my grandmother more than any other human being because she never lied, never told you what you wanted to hear, never compromised," Roseanne wrote.[22] Not a particularly tolerant person—she hated all systems of government and all religions, "except her own"—Bobbe Mary imbued Roseanne with a pride in Judaism and a refusal to believe that Gentiles could ever respect Jews.[23] In Utah, this was an important lesson, and one which differed from Roseanne's mother's compromise with Mormon ways.

Bobbe Mary gave Roseanne many lessons in Jewish observance. She said morning prayers, kept her rent money in piles of 18 cents (the number corresponding to the Hebrew letter *chai*), and filled *tsedakah* boxes (Roseanne knew them as *pushkas*) on behalf of each of her children and grandchildren. Refugee families filled her grandmother's building, and on Friday nights, when many joined the family for Shabbat dinner, Roseanne and her siblings heard stories about the Holocaust. Especially frightening was the dreadful tale of Bobbe Mary's own family being burned alive by the Nazis; the grief of that grotesque event led to Bobbe Mary's incessant weeping, a sound that haunted the girls' mother and frightened the children.

Roseanne herself became extremely paranoid. As the only Jew at school— the "designated Heathen, the Other"—she felt the onslaught of the Nazis was very close; "these horrible things had happened just down the street," she believed, "one breath away."[24] When her friends sent their Barbie dolls out on dates, Roseanne wanted hers to be a resistance fighter parachuting behind enemy lines. Her dreidl song at Chanukah time incorporated a similar theme about Jewish resistance.[25]

"There was only one safe place on earth to be Jewish," Roseanne recalled, "one safe place against the imagined and real onslaught of terrorism, and that was at my Grandma's house, at her oil cloth-covered kitchen table, where she, as Resistance fighter, listened constantly to the talk radio show, and when there was anything anti-Semitic in the conversation (i.e., everyday) she would call in, and using a secret code (wisdom, truth) set them straight." The second place in Utah where Roseanne felt safe was on the stage: "I entertained like mad, because I was afraid if I didn't everyone would start to talk about the Holocaust."[26]

Roseanne's mother, Helen, offered little protection. Bobbe Mary's stories of the Holocaust, and her weeping, terrified Helen, and she suffered for years from terrible nightmares. As a Jew in Utah, she felt especially vulnerable, reviled, always an outsider; when the doorbell rang unexpectedly, Helen would hide in the basement for hours with her children. Rather than take pride in her religious difference, as did Bobbe Mary, Helen sought safety for her family by joining the Mormons. "Don't ever tell anyone you're Jewish," she told Roseanne. But afraid of Bobbe Mary's reaction, Roseanne's mother split the difference, allowing her children to be Jews from Friday through Sunday morning and to act as Mormons for a few other days. Helen Barr, the "Jewish Mormon," became a sought-after Mormon speaker, and Roseanne—president of the Youth Group and leader of its choir—was the "darling of the Mormon hour." But even as a Mormon, she was always the "little Jeweeeesh girl, not even a member, really."[27]

Roseanne has written that the "story that taught me the most in my life" was not about her mother and grandmother's grief about the Holocaust—a story of victimization—but, rather, it was the "Showdown at Park Street": Bobbe Mary's standing up to a man—her son-in-law (Roseanne's father)—after he hit Rosanne's toddler brother for a minor infraction. "Like a Goddess," the three-hundred-pound Bobbe Mary rose from her kitchen chair and proceeded to slap her father across the face. "You do not hit my grandchildren," she told him. "Do you understand?"[28] When her grandmother died years later, Roseanne paid tribute to her with a poem she wrote—"because I could find no prayer in all of Judaism to thank her (or any Jewish woman)"—that praised her strength as a woman and deep sense of Jewish commitment.

> As Rachel and Esther
> she was a Jew and a woman
> A keeper of the Holy flame

> the guardian of commandments
> Handed down from
> mothers to daughters. . . .
>
> She gave birth to us all and
> wrapped her strong arms defiantly
> around our history
> Sure of her birthright
> She created Proud men
> Her strength would seize my young heart
> as I watched her create fire and pray[29]

In looking back over her life, Roseanne wrote that she molded herself after two women: one was a neighbor, Robbie, who had been her babysitter—a tough Appalachian woman who wore overalls and chewed tobacco; in the 1950s, she was a clear "social misfit" whom Roseanne admired for her nonconformity. The second was Bobbe Mary. Her grandmother's strength and convictions shaped Roseanne's sense of personal identity and, along with Robbie's "white trash" legacy, became the backbone of her most famous comic creation. As "one half Tennessee Hillbilly and one-half Jewish Matriarch," Roseanne Barr would grow into adulthood and start her career as a performer.[30]

Comedy became Roseanne's route to success. At age nineteen, she left home ("for my own life, my own self") and settled in the mountains of Colorado, where she married quickly and had three children.[31] Roseanne and her husband struggled to make ends meet; for a time they lived in a trailer and Roseanne worked as a waitress. Her sharp barbs to customers, rude but funny, eventually turned into a comedy act. With the help of her sister Geraldine, Roseanne created a stand-up routine about her travails as a working-class housewife and young mother; it wasn't long before she was known as "the Queen of Denver Comedy."

Roseanne's act owed much to the feminist movement. In 1980, Roseanne and her sister joined a feminist collective in Denver organized around a woman's bookstore; Geraldine recalled the group as similar to the "B'nai Brith girls" of her childhood.[32] As a Jew from Utah, the experience of discrimination Roseanne knew best was anti-Semitism, which she insisted that the collective discuss openly, as well as other experiences of racism and sexism, and the group began to hold seminars on "racism, classism, anti-Semitism, pornography, and taking power."[33] But Roseanne still felt like an outsider who threatened everyone—whether from "my fat, my culture, my ideas, my marriage or my motherhood"; in fact, she was the only housewife in the collective.[34] Despite her feelings of marginality, she became a core member and, with the group's support, an avid feminist as well, reading widely in women's history, mythology, and literature. Enthused, she wanted to spread the word about women's oppression and her opportunities for liberation—to "speak about what was be-tween, beneath, hidden" to others.[35] She found herself "re-created" by the group.

Rosy could be "trailer park mama one minute, an intellectual the next," re-called her sister. Roseanne was hooked on comedy as a way of changing the thinking of women and as many men as possible. Trying out her feminist rou-tines on the bookstore collective, Roseanne was "using humor in a consciously subversive way," as Geraldine put it. In a word, "we began exploring feminist theory expressed as humor. . . . We found that humor was a good common ground . . . acceptable to the woman who worked as a janitor and the woman who worked as a professor."[36] Through laughter, they could institute social and political change. This was the lesson Roseanne had learned from her sojourn at the Woman to Woman Bookstore, but it was a lesson that took because it rein-forced the vital experiences of her childhood.

Both her parents, who had wanted to be writers, had reveled in storytelling and encouraged Roseanne's earliest efforts. Her father's favorite stories were about his father—an atheist and Bolshevik; her mother told her stories "in the style of Midrash"—according to Roseanne, a "story that has both schmaltz and morals"—and favored stories about Bobbe Mary fighting off ex-tenants, beat-ing them up, "never backing down."[37] At the Barr house, whenever a comic would appear on *The Ed Sullivan Show*, her father would call the children, "Co-median, comedian," and while they watched, he would "pass down his Rashi-like commentary on the comedic texts." Her father enjoyed women comics such as Moms Mabley, Totie Fields, and Phyllis Diller and impressed upon Roseanne that comedy was funny when "speaking up for the little man or killing sacred cows."[38]

By the time she was an adolescent, Roseanne had developed deep respect for comedy as a mode of expression and as a site of respite from the horrors of the Holocaust. "The thing that calmed the terror for a while was the joke, the laugh," she said of her childhood; comedy also provided a path for renewal. It was about "politics, and somehow about rebellion, and resistance and anarchy." Comedy, in fact, had become "the word of god incarnate." It was "some Jewish thing," she thought at the time, "something that Jews really owned and knew about and did better than almost anything else. It was the Midrash, it was about connection, and the symbolic murder of the status quo, and the blurring of what is sacred and what is profane."[39]

But watching the Ed Sullivan comics—especially the Jewish men who mined insider Borscht Belt humor for a mass audience—she immediately understood the limits of their chauvinistic comic narratives: "It was sad, angry, misogynistic, defiant, misogynistic, titillating, almost obscene, and misogynistic." Roseanne was developing a sense of comedy as a "super-political act, the power of creating a new point of view."[40] But she would perform it in a way that privileged her marginality—fat, rude, Jewish, and female—reversing the male-centered,

Catskills-style comic shtick that had kept her family enthralled. The vehicle for her subversive humor was her new creation, the "Domestic Goddess."

The idea came from a book, *Fascinating Womanhood* (1974), popular among her mother and her Utah friends, which told women they could become perfect wives by manipulating their husbands; in so doing, they would gain control of their marriages. Roseanne turned this advice on its head, using the Domestic Goddess idea for "self-definition, rebellion, truth-telling." It became the center of her stand-up act, and eventually her television sitcom. Roseanne's Domestic Goddess built on the ideas she had brought to the bookstore, taken from personal experience and women's movement theory, and it emphasized the strength of blue-collar women—welfare mothers and women in poverty— as the true "voice of the movement."[41] Rejecting the self-sacrificing mode of traditional domestic ideology, Roseanne's "goddess" notion put women's needs and emotions at the center of family life and did so with gusto rather than grace. Like Roseanne, the Domestic Goddess exalted excess—verbal and physical—and privileged "unruliness." Kathleen Rowe Karlyn has described Roseanne's Domestic Goddess as follows: "A fat woman who is also sexual; a sloppy housewife who is a good mother; a 'loose' woman who is also tidy; who hates matrimony but loves her husband; who hates the ideology of True Womanhood yet considers herself a domestic goddess."[42] These contradictory traits help explain why Roseanne was beloved by a mass audience despite her transgressiveness. Thumbing her nose at the sentimental family ideal that fueled prime-time television comedy and exploding class-based stereotypes of women, *Roseanne*'s rebuttal of domesticity ushered in an awareness that even on screen, mothers could be sassy, sloppy, and lazy. "Instead of homemade chicken soup and matzoh balls," notes David Marc, Roseanne fed her family with "meat byproduct hot dogs and barbecue flavor Doritos—and they had better like it."[43] At the Conner household, "parenting was a sport conducted with brute sarcasm." "Why are you so mean?" her young son asks in one episode. "Because I hate kids and I'm not your real mum," she retorts, threatening to give the children back, but the audience knows she doesn't mean it.[44]

Roseanne was the "second wave feminist coming to power—actively rebellious, indifferent to standards of body image and dress, liable to say or do *any* damn thing."[45] Yet many critics have noted that despite its rejection of conventional domesticity, the show nonetheless became what Hal Himmelstein calls a "traditional suburban-middle-landscape comedy of reassurance," continually demonstrating the strength of love and of family bonds. In David Marc's view, after a courageous start, Roseanne succumbed to the "hypersentimentality" of sitcom: Domestic Goddess jokes could be told but not acted out. They became "wisecracks laughed at not only by the audience, but also by Roseanne's family." Roseanne had learned that "bad (meaning unloving) mothers are not compatible with situation comedy," but "bad-mouthed" mothers can be, as long as they are not abusive in any lasting way.[46]

Feminist critics gave the show mixed reviews on the question of whether it rehashed perennial sitcom ideals or engaged maternal issues in a new way. Several believe that Roseanne did transpose "feminist discourse and women's knowledge into mass entertainment."[47] But others argue that while the show rendered the expression of maternal frustration safe by making it comic, *Roseanne* ignored issues that oppressed all women and reasserted women's traditional maternal power. In the process, the character tyrannizes her children, who resent her control. Ultimately, then, *Roseanne* merely replaces the "fifties wife and the sixties rebel with a new improved powerful mother," revalorizing the ideology of motherhood by rendering it heroic and utopian.[48] Roseanne may have started as an anti–Molly Goldberg, but she finished with no less claim to authorizing motherhood and matriarchy as a powerful influence in the family and the world.

In real life, Roseanne certainly mythologized the ideal of motherhood. She writes: "Sisterhood's Dead. Motherhood is where it's at." It is only as a mother, she acknowledges, that she can fulfill her feminist goal of speaking out and changing the world:[49] "MOTHER," she writes:

> To give birth to; to create; the act of giving birth or creation (not necessarily offspring). To accept responsibility for that which you create. To mold, nurture, connect with on a spiritual, psychic, emotional and physical plane, and continue to guide, protect and feed. To give form to, to invent, to assume the ultimate innate power of humanity, the act of replication. The physical, personal and political act of caretaking—to bring forth the primordial. To oppose carnage and destruction, to set the physical world right.[50]

This visionary mother may seem a far cry from the cynical, vulgar Roseanne Conner, yet the sitcom character connected as a mother. The power, strength, and self-sufficiency of the mother's role links *Roseanne*, the television show, to Roseanne, the artist.

Neither Roseanne Conner, the television character, nor Roseanne Barr, the name the star used in her real life, identified as Jewish mothers. The sitcom Roseanne, so pronounced in her blue-collar maternalism, lacked any specific ethnic coloration; she stood as a universalized mother, large in her person and personality, above and seemingly beyond any narrow identification. As opposed to comics such as Gertrude Berg, Milton Berle, Sid Caesar, and Joan Rivers, she used no Yiddishism or any other kind of phonetic indication of Jewish roots, nor were any other references to Jewishness expressed. As David Marc has noted, like Jack Benny (née Benny Kubelsky) and George Burns (née Nathan Birnbaum), Roseanne became a *juif manqué* whose "middle-American" sitcom setting led to a "reconstruction of self"—"from a culturally marginal Jewish-American personality into an unhyphenated American."[51] Marc suggests that this strategy was particularly resonant for Jews such as Benny and Roseanne, who came from Waukegan, Illinois, and Salt Lake

City, rather than cities with strong Jewish neighborhoods that could have supplied solid Jewish American identities.[52]

Despite the lack of expressed ethnicity in *Roseanne*, there is no reason to
disavow the actress's assertion that her sitcom character, the white trash Domestic Goddess, is in actuality a "Jewish mother," or at least that the character
was deeply influenced by Roseanne's upbringing and the central influence of
Bobbe Mary. In fact, on the show, Roseanne's free-spirited maternal grandmother is also named "Nana Mary," played by Jewish actress Shelley Winters
(the nagging mother in *Next Stop, Greenwich Village*). Bobbe Mary's strength
and honesty, her unconventional role as breadwinner, and her deep connection
to her family modeled Roseanne's vision of what Jewish mothers could accomplish.

Roseanne pushed the boundaries of the domestic comedy genre with its
portrayal of a confident, compelling—albeit universalized—mother. In this
way, the show's key character may perhaps be considered a non-Jewish "Jewish
mother." A product of Roseanne's creativity, her childhood influences, her life
experiences with feminism, and her own marriage and motherhood, it turned

Shelley Winters plays Roseanne's free-spirited grandmother, "Nana Mary," in this 1996
episode of her TV show. Roseanne, who quips that her "Domestic Goddess" character
was actually a "Jewish mother," was deeply influenced by her powerful "Bobbe Mary," a
Holocaust survivor who shared her granddaughter's interest in show business and
taught her about Jewish rituals and customs. (ABC/Photofest)

the tables on the stand-up Jewish comedians' portrayals, which Roseanne considered funny but fundamentally flawed and terminally "misogynistic." With her own depiction, Roseanne opened a new and potentially fruitful path for media presentations of strong women that interrupted and redirected male paradigms.[53] The narcissistic, overprotective Jewish mother disappeared in Roseanne's portrayal, but the elements of her behavior that carried on in this new guise accurately reflected the experience and insights of one notable Jewish and feminist model of a modern mother.

Jewish Mothers on TV: "Neurotically Overprotective, Brash, and Often Garish"

Roseanne's revision of television's maternal archetypes bore some resemblance to second-wave Jewish feminists' portrayals of motherhood, which also minimized ethnic—and particularly Jewish—connotations. Yet the majority of television and film representations of Jewish motherhood followed a different path, one which exaggerated, rather than erased, Jewish specificity. Following *Roseanne*, television depictions of Jewish women, many of them mothers, were almost always depicted in a harsh and unflattering light. In one scholar's opinion, television images of Jewish women were as disturbingly stereotypical as those of blacks on the old *Amos and Andy* shows.[54] In 1993, *New York Times* television critic John J. O'Connor, describing himself as a "puzzled goy," wondered why television seemed "curiously partial to neurotically overprotective, brash and often garish mothers of the unmistakably Jewish persuasion." O'Connor noted that previously, "white Anglo-Saxon mothers in shows like 'Father Knows Best' were models of decorum. Today, black mothers . . . are paragons of warmth and nurturing. But too many Jewish mothers . . . become props for humor that often teeters on outright ridicule or even occasional cruelty." Even acknowledging that "caricature is endemic to prime time," he asked, "why do Jewish mothers seem to have a monopoly on its more extreme forms?"[55]

In television in the 1990s, the Jewish mother figure is usually a total nuisance in the lives of her children.[56] Although rarely a central character, as was Molly Goldberg, she impinges on her children in other ways, nagging, whining, annoying. Almost all TV Jewish mothers fall into this stern-faced, nagging, guilt-tripping caricature. Witness the Sylvias—Sylvia Buchman (Cynthia Harris) on *Mad About You* and Sylvia Fine (Renee Taylor) on *The Nanny*; Jerry's mother (and Estelle, George Costanza's crypto Jewish mother) on *Seinfeld*; Conrad's mother on the short-lived *Conrad Bloom* (Linda Lavin); Grace's mother (Debbie Reynolds) on *Will and Grace*; and Vicki Groener's mother, Edie (Joan Rivers), on *Suddenly Susan*. Even cartoon character Kyle Broslovski's mother, Sheila, on the animated show *South Park*, is drawn as a pushy yenta who calls Kyle "bubbie" and orders him around.

How stereotypical are these portraits? Sylvia Buchman, the mother of Paul Reiser's character in *Mad About You*, is so obsessively protective of her son that she sends food along when he goes to his wife's parents for Thanksgiving. It is implied that when her mild-mannered husband gets a heart attack, she caused it. Mrs. Seinfeld, a dour, unsmiling, character, is "nagging, smothering, and suffering."[57] Mrs. Costanza, says one critic, is "a fingernail scraping against the scattered life of her son George" (according to Jerry Stiller, who plays George's father, George is in fact a Jew in a "witness protection program"). Mrs. Costanza is domineering to the extreme:

> Her love is as soft as a pillow used to smother his dreams and drive . . . she owns a "mutual fund" of guilt, trading shares for shame and embarrassment. She loves her son so much it hurts—everybody. He's bald because his hair couldn't survive the heat of his mother breathing down his neck.[58]

A particularly offensive caricature is that of Edie Groener (Joan Rivers), the mother of Vicki (Kathy Griffith), on *Suddenly Susan*. For a short time, Vicki and her rabbi husband were one of the rare Jewish couples on TV, but Edie actually precipitates her son-in-law's death from a heart attack by insisting that the couple have sex to give her a grandchild. Loud, whiny, nasal-voiced, and dressed in bizarre, tacky outfits, Edie is an ever-worse caricature than Joan Rivers playing herself.

Debbie Reynolds, the actress who plays Grace's Jewish mother on *Will and Grace*, the breakthrough, gay-themed sitcom, is a much more refined type than the Joan Rivers character. Yet even on a show that prided itself on breaking gender stereotypes, this mother fits snugly into the pushy, interfering, overcritical Jewish mother caricature.

The Nanny, especially, has received a great deal of critical comment for its portrayal of Jewish women—much of it negative. The outlandish Sylvia Fine nags her daughter, the Nanny (Fran Drescher), about landing a man. The running joke is that this Jewish mother stuffs herself rather than her child. Although she was more svelte in the show's final season than in previous years, Sylvia is invariably dressed in glitz, miniskirts, and open blouses that a woman of her age and shape would best avoid.

The Jewish press see Drescher's character as a "princessy, irritating, Jewish woman," a "whiny, manipulative, clothes-horse hunting rich (nonJewish) men," a "flashy, materialistic, and champion whiner." With *The Nanny*, comments one source, "the woman of valor has become the woman of velour,"[59] one who "loves shopping, gabbing, whining, polishing her nails at every moment, spouting 'Oy!' after every sentence, searching for a rich husband, and putting plastic seat covers on the furniture."[60]

An exaggerated Jewishness certainly provides the central image and dramatic device of the show—exemplified in an episode in which the Nanny is dating the young cantor of her mother's synagogue. When Mr. Sheffield (the Nanny's boss) discovers that the star of his forthcoming Broadway musical has fallen ill, he taps the cantor to play the lead. "God has sent us a nice Jewish boy," Mr. Sheffield intones. But Fran's mother Sylvia is deeply agitated that no one in her temple will talk to her since they blame her for the loss of their cantor. Sylvia threatens her daughter that she will get even: "our God is not a merciful God," she warns. With that, locusts appear and there is lightning and thunder. Overlooking the disturbances, Fran's eye falls on an advertising circular on the hallway table. "Oh my God, I missed the Loehman's yearly clearance," she wails. "God, why are you doing this to me?"

In the final scene of the episode, Fran, dressed in a hot pink miniskirted suit, and her mother, in a loud yellow one, enter their temple and take seats in the last row. "We've been exiled to Siberia," Fran moans as her mother takes out a ham-and-cheese sandwich. "At temple?" Fran asks incredulously. "Nobody can see us here," Sylvia replies. "I can [even] throw a luau." Fran's discomfort increases when she sees a friend, proudly sporting an engagement ring, seated a few rows ahead. Envious, she asks what she ever did to God to deserve such neglect. Remembering that she scammed $500 from an airline, Fran goes up to the rabbi to contribute the airline's check to the temple. Immediately her luck changes. Her friend Debby is overheard in a dispute with her fiancé and returns the ring, while another congregant tells Sylvia that she can be first for the front-row seats she no longer needs for the high holidays. Thankful, Fran and her mother bow their heads: "Find her a doctor," the mother prays. "Find me a doctor," Fran says simultaneously.

Here, not only Jewishness, but Judaism as a religion, is portrayed stereotypically and disrespectfully. The Jewish God is vengeful, the synagogue is a place for lavish and competitive display, and prayer itself is merely a means for special pleading regarding dating and marriage. The violation of religious norms apparent in eating a sandwich during a service (the running joke has Mrs. Fine an out-of-control eater at all times) is exaggerated by having the sandwich consist of a food that observant Jews strictly avoid; even Reform Jews, which presumably the Fines are, might well balk at taking pork into the sanctuary.

For the most part, the Nanny's Jewishness lies in her inflection, her whine, her Yiddishisms, her mania for shopping and for men, and her funny Jewish family. Like Fran (who becomes a mother—of twins—in the show's finale), they are originals, whether her gaudily overdressed canasta-playing mother or her chain-smoking Grandma Yetta. But these female relatives are without taste and refinement, even without manners, as in "A Fine Family Feud," when Fran's Aunt Frieda (played by Lainie Kazan) and Fran's mother carry on a long-standing feud by throwing cream pies down each other's bare bosoms at a sweet sixteen party in a nightclub.

Televised Jewish mothers, in short, are easy targets for laughter because of their excess. At times the affection between mothers and their offspring comes

With her excesses, whining, and guilt tripping, the Nanny's mother, Sylvia Fine (Renee Taylor), embodied the image of the stereotypical Jewish mother in the mid-90s sitcom *The Nanny*, starring and co-produced by Fran Drescher. (CBS/Photofest)

through all the meddling, as was the case with Molly Goldberg, and even Ida Morgenstern, the rough-mannered mother of the 1970s television character Rhoda, who demonstrated her love and concern despite her often overbearing manner. It is the case with the Nanny and her mother as well. But for the most part, television ridicules the Jewish mother, stripping her of her humanity.[61]

The New Lives of Jewish Mothers on Screen

Recent films with Jewish mother characters have had a similarly complicated trajectory. The vicious portrayals of the 1970s, seen in such mother-bashing films as *Where's Poppa?*, *Portnoy's Complaint*, and *Next Stop, Greenwich Village*, have been softened, yet the stock character lingers on, appearing in many films of the 1990s. Female directors, including two of the most innovative contemporary Jewish filmmakers—Nora Ephron and Barbra Streisand—join Roseanne Barr and Fran Drescher as prominent Jewish female auteurs who have translated their personal visions of Jewish family life to the screen. Their works replace the oedipal narratives shaped by Philip Roth, Allen, Reiner, and Mazursky with female-centered dramas and comedies that often highlight mother-daughter relationships. Yet as we have seen in the case of Barr and Drescher, the rudiments of the manipulative mother profile often remain, though with considerably less trenchant mother-blame.

One of the most positive portrayals of the postnuclear Jewish family occurs in *This Is My Life* (1992), the directorial debut of writer Nora Ephron, who cowrote the screenplay with her sister Delia, adapting Meg Wolitzer's novel of the same name. Ephron has said that the story of the two siblings and their working mother resembled her own childhood; while the Ephrons' mother was a notable writer, the film mother is a stand-up comic.[62] Investing Jewish comedy traditions with contemporary meaning, Ephron's mother-comedian heroine represents the wider problems of working mothers.

The film focuses on Dottie Ingels (Julie Kavner), a single mother in her midthirties trying to make it in New York as a stand-up comic, and her two daughters, sixteen-year-old Erica (Samantha Mathis) and ten-year-old Opal (Gaby Hoffman). As the film opens, Dottie is selling cosmetics at a department store and raising her daughters with the help of an aunt. We see Dottie's comic talent as she demonstrates cosmetics: "This is probably a Jewish placenta," she wisecracks as she holds up some placenta-based cream. When Aunt Harriet dies, Dottie siezes her big chance. She moves to Manhattan and begins to haunt the city's comedy clubs. With the help of a big-time agent, Albert Moss (Dan Ackroyd), with whom she eventually has an affair, Dottie enjoys rapid success. At first, the girls are excited by their mother's career. But as Dottie spends more and more time traveling to gigs in Las Vegas, even making it to TV, with stories about the family filling the core of her act, Erica becomes resentful. The emotional center of the movie occurs when Dottie comes home one night while Erica is impersonating her, very sarcastically, and the two fight, Erica angry at her mother's leaving her and Dottie asking why she can't have a life of her own. The two daughters then set out to find their father, who has abandoned them; when they locate him, he is cold and remote, not even remembering their names. Ultimately they are reunited with their mother. Presumably both the daughters and mother now recognize each other's right to lead independent lives while supporting each other.

While the structure of this family is postnuclear, the film expresses strong family values informed by the dual needs of working parents and children. Dottie's love for her daughters is powerful, despite her determination to lead her own life. When she tells her studious older daughter, "let's face it, Erica, you'll never be a conventional beauty, but you'll be special," her daughter takes heart from Dottie's honest caring. And although quite secular (Thanksgiving is the major holiday celebrated, in this case by Dottie, her children, and her informal family of comedian friends), the family's Jewish identity is never in dispute. As a divorced Jewish mother who struggles to make good in the male-dominated, misogynist stand-up world, Dottie stands out as a wise and loving Jewish mother.

The Mirror Has Two Faces (1996), with Barbra Streisand as producer, director, and star, is less successful in its portrayal of a nonstereotypical Jewish mother. Streisand plays Rose Morgan, a wildly popular professor of literature at Columbia University who has been unsuccessful in love. Still living with her mother, played by a tart-tongued Lauren Bacall, Rose finds herself in a platonic relationship with a Columbia math professor, Gregory (Jeff Bridges), when her sister answers an ad he places for a date. They marry on his terms: no sex, no physical relationship, just a "meeting of the minds."[63] Rose, however, finds herself unsatisfied with the arrangement. After she transforms herself into an alluring beauty by means of exercise, diet, makeover, and a sexy new wardrobe, Gregory learns how misguided he has been to desire love without passion, and the two reconcile, with feeling.

The portrayal of Rose as a frumpy but stellar teacher who becomes a sex kitten is certainly exaggerated. But even more problematic is the film's portrayal of Bacall as Rose's mother, Hannah, and Mimi Rogers as her sister, Claire. Materialistic, superficial, and self-centered, both women fit the unpleasant stereotypes of Jewish women, though in their manner, tones, and appearance, neither seem in the least related to Streisand's familiar Brooklyn-accented heroine. Like Dottie in *This Is My Life*, Hannah loves her daughters but also fights them. While it is Dottie's ambition that riles her daughters, in Hannah's case, it is "excessive vanity" that interferes. Like Dottie, Hannah also works in cosmetics, and she knows a great deal about beauty. Indeed, Hannah's criticism of Rose for her supposedly dowdy appearance is nonstop. "Get that mask off your face," she harps, "it will clog up your pores." This is a family in which Rose's professional achievements pale in comparison to her sister's good looks and success in trapping a debonair husband (with whom Rose is secretly infatuated).

In one of the film's poignant moments, Rose and her mother talk about beauty. The daughter asks, "How did it feel? Being beautiful?" "It was wonderful," her mother says. Showing Rose a photo of a cute baby, Rose mistakenly assumes it's her sister but learns it is herself. "You were such a beautiful baby," Hannah croons, and the grateful Rose thanks her for providing some new self-esteem. Of course, the theme of the ugly duckling's inner-and-soon-to-become-outer radiance is a familiar one for Streisand; here, however, played off against the mother's and sister's vanity, it only adds to pejorative notions of Jewish women.

Barbra Streisand took a hiatus after *The Mirror Has Two Faces*, returning to film eight years later in the 2004 comedy, *Meet the Fockers*. No longer playing a Jewish daughter, in this film she is cast as the eccentric Jewish mother, Roz. A sex therapist for senior citizens who writes sex manuals with titles such as *Meet Your Orgasm!* and collects erotic wood carvings, she is a middle-aged, hippie version of Dr. Ruth Westheimer, the diminutive, popular sex therapist. Roz enthuses about sexual passion and is still excited about her husband (Dustin Hoffman). (In one unforgettable scene, Hoffman emerges with his face smeared with the whipped cream covering Streisand's bosom.) No nagging Jewish mother here, the outrageous Roz is loving and warm, inviting her son to leave his repressions behind and join in life's fun.

Another recent film, *Prime* (2005), offers an intriguing portrayal of a Jewish mother who combines tradition with modernity. The character Lisa Metzger (Meryl Streep) manifests elements of the stereotypical Jewish mother's suffocating control of her son but eventually transforms into a more open character. Like *Meet the Fockers*, the film presents a son in a relationship with a Gentile woman, but with the complication of a sizable age difference between the lovers. Moreover, the older woman, Rafi, a beautiful thirty-seven-year-old model played by Uma Thurman, is in therapy with the twenty-three-year-old Dave's mother. Lisa is a modern Jewish mother—well educated, well read, with all the accoutrements of the cultured, professional woman (flowing scarves, colorful interesting jewelry, shopping trips to Crate and Barrel). Yet despite her modernity, she harps on tradition and the past, especially in regard to her son.

The first conversation we hear between mother and son is from Dave's point of view. "No, she's not Jewish," Dave speaks into the telephone. "No I'm not trying to kill you. Yes, I want you to be alive to see your grandchildren, your Jewish grandchildren, Mom. No, I didn't know that you wanted to be buried in Israel, Mom." From this conversation, heard before we know that therapist Lisa is Dave's mother, the viewer imagines an excitable, dominating mother, very much in the Sophie Portnoy vein. Dave does not like her lecturing him, accusing her of sounding "like an after-school special." And he dismisses her concerns about his romance with a Gentile woman. "You make it out like

In the film *Prime* (2005), Meryl Streep plays an Upper West Side psychiatrist who manifests elements of the stereotypical Jewish mother's suffocating control of her son. Yet the collision between her professional and maternal instincts—and her ability to learn from each—gives the portrait a new dimension. (Focus Features /Photofest. © Focus Features Photographer: Andrew Schwartz)

it's the Warsaw Ghetto," Dave tells her. "It's not; it's the Upper West Side. We're strong in numbers here."[64]

Lisa is much more permissive as a psychotherapist than as a parent. She encourages Rafi, who has just ended a long, loveless marriage, to delight in her sexuality. "Enjoy yourself . . . just get messy in life," she tells her. Intelligent and sympathetic, Lisa is a toned-down version of Roz Focker. But when Lisa learns that her patient's lover is her son, her professional advice wars with her maternal instincts; she threatens to cut her son out of the family if he continues with the inappropriate liaison. In the end, however, Lisa learns from the affair, and from the relationship with her patient, for whom she wants only the best. She is an authentic, caring, professional, but also an authentic Jewish mother, intense and involved.[65]

While these and other recent films do not avoid Jewish mother stereotypes, several of the new films raise significant questions about the changing structure of Jewish family life, the new roles that mothers are playing as parents and professionals, and the nature of family continuity and Jewish identity.[66] Jewish women writers, directors, comics, and producers, and a new generation of male filmmakers as well, have enriched the repository of screen images from which contemporary audiences draw meanings. Although the

Jewish mother caricature has not been eliminated, these new artists have helped to create a more complex canvas.

It remains disturbing that many screen depictions continue to showcase the Jewish mother as "other"—different, excessive, venal, manipulative, and crude. These portrayals are in some ways a consequence of the lag between the formulaic conventions of popular media and the changing conditions of Jewish mothers in contemporary life. Fiction, historical scholarship, memoirs, and religious studies, influenced by new feminist research, offer a more compelling, up-to-date vision of Jewish mothers in interaction with culture and society.

"You are a writer," she says. "So, do you want to take down the story of my life?"

I am torn by contradiction. I love this woman. She was my first great aching love. All my life I have wanted to do whatever she asked of me, in spite of our quarreling. . . .

But . . . I'm afraid. I fear, as any daughter would, losing myself back into the mother.

—Kim Chernin, *In My Mother's House: A Daughter's Story*

8

FROM SECOND-GENERATION MEMOIRS TO WOMEN'S HISTORY

Reclaiming the Missing Mother

IN THE POSTFEMINIST 1980s AND 1990s, Jewish daughters intensified their quest to come to terms with their mothers. The struggle to connect with mothers took various forms. Some "re-storied" their mothers, breaking the silence and exclusion about women's lives that characterized traditional Jewish texts, by writing directly, in fiction and memoirs, of their desires and experiences as Jewish women, both as daughters and mothers. Different from the abrupt estrangement from mothers that often characterized their male counterparts' writing, Jewish women revealed the complexity of "sustained, conflicted engagement" with their mothers.[1] And while male writing could also draw on sober nostalgia, female writers drew from the reality of their personal journeys, and joined with a vast outpouring of reflections about the history of Jewish women and maternal role models in Jewish texts and traditions. These voyages of discovery proved transformative.

The popular play *The Sisters Rosensweig*, by the late Wendy Wasserstein, is an apt example of how Jewish mothers were reinterpreted and transformed as part of the effort to understand and connect to them in more positive ways. The drama presents three unlike sisters: Pfeni, the youngest, an unmarried, eccentric, world-traveling journalist (most like Wasserstein herself); middle sister, Gorgeous Teitelbaum, a chatty mother of four from Newton, Massachusetts; and the eldest, expatriate Sara, a divorced banker with a skeptical college-aged daughter, Tess, who is writing a biography of her mother's early years. During the course of a brief family reunion in London, the sisters explore questions of marriage, motherhood, sex and selfhood, and their connections to religion and heritage. A central theme is Sara's coming to terms with the Jewish roots she abandoned on her route to achievement. Because of her daughter's quest to record her mother's story, Sara is finally able to embrace her identity as a *Jewish* mother.

The "funsy" sister, "Gorgeous," brilliantly played in the 1992 Broadway production by comic actress Madeline Kahn, is another lesson in positive interpretation. Gorgeous was a mixture of Wasserstein's mother, Lola, her sister Georgette, and the women Wasserstein fondly remembered from growing up in Brooklyn: women proud of the bargains they got at Ohrbach's or Klein's department store, "women who knew their moisturizer," Wasserstein observed. Gorgeous is not only a consummate shopper, but also president of her temple, and so winsome that she hosts a call-in radio talk show where she offers advice as "Dr." Gorgeous. In spite of the character's eccentricity, Madeline Kahn intuitively understood that many people in the audience would identify with Gorgeous. "I'm going to give them their dignity," she told the playwright. "That's why I wrote the play," Wasserstein responded. Gorgeous was "not a joke," not the extreme JAP or Nanny caricature rendered by so many other comic writers, but a character with familiar Jewish traits, at last rendered sympathetically.[2]

Known primarily for her portrayals of intelligent, modern—and usually single—women, struggling to balance independence with desires for family and nurturance, here Wasserstein offers a fresh interpretation of two Jewish mothers. And although the mother of the three sisters never appears, Mrs. Rosensweig's influence on her adult daughters is palpable. Daughters and mothers are irrevocably intertwined, the play seems to tell us; daughters who will one day grow into mothers must understand and appreciate their forebears. And for mothers to live their fullest lives, they must also understand and appreciate themselves, a task which daughters can aid immeasurably.

In fact, the fictional Sara Rosensweig and her biographer daughter found a whole generation of real-world counterparts. The attempt by second-generation offspring of Holocaust survivors to reckon with the complex legacies of their parents provided a rich vein of real-life biographies and narratives that looked anew at Jewish mothers. Helen Epstein, the daughter of survivors from Czechoslovakia, unlocked her parents' "iron box" of secrets by collecting the stories of other children of survivors like herself. Her influential book, *Children of the Holocaust: Conversations with Sons and Daughters of Survivors* (1979), is the remarkable result of her efforts to break the silence and give a name to a previously unacknowledged generation: Epstein called it the "second generation," sometimes dubbed the "2Gs."[3] In a later book, *Where She Came From: A Daughter's Search for Her Mother's History* (1997), Epstein sets out on

Madeline Kahn, playing Massachusetts mother and talk-show host Gorgeous Teitel-baum in Wendy Wassserstein's play *The Sisters Rosensweig*, wanted to give "dignity" to her character. For Wasserstein, and scores of writer-daughters seeking role models, the Jewish mothers they had known were "not a joke." (Associated Press/Marty Reichenthal)

an extended odyssey to Europe to confront the sites of her mother's life in or-der to repair "the most passionate and complicated" relationship of her own existence.[4] She is one of many adult second-generation children who came to recognize their mothers as "heroine[s] more compelling than any in the Bible, any novel or myth."[5]

Daughters of Jewish mothers who were not directly affected by the Holo-caust came to similar revelations. They too initiated journeys—metaphorical and actual—to reckon with their mothers' hidden legacies. Others used their writing to explore the rage and antagonism caused by "fierce attachments" to their mothers, to use the title of Vivian Gornick's 1987 acclaimed mem-oir. They were "torn by contradiction," afraid of losing themselves "back into the mother," author Kim Chernin admitted, in her case to a mother whose influence and power as a Communist Party organizer she admired and feared. Chernin's *In My Mother's House: A Daughter's Search* (1983), was the first of several literary attempts, like Epstein's, to fully know her mother.[6]

A third set of writings came from daughters and granddaughters who endeavored to connect to mothers and grandmothers through remembering—or reconstructing—domestic experiences, particularly regarding food. In memoirs and cookbooks, they sought to bind themselves to maternal ancestors through the recollection of shared recipes and stories of the family table.

These personal accounts have been complemented by a torrent of writings about Jewish women from fiction writers as well as scholars in disciplines as diverse as history, literature, sociology, anthropology, philosophy, and religious studies. Drawing on feminist research as well as Jewish studies, these scholars asked new questions about the lives of Jewish women—and Jewish mothers—and their textual and cultural representations. The Jewish Women's Archive, a national organization established in 1995 to uncover, chronicle, and transmit the lost stories of American Jewish women, provided an institutional base for the recovery of materials about Jewish women and their promulgation to the wider public. Through all of these works, the reclamation of the Jewish mother proceeded apace.

"Why Does Your Mommy Wear That Number on Her Arm?"

As most accounts of second-generation children make clear, survivor parents frequently passed their suffering on to their children in the form of heavy silences and residual fear. In the face of their "cosmic responsibility" to bear witness to their parents' awful past, the children were marked by their elders' experiences in traumatic ways, the more profound because they were not acknowledged.[7] "Deeply internalized" in their lives, yet "strangely unknown," as Eva Hoffman recounts in *After Such Knowledge*, the Holocaust cast its long shadow on "2G" offspring, who found themselves unable to rebel in typical ways against their parents.[8] Some found themselves jealous of the intensity of their parents' experiences; others stayed too close to their parents' pain, guilty and sorrowful, ever watchful for signs of anguish. "Looming over every conversation, every interaction, was her anguish," Fern Chapman wrote of her survivor mother. "Her past minimized, even negated, my own emotional life. As an adolescent, I couldn't challenge her; she had suffered enough. Rebellion was a luxury—a right for other American teenagers, but not for me. From the perspective of her loss, no minor problem I might present would matter."[9] The burden of loss passed on from survivor parent to children lasted a lifetime.

According to Helen Epstein, the common element among survivor children was "enormous physical and psychic disruption in our family history because of great catastrophe."[10] Children were fearful of discussing the war—especially when friends asked questions such as "Why does your Mommy wear that number on her arm?"—and grew up ashamed of their parents' victimization and simultaneously guilty about such feelings.[11] In spite of parents' attempts to provide secure berths for their children in the aftermath of their own tragic pasts, many failed to pass on what their children needed. "Some of the mothers, having undergone so much loss, clung too closely, too insistently to their infants—clung to them for dear life," Hoffman speculates, while others were "too numbed or too afraid to make much physical contact with their children at all."[12] Afraid of loss, hugging their secrets deep within, Jewish survivor mothers affected their children's lives in difficult and complex ways. The search to recover their mothers' stories proved an effective way to reverse the "transmission of trauma" that many of the second generation experienced. In re-creating the life of her mother, Franci, and grandmother, Pepi, who had migrated from Brtnice, Czechoslovakia, to Vienna and then Prague, Helen Epstein loosened the engulfing grasp of her mother's hidden secrets on her own life. By fleshing out her mother's history before and after Auschwitz, to which she had been deported, Epstein came to acknowledge the powerful feelings she had for her mother that lay buried within that "iron box" of family secrets.[13] The journey would be repeated by other second-generation daughters.

In *Motherland*, Fern Chapman conveys how centrally the Holocaust experience stalked her relationship with her mother, Edith. Edith's parents had sent her to America when she was twelve to escape the Nazis, but most of her family was killed in concentration camps. Though she refused to discuss it, Edith was never able to forget the past; she lived her post-Holocaust life "with an eye on the rearview mirror," her soul "forever held hostage to another world." The result was that Chapman knew little about her mother:

> Most mothers and daughters . . . observe each other in a mirror, reflecting one another at different stages of life. They are bound to each other by blood, by emotion, and by that mirror which reminds the mother of what she once was and shows the daughter what she will become.

For Chapman, however, the mirror between them was "one-way": mother could see daughter, but daughter could not see much of her mother and so had to read meaning in her mother's gestures and expressions—like "decoding hieroglyphics."[14]

Expressing the desire for separation was especially difficult for Fern. Unable to accept the fact that her parents had sent her away, albeit to save her life, Edith saw her daughter's growing independence as a betrayal. Chapman recalls her trip to college, with the car ride taking on "a doomed, claustrophobic mood as she stared out the window, never saying a word, her tears, sighs, and quiet gasps punctuating the silence."

> Surely, in any parent's life, joy and sadness fill these moments when a child begins to establish an independent life. But for my mother, this parting was much more than that; it was a funeral procession, a break like the one years earlier, when her parents took her to the boat."[15]

Compared to the overbearing behavior of "Joseph's mother" who follows her son to college in Bruce Jay Friedman's *A Mother's Kisses*, Chapman's poignant account of her mother's heartbreak over her own departure suggests that such clinging was the result of deep psychological trauma—not some foolish empty-nest syndrome.

Only late in her life did Edith come to understand that she could release the past by confronting the nightmares of her childhood. Journeying back to Germany helped heal her pain and allowed mother and daughter to overcome the distance in their relationship. For Chapman and her mother, "motherland" was a geographic place that allowed repair. For all mothers and daughters, Chapman wrote, it was "a country of the heart—the one to which we return when, transformed, we ourselves have become the mothers."[16]

Another story of transformation comes from Ann Kirschner, author of *Sala's Gift: My Mother's Holocaust Story*. Media consultant, literary scholar, and mother of three, Kirschner was startled when in 1991, her mother, Sala Garncarz Kirschner, revealed to her a secret she had kept for nearly fifty years. In 1991, shortly before going to the hospital for triple bypass surgery from which she feared she might not recover, Ann's mother took her to the bedroom closet of her Queens apartment where hidden in a red box that once contained Ann's old "Spill and Spell" game was a leather portfolio full of hundreds of yellowing postcards and letters that Sala had saved for decades. "It was like an electric shock," Kirschner wrote later, "and at the same time it was like something I had been waiting for my whole life." She resolved to tell her mother's story, translating, interpreting, and fleshing out the contexts of the tattered documents. In so doing, she deepened her relationship with her reluctant mother, with whom she sat for years trying to piece together the events behind the letters. Imprisoned in 1940 when she was only sixteen, Sala endured seven forced labor camps, in Germany, Poland, and Czechoslovakia, before she was liberated in 1945; Sala had defied her captors by hiding these letters from family and friends, which prisoners were allowed to receive but not keep. Written in Polish, Yiddish, and German, they provide a portrait of a young woman desperately trying to keep in touch with her collapsing world. Sala's separation from her mother and sister, and later from an older woman who acted as a mentor to her in the camps, is heart-wrenching, revealing her own bravery and determination. Sala's is the sole *collection* of letters—not just individual letters—from the Nazi labor camps to

For nearly fifty years, Sala Grancarz Kirschner hid a unique collection of letters she saved during the time of her wartime imprisonment in Nazi labor camps. After she revealed their existence to her daughter, Ann, they became the subject of an exhibit at the New York Public Library and of Ann Kirschner's book, *Sala's Gift: My Mother's Holocaust Story.* (Courtesy of Ann Kirschner. © Joyce Ravid. All Rights Reserved)

survive. The remarkable letters became the subject of Ann's compelling memoir and a major exhibit at the New York Public Library.[17] Sala had hid the letters because she wanted to protect her children from the nightmares and guilt. But in passing the letters on to Ann and in permitting her story to be told through her daughter, she offered a gift to history as well as her family.

No one better understood the importance of retrieving women's experiences than distinguished scholar Gerda Lerner, the founder of the first Ph.D. program in women's history and the author of a dozen volumes in U.S. women's history. Forced by the Nazis to leave Vienna, Lerner fled to the United States in 1939, still in her teens. But her mother, aspiring artist Ilona (Ili) Kronstein, refused to leave Europe: "I will survive—on my own terms," she told her daughter, adding that her best work had not yet been done.[18] Lerner never saw her after their leave-taking in the South of France; Kronstein survived the war but died from multiple sclerosis a few years after the war's end. For fifty years, Lerner remained critical of her mother's decision to remain in Europe but blamed herself for failing to understand and connect to her mother before her death.

Lerner's sister, Nora Rosen-Kronstein, an artist who emigrated to Israel, managed to save her mother's paintings, and in 2000, both daughters arranged for the first exhibition of Ili's work at the Jewish Museum in Vienna. Through the prism of her critically acclaimed canvases—colorful abstract compositions, landscapes, nudes, and self-portraits—Lerner saw her mother's life in a new light, appreciating the spark of hope that allowed her to separate from her family for the sake of her belief in her art. "Like the good fairy in the tales," she wrote in her autobiography, *Fireweed*, "my mother had equipped me, the adventurous child poised for a long and hazardous journey, with magic sources of strength in the face of danger."[19] Lerner would need this fortitude to escape the Nazis and in her life as a refugee in America, where she became a grassroots activist, member of the Communist party, and pioneer in the women's movement and women's studies. Her biographical essay about her mother in the museum catalogue pays tribute to Ilona Kronstein's uncommon life and work, acknowledging the complex legacy she provided.[20]

The extraordinary women who survived the Holocaust and bequeathed mixed and often puzzling legacies should rightly be seen as "heroines" more compelling than those of myth and literature—and certainly those of comedy. The daughters' memoirs, histories, films, and art offer us new images of Jewish mothers enriched by the dramatic stories of their pasts.

"Torn by Contradiction": Daughters Search for Balanced Connections

While 2G daughters struggled to overcome their survivor mothers' remoteness, some third-generation daughters ached for more distance from mothers.

In their 1980s memoirs about their mothers, Kim Chernin and Vivian Gornick told of constant fighting with their mothers, mostly because of the mothers' intense and continuing emotional presence in their lives. Growing up, the stories the mothers told them deeply influenced their outlook and values, even as they fought to reject them. In response to their mothers' urging to write down their stories and pass them on to other generations, Chernin and Gornick took the occasion to examine the connections they had to their mothers, as well as the legacies the mothers had passed on.

"I am torn by contradiction," Chernin writes, after her mother asked her to take down the story of her life. "I love this woman. She was my first great aching love. All my life I have wanted to do whatever she asked of me, in spite of our quarreling."[21] Yet she feared that coming to know the full story of her mother's life would force her to confront all the "secrets and silences" they had lived by. "I fear, as any daughter would, losing myself back into the mother," Chernin admits.[22] Gornick's mother told her, "So you'll write down: From the beginning it was all lost." Gornick despised the deprivation litany of her mother's life but acknowledged her role in transmitting her mother's story: "I am the repository of your life now, Ma."[23]

Chernin and Gornick found much to admire as they rediscovered their mothers' lives. Chernin heard a "story of power" stretching over four generations of women, from her grandmother to her own daughter. The narrative of immigrants and their descendants, it was "a tale of transformation and development—the female reversal of that patriarchal story in which the power of the family's founder is lost and dissipated as the inheriting generations decline and fall to ruin."[24] Although she had fought against her mother's politics, Chernin wanted to be "just like her" when she learned the full story of her mother's courage and conviction as a Communist Party organizer. In bringing her mother's past to light—the "history of separations in her life, the loss of her first home, the shtetl, grandfather," the "loss of her mother, who could not be a mother to her in America" "—Chernin understood what she had wanted to distance herself from: "This knowledge of loving, the depth of this love, our love so terrifying for us both."[25] To use scholar Janet Burstein's word, "restorying" her mother allowed Chernin to reverse her "long and troubled struggle for separation" and embrace her mother's influence and strength.[26]

Gornick's memoir depicts a similar struggle. Also a Communist Party supporter, Gornick's mother headed the Tenant Council in her Bronx tenement. With the birth of their first child, Gornick's husband insisted that she quit her organizing activities. But Mrs. Gornick never tired of telling the story of how she ran the Tenant Council. " 'Every Saturday morning, . . . the way other mothers told their children Mary had a little lamb," mother would tell daughter what became a personal "childhood classic":

"I would go down to the Communist Party headquarters in Union Square and receive my instructions for the week. Then we would organize, and carry on." How she loved saying, "Then we would organize, and carry on." There was more uncomplicated pleasure in her voice when she repeated those words than in any others I ever heard her speak.

Her mother's example no doubt shaped her own childhood fantasies. "I never daydreamed about love or money," Gornick remembered. "I always daydreamed I was making eloquent speeches that stirred ten thousand people to feel their lives, and to *act*."[27]

But her mother's life had grown narrow and "unlived" as she retreated from the world to raise her children. Frustrated and unsatisfied, she left little for Gornick to imitate. After a lifetime of "accusation and retaliation," leading to cycles of "Silence. Anger. Separation," the two had become "locked into a narrow channel of acquaintance, intense and binding." For Gornick, the depth of the connection between them, the passionate rages, had been maddening. But she increasingly came to understand her mother's choices, believing that they had survived their "common life." At the end of the memoir, Gornick's mother asks her: "Why don't you go already? Why don't you walk away from my life? I'm not stopping you." "I know you're not, Ma," Gornick responds, for she admits that she is "half in, half out," of the story yet to come.[28] Although the future of their relationship was unclear, Gornick reached the "single insight" that led her to write the book: "I could not leave my mother because I had become my mother."[29]

Both writers seemed to say that there is no closure to the task of writing their mothers' lives. Four years after she completed her memoir, Chernin wrote in an article that despite the years she had put into writing, "something was missing, something had not yet been said." For Chernin, it was "the tale of the missing Jewish identity," an inheritance which, because it was not handed down by her mother, she had to learn "at a slant."[30] She was able to recover that tradition by writing it into another exploration of the generational connection between Jewish women, this time in a novel. *The Flame-Bearers* (1983) told the story of a young Jewish girl who hears from her grandmother stories of Jewish women who worship a female God and who in other ways offer a radical critique of Judaism. Through these myths, the granddaughter confronts her own spiritual needs and the legacy of her foremothers. As did the memoir, *The Flame-Bearers* acknowledged that "women must define themselves with reference to the past." But it went beyond *In My Mother's House* to link the personal legacy of her mother with the Jewish tradition Chernin believed Rose ultimately embodied. "Tradition is the mother one finds oppressive," Chernin declares; it is both "the source of one's inspiration and intolerable."[31]

The 1991 memoir *Deborah, Golda, and Me* by feminist activist and writer Letty Cottin Pogrebin, continued the quest to locate an empowering tradition within Judaism. Combining a personal exploration with a deeper historical interrogation of Jewish women's tradition, the book had a profound effect on readers' struggling with their own Jewish identities. Pogrebin's mother died when the writer was a teenager. Grieving for her mother, but not allowed to say *kaddish* (mourning prayer) because she was female, Pogrebin refused to accept her father's male-dominated Judaism. Her alienation from the religion continued for two decades, until feminism motivated her to fight "for my mother's rights" and reclaim an alternative, egalitarian Judaism by identifying with the biblical Deborah and Israeli Prime Minister Golda Meir.[32] She discovered that her mother had been

> a brave pioneer in the new world, a female wage earner unbowed by a grade-school education, a single parent who supported and educated her child through the Depression, a gifted artist and designer, an intrepid student, a maker of feasts and celebrations, a relentless optimist, a nourishing mother, and a true and giving friend.

Connecting to Jewish tradition through her foremothers helped Pogrebin accept her own mother and understand that she had passed on "what success means."[33]

Paradise Regained: Pots, Recipes, and Maternal Legacies

In the 1990s, another group of Jewish daughters found their connections to Jewish tradition by exploring the neglected and often hidden legacies of Jewish women. Food and memoir writers such as Elizabeth Erlich and Joy Horowitz put behind them the many negative stereotypes of Jewish mothers force-feeding their children with guilt through food, instead reclaiming the recipes, utensils, and cooking styles of their families, and in particular their Jewish mothers' ancestral pasts.

Nonobservant and married to a non-Jew, Joy Horowitz increasingly became concerned about her children's education and her own lack of connection to her heritage. "As a Jew," she acknowledged, "my spiritual search will have to be one of my own making."[34] In the interest of tradition, she reached out beyond her mother to her grandmothers, spending time with them and asking them for their favorite recipes. *Tessie and Pearlie: A Granddaughter's Story* (1996) recounts this spiritual journey into her grandmothers' immigrant past and the food they lovingly cooked for their families.

Among the recipes offered in the book are Grandma Pearlie's and Grandma Tessie's stuffed cabbage. Grandma Pearlie says hers is the "most wonderful thing for freezing. You can make it exotic with raisins—white or red. There's so many ways to make it tasty. . . . It's always ready for ya." Grandma Tessie observes that it's "really a chore to make cholipshes . . . you take a day off just to prepare yourself. . . . How much rice? I don't know. A half pound is too much. Two handfuls, two fistfuls of rice is good. Of course if you want you can wash it. Then, you chop up an onion or two, whatever you like."[35] Transcribed in her grandmothers' voices, these recipes convey the collaborative tone and democratic flavor of her grandmothers' lives. Antiauthoritarian and imprecise, they are full of the colorful ethnic observations that mark the world of *yiddishkeit*.

One Mother's Day Pearlie gives Joy "a most remarkable present: her mother's aluminum pot for stuffed cabbage . . . more than a century old." Although this "family heirloom . . . would be thrown in a junk heap by anyone else," it is precious to Joy, but she feels guilty, "worried about my place in the family. . . . Shouldn't my mother be next? Or my aunt? Or my older sister? . . . But, I think, Grandma has given this to me because I'm the one who's asked to learn how to make her stuffed cabbage."[36]

But more than recipes and utensils are passed on to Horowitz during the course of her culinary collaboration with her grandmothers. "[E]ach of their memories is like a gift of hope. Their stories and reminiscences transmit values that have grown anachronistic: Loyalty. Continuity. Faith. A belief in what is simple and true—the love of family."[37] In her grandmothers' lives, love has been most often expressed through the preparation of food. "Not that they're book-smart or intellectually brilliant," Horowitz writes of her grandmothers, but they are "the smartest women I know. . . . In the ways of life—in the stuff that matters—they're geniuses."

Through her grandmothers Horowitz comes to a greater understanding of who she is as a Jew in cultural and spiritual terms. "It is impossible for me to spend time with Pearlie and Tessie and not believe in something bigger than ourselves," she writes. Spending time with them, she concludes, is "as holy as anything I know."[38]

Elizabeth Ehrlich also connected to her spiritual heritage through recipes but "grew up at a distance" from her grandmothers:

> I forgot the childhood appetites that could only be satisfied in my grandmothers' kosher kitchens. I forgot the practical, mystical teachings, spiraling back through time, that my grandmothers had once dished out with their soup. I forgot the dignity my immigrants had, that comes with the connection to something larger than everyday life, even when you are doing nothing more than stirring soup. I had the bequest of my grandmothers' details, but I devalued all this for many years.[39]

Ehrlich has to go through her mother-in-law, Miriam, to reconnect to this legacy because even her own mother—who could only recall her mother's kitchen—had let tradition slip away:

Her vegetable and barley soup, chicken soup, *gedemfte fleysh* (pot roast), chicken roasted with potatoes or lima beans, potato *kneydlekh* (dumplings), *kreplekh* (filled dumplings), *lungen un milts* (chopped and sautéed lung and spleen), roast *heldzl* (stuffed poultry neck), chicken fricassee, *gefilte milts* (stuffed spleen), meat loaf, *Kokletn* (spiced ground-beef patties fried in oil), *meyrn tsimes* (carrots simmered in honey), chopped liver, roasted *kishke* (stuffed derma), baked fish with string beans, baked carp, gefilte fish, potato pudding, rice pudding, noodle pudding, potato pancakes, cheese blintzes, chili sauce, sour pickles, pickled green tomatoes, canned fruit, farmer cheese, chocolate cake, spice cake, apple pies, apple strudel, and cookies, were legendary. . . . I am so sorry I failed to ask for the recipes.[40]

Like Horowitz, Ehrlich began to wonder about her heritage when as a mother herself she wanted to teach her children how to "build a floor . . . something strong and solid" under them. Without access to the "wisdom and innovations" of her mother and grandmothers, Ehrlich could draw on her mother-in-law's legacies.[41] While the cadence of the recipes from Miriam, a Holocaust refugee from Germany, differed from those of her East European immigrant grandmothers, Ehrlich nonetheless recognized many of Miriam's "dishes, expressions and perceptions" from the kitchens of her childhood. The culture of Jewish women's food crossed boundaries of time and place.

A mix of personal and family narratives and formal recipes, *Miriam's Kitchen* is a culinary autobiography. "I light a candle, recite a prayer, grate a potato, and move toward making my kitchen kosher," she writes. "Thus, I forge links from my grandparents, and my husband's grandparents, to my children."[42] The history she recovers becomes her "own little temple" where she can measure her life against a "reliable standard" and "increasingly . . . find meaning." Guided by the "sinkside, stoveside" personal perceptions of her foremothers, not a "rabbinic one," Ehrlich reproduces and maintains the culture of women that she has come to recognize as the most significant aspect of her spiritual nature.[43]

As distinguished from earlier feminists who scorned their mothers' ways of life, Jewish culinary writers of the 1980s and 1990s used traditional domestic concerns to link to their mothers' and grandmothers' pasts. In sympathy and with respect, they stood watch over their ancestors' stoves and sinks. These varied memoirs joined those of the daughters of Holocaust survivors, radical activists, and other New World "pioneers" who rescued their mothers' stories from oblivion. In so doing they fashioned a new portrait of the Jewish mother.

"Mirror, Mirror on the Wall, Am I My Mother After All?"

Jewish women, of course, also turned to the more traditional formats of novels, short stories, and plays to transmit the heritage passed on by generations of Jewish mothers. One of the first of these was the pioneering 1975 novel, *Her Mothers*, by E. M. Broner. Written from a mother's point of view, Broner's novel tells the story of Beatrix Palmer, a mother and a writer who researches the lives of women but finds no heroines. Her Jewish mother failed to provide friendship and kindness, and she learns from her only that "woman is nothing, only her husband is something." Without a model of successful parenting, Beatrix cannot provide for the needs of her daughter, who has run away and is missing.

In the hope of finding guidance, Beatrix turns to history. But she is disappointed to learn that the historical mothers she investigates—abolitionist Charlotte Forten, writers Emily Dickinson, Louisa May Alcott, and Margaret Fuller—were all "Father's Daughters," carriers of their fathers' dream, who humbled and dissembled themselves before the men they loved. Beatrix turns next to the biblical matriarchs, but again she finds only flawed women. Sifting through the stories of Sarah, Rebecca, Leah, and Rachel and the lives of contemporary Israeli women, Beatrix's outlook only gets bleaker. The Bible tells her that "a woman is as good as her womb," that "women fight for the penis of a man," that "menstruating women are as camel dung," damaged by the patriarchal demands of what Broner wickedly terms the "Old Testicle." "What do I learn from my mothers?" Beatrix asks. The answer is only, "Sister against sister, woman betrays woman."[44]

At the conclusion of the book, Beatrix and her daughter meet and reconcile—almost; because of their own struggle to connect, the future seems promising even if there are few role models available in the long record of Jewish and American history. "It is the final generosity to embrace one's mother," Broner writes, and that effort had to come both from individual and collective effort.

Written out of her own experience as mother of two daughters and two sons, *Her Mothers* poignantly expresses Broner's belief that in a patriarchal society, the failure of mother to nurture daughters is inevitable. "The cycle continues because women give to their daughters exactly what they've learned from their mothers." The solution: "Women must connect to other women—and to themselves" if they wish to become agents of their own lives who could nurture others effectively. Never taught how to mother, they had to find out, as Beatrix did, through their personal quests.[45]

The struggle of mothers and daughters to find common ground has been a central theme in the crescendo of fiction by Jewish writers in the thirty years since the publication of Broner's breakthrough novel.[46] One of the most influential of these works was Anne Roiphe's *Lovingkindness* (1987), which told the story of Annie Johnson, a professor of women's history and a staunch feminist who must come to terms with her daughter Andrea's rejection of her own secular, liberal values, which Andrea finds hollow and even destructive. To escape her own alienation, which led her as a teenager to drugs, abortions, and a suicide attempt, Andrea flees to Israel where she studies at a yeshiva, joins an ultra-Orthodox sect and plans to take a husband in an arranged marriage. Rejecting her initial impulse to rescue Andrea (now renamed Sarai) and spirit her away, Annie accepts her daughter's choice to become a *ba' alat teshuva* (an adult woman, not brought up Orthodox, who chooses Orthodoxy). Letting her go—that is, letting her stay in Israel, where she has found the community that is an antidote to her spiritual wandering—is an act of maternal "lovingkindness."[47]

Almost a decade later, Allegra Goodman's debut novel, *Kaaterskill Falls* (1998), presents another rich portrait of a mother's struggle to reconcile the religious and secular aspects of modernity. Set in the Catskills, now home to dozens of Orthodox communities, the novel tells the story of Elizabeth Shulman, a devout wife and mother of five daughters, who becomes a "tourist in the other direction," yearning for new roles beyond her traditional, domestic one. Though ultimately she remains in her limited world ("there is beauty in it," she concedes), the rebellious spirit that lies inside her passes on to Chani, her outspoken daughter.[48]

Connections between mothers and daughters—and the differences between them—take center stage in Rebecca Goldstein's vibrant *Mazel* (1995), an exploration of three generations of talented, unconventional women: Sacha Saunders, a leading actress on the Yiddish stage in prewar Poland, now living (in "exile") on Manhattan's Upper West Side; her daughter, Chloe, a 1960s "freethinker" who teaches classics and "dead languages" at Barnard; and her granddaughter, Phoebe, a mathematics professor at Princeton, specializing in the theory of soap bubbles. Although Chloe's Jewishness, derived from her mother' stories, is elusive, the brilliant, rational Phoebe chooses to become observant and marries, at the novel's end, in a traditional Orthodox ceremony. The women of Sacha's family are "sealed together, worlds apart."[49]

Many recent novels similarly expose the differences and the aching for reconciliation that motivate mothers and daughters and their relationships to sisters, husbands, friends, and lovers. In Rosellen Brown's *Half a Heart* (2000), a Houston wife and mother, former civil rights activist and teacher, sets out to find her eighteen-year-old biracial daughter who has grown up with her father, an African American musician and black power radical. In Marge Piercy's *Three Women* (1999), a grandmother who is a union organizer, her daughter (a law professor), and her granddaughters (one studying to be a rabbi and the other a troubled "drifter") find a way to connect and redefine what it means to be "good mothers" and good daughters. In Letty Cottin Pogrebin's *Three Daughters* (2002), each adult daughter, now a mother herself, draws on the inheritance of her flawed mother—the "old Jewish Mama"—as she confronts a painful crisis in her life. "Mirror, mirror on the wall," one daughter asks, "am I my mother after all"?[50]

The search of Jewish daughters, sisters, mothers, and grandmothers in fiction to enrich their personal identities as Jews and as women spans several continents as well as generations. For example, Erica Jong's *Inventing Memory* and Goldstein's *Mazel* are set in Europe and the New World, while Anne Roiphe's *The Pursuit of Happiness* begins in a tiny Polish town and takes its characters to America and Israel. Like the stories told in the cookbooks and memoirs, these excursions into the times and spaces of family history are explorations in self-identity, and they permit a recovery of previously lost connections that enable young and older women to establish themselves as Jews. Jong says, "What we learn from our mothers and grandmothers stays in the bone marrow. It surfaces as soon as you become a mother yourself. And what you sow as a daughter, you will inevitably reap as a mother." The "mother-daughter dance" repeats itself over the generations.[51]

In their complex portrayals of family relationships and of Jewish mothers' and daughters' "multiple homes and selves," this recent fiction has moved a "giant step" even beyond previous writings of Jewish women through the 1970s.[52] Fiction has completed the work of memoirists and autobiographers by allowing writers some distance from their own pasts, but it has also permitted them to imaginatively reconstruct maternal desires, impulses, and legacies.

"The Majority Finds Its Past"

Fresh interpretations of the Jewish mother's role in history came from the feminist academy as well. Beginning slowly in the late 1960s and early 1970s and intensifying in the 1980s and 1990s, women's studies as an academic enterprise uprooted traditional paths to knowledge in many disciplines. Historians, sociologists, anthropologists, literary critics, and philosophers were among the scholars who began to ask new questions and devise new methodologies in order to render visible the contributions of the "majority" sex, as Gerda Lerner put it in her influential volume, *The Majority Finds Its Past* (1976).[53] To give meaning to the lives of women of the past meant chronicling women's contributions to the culture and politics of their times, turning the spotlight as well on nontraditional arenas where women had been central participants. Faced with a wealth of diverse stories of previously unappreciated women, scholars soon recognized that they could not universalize or encapsulate women's experiences. A new direction in women's scholarship, focused on distinctions among different groups of women, took center stage.

The study of Jewish women in culture and history benefited from this new emphasis. Historians focused in new ways on Jewish women's experiences, highlighting their roles in immigrant culture, voluntary and professional life, politics, culture, the arts and religion. In her 1988 volume, *The World of Our Mothers*, Sydney Stahl Weinberg reframed Irving Howe's landmark (but virtually womanless) study of Jewish immigrant culture, *World of Our Fathers*, by conducting oral histories of female Jewish immigrants. Weinberg dwells prominently on the close relationships of mothers and daughters, seen in mothers' encouragement of daughters' ambitions and in the examples mothers imparted of "competence, pride, and strength." Among other skills, daughters learned from mothers "how to 'manage,' how to act as mediators and play an important role in running families behind the facade of paternal authority." Daughters were deeply affected by mothers' models of "service and self-sacrifice"; most learned from them "to achieve satisfaction from such a life." While not all the daughters had warm relationships with mothers, over the course of a lifetime, as the daughters became mothers themselves, they drew closer to them.[54]

Susan Glenn's 1990 work, *Daughters of the Shtetl*, revealed the importance of daughters' participation in the industrial labor force to social and political advances. After immigration, daughters replaced mothers as primary bread-winners, allowing mothers to remain at home. Although most daughters quit the labor force after they married, the activism and mutual support that char-acterized their work experience carried over into their later lives as mothers. Some returned to paid work while most "moved in and out of political life as easily as they dropped in and out of breadwinning." Always their identities re-mained "complex and fluid"; their life course "moved not in a straight line to-ward one identifiable model but back and forth like a pendulum." Helping to create a Jewish immigrant version of the "New Woman" who came to promi-nence in the early twentieth century, these women played vital roles in the community as they matured and became mothers themselves.[55]

A third example of the new historical scholarship about Jewish mothers is Ruth Markowitz's study of Jewish women schoolteachers in New York City from the 1920s to the 1960s. Many were daughters of trade-union activists like those chronicled by Glenn; although they entered white-collar rather than fac-tory work, they resembled their mothers in their simultaneous commitment to family life and to activism for social justice. Markowitz's interviews with these teachers revealed that Jewish mothers played critical roles in supporting daugh-ters' desires to become teachers. "Study, study, so you can become a teacher" was a typical refrain in immigrant homes, often in the face of fathers' disap-proval. "It was the only time I remember my mother taking a stand against my father," reported one narrator.[56]

Parallel to the recovery of Jewish mothers' experiences in modern American history, feminist scholars turned to ancient texts—and to the silences they found therein—as another site for reclaiming the Jewish mothers missing from tradi-tion. In her influential *Standing Again at Sinai* (1990), Judith Plaskow sought new meanings of Torah by looking at discrepancies between the "holes in text"—where women were selected, edited, obscured, and erased—and women's actual "felt experience." Through innovative use of midrash to interpret texts, and new modes of liturgy and ritual, she offered ways that Jewish women could connect to their foremothers.[57]

Following Plaskow, many scholars and theologians have reinterpreted women's roles in the Hebrew Bible and religious tradition. The result has been new accounts of the matriarchs themselves—Sarah, Rebecca, Rachel, and Leah—as well as arresting interpretations of the experiences of other Jewish foremothers (Ruth, Esther, Miriam, Deborah, and Tamar, to name a few).[58] In these studies, Jewish women emerged as strong and assertive, often defying patriarchal power and helping to establish divine authority.[59] Though they possessed little de jure political or economic autonomy, they used their wit to derive some benefit from those in control, usually in areas related to children. *The Red Tent*, the 1997 novel by Anita Diamant that became a best seller largely through word of mouth, is a remarkable effort that reimagined the biblical mothers as they might have been. Diamant's retelling of the Genesis story, narrated in the voice of Dinah, opens with the tale of her four mothers, the wives of Jacob—Leah, Rachel, Zilpah, and Bilhah—and illuminates in engrossing detail how mothers and daughters lived their everyday lives, particularly in the society of other women, in biblical times.[60] In such works as well as in new ritual dimensions of women's religious practice, Jewish women discovered new sources of spirituality that connected them to earlier faith-based women's traditions while carving out an arena for innovative approaches.

The determination to remember the lives of Jewish mothers of the past took disparate forms in the 1980s and 1990s, but whether embodied in a personal or spiritual quest or an attempt to restore the experience of larger groups of female actors to collective memory, these efforts changed the lives of those who re-storied their Jewish mothers and pointed the way to a new future.

"Where History Lives and Grows"

A new and visionary approach to remembering Jewish mothers came in 1995 with the founding of the Jewish Women's Archive in Brookline, Massachusetts. Started by Gail Twersky Reimer, the daughter of Holocaust survivors and a scholar who has reexamined biblical women's lives, the archive hoped to change future generations' legacy by collecting Jewish women's stories that might otherwise be lost to history. Reimer had been inspired by her mother, Natalia Twersky, a "strong, courageous, determined woman who held our family together."[61] Born in Kracow, Poland, in 1914, Natalia married shortly before World War II and bore a son in 1941, whom she sent into hiding for the duration of the war. (Reimer was born after her parents emigrated to the United

States.) Although her mother did not fully share the story of how she hid her son, neither did Natalia deliberately keep silent about the Holocaust. Many times Reimer heard the story of how her mother had removed herself from Schindler's list so that she might protect her siblings and friends and about how she was sent to Auschwitz. And she heard her mother admit, without guilt, that she had served as a kapo—an overseer recruited from among the prisoners—at the camp, using her "privilege" to save as many women as possible. Growing up, Reimer met numerous survivors who told her about the many people her mother saved.[62]

Once in America, Natalia continued to serve as family matriarch for her five surviving siblings, creating a new home and community for them. Reimer believed that her mother experienced no survivor's guilt; rather she was "propelled by her sense of mission to keep Judaism alive despite Hitler. Surviving just to tell the story was simply not enough; you had to survive as Jewish and repair the community and the world."[63] This lesson would stay with Reimer throughout her life. By the time she began to teach at Wellesley College in the 1980s, she felt that her attachment to Judaism was out of sync with many feminists in her generation.

Her mother's death after an operation that left her without her voice, unable to respond to her family, was the catalyst that brought Judaism and feminism together for Reimer. "You wait and wait to ask certain questions, to hear certain stories, to get certain facts straight, and then it's too late," Reimer recalled. "I was very aware of this loss, and I realized that it was being directed to my future." Her bereavement was compounded by the fact that she was left out of the mourning services for her mother, which, according to Orthodox tradition, meant that women could not recite the kaddish.[64] At this point, Reimer decided to move ahead with a project that would explore the remarkable relationship of the biblical Naomi to her daughter-in-law Ruth through a series of commissioned essays. *Reading Ruth*, coedited with Judith Kates, was dedicated to the memory of Reimer's formidable mother.[65]

Despite the importance of this scholarship, and another book with Kates that focused on women in High Holy Day texts, Reimer's dream went beyond the re-storying of women's individual contributions.[66] Her fear was that unless the stories of Jewish women, largely hidden from the narratives of American and Jewish life, were to be deliberately collected and preserved, the history of Jewish women in the contemporary world, like the real stories of the biblical women whom she had written about, would be lost forever. What was unique about the idea was that the Jewish Women's Archive, as it came to be called, would be "virtual": materials would be collected online, and they would be transmitted in a variety of unconventional ways to a diverse audience through a state-of-the art website and community programs, as well as through posters, images, oral histories, films, curriculum materials, and other documentary resources. Equally unusual was the second part of Reimer's plan: the archive would be independent, unconnected to any umbrella institution within the Jewish or academic communities. Attracting a committed group of founding board members and a small staff, Reimer created a fledgling organization that grew into a powerful institution—the only national organization dedicated to the history of Jewish women.

In its short lifetime, the archive has gathered an extensive range of materials about Jewish women that it has made available in both virtual and nonvirtual forms: exhibits in such areas as politics, the arts, religion, business, academic life, and sports; oral histories of "ordinary" women notable for their community activism; curricula materials; artistic and photographic exhibits; and information about nearly a thousand archival collections relating to Jewish women across the United States and Canada. Fueled by contributions from both scholars and ordinary women, it is a site where "history lives and grows."[67] Beyond its website, the archive has developed a lively outreach to Jewish educators and community leaders, encouraging the creation and collection of resources about Jewish women.

These collections do not focus on mothers per se, but include information about Jewish women whatever their marital and child-rearing status. In addition to the life stories of mothers told in these sources, archive materials reveal that the rhetoric of motherhood carried over to single, childless women. Of the JWA's eighteen prominent "Women of Valor," for example, Emma Lazarus, whose famous poem "The New Colossus" is engraved on the Statue of Liberty, created an enduring symbol for immigrants and all Americans, describing a "mighty woman with a torch . . . the Mother of Exiles"; anarchist Emma Goldman titled her influential magazine about culture and politics *Mother Earth*; and Henrietta Szold, who founded Hadassah as the "healing of the daughter of my people," inspired generations of Zionists as the "Mother of Israel." The work of the archive and of women's history scholars demonstrates that Jewish motherhood has served broadly as a metaphor for the act of creation and of engagement in the world. Engraved in Jewish tradition and the experience of Jewish women of different religious and family backgrounds, images of Jewish mothers can now be chronicled and transmitted as historical artifacts of great import.

Furthermore, it is not only women who are taking the journey to find and promulgate the stories of Jewish mothers. The reclamation of Jewish mothers' lives has been aided by male writers, artists, and social scientists who have committed the story of their mothers' lives to the public record. In addition to sons of Holocaust survivors such as Art Spiegelman, who began this reclamation with the allegorical cartoon book, *Maus*, partly to tell the story of his mother's depression and suicide after Auschwitz, Jewish male writers are providing important new memoirs that place Jewish mothers into living, vital historical contexts.[68]

These biographies and memoirs, like recent histories, cookbooks, and novels, are among the deeply felt acts of rescue that collectively contribute to a broader set of images of Jewish mothers, further distancing them from the monolithic stereotypes of the past.

My mother—and I think all Jewish women—took a chicken and made twelve different dishes out of it. You made the soup, and then you roasted the chicken, and you chopped the liver. They took that neck skin and they stuffed it with flour and pepper, and sewed it up and roasted it with the chicken. I'm telling you—twelve different dishes.

—Selma Litman, *Weaving Women's Words*,
Jewish Women's Archive

In my parents' will, they said, "We're not leaving any money to our children or grandchildren. Instead, it's going to be in trust for all the family." We have sixty-eight at our seders—brothers, sisters, children, grandchildren. Before the seder starts, my brother makes a tribute to my parents, who made this possible. And when I'm no longer here, I know and feel very strongly that my children absolutely will continue that.

—Elsie Miller Legum, *Weaving Women's Words*,
Jewish Women's Archive

9

"THEY RAISED BEAUTIFUL FAMILIES"
Jewish Mothers Narrate Their Lives

IN HER 1989 TREATISE, *MATERNAL THINKING*, Sara Ruddick lamented the absence of a realistic language that captured maternal experience as expressed by mothers themselves. "Drowned by professional theory, ideologies of motherhood, sexist arrogance, and childhood fantasy," Ruddick wrote, maternal voices had been "alternatively silenced and edging towards speech."[1] But as memoirists, writers, historians, and activists struggled to connect to their own Jewish mothers and the mothers of Jewish tradition, they also sought to empower Jewish mothers as storytellers and historians in their own right. As a result, the last decade and a half has seen a burgeoning of narratives told by Jewish mothers.

Jewish mothers have been given voice in an elaborate series of oral histories, surveys, and questionnaires that asked them to narrate the circumstances of their lives and to express their opinions about their roles as women and mothers. Most of the women interviewed in these projects came from the immigrant generation or their second-generation offspring; the experiences they relate take us back at least a generation ago, usually more than that, when their children were young, but they also speak of their experiences as mothers of adult children.

How do the stories Jewish mothers tell about themselves contrast with those told in fiction and memoirs or in Jewish jokes? Do they validate the stereotypes or challenge them? In one respect, studies point to some similar elements in the stereotypical portraits. In one of the most extensive surveys, mothers reported their disappointment if their adult children did not call them frequently. Many said they spoke to their children daily, or at least several times a week. They strongly objected to a child who "moves out of the house and forgets about you"; this was not a "good" son or daughter.[2] Interviewed in the twilight of their lives, they might well have complained to their busy children, "You never call! you never write!" But when the mothers recalled their relations to their own parents, many of whom they left behind in the Old Country, they also complained that parents had asked too much of them by expecting them to write (as well as send support). Expectations of filial closeness had been passed down—and sometimes resented—through the generations.

Despite this lament, mothers in these surveys voiced extremely positive views of parenting. Taken collectively, they present a view of Jewish motherhood almost entirely at variance with stereotypical images. If they recognized a negative image of the Jewish mother as "possessive" and "nagging," it was, they said, "thanks to the Jewish comedians."[3] In their own words, these mothers told of Jewish mothering that was engaged, spirited, flexible, and in large degree modern, attuned to the needs of their children and not—in their own opinion—to their desire to be "right." Although these studies probed only the mothers' views, and not those of their children, the informants also spoke as daughters about their own mothers, providing another perspective. No attempt was made to empirically validate the data as evidence of actual child-rearing behavior, but the studies do represent actual retrospective attitudes and mothers' current beliefs.[4]

Three such studies illuminate how Jewish mothers recalled their lives. The first, conducted by a team of sociologists and historians under sociologist Rose Laub Coser's leadership in the early 1980s, took aim at what she considered the misogynistic work embodied in Irving Howe's *World of Our Fathers*. Under a grant from the Russell Sage Foundation, Coser, historian Laura Anker, and their associates interviewed one hundred immigrant mothers (sixty-one Jewish and thirty-nine Italian), who had moved from Eastern and Southern Europe to the United States before 1927 and who were at least thirteen years old at the time of resettlement. Due to Coser's illness and eventual death, the study that resulted from this survey, *Women of Courage: Jewish and Italian Immigrant Women in New York*, was not published until the end of the 1990s and includes information primarily about respondents' workplace experiences.[5] In order to ascertain attitudes about these mothers' parenting, I returned to the original raw data and gathered extensive material about the Jewish women's stories of motherhood.[6]

A second study of sixty older Jewish women in Seattle and Baltimore conducted by the Jewish Women's Archive in 2001–2002 similarly demonstrates the power of women's words to illuminate Jewish mothers' lives. I had the opportunity to work with the archive to develop a framework for exploring the context of women's lives that spanned the twentieth century. The survey framework focused on the interlocking experiences of marriage, child-rearing, education, work, leisure, cultural and volunteer activities, and women's networks.[7]

The third study was one I conducted in 2003 of one hundred women who came to hear my lectures on Jewish mothers to the Florida Region of the Brandeis University National Women's Committee in Broward and Palm Beach Counties, Florida.[8] The survey was designed to elicit the women's first reactions to a range of questions about their mothers, their own and their children's parenting, and reactions to standard images of Jewish mothers.

Responding at a time when narrators might have long since come to terms with the difficulties of motherhood, the claims made by women in each of the studies must be greeted with a degree of skepticism. However, the results of all three of these surveys corroborate each other and help build an important mothers' perspective. Seeing themselves as enablers who raised their children with moderate and flexible methods of child-rearing, encouraging them to do well in school and in life, these Jewish mothers took pride in their parenting and their offspring's achievements, expressing optimistic views about family experiences and indicating a high degree of connection to children.[9] They suggest clear attitudes that go against the grain of the predominant stereotype.

"Mothers Have to Be Friends to Their Children, Not Dictators": Coser's "Women of Courage"

At the time Coser and Anker began the interviews, a new wave of research about immigrant lives had begun to focus on female labor as a motivation for migration. But as Coser and Anker recognized, "immigrant women themselves—their particular perspectives, motives and constraints, remained invisible."[10] As a corrective, Coser and Anker determined to interrogate Jewish and Italian mothers in an extensive series of in-depth interviews in order to provide the basis for a thorough "theoretical, historical" account of immigrant women's lives.[11]

Coser had come to focus on Jewish women's oral history through her long-standing work on the structural roles of women in the family. Blaming the influence of Freudian psychoanalysis for the post–World War II attack on mothers, including the Jewish mother caricature, Coser abhorred the psychological behaviorist framework according to which "mothers were damned if they did and damned if they didn't."[12] In its place, she substituted a concern for social structure that focused on role complexity, postulating that in modern societies women as well as men operated in multiple groups, with multiple expectations and needs.[13] In narrating their own stories, women emerged as "reflective thinkers who fashioned life strategies in response to the changing social, economic, political and familial circumstances that constrained their actions and choices."[14]

"You gotta be a diplomat. A mother has to be everything," reported a typical mother, then in her eighties, in the Coser survey. A former union organizer, a PTA volunteer, and an unofficial foster parent, this mother still practiced her special form of maternal diplomacy as a volunteer at a Jewish Workmen's Circle home. She described the women she ministered to as mothers who "worked their lifetime[s]. They never had an education, they never had anything nice, like mink coats, but they raised beautiful families."[15]

At home as well as at the workplace, these Jewish immigrant mothers attempted to ensure the welfare and survival of their families. Fully 88 percent of the Jewish women in the survey worked before marriage. The social relationships they forged in the workplace became a significant part of their ethnic identity and helped them extend their networks. These women took back to their homes and families the communal ties and solidarity they discovered on their jobs. About one-third of the Jewish women surveyed continued to work when their children were young, with community support helping to provide child care; 54 percent worked outside the home when their children were grown.[16]

Education for their children was one of the mothers' highest priorities. "In the four years he went to City College," one mother remarked, "I didn't buy myself a dress." When the Jewish mothers were asked which kind of child they preferred—one who did well at school or one who helped at home—they overwhelmingly rated performing well in school much higher than good conduct at home. Another question asked whether a child should miss his exams to attend a grandparent's funeral; almost all mothers responded that the child should remain in school. As one mother put it: "Education is for the future and it gives them a broader outlook on life." "I always said to them, 'learn, learn, learn,' " replied another. With rare exceptions, the women agreed that because daughters' education was equally important as sons', parents should make the same sacrifices for them as for their male offspring. Because she had not had an education, one woman explained, "My ambition in life was to have my daughters educated."

Jewish mothers' championship of education apparently paid off. Of the approximately seventy-five children of the Jewish mothers in the Coser survey for whom information was available, more than two-thirds had completed college, with only one-fifth completing high school or less. The largest group of children had completed postgraduate or professional degrees: several had Ph.D.s and master's degrees, others were doctors, lawyers, dentists, and nurses. Almost all the children had careers that could be characterized as professional, although there were a handful of secretaries and businesspeople (insurance, office manager, controller, advertising). The most common occupation was teacher or professor; one or two were deans, and another few worked in government or were engineers. An astonishing 75 percent of the female children, mostly born in the 1920s or 1930s, had occupations distributed in these areas.

Attitudes toward parenting were reflected in child-rearing styles as well as educational values. Generally, respondents saw themselves as moderate and permissive. Although mothers had been the primary disciplinarians because fathers worked long hours and were rarely at home, in looking back, the mothers emphasized that they aimed to base relationships on mutuality rather than discipline. As one woman put it, "Mothers have to be friends to their children. Not dictators." "The only way you can really hold onto your children is to let them go," suggested another. "Give them as much freedom as possible, as long as they don't abuse it," replied a third. When asked how they had been most helpful to their children, the mothers had a variety of responses: providing "proper morality" and financial assistance; taking care of children and listening to them; supporting their education; acting as role models; and showing them how to "grow up to be good citizens." Mothers prided themselves most when their children considered them "best friends."

The Jewish mothers distinguished between interfering in their children's lives and being asked for advice. They commented on their children's independence, noting that "they do what they want anyway. It would be a different life if children listened to parents." Not only did children have "their own brains," but they also often had "more knowledge" besides. Mothers could give good advice, but it wouldn't necessarily help. "She had to see for herself," one mother remarked. For many mothers, persuasion was a more effective strategy than coercion, listening better than nagging. "Treat them like you want to be treated yourself," said one mother. In the words of another: "Have the patience for your children. . . . Try and listen to them and understand them. What they feel [and] think." One mother thoughtfully summarized this view:

> A mother should realize that her children are independent individuals, and they should realize that they have their moods and their problems which are different from the mother's. . . . And not to put herself on a pedestal—"I'm the mother, you listen to me!" That is not the way to improve a situation, and it's the opposite! And a mother should feel, if she's sincere and unselfish, the children need her affection and her friendship. They need it. A lot of them are starved for a mother's love! . . . Giving love and tolerance . . . makes healthier people of your children. . . . They make mistakes and you are not to harp on it. None of us are angels—we commit mistakes, we make wrong, that's all part of a human being.

There is no way to confirm whether and to what degree survey mothers acted in the tolerant, permissive fashion that these remarks describe. But it is clear that the ideal lay in a more hands-off attitude.

The Coser survey also asked about worrying, another core element of the Jewish mother stereotype. One respondent commented that "mothers always worry," but most believed that they had not had any special concerns about their children. When prompted, they did recall anxieties about children crossing streets, getting into car accidents, returning home late at night—in other words, situations where some elements of unusual harm or danger could be present—but generally they answered that they did not worry much because their children had been responsible and well-behaved. "They were model children," was a typical sentiment. Because they trusted neighbors and the children's peers, mothers did not believe that they had to be especially vigilant on behalf of their children's safety. Such sentiments display confidence in their children and the sense that in their opinion, the children had been "special."

Mothers spoke of strong community bonds and deep networks of friendship and support outside the family. In the Coser team's words, respondents were not at all "homebound." They went to meetings of the PTA, the Yiddish shul parents' group, women's groups, or unions; they were "bustling with activities," both political and cultural. "We went to meetings, Broadway shows, restaurants, and concerts," reported one woman. "Went to shows, weddings, open meetings of the union, *shul* benefits with other people in the neighborhood," recalled another.[17] Even as the women aged, they spoke of continuing involvement in civic life.

When asked about the transmission of Jewish values across the generations, mothers spoke of pride in raising their children as Jews. Others spoke of the satisfaction they felt that their grandchildren were raised Jewishly—attending Hebrew schools, observing holidays. Jewish values deeply affected respondents' sensibilities as they raised their children, whether or not mothers mentioned synagogue affiliations. Most of the organizations in which respondents participated—Hadassah, National Council of Jewish Women, and Women's American ORT—had a strong Jewish and, most frequently, a Zionist component. One woman worked for Hadassah for many years "because I got a Jewish heart. I always feel I have to do something." One member of Pioneer Women explained that she joined the organization "to help people here [and] in Israel"; another member preferred to emphasize the benefits of belonging to a women's Zionist association: "Men didn't have the right to tell us what to do."

Interviewers attempted to elicit how experiences of the Holocaust and anti-Semitism may have affected child-rearing. One mother who lost relatives in the Holocaust explained how the tragedies of World War II influenced the values she taught her children. "I tried to make them realize that the world is small and it can reach anybody and that they should be good people. They should be good Jews. And they should be good to each other and to the whole . . . everybody around them. Not to mistreat anybody." Another responded that the "killing of Jews in World War II" definitely affected the way she raised her children. This mother sent her children to Hebrew school to bring "Jewish life to them" and encourage their Jewish connections. Another took her children every Saturday to the library "to read about Jewish history and culture." But just as importantly, "we lived it." Another mother explained that she sent her son to school and camp for extra Jewish education and "kept talking and discussing with him Judaism, what Judaism stands for," trying "to put a love into him for Jewish life. . . . The way I raised him made him feel that he has to help Jews."

Connecting the world outside to parenting, one mother spoke of how the dark forces of fascism became the "stunning" force that affected her mothering. She recounts that when in 1933 she gave birth to her son,

> I noticed the newspapers mentioned the fact that Hitlerism came into power and what they're doing in Germany. I felt, "My God, what have I brought a child into the world for?" And it was revolting to me. And, that was my answer, getting into, fighting for, Zionism. I am of Jewish extraction and my son is, and I feel that he's entitled to live in a righteous world.

Her son became "a very good human being," an "ardent" member of his temple, deeply involved in the UJA (United Jewish Appeal)—perhaps, his mother speculated, because "he's seen me work in Hadassah and work hard on it."

While narrators revealed that they took pride in their achievements as workers, citizens, community activists, and as Jews, success in parenting loomed especially large as they looked back on their lifetimes in America. Although being a mother was hard—especially the responsibility "to make sure to bring up as good a human being as possible"—the mothers in the survey believed that the rewards were well worth the effort. Overall they expressed deep satisfaction with their child-rearing, remarking on their children's success as family members, in their work and professional lives, and as citizens and community members. "They participate in the community," one respondent acknowledged with pride. "And they teach their children the right way to live . . . and that's all you can want from your children." As Coser explained it, Jewish women's communal activities incorporated a "moral value," "sense of obligation."[18] Mothers spoke specifically of their efforts to transmit values, and husbands also recognized their wives' activities as a major part of family ethics. In the view of Coser and her coauthors, Jewish women's multiple contacts with the outside world provided important "social capital" for their families.[19]

Finally, the survey asked about respondents' ideas about their representation in popular culture: did they know of any novels with a Jewish mother in them? Had they heard any jokes or stories that people tell about Jewish mothers? How did they feel when they heard such jokes? Did they believe those stories were true? In their responses, mothers referred to the specific humor of writers and comics such as Philip Roth, Mel Brooks, or Joey Adams, along with a general body of jokes that poked fun at the manipulative, overzealous Jewish mother. Some thought that every such joke contained some kernel of truth, however exaggerated, while others denied that Jewish mothers were distinctive in *any* aspect of their behaviors. "Every mother feels for her child in the same way," one mother responded, "there is no difference." While many believed that the jokes denigrated Jewish women and felt offended at hearing them, a good number had no adverse reaction. And several saw the humor as testimony of the Jewish mothers' strength and importance. "The mother in the jokes is 'forceful,'" one respondent commented. "We have that forcefulness. We want . . . the best for our children, and we must be forceful to assert ourselves."

Even while denying that Jewish mothers were fundamentally different than other mothers, the narrators expressed great admiration for the Jewish mother's commitment to her children. One mother recalled:

> I used to run home to give the lunch while the others sat and then my boss said to me, "Alice . . . where are you going . . . every day." I says, "Well, I run home every day to give my kids dinner-lunch." He says "your children can't take it themselves?" They could, but all my life I took care of the kids. . . . He says, "Do me one favor. I don't want to see you run home. I want you to take 15 minutes more. . . . When I see you running to the job . . . it makes me sick, Alice. Take 15 minutes extra and then at night you will work the 15 minutes more." To please him I done that. Two stations I used to go every day.

Alice's story recalls that of my colleague whose immigrant mother brought lunch to her sons in Yankee Stadium (and my own habit of packing lunch for my teenage daughter). To Alice, too, making lunch was a critical ingredient in how she defined her mothering; it reflected a positive sense of devotion more than it did unwelcome interference or overprotection. Like Alice, mothers in the survey seemed to find no contradiction in their ardent attention to their children and their belief that they had given their children room to grow. If they were not particularly bothered by the Jewish mother stereotype, it was because they felt confident in their own parenting skills—especially the belief that they had established democratic relationships with their children—and in the kinds of adults their children had become. "A Jewish mother is a good mother," one respondent put it simply.

"A Paradise in My House": *Weaving Women's Words*

The Jewish Women's Archive's (JWA) oral history project, *Weaving Women's Words*, conducted in Baltimore and Seattle some twenty years after the Coser study, turned up similar themes, including pride in parenting, strong community and civic activism, and satisfying workplace experiences.[20] For these women, each of whom was interviewed for two to three hours in her home, affection and respect for their own mothers was deep, and many spoke of inherited maternal legacies. The sixty respondents to the JWA survey, born before 1927, were half or a full generation younger than the women of the Coser survey, and most were the children of immigrants, rather than immigrants themselves. While the majority came from Ashkenazi families primarily of Russian or German descent, about one-third of the Seattle narrators had Sephardic roots in Rhodes or Turkey (Seattle has the second largest Sephardic population in the United States). All but two of the respondents married, and over two-thirds became mothers, with almost all having more than one child.[21]

At the end of long lives, these narrators took the long view of themselves, and the way the world had changed, both for better and worse. While their views of their own mothers were largely positive, they also recognized their mothers' flaws and understood that their mothers had been products of their own times. And while they expressed satisfaction with their children's lives, views about their daughters and granddaughters were tempered with concerns: although narrators appreciated the ways that options for women had improved in the workplace, home, and in the religious realm, they also saw the costs of such changes.

Overall, however, it was not the hardships, either in their parents' generation, their own, or their children's, that stood out. The decidedly affirmative views these women held suggest that whatever challenges they had to cope with, their own self-representations as daughters, mothers, and grandmothers minimized negative environments and accentuated achievements. The preponderance of these views, resembling the attitudes of the Coser narrators, suggests that optimism may well have been a characteristic of these women's Jewish inheritance, determining their actions as parents and citizens as well as their recollections of their past. Seeing their mothers as positive role models, appreciating their legacy of civic engagement and involvement with Jewish tradition, they drew a portrait of Jewish motherhood deeply at variance with the traditional stereotype. While their own memories and attitudes are themselves constructions, they offer a corrective to the vision of Jewish motherhood conveyed in standard accounts.

Many respondents spoke about their mothers' devotion to others, both their families and outsiders, which often manifested in creating important Jewish institutions in the community. One woman from Seattle recalled her grandmother as

> the true matriarch of the Sephardic community. She quickly organized a few men and they found a little tiny place to have services. . . . [She] was president of the Ezra Bessaroth Women for ten years. She organized the Red Cross. . . . She used to go door to door collecting money for the poor. Nobody would ever say no to her. She was wonderful with herbs. She was a healer. Everybody used to come to our house, it was like a hospital.

This respondent's mother had been a role model for her daughter, teaching her to sew and to make bags for "Neighbors in Need." One day, when the respondent was seven months pregnant and chairing the Jewish Federation campaign, she went into a home in a poor section of Seattle on behalf of the campaign. Although the homeowner, Mrs. Barlia, was poor, she greeted the visitor with the words "*Sus bendicha hija de bendicha madre* ('You're a blessed daughter of a blessed mother'). . . . And she gave me twenty-five cents. Now that twenty-five cents from Mrs. Barlia was like twenty-five dollars from somebody else."[22] As is the case with this narrator, devotion to volunteering was often attributed to maternal influences.

A Baltimore narrator, the daughter and wife of Orthodox rabbis, told an anecdote about her mother's strong values and insistence on standing up for them as a spur to her own religious activism:

> My mother was very principled. I remember a rabbi who always carried a little doctor's suitcase. It was his chicken! He only ate his own food. Once, my mother served everybody on china dishes. But for him—plain melmac. And he said, "How come everybody gets the beautiful china and to me you give this?" So she said, "Rabbi, if you can't trust my *kashrus*, I can't give you my dishes."

In addition to her role as *rebbetzin* (rabbi's wife) and mother of six children, this narrator worked as a Hebrew teacher, coordinated volunteer services at the Jewish Convalescent Home, and founded Bikur Cholim, a network of volunteers who care for Jews who are ill and their families. She also created an outreach program to help Jewish victims of domestic violence. In Europe, her father told her, "the windows were over a courtyard, and you could hear the slaps and screams and the dishes breaking." Her father closed the shutters to keep out the terrifying noises; she took a different path. "My work with domestic violence has been about opening the windows," the narrator reported.[23]

Bequeathed with a legacy of charity, honesty, and service to the community, the Jewish women in the survey were often heirs to a strong tradition of women participating in family businesses. A Baltimore narrator spoke of her immigrant mother who, upon arriving in the United States, worked in the tie factory of her father's *landsman* (fellow countryman). After she married, she worked with her husband in a little confectioner's store, then went into the used furniture business with him; later they bought and sold real estate. In each business, the father did the "outside" work while the mother "ran the inside." A hard worker, the narrator's mother carried rugs on her shoulder in the furniture store and nursed all her four children there, usually working around the clock. Another example of female business sense was seen in the narrator's grandmother, who started the first *mikveh* (ritual bath) in Baltimore, using profits from the business to buy real estate. The narrator herself followed her grandmother and mother's example and became a chief buyer for the family's clothing business.[24]

Other mothers in the survey entered the workforce in professional fields. One Seattle narrator, born in 1922, became one of the state's first women pharmacists: her mother, "proud of working," had encouraged her into the trade. "She always said to me that you should be able to support yourself and your kids, and she thought everybody looked great in those white uniforms. She thought it would give us a little bit of credibility."[25] Many held professional and managerial positions at a time when it was uncommon for women to do so. Doctors, lawyers, legislators, judges, teachers, social workers, therapists, writers, government employees, artists, dancers, businesswomen, and more, they substantially contributed to family incomes. Many experienced discrimination on the basis of their gender, both in education and work opportunities—but they usually persevered and found ways to pursue their interests.

Growing up during the first decades of the twentieth century into the Depression years, most of the women were raised in families that upheld traditional cultural norms. Nearly all remembered their mothers—even those who worked for pay—spending most of their time taking care of the house and the children. Mothers were commonly described as "the soul of the household," "a queen in her house." The most frequent adjective interviewees used to describe their mothers was "kind." Some spoke of their mothers as teachers, instructing them about "the value of education, kindness, and compassion." Others spoke of their competence—"manager of everything that was to be done in the home."[26]

Louise Azoze, a Sephardic Jew who was ninety-seven years old at the time of her interview, had emigrated from Turkey to Seattle, where she married and had five children, a daughter and four sons (one became a rabbi, another a cantor). She spoke fondly of both parents, "the best in the world." Louise felt herself doing the "same like my mother," never working, taking care of the children, which she never considered work, since they were "very, very good."[27] "I had a paradise in my house," she recalled. Though she never worked for pay, Louise was typical of this group of mothers in her volunteer work for her Orthodox synagogue, where she displayed her skills cooking Sephardic specialties.

While narrators had great respect for their mothers, they also could experience them as conservative forces—upholding standards of respectability, warning them not to become so educated and professionally focused that they wouldn't be able to find husbands. Others felt their rules were too rigid. One Baltimore narrator eloped to avoid her mother's displeasure at her marrying at a young age but later agreed to the full-scale wedding her mother wanted. "I think a lot of things that my mother did were wrong," one Seattle narrator acknowledged, "but she didn't do anything out of malice, just the best that she knew." Each generation thinks "they're going to be a better mother," the narrator noted. "I know my daughter thinks that she's a better mother than I was. You just make 'different mistakes.'" On the whole, these women's devotion to their homes and children mirrored that of their mothers. Even among the women who worked outside the home, children were their first priority. "Their

Louise Azoze was one of sixty elderly Jewish women who told their stories of being Jewish women and mothers in an oral history project conducted by the Jewish Women's Archive in 2001. Although nearly one hundred years old when this picture was taken, she continued to pass on her Sephardic Jewish culture to her children and grandchildren through traditional recipes and folksongs. (Joan Roth)

wish was my command," said one Seattle woman of her devotion to her children. When her husband went on vacation, she "stayed home with the kids so he would know that they were properly taken care of." Another, a professional musician, spoke of her children as the "primary object" and "focal point" of her life; she, too, always stayed home when they were at home.[28]

While most women felt that their child-rearing had been fulfilling and experienced no conflicts about their roles as mothers, others noted the sacrifices they had made for their children. Yet although they spoke of educational or professional goals that had to be put on hold while their children were young, most seemed to have taken this delay in stride.

Nearly all the women interviewed expressed excitement about changes in women's roles from their generation to their daughters' and granddaughters.' Some were wistful about the different paths they might have taken in terms of careers if more choices had been open to them; a number did take degrees later in life and started on second careers or moved from volunteer to professional positions, after their children were grown. At the same time, they were also able to look at the changes feminism had wrought with a mature eye, seeing the complications wrought by changing gender roles. Some interviewees worried about the effect on young children of women working outside the home and trying to juggle careers with child-rearing. Others worried about the stress that balancing work and career placed on the mothers. One woman was glad that women "have a chance to be equal to men" and felt that women's new roles are "so exciting" but worried that "they're not doing justice to their families." And although many felt that women with young children should stay at home with them if at all possible, others advised them to hang in there. As one Baltimore mother put it, herself a highly successful working mother: "The women one respects are always going to be the best nurturers and the best lovers and the best at whatever they do . . . that is going to make for stress. I hope it doesn't mean that they are going to give up any of those roles."[29]

Finally, many of the women spoke about the importance of Jewish tradition. Several described gathering their families on Friday nights and expressed pleasure that their daughters were carrying on the tradition of family Shabbat dinners. *"Hijicas mias, canta"* (My daughters, sing) was a fond refrain around her family table, Louise Azoze recalled. This was the "work of love" designed for family togetherness over the generations, and they undertook it with devotion.[30]

The images of Jewish mothers painted in the *Weaving Women's Words* interviews are not without shadows, but the rosy hue that characterizes them overall suggests a celebratory attitude toward the past and optimism about the future that overrode memories of hardship or contemporary difficulties. Extending from their mothers' and grandmothers' generations to the lives of their daughters, they voiced respect, concern, and admiration for Jewish mothers.

"The Antithesis of What the Caricature of a Jewish Mother Is Supposed to Be": The BUNWC Survey

Women who attended my lectures to the Florida Region of the Brandeis University National Women's Committee in 2003 were asked to complete a questionnaire about Jewish mothers that probed memories of their mothers, perceptions of their own experiences as mothers (if they had children), and those of their children as parents, as well as views about images of Jewish mothers. With an average age of seventy-six, like the *Weaving Women's Words'* respondents, the group was approximately one generation younger than the Coser women. Attracted to a professor's lectures, this accidental sample of one hundred was not a cross section of the general population of elderly Jewish women. Generally, they had a high degree of education and work experience. Over half had attended college, and three-quarters had worked in a managerial or professional capacity at some point in their lives; most were from the northeast or central United States and had retired to Florida.[31] Nonetheless, their views are remarkably consistent with those of the previous oral history respondents.

When asked to recall their mothers in several types of questions, more than two-thirds of the women remembered mothers with great fondness, bringing to mind the following responses:

> "A warm, wonderful person who everyone loved"; "a small dynamo!"; "A beautiful woman"; "Good sense of humor"; "hardworking, social"; "Soft-spoken"; "Protective of me and two sisters"; "thoughtful"; "Vibrant"; "Always being there for me"; "How understanding she was"; "She never pushed advice"; "kind to all, home open to all, charitable. Generous with her time and always there for her three daughters"; "Dignified, encouraging, inspiring, a perfect role model"; "I adored her! And the feeling was mutual!"

Responses to the question, "What were some of the typical things your mother said to you?" exemplify these positive recollections. The most popular categories of response were manners and morals ("be good . . . be honest"; "don't swear to anyone but yourself"; "be careful"; "be kind"; "don't sit on the bed—beds are for sleeping") and advice to build self-esteem:

> "Be and do the best that you can"; "You are strong and can accomplish whatever you set your mind to"; "Have confidence in your self"; "Always reach high"; "Be true to yourself"; "Be independent. Try different things"; "Follow your dreams."; "Follow your heart"; "Be individuals." "Following the crowd leads nowhere"; "Develop to your own potential."

Education was the next largest advice category: "Education is the most important thing." "Study. Practice." "Always do your homework." "Finish college before you get married." Many similar remarks highlight the fact that through their strong support of education, as well as in their advice to daughters to "fly to the moon" and develop their own potential, mothers were remembered as consistently nurturing their daughters' aspirations.

Respondents also recalled mothers' advice about social relationships: friendship was highly valued, and marriage was a frequent topic for motherly concern. Daughters were told that their husbands should be first in their lives, but also that "men are like streetcars—miss one another will come along." They were warned to avoid premarital sex: "sex is great . . . and worth waiting for!" Another mother's remark, noteworthy for its breaching a taboo subject, as well as its negative view of sex, was that her daughter should take petroleum jelly on her honeymoon, because "it hurts."

Mothers offered a wealth of practical wisdom about health, hygiene, and deportment. Daughters were told to eat well, take care of their health, exercise, and stand straight. Several received advice to "always make sure you wear clean underwear" (added one mother, "You may be in an accident"). Other advice concerned fashion and style: "Be sure your shoes and bag match"; "never leave the house without your earrings." Finally, mothers gave frequent advice about serving the community and being charitable. They instructed daughters to be proud of their Jewish identity and to help Jews in need, but also told their daughters that charity should extend to the "general" community. "Everyone is equal," one respondent recalled her mother's words. "There is good and bad in all religions and all people."

Whatever the specific area of concern, the most common response indicated that these Jewish mothers had attempted to pass on to their daughters their own sense of the most important rules for life. Concern for morals and values, the centrality of family, and the importance of personal growth and achievement loomed large in the mothers' eyes, and more than a half century later, in the daughters' recollections. While only a minority of mothers spoke specifically of "Jewish" values, their concerns about ethical behavior, charity and community, and individual and family development might well be considered to reflect Jewish teachings.

When asked to describe their own parenting, respondents again offered extremely favorable recollections: more than 80 percent used positive adjectives (for example, affectionate; loving; caring; flexible; forceful; involved; supportive) while less than a fifth used negative ones (about 5 percent considered themselves to have been "nagging," "overprotective," or "possessive"). Representative comments came from a mother who remembered herself as "supportive and involved to this day," and another, who viewed herself as "always there to help, advise or just talk." Although comments most often suggested a moderate child-rearing style—for example, "give them freedom of choice"; "expect children to pursue their lives and not be a *rubber stamp* of their parent"— some mothers acknowledged that a hands-off approach did not always work.

"I do try to let them lead their own lives in their own way," a mother wrote, "but I will 'nag' if they do not keep in touch with each other enough or write 'thank you notes' to certain people. I was raised to be 'proper' and I occasionally have to remind my son." "Give your children advice *once* and don't push it on them," another commented. "Let them learn from their mistakes. *Listen* to them; you may learn something!" A few mothers admitted that children may have seen their child-rearing in different ways than they intended. "My daughter claims I was possessive," wrote one woman. "Probably so." Another remembered herself as "respectful—when I'm at my best." A little less than a third of the mothers used both negative as well as positive adjectives in recalling their own mothering. But twice as many respondents referred to their child-rearing in only positive ways.

Respondents generally reported their child-rearing practices to be similar to those of their own mothers, although there were some differences: they emphasized the importance of discussing feelings more than their mothers, allowing children to get angry when necessary; they talked more to their children than their mothers did; and they were less likely to use guilt than their mothers. Beyond these differences, there were wide areas of agreement between the child-rearing styles of these mothers and their own mothers. Both generations did not consider themselves to be passive figures in their children's lives; rather, they were actively engaged with their children and usually proud of their involvement. Indeed, only a small fraction of total respondents described themselves as not being involved—most considered themselves highly interested in their children's lives and supportive. But whether positive or negative, these mothers characterized themselves as concerned with their offspring; a report of distance between the generations was so rare as to be unheard of.

In response to a question that asked respondents what made them most proud of their own children as parents, the mothers reported the kinds of achievements consonant with the goals they had hoped to instill in their children. High on the list were morals and values (including charitable endeavors and being part of the community), devotion to family, and educational and professional success. Mothers reported that they gave their children advice on how to be self-reliant, good and decent, and supportive of their own families, as their own mothers had endeavored to teach them; now as they looked at their children's achievements, they pronounced themselves satisfied. The continuity between their mothers' values and goals, their own, and their children's is noteworthy.

Finally, in their comments to a question about images of Jewish mothers, there was little consensus. Jewish mothers were defined in various ways, although two-thirds preferred to offer a positive definition of their own. They often noted the disparity between media images of the Jewish mother and experiences of their mothers and themselves as parents, as in the respondent who recalled her mother as "gentle and loving"—"the antithesis of what the caricature of a Jewish mother is supposed to be." Others responded: "It is most unfortunate that the pushy, possessive and generally negative images prevailed. I thought of my own mother and tried to be a mother that reflected positive images." "I think Jewish women have negative images thanks to the Jewish comedians. For the most part, I do not believe the modern young Jewish woman reflects so many of the negative stereotypes." "The image of the traditional Jewish mother is possessive, nagging, forceful and is in general, a pejorative type, which does rarely apply today. I think it is a stereotype. I have been very loving and attentive to my daughters and have instilled a love of learning and achievement."

These women largely saw their mothers and themselves as the "antithesis" to the Jewish mother stereotype. The mother-daughter relationship they enunciated in their role both as daughters and as mothers was one that was based on connection rather than on anger or separation, and they indicated their belief, or at least the hope, that their own mothering may have been received by their offspring in similarly appreciative ways.

Even allowing for the distortions of time, these respondents' memories of their mothers, like those in the Coser and JWA surveys, may be no more suspect than the writers of memoirs who offer their recollections as truth. It is unlikely that most respondents' memories, even if tinged with nostalgia, would reflect views greatly at variance with their own past histories. That the preponderance of respondents saw their mothers as loving and supportive is significant, for it puts in perspective the mother-blaming so endemic in American popular culture, especially where the Jewish mother is concerned. The interpretation of respondents' own mothering—with its even more rosy valance—may reflect aspiration more than memory, but despite the lack of corroboration from respondents' children, these personal testimonies provide noteworthy evidence about the subjective experience of Jewish mothers, as told by mothers themselves. When asked to construct their own ideas of mothering, the story they narrate is a prideful one. Cognitively, affectively, emotionally, motivationally, and attitudinally, the women believed that they had successfully shown their children the way to the future.[32]

MOTHER: Hello, Amila. I don't know if you heard the latest on the portable stereos, but they're saying that the foam earpiece on the headphones is a prime breeding ground for bacteria. So if you still insist on walking around with the headphones on, you may wanna take an antibiotic. OK, hon? Talk to you soon. Bye.

MOTHER: Hi, Amila. It's me, honey. If you haven't already left to go to the motor vehicle bureau, keep in mind that the wait is very long. So before you get in line, you may wanna empty your bladder. All right, honey, that's all for now. Bye-bye.

MOTHER: (singing) . . . How old are you now? How old are you now? Better hurry and find a husband before your ovaries shut down. All right, that's just a little creativity for my birthday girl. I love you, sweetie.

—Amy Borkowsky, *Amy's Answering Machine: Messages from Mom*

10

WE ARE ALL JEWISH MOTHERS

Mothering in the New Millennium

IN 1969, WITH THE SCANDALOUS *PORTNOY'S COMPLAINT* RIDING HIGH on the best-seller lists, Philip Roth's mother received a telephone call from a *New York Times* reporter, asking her, in Roth's words, "the needling question": was she like the "Jewish mother" portrayed by her son? Too respectful to refuse to answer, Mrs. Roth placed the book in the only context that made sense for her. "All mothers are Jewish mothers," she replied.[1] Given Sophie Portnoy's negative resonance, the remark may have antagonized Gentile mothers all over the country, or so Roth thought. But his mother's words embodied more than a grain of truth: even if Roth had identified Sophie Portnoy as part of a particular Jewish cohort, the character writ large the universal type of the overinvolved, dominating, intrusive mother.

In the decades since the novel's publication, Mrs. Roth's comment has shown itself to be unwittingly prescient. Ironically, transformations in the roles of American mothers have affected a growing convergence between images of "bad" Jewish mothers and contemporary, well-intentioned, but equally overprotective, "good" American mothers. In addition to the dramatic shifts in behavioral patterns that have promoted new parenting ideals, a demographic revolution in dating, marriage, childbearing, and child-rearing has fostered a significant reorientation of modern family life. Jewish families have been altered as well. Because of current trends regarding single- and dual-career parenting, interracial and interfaith marriage, conversion, and cross-cultural adoptions, the traditional, monolithic Jewish mother "type" has been replaced by a much more diverse, pluralistic, and universal model.

It might be expected that these new social realities would challenge and displace the old stereotypes. However, despite compelling new depictions of Jewish mothers, including a flattering portrayal from Philip Roth himself, the caricature lives on, most notably rendered in the 2000s by hip Jewish female comedians. Yet in the cultural climate of postfeminism, the significance of Jewish mother humor has been irrevocably altered. The jokes and the stereotypes remain, but with new and complex social relationships behind them, they suggest a very different understanding and appreciation of the caricature. In the new contexts in which it has been expressed, the Jewish mother joke represents a "cultural seismograph" of our changing times.[2]

You Don't Have to Be Jewish to Be a "Helicopter" Mother

The mothering role has undergone a drastic revolution in the last quarter of a century. For the first time in history, more mothers of infants and young children participate in the full-time labor force than stay at home. And Jewish women are no different: very high numbers of Jewish women have trained for careers in the professions and business and are combining work with family responsibilities. The growing numbers of women in the Reform and Conservative rabbinates, including a large proportion of wives and mothers, is one example of the strides Jewish women have made in entering high-status professions that were closed to them until the last few decades. Although female rabbis often confront gender discrimination at work and face daunting struggles to balance career and family, the new image of *"ima on the bima"* (mother on the pulpit)—the title of a children's book about a rabbi mother—encapsulates the fact that the next generation is growing up with very different images of Jewish mothers than previous ones had.[3]

Female rabbis themselves have provided more positive images of Jewish mothers than have been common in previous generations. For example, a recent Mother's Day sermon by Rabbi Judy Chessin in Ohio gleefully discussed the new scientific discovery that some 3.5 million, or 40 percent, of Ashkenazi Jews are descended from just four "founding mothers" who lived in Europe one thousand years ago; the mothers were part of a small group who founded the European Ashkenazi Jewish community as a result of migration from the Near East. "While it takes no women to screw in a light bulb," Rabbi Chessin proclaimed, "it *is* possible that our four matriarchs populated our Jewish nation."[4] For more than the thirty years that they have been ordained, women rabbis have used the matriarchs and their descendants, like these four genetic ancestors, to provide examples of women's contributions to Judaism and the wider world.

Accompanying the social transformation of women's roles in the workplace and community has been the growth of a new ideology of motherhood which posits that good mothers must pay ever more devoted, critical attention

IMA ON THE BIMA

MY MOMMY IS A RABBI

Written by
MINDY AVRA PORTNOY
Illustrated by
STEFFI KAREN RUBIN

Ima on the Bima (mother on the pulpit), the title of a 1986 children's book, suggests the many new roles that Jewish mothers play in contemporary life. In their sermons, women rabbis draw on positive images of the Biblical matriarchs and other historical Jewish mothers. (Steffi Karen Rubin)

to the tasks of child-rearing. With middle-class families becoming more affluent and educated, the benefits of privileged child-rearing that once accrued mainly to the wealthy and those deeply motivated to sacrifice their own comforts for their children's success have become more widespread. The result is that an increasing number of mothers feel compelled to offer the best resources, and much of their time and effort, to raise achieving children. These determined mothers are said to "hover" over their children at all stages of their development, managing class schedules, extracurricular activities, laundry, e-mail, even job interviews. Their children, called "echo-boomers" to distinguish them from their "baby boomer parents," have become the most watched-over generation in history.[5]

Variously known as "intensive mothering," "helicopter," or "hovering" mothering, or simply "the new momism," the developing ideology that promotes such parental overwatchfulness is spawning a new generation of guilt-ridden mothers concerned that their failure to become perfect parents will stunt the social and emotional growth of their youngsters.[6] Unrealistic motherhood goals, coupled with increasing pressures on children to achieve, have made both parenting and childhood the subject of growing anxiety.[7] Consumed with protecting her children, "inflating their egos," "massaging them, fighting their battles for them," any mother who follows these dictates finds herself deeply embedded in every aspect of her children's lives. Describing "how we all became Jewish mothers," historian Steven Mintz in fact declares that today's incessantly agonizing parents are exactly like the storied Jewish mothers of comic lore.[8]

Have the pressures of contemporary child-rearing really turned modern parents into stereotypical "Jewish mothers"? In the sense that today's parents are deeply, and perhaps inappropriately, involved in all manner of their children's daily lives, even those of adolescents and older children, the anxious modern middle-class parent may be said to resemble caricatures—if not the real-life Jewish mothers—of the past. Self-sacrificing, overprotective, deeply identified with her child's success, and tending to focus on the child's vulnerabilities, this mother has been convinced—or manipulated, in the views of such critics as Susan Douglas and Meredith Michaels—to put her own needs aside and find full satisfaction in the mothering role, "24/7." One difference between the Jewish mother icon and the representation of the contemporary helicopter mother is that the latter is less likely to stoke the flames of guilt in her children than to feel the heat herself for neglectful (that is, less than 24/7) parenting. Like Jewish mothers in the past, they are being blamed for being too overprotective, but on the other hand, not being concerned is seen as equally detrimental. Today's mothers, too, are caught in an oppressive double bind.

Though the new "mommy myth" of perfect parenting touches mothers of many different ethnic and religious groups, one notable response has come from psychologist Wendy Mogel, a formerly secular Jew who turned to Jewish religion to find help for her patients. Confronted with overprogrammed children and anguished parents who were used to taking their children's "emotional, social and academic temperature every four or five seconds," Mogel found that the standard repertoire of psychological interventions produced little change.[9] She began to study Judaism, in part because many of her clients, in fact, were overwrought Jewish mothers, and discovered that traditional Jewish texts could provide an antidote to the problem of too-perfect parenting. Bridging Jewish philosophy and psychology, she developed a series of parenting classes and wrote *Blessings of a Skinned Knee: Using Jewish Teachings to Raise Self-Reliant Children*; it has now gone through more than a dozen printings and is in wide circulation today. "If you have children of a certain age," a reporter commented in 2006, "chances are that someone you know will own a copy or have lent one away."[10]

Mogel's guide uses lessons from the Torah and Talmud to help parents "escape the danger of overvaluing children's need for self-expression so that their kids don't become 'little attorneys,' accept that their children are both ordinary and unique, and treasure the power and holiness of the present moment." Believing that the three cornerstone principles of Jewish living—"moderation, celebration, and sanctification"—can help people achieve a "balanced life, no matter what culture we happen to inhabit," she urges parents to incorporate them in their daily life, emphasizing "deed over creed."[11]

Although the guide is based on strictly Jewish teachings, Mogel has attracted a devoted general readership and has become a sought-after lecturer among nondenominational as well as Christian and Jewish groups; the book itself is used as the basis for discussion groups in churches and schools.[12] The success of her Jewish parenting philosophy among this broad population confirms that the dilemmas of overanxious parenting are relevant not only to the Jewish mothers Mogel sees in her practice, but also to parents of all backgrounds.

Mogel's attempt to bring mothers back into a more grounded approach to parenting through traditional Jewish texts is one of several recent efforts to remind mothers that parental responsibility is, in fact, finite and that perhaps the best parents can do is help maximize strengths and provide a forgiving environment for limitations.

"Yiddishe mamas" of the immigrant generation and their postwar successors also confronted this underlying psychological truth. But metaphorically, many did, in fact, "go to school" with their children even if they did not physically attend classes. Encouraging them, demanding that their kids do their best, they straddled the boundaries of concern and overinvolvement; they did not feel guilty as much as they felt the desire to allow their children a better future.

As contemporary "intensive" mothers search for models to guide their efforts, the confidence, energy, and assertiveness that "real" Jewish mothers exhibited may prove instructive. If truly "we are all Jewish mothers today," we might learn from the lessons of this early generation's contributions to their children's well-being and achievements.

The New Face of Jewish Mothers

At the opening of the new millennium, some 3.6 million American adults had a Jewish mother; for almost a quarter of these, their mother was their only Jewish parent. Although slightly fewer had a father as their only Jewish parent, twice as many offspring with a mother as their sole Jewish parent identified Jewishly than the reverse.[13] As many studies have confirmed, even beyond the principle of matrilineal descent (whereby the mother's ancestry determines a child's Jewishness), having a Jewish mother correlated most positively with the child's personal identification as Jewish.[14]

In the new millennium, there will be even more varied kinds of Jewish mothers than in the past. In addition to new work patterns and the new ideology of intensive mothering, a major shift in the demography of Jewish family life due to intermarriage, conversion, adoption, and single-parenting is changing the face of Jewish parenting. Given the probability that a shared ethnic heritage will become less likely in the future, modes of "looking" and "acting" Jewish will also diversify. Although it is unlikely that the passing on of Jewish identity to children will shift in dramatic ways, the new Jewish mothers face different challenges than those of prior generations.

According to one recent estimate, at least 20 percent of the Jewish population is racially and ethnically diverse, including African American, Asian, Latino, mixed-race, and Sephardic Jews. This number includes Jews who are converts; those adopted into Jewish families and raised as Jews; multiracial children born to Ashkenazi Jews and people of color; individuals who descended from Jews of color; and Jews of Sephardic and Mizrahi heritage.[15] Examples of the new faces of modern Jewry are everywhere. There is Patricia Lin (Chava Esther bat Avraham), a Chinese American Jew raised by Taiwanese emigrants in Wayland, a suburb of Boston, where she had many Jewish friends and teachers. Lin converted to Judaism, joined a Reform synagogue in San Francisco, and serves as surrogate big sister to two adopted Asian American Jewish girls with Ashkenazi parents; she is completing an in-depth study of the rapidly growing Asian American Jewish population in the United States.[16] Angela Warnick Buchdahl, daughter of an Ashkenazi Reform Jewish father and Korean Buddhist mother, grew up in Tacoma, Washington; a member of the Multiracial Jewish Network, she is a Reform rabbi and cantor in Scarsdale, New York.[17] Alysa Stanton, an African American woman raised in a Pentecostal household in Cleveland, Ohio, is a convert to Judaism who has been ordained as a rabbi. She considers herself and her daughter "both Jewish and black."[18]

And there is Jamaica Kincaid, the Caribbean-born author who converted to Judaism after marrying a secular Jew and becoming the mother of two children. Now divorced, Kincaid served as president of the synagogue in her small Vermont town, where she is the only black congregant. Having written vividly about motherhood from the point of view of a rebellious Caribbean daughter, in her own life today she considers herself "deeply proud" to be a Jewish mother.[19]

In a recent book about the experience of being a white feminist mother of two black sons, Jane Lazarre discloses the difficulties her own family had in reconciling the dual identities of black and Jewish. Although she and her husband raised their sons in a biracial household that celebrated both their Jewish and African American backgrounds, Lazarre watched the boys move further away from a sense of Jewish identity as they grew into young adults and experienced the blunt force of racism. Lazarre learned to "see the world more truthfully." While she has given up the ideal of a biracial identity as too simplistic, Lazarre's reexamination of child-rearing in a multiracial context gave her Jewish mothering "renewed life" and passion.[20]

Children's perspectives on growing up in interracial families have deepened the understanding of the changing dimensions of Jewish motherhood. In *Black, Jewish and Interracial*, Katya Gibel Azoulay, the daughter of a Jewish mother and black father, interviewed adult children with similar black-Jewish backgrounds. The interracial identities they describe led Azoulay to fasten on the complexity of black-Jewish heritage and to acknowledge that in these families "Jewish," "white," and "black" often come together in ways that simultaneously respect "unity" and "plurality": for children growing up in such families, the process of identity-formation can be "open ended, plural, malleable" while nonetheless offering "stability and continuity."[21] James McBride's 1997 best-selling memoir, *The Color of Water*, personalizes the amalgam of traits in families with black and Jewish roots. McBride pays warm tribute to his eccentric, dynamic mother, a rabbi's daughter who fled her rigid Orthodox family to marry an African American with whom she started a Baptist Church. Although McBride's mother kept her Jewish background hidden, in uncovering her past McBride paints a portrait of a mother whose Jewish values, especially her willingness to make sacrifices for her children, reigned supreme. Despite growing up in poverty, all twelve of the family's children went to college and achieved remarkable professional success. "It was in her sense of education, more than any other, that Mommy conveyed her Jewishness to us," McBride thought.[22]

Intermarriage has also rewritten the rules for Jewish mothering. While many community leaders bemoan the high rate of intermarriage, now more than 50 percent, and the fact that overall only one-third of the children from mixed marriages are raised as Jews, researchers have begun to discern that child-rearing outcomes change dramatically when the gender of the intermarried parent is taken into account. In fact, says Keren McGinity, who has interviewed Boston-area intermarried Jewish women, when compared to intermarried Jewish fathers, Jewish mothers in mixed marriages are overwhelmingly likely to raise their children as Jews and to create a proud and personally meaningful Jewish identity for themselves.[23]

For these women, the convergence of feminism and motherhood made it likely that they became more observant and more involved in their Jewish communities after they married out. Jewish women's identification with Judaism "sometimes lay as if dormant during the dating and engagement period," says McGinity; it was a "Sleeping Beauty awakened by the kiss of a Gentile husband," and enhanced by concerns for offspring. In some cases, the "December

Dilemma"—whether or not to have a Christmas tree—became the lightning rod that set off the mother's determination to "come out" Jewishly.[24] But if intermarriage led to deeper Jewish identity, it could also define women in unenviable ways; "anti-intermarriagism" became a bias within the Jewish community especially harmful to women. McGinity's respondents spoke of a "triple marginality"—as Jews in a Christian world; women in male society; and as Jewish women married to Gentile men. Many resented being labeled "intermarried," an identity they felt was imposed upon them and was not the way they saw themselves. They and their children were fully Jewish, they believed, not "half and half."[25]

McGinity's research suggests that contemporary Jewish mothers in mixed marriages have found a way to redefine the meaning of Jewish motherhood. They have created what McGinity calls a "Jewish-feminist modus-vivendi," in which they are the "gatekeepers and the door-openers to Jewish life for their families." From within their intermarriages, they may be responsible for a "renaissance of Jewish religious and cultural identity formation and practice."[26] This achievement, if it comes, will carry with it a necessary condition: like other new Jewish mothers of this millennium, these mothers insist that narrow cultural definitions must not limit their own or their families' self-definitions. They will raise their children assertively, refusing to be stereotyped in the process, creatively passing on Jewish and maternal legacies.

Adoption practices have also diversified traditional modes of Jewish parenting. Because of the dearth of Jewish children available for adoption, the relatively late marriage age of Jewish women and concomitant problems of fertility, and a growing interest among gay and lesbian Jews in adoption, Jews are disproportionately represented as adoptive parents relative to their percentage of the population; approximately 5 percent of Jewish households currently report an adopted child at home. One-quarter of these children are estimated to come from overseas.[27]

Parents who have adopted children overseas may have had reason to contact Jane Aronson of New York, known as the "Orphan Doctor." One of about a dozen American physicians working in the field of international adoption medicine, Aronson has visited orphanages in Russia, Bulgaria, Romania, China, Vietnam, and Latin America and evaluated thousands of children adopted from abroad in her pediatric practice. She and her partner, Diana Lee, are the parents of two children, Benjamin, adopted from Vietnam, and Desi, adopted from Ethiopia.[28]

Aronson believes that it is particularly important for the Jewish community to welcome children born overseas and to learn from them new ways of becoming Jewish parents. She takes her Judaism seriously—at one point she even considered becoming a rabbi—and her concept of being a Jewish mother is a positive one. Yet although she grew up with several different kinds of Jewish mother models, it was not until she became a mother that she fully understood the meaning of good parenting.[29] Raising her children as a lesbian mother in a multiracial community, she acknowledges that her own generation of Jewish mothers, many of whom like herself have confronted the problem of difference openly and positively, will nonetheless have to learn how to deal with problems that have faced every successive generation of Jewish mothers: what is best for their children, how to nurture and protect them, and how to separate from them as well.

The new face of Jewish motherhood is also that of single mothers who have decided to have biological children, or to adopt children, outside of marriage or other partnerships. The late playwright Wendy Wasserstein, who gave birth to her daughter Lucy in 1999 when she was forty-nine, was one of the most celebrated of these new Jewish mothers. Having succeeded in the work world, her female characters acknowledge gaps in their personal lives; quite often, they dramatize the pressure Wasserstein felt in her own life to "get married, get married, get married."[30]

Wasserstein proclaimed about her own parenting that "I'm a Jewish mother, but I'm not Molly Goldberg."[31] Nor did she see herself following the model of her mother, Lola, who encouraged Wasserstein's dramatic talent through her own interest in theater and dance but continually carped about her daughter's unmarried status. Giving birth as an unmarried mother, Wasserstein believed that she finally became a "walking shandeh" (shame, or embarrassment).[32] Yet as a mother, she drew closer to her mother. "For all the nagging, you look at your mother as someone very precious," Wasserstein commented, although she acknowledged that the difference in their values remained. "Lucy and I were looking at the Hope Diamond in Washington, D.C.," Wasserstein recalled. And she found herself speaking in her mother's voice: "Darling, when you grow up you meet somebody nice to get you something like that." But she immediately recovered, expressing the new mother's point of view: "Or, you can buy it for yourself."[33]

In some cases, new kinds of Jewish mothers have even crossed the gender divide. Transgendered performance artist Kate Bornstein talks of her mother Mildred's reaction to Kate's gender change, and her request that she call her by her new first name. "Kate!" scoffed her mother at first, "Only when you call me Mrs. Bornstein." But the very next day there was her mother on the phone, "Kate?" she inquired. "It's your mother." In a moving column in the *New York Times Sunday Magazine* Bornstein described her conversation with her mother shortly before the latter's death. "Who are you?" asked Mildred (heavily drugged). "I told her the truth. I was her baby. I always would be. . . . I was her little boy, and the daughter she never had. I told her I loved her. 'Ha!' she'd exclaimed . . . 'That's good. I didn't want to lose any of you, ever.'" Herself a parent, Kate identifies with the loving qualities of her Jewish mother and marvels at the story she has to tell: that of "a nice Jewish boy who grew up to be a Jewish mother."[34]

The growing diversity of contemporary Jewish motherhood and the convergence of traditionally involved Jewish parenting with parenting patterns of modern America have created a profile of the new Jewish mother quite different than that of her fabled predecessor. The new trends are changing how the Jewish mother is represented in our culture—gay Jewish mothers, Jewish mothers of gay daughters and sons, single Jewish mothers, Jewish mothers in mixed marriages, Jewish mothers by choice, Jewish mothers of color, and working and professional Jewish mothers have already made their appearance in popular culture. One example is provided by Esther Paik Goodhart, a Korean-Jewish mother who converted to Judaism eighteen years ago. A Hebrew teacher and the mother of two teenage sons, Goodhart is also a comedian who treasures her membership in the Friars Club. Korean mothers and Jewish mothers are very similar, she quips. "They both say, I will give you the best pieces of meat; oh, don't worry, no shoes for me, I don't need shoes, so long as we can have money for you to learn; or no . . . no . . . eat this one full piece of bread. I am not hungry."[35] While the Jewish mother is still fodder for comedians' antics, underneath the stereotype, more varied renderings have emerged.

Contemporary Artists Re-vision the Jewish Mother

KISSING JESSICA STEIN

Several of the new portrayals in film, fiction, and on the stage depict sympathetic Jewish mothers of daughters who are lesbian. A lighthearted romantic comedy about an affair between two women, *Kissing Jessica Stein* (2001), pairs Jessica Stein (Jennifer Westfeldt), an ordinarily straight proofreader-cum-artist, with Helen Cooper (Heather Juergensen), a bisexual gallery manager; Westfeldt and Juergensen cowrote the film. In a bravura performance as Jessica's nagging Scarsdale mother, Tovah Feldshuh (as Judy Stein) reveals the depths of emotion and understanding that reside beneath the layers of a Jewish mother's shtick. At the beginning of the film, Judy Stein appears as a prototypical Jewish mother. Drawn precisely to type, Mrs. Stein tries to fix up Jessica with any available male. At High Holiday services, Jessica's mother points out eligible Jewish men to Jessica, until Jessica shuts her up. When Jessica reluctantly obeys her mother's command to appear for Friday night dinner, Judy seats her next to an eligible computer dork, whom Jessica detests.

Judy Stein's matchmaking and her relentless pressure for Jessica to marry is one reason Jessica seems so uncomfortable and rigid in her social relations; she also has had such poor luck with men, as a sequence of blind dates early in the film makes appallingly clear, that it is no mystery why she impulsively responds to a romantic ad placed by Helen. When Helen finds that the "Jewish Sandra Dee" to whom she is attracted is too fearful to give in to her feelings, it is Judy Stein, intuitively understanding the situation, who gives Jessica the courage to proceed. In a moving scene on the porch swing in their Scarsdale backyard, a sobbing Jessica confesses to Judy her fear that she will always be alone. Judy recalls a time when Jessica dropped out of playing the lead in her fifth-grade class play, but she makes Jessica understand that she would have been much happier to have persisted in the role. Jessica understands that her mother is giving her permission to take the risk of pursuing Helen; she is urging her to be her authentic self.

The message changes Jessica's life, allowing her to move forward and open herself to a greater degree of intimacy, self-expression, and creativity. This Jewish mother is meddlesome and nagging, but the bond she forms with her daughter is life-affirming. Caring and devoted, she facilitates her daughter's deepest desires. In embedding such deeply nurturant and insightful maternal behavior within the shell of the old nagging Jewish mother caricature, the creators of *Kissing Jessica Stein* show how film formulas can be modified from within to reflect the more progressive, feminist ideas of mothering.

WELL

Lisa Kron's autobiographical play, *Well*, received excellent critical reviews and several awards when it opened at the Public Theater in New York in 2004. Kron, who performed as a member of the Five Lesbian Brothers, has written several other well-regarded dramas, among them *2.5 Minute Ride*, a monologue that weaves together autobiographical stories, including Kron's pilgrimage to Auschwitz with her Holocaust-survivor father. In *Well*, the character Lisa Kron (played by Kron) futilely insists that "the play is not about my mother and me" but about illness and health, yet the play thrusts the story of Lisa's relationship with her mother into the narrative's center. Lisa explains to the audience that she wants to tell the story of how her chronically ill mother healed a sick community but never was able to rid herself of her own sickness. Lisa, who suffered from severe allergies all through college, refuses to follow in her mother's footsteps.

Lisa describes her childhood as filled with two subjects: allergies and racial integration. In the 1960s and 1970s, Lisa's mother was president of the West Side Neighborhood Association in Lansing, Michigan; she believed that integrating the neighborhood would end its steep decline and took her young daughter to a "million meetings." The only Jewish children in the neighborhood, Lisa and her brother grew up with many black friends. As the playwright, she shows scenes of her mother's social activism; her mother, who cannot understand the rules of the stage and constantly interrupts the action, spoiling Lisa's play, comments that the scene seems "awfully compressed," while befriending the stage actors.

But Lisa's mother, Ann (Jayne Houdyshell), steals the show. For most of the play, Ann sits in stage left on a La-Z-Boy recliner in housedress and slippers amid the clutter of Lisa's childhood home. Although Ann is sloppy, obese, and complains a lot, the play's other characters sympathize with her. "You're not writing a play about me?" she querulously asks her daughter.

"My mother is a fantastically energetic person trapped in an utterly exhausted body," Lisa explains.[36] "I am not like you," she tells her mother, "I have chosen to be healthy." Ann understands that behind Lisa's play of "illness and health" is her barely submerged anger: "Go ahead and say whatever you're afraid to say to me; stop hiding behind the play and talk to me." Confused, Lisa admits that she is worried she will become like her mother. "How can you think I was choosing this?" her mother asks. Lisa is abandoned in her own play as the other actors take her mother's side and stage a walkout.

The play concludes with the characters handing Lisa a copy of a moving speech that Ann gave at a meeting in the high school cafeteria in Michigan. "This is what integration means," it says. "It means weaving into the whole even the parts that are uncomfortable or don't seem to fit. Even the parts that are complicated and painful."[37] By listening to her mother's words, at last trying to hear her mother on her mother's terms, not filtered through her own experience, Lisa achieves an understanding of who her mother is. And her mother emerges as a charismatic figure, in spite of her very noticeable flaws. According to Kron, "this capacity to reimagine my life, to make changes, to be different from my family . . . my mother gave me permission and encouragement to do all these things."[38]

Jewish mothers, these two stories tell us, are not what they appear to be: the flawed outer shell of the Jewish mother is seen to hold within it a sympathetic, even noble, character. In the works of these women, popular culture formulas that tightly constrained the Jewish mother are being stretched to include more positive renderings; this is achieved not through nostalgic looking back but from harsh confrontation. Critical of their mothers, these Jewish daughters learn to see beyond the perimeters of the apparent "bad" mothering to appreciate the wisdom that lies beneath. The cultural portraits that emerge are complex and nuanced.

JEWISH MEN HAVE ALSO CONTRIBUTED to rewriting the Jewish mother narrative. In addition to works of biography and memoir, new portraits of loving Jewish mothers have emerged in the fiction of Philip Roth, who did so much to put the monster Jewish mother into the American vocabulary, and the comedy of Billy Crystal, suggesting that at least in the works of older Jewish culture-makers, the Jewish mother caricature may have run its course. Roth and Crystal join writers of a previous generation such as Alfred Kazin and Michael Gold who recalled mothers through the rosy hue of time and distance. Imagining and recalling themselves as boys, they place their mothers in a personal and historical context that parallels the emerging representations occasioned by lifestyle and demographic changes.

The Plot Against America

Philip Roth's *The Plot Against America* is a tense, chillingly etched, political novel embedded in a compelling family drama set in Roth's own environment of lower-middle-class Jewish Newark. In fact, a young "Philip Roth" is the narrator of this story: just seven years old at its start in 1940, he sees the world through the eyes of his "energetic" and "optimistic" young parents, "Herman" and "Bess" Roth, only to endure a historical cataclysm during the next two years that places American Jews—and young Philip's faith in the rectitude of his parents—in deep jeopardy.

The story begins when presidential candidate Charles Lindbergh defeats Franklin Roosevelt on a peace-with-Hitler platform, receiving 57 percent of the popular vote and winning every state except New York and Maryland. Deeply anti-Semitic and isolationist to boot, President Lindbergh institutes an Office of American Absorption that sends Jewish city children to spend their summer on Southern farms and later attempts to break up Jewish "ghettos" by removing Jewish families from neighborhood enclaves and placing them in "American" communities; the Roths, from Newark, are slated for Kentucky. More restrictive measures—including violent pogroms—follow. The fiercely ethical Herman Roth fights these government policies from the beginning, outspoken in his contempt for Lindbergh's destruction of democracy and his blatant anti-Semitism. Other family members—including nephew Alvin, older son Sandy, and sister-in-law Evelyn, who marries Rabbi Lionel Begelsdorf (Lindbergh's Jewish shill) collaborate with the Lindbergh administration, not understanding the detrimental effect of its actions on Jews. Bess Roth urges her husband to flee to Canada, but he is ultimately too proud and too much a believer in America's bedrock values to do so.

The author paints the "Roth" parents as decent and even noble. But it is Bess who is the main surprise. Nostalgic and affectionate, Roth's portrait of Bess as a 1940s urban Jewish housewife lacks the mocking irony of the author's earlier Jewish mothers, in particular, Sophie Portnoy. As Roth describes her, Bess is "slender but strong and . . . tidily dressed, with a lock of her wavy dark hair over one eyebrow and roundish cheeks a little rouged and a prominent nose and chunky arms and shapely legs and slim hips and the lively eyes of a girl half her age." Like Herman, Bess offers both "a surfeit of prudence and a surfeit of energy."[39] She carries out her domestic functions flawlessly; she is devoted to her family, effective, and smart. Above all, Bess can be relied on: even after she takes a job as a retail clerk in the face of Lindbergh's threats (so she can put away money in case the family has to flee to Canada), she "gets up early to eat breakfast with father and to make our lunch sandwiches and wrap them in wax paper and put them in the refrigerator."[40] Bess relishes household routine; in the face of the alarming political events that are pulling the family apart, she finds solace in the daily events of her motherly role even when they no longer make sense. Her function as Jewish mother is to shield the family from harm, providing calm and steady reassurance and an "orderly existence . . . full of purpose."[41] Performing each day "in methodological opposition to life's unruly flux" (the trait that the writer acknowledges as key), Bess is the bedrock of the family—"her job was to hold our world together as calmly and as sensibly as she could; that was what gave her life fullness and that was all she was trying to do."[42]

Bess inhabits this role confidently, and it provides her with deep satisfaction, even though Roth indicates that she has a life outside her family. Once an office secretary, Bess now serves as president of the boys' PTA; she is often out at meetings. Her civic interests are indicated as well by her work as poll watcher at election time; when she can, she enjoys reading the mid-level fiction of "Pearl Buck or Fannie Hurst or Edna Ferber," borrowed from the local rental library. This is no desperate, unfulfilled housewife living out her life subordinate to those of her husband and children. An energetic and "untiring mother full of contentment," she nurtures them all and is deeply attached to them; she can't quite hide her loneliness when Sandy spends the summer away.[43] It is Bess who is responsible for Philip's prized stamp collection, having started him off collecting and contributed to the purchase of his most sought-after acquisitions. Bess's mothering is "gentle, kindly," but authoritative: she doesn't hesitate to smack Sandy when he defies his father by calling him a "dictator *worse* than Hitler"; Herman merely walks away in disgust.[44]

Bess's finest moment comes at the end of the novel. President Lindbergh has disappeared, martial law is declared, and killings and riots have begun. With the closing of the Canadian border, the family realizes that Herman's refusal to listen to Bess and get them all out of the country months before was the "gravest mistake" he has ever made.[45] Tragedy strikes their former neighbors, the Wishnows. Late one night Bess accepts a collect call from ten-year-old Seldon in Kentucky, who, frightened, tells them that his mother has not returned home from a trip. Bess calms Seldon down (though in fact the widowed Mrs. Wishnow has been killed), meticulously instructing him to make himself dinner with the little food left in his refrigerator. "You have to eat. . . . I want you to sit down first with everything you need at the kitchen table. I want you to use a spoon and a fork and a napkin and a knife. Eat slowly. Use dishes. Use a bowl. . . . Make yourself some toast, with the cereal. And use the butter. Butter it. And pour yourself a big glass of milk."[46] Then she arranges for the family that son Sandy had stayed with in Kentucky to pick up Seldon.

No Sophie Portnoy nagging her son to eat his liver, Bess insists that Seldon eat in order to comfort him and keep him safe. Like the mothers of Eastern Europe who courageously protected their offspring from hostile neighbors, Bess's mothering rises to the occasion when Jewish children are threatened, even if not her own. Roth makes very clear that the mothers of the community were "close and reliable friends who . . . looked after one another's children" when necessary.[47] Beyond the "watch-its" and "be-carefuls" of Mrs. Portnoy and her circle, the "generic maternalism" that Mrs. Wishnow and his mother shared offered their children a "succoring warmth . . . as a matter of course."[48]

If American women might be said to have enjoyed their domestic roles in the early and mid-twentieth century and found themselves fulfilled by serving as the linchpins of family order, then Bess Roth is the epitome of this type. Secure in her Americanism and relishing her Judaism (Mrs. Roth lit Sabbath candles every week though she had no "doctrinal creed"), Bess Roth made the most of domesticity. Before the supposed Lindbergh catastrophe, she, Mrs. Wishnow, and their neighborhood friends were "watchful members of the local matriarchy whose overriding task was to establish a domestic way of life for the next generation."[49] Roth makes clear how significant, and how courageous, a Jewish mother's actions could be.

700 SUNDAYS

Roth's admiring portrait of the fictional "Mrs. Roth" in *The Plot Against America* is matched by comedian Billy Crystal's sentimental tribute to his mother, Helen, in Crystal's award-winning one-man Broadway show, *700 Sundays*. Crystal's father, who died of a heart attack when Crystal was only fifteen, dominates the first act of the play, which derives its title from the finite number of Sundays Crystal was able to spend with his father. After his father's death, Helen Crystal became her son's "greatest hero," commuting two hours round-trip every day to secretarial school, learning the skills that would ensure she could provide for her family and send her youngest son to college, even becoming Billy's Cub Scout leader.[50] Crystal's mother is given her dramatic due in the second act; her death, when Crystal is fifty-three, leaving him a grieving "orphan," becomes the moving finale of the play. Crystal recalls his mother as "tremendously funny, strong, very much a performer"; for a while she was the voice of Minnie Mouse in the Macy's Thanksgiving Day parades in New York.[51]

Crystal, born in 1948, was not part of the first generation of Borscht Belt comics, although he was inspired to become a professional comedian after visiting the Catskills. His lavish praise for both his parents, and his deep attachment to them, separates Crystal from the Catskill forbears who had such a deep influence on him, as they did on Roth.

In *The Plot Against America* and *700 Sundays*, two of the funniest Jewish men in contemporary American culture present loving portraits of functional, caring Jewish families, each of them anchored by strong, decent, competent Jewish mothers. Along with *Kissing Jessica Stein* and *Well*, these characterizations indicate a growing willingness on the part of popular culture's movers and shakers to probe more deeply and realistically into their own backgrounds. But it may be too soon to expect that the turn away from Jewish men's "insult"

humor directed at Jewish women, along with a more generous theatrical caricature from Jewish daughters, portends a growing trend in entertainment and
fiction—for the tradition of negative Jewish mother humor is insistently being
carried forward by able and witty Jewish women comics.

"Her Daughter Gives Her Heartache": Jewish Women Comedians and the Jewish Mother

In March 2005, the Jewish Women's Archive presented a night of Jewish
women's comedy at the Copacabana in New York City. Seven hundred guests
enthusiastically welcomed the six comedians who entertained that evening—
the award-winning Jackie Hoffman, Judy Gold, Rain Pryor, and Wendy Liebman, all of them in their forties, and two younger comics, my own daughter,
Lauren Antler, and Catie Lazarus. Although the laughs were plentiful, many
audience members were puzzled at the overwhelming presence of Jewish
mother jokes by two of the best known of the performers, Hoffman and Gold,
while Pryor, daughter of comedian Richard Pryor, offered a storytelling routine about her Jewish grandmother that also teetered on the stereotypical. The
nagging, whining, manipulative Jewish mother of old had returned, although
as the comedians might have argued, at least she was there in an affectionate,
respectful guise.

Hoffman, eight-year veteran of Chicago's famed Second City improvisa-
tion group, Obie Award best-actress winner, and recipient of much acclaim for
her performance as Jessica's pregnant coworker friend, Joan, in *Kissing Jessica
Stein*, told many jokes about her widowed, senior citizen mother who she
phoned every day. Her mother called her too, leaving messages frantic with
worry whenever Jackie didn't answer right away. Then she called the police,
who asked her to describe her daughter. "She's not married," replied the mother.
"She has a filthy mouth. If she took her hair out of her eyes she'd be a beautiful girl."[52] Another mother joke came with Hoffman describing the language
tapes she played to learn Yiddish. Rather than the standard phrases for language instruction, these tapes conveyed key phrases of Jewish life: "Her
daughter gives her heartache. I feel sick."

Comedian Amy Borkowsky created another nagging mother in her recorded
tape messages from her best-selling CD set, *Amy's Answering Machine*, which
were played in segments throughout the night of Jewish women's comedy at
the Copacabana. With the heavily Jewish-accented voice of the invisible Mrs.
Borkowsky filling the entire airspace of the huge ballroom, it seemed as if
Woody Allen/Sheldon Mills's mother had returned. "Hi Amila," intones the
voice, "I was watching the news, and I heard about the little girl who was alone
in an apartment for nine days without food, and it made me think of you.
Honey, please, be sure you have what to eat in the fridge, 'cause last time you
came to visit, you looked like Olive Oyl." The voice warns about all kinds of

lurking dangers—nylon-crotched panties; the foam earpiece on headphones ("a prime breeding ground for bacteria"); even lambskin condoms—and gives her thirty-something daughter practical advice she surely doesn't need, like emptying her bladder before standing on line at the Motor Vehicle Bureau or "which side to wear your purse so your shoulders don't get uneven." Welcome to the "land of Overprotection," Amy writes in the print version of *Amy's Answering Machine*, as she introduces the messages from her mother, "who seems to think the phone cord is an umbilical cord."[53] Despite the umbilical telephone cord, which seems to strangle her independence, Borkowsky declares that she is lucky to have a "classic Jewish mother" "who cares so much."[54] Yet this qualification does not completely absolve Borkowsky, like Hoffman, from having created a stock figure. Indeed, her nagging, worrying mother might well be the stick-figure centerpiece of a latter-day "how to be a Jewish mother" manual.[55] Even though the portrayal is essentially loving, Borkowsky's mocking routine echoes the objectification of mothers so familiar from the performances of her male comic predecessors.

Judy Gold's performance at the Copacabana and in her one-woman show, *25 Questions for a Jewish Mother*, makes good use of jokes about the Jewish mother's phone calls, but in her show, the stereotyped mother's overprotectiveness becomes the basis of a much more fully developed persona. Gold, who won two Emmy Awards for writing and producing the *Rosie O'Donnell Show* and a Cable Ace Award for her own HBO special, was twice nominated as funniest female stand-up by the American Comedy Awards. At the Copacabana, her performance was a stream of Jewish mother jokes. "My mother is the most annoying person on the face of the earth," she says, "a miserable human being." "You can say something to her and she cannot only make it negative, she makes it about herself. What are you having for New Year's, filet mignon? I'll be eating shit." (Her mother's just-published autobiography, she has quipped, is titled *I Came, I Saw, I Criticized*.)[56] At stand-up performances and on Jay Leno's *Tonight Show*, Gold plays her mother's "crazy" tape-recorded phone messages; she also tells jokes about her son, Henry, imitating his grandmother's phone message, in a Yiddish accent, saying, "Judith, where are you? I'm a wreck." A lesbian who is raising two sons with her former long-time partner, Gold often quips that she feels sorry for her kids because they have two Jewish mothers.[57]

But in her sold-out one-woman show, cowritten with Kate Moira Ryan, Gold turned a new light on her Jewish-mother one-liners. This performance elaborated the Jewish mother joke into an expansive routine, drawing on Gold's own biography and on interviews with Jewish mothers across the country. The backstory of the show is that after some earlier stand-up routines, a reporter from the *Jewish Daily Forward* asked Gold to stop promoting stereotypes of the Jewish mother; "They don't need any help from me," Gold protested. Nonetheless, to find out what the Jewish mother was really like, she interviewed different types of Jewish mothers around the country; in her show,

Comedian Judy Gold, shown here with sons Ben and Henry, represents the new breed of Jewish stand-up. In her one-woman show, *25 Questions for a Jewish Mother*, she jokes about her over-protective mother, Ruth, but proclaims her own identity as a proud lesbian "Jewish mother." (Courtesy of Judy Gold. Photo: Shari Manko)

characters based on these interviews alternate with stories about her mother, Ruth, and her own experience as a mother.

The portrait of Gold's mother that emerges is of an excessively protective woman consumed with maternal worry. Every time the young Gold left the house, her mother feared something was going to happen; when once she came home forty-five minutes late, her mother had already called the police and was serving them her homemade *rugaleh* in her living room. Judith's tardiness led her mother to attach an egg timer to her belt to remind her to get home on time. No fun and games in this family: Mrs. Gold's favorite read-aloud story to the young child was the pop-up version of the *Diary of Anne Frank*. So the comedian grew up experiencing a "tortured" childhood and adolescence during which she and mother communicated only through sticky notes on the refrigerator from Ann Landers columns. To this day, Gold's mother calls many times a day and panics if she doesn't hear from her daughter; "You never call" is her true mantra. "How are Jewish mothers different from non-Jewish mothers?" Gold asked her interviewees. "I look at my children and I feel afraid," says one of them.

Despite their anxieties and the guilt they instill in their children for simply leading their own lives, the mothers in Gold's show emerge as appealing women with distinct voices—each has her own story: the mother who as a thirteen-year-old drew on her mother's strength in the concentration camps, allowing both of them to survive; the Chinese Jewish girl who prepares matzo ball soup in a wok; the Orthodox mother of seven who loses a son from AIDS but accepts his sexual orientation.[58] Hearing their tales, Gold begins to understand her own mother, who belatedly tells a story that helps put her manipulations and intrusiveness into perspective: Gold learns about the death of Ruth's fifteen-year-old brother, Stuart, who died in a freak accident after bumping his head on a marble lobby floor. That Gold's mother gave up her own dreams of attending college after her brother's death for fear of leaving her grieving parents is another revelation that humanizes her for the audience. She becomes more than a nagging cardboard figure on the other end of a telephone.

Gold's understanding of her mother's pain eases the disappointment that for a long time, her mother refused to acknowledge her choices as a lesbian: "You two care only about yourselves," she responded when Judy told her that her partner was pregnant; "leave me out of it." And no member of the family attended her first son's bris. But at a poignant moment at the end of her performance, Gold confesses that the support that her mother proffered after Gold's painful break-up with her partner showed her ultimate acceptance of her daughter's nontraditional lifestyle—and her friendship. Together with the stories of the women she interviewed, her mother's love allows Gold to ultimately "come out"—not as a lesbian, but as a Jewish mother. This means adopting and taking pride in the stereotype, even while admitting to ambivalent feelings about the Jewish mother's characteristic mix of overprotection and affection.

In the last story Gold tells, about the mother whose son died of AIDS, the mother asserts that although G-d may reside with her, "G-d doesn't pay the rent": it is the Jewish mother, with her endless worrying, nagging, and love, who must pay. The mothers' stories teach Gold about suffering, but also about defiance. And she understands what has been true as well in her own experience: that daughters may seem to hate their mothers, but they really love them, even when they remain in absolute fear of becoming like them. (Gold also called the police when recently her octogenarian mother failed to call her—she was at a bingo game at her synagogue.)

In addition to maternal paranoia, Gold acknowledges that she inherited other legacies from her mother.[59] Gold grew up in a kosher home, keeps kosher today, and considers herself religious, a treasured inheritance passed on by her mother, who served as president of her local B'nai Brith chapter and is a life member of Hadassah. In addition to her "hysterical" overprotectiveness, which Judy found herself channeling when she herself became a mother, Ruth taught her daughters to "speak up," to "never be a victim." So adamant was she about "standing up for yourself" that Gold hid from her the fact that she was the frequent target of jokes because of her unusual height; she knew her mother would embarrass her by immediately taking on the perpetrators. Because she felt loved and safe, Gold felt secure enough to develop her personality based on "being an outsider and being ridiculously ostracized."[60]

It is this persona she incorporates in her performances today as a fast-talking, outsized (six-foot-three-inch) comic. And Gold insists that although her mother is a tough audience, she doesn't mind being the butt of her daughter's humor. "She thinks it's hilarious. And it comes from a really good place." "To be a great standup," Gold adds, "you have to tell the truth and you have to draw upon your own experience. . . . Otherwise there's no passion."[61] She believes that her Jewish mother jokes challenge rather than reify the stereotype, illuminating the real women behind them—women like her mother. "For me to say I'm a Jewish mother," she says, "it's an honor."[62]

Appreciative audiences agree with her positive interpretation: in the words of critics, Gold truly knocks Jewish mother jokes "out of the park" because of tight writing, perfect timing, and the "modern gloss" she puts on old canards.[63] Jewish mothers, even well-worn Jewish mother jokes, can be funny, especially when they are innovatively packaged—and as Gold slyly winks to her audiences, after all, she is a single mother, and she needs to make a living.

Some forty years after Dan Greenburg's famous guide to Jewish mothers' guilt-producing manipulations, Jewish women comics have taken possession of this comic mantra. The question is, why? One reason that female comedians employ the Jewish mother joke is that it has a continuing bearing in reality. Equally important is the fact that it *is* a stereotype, easily recognizable as a Jewish comic shtick. As such, it has an immediate payoff, calling forth an automatic response that makes spectators laugh at this "insider" humor. Starting with Freud, psychologists and humor theorists have argued that Jews use self-mockery as a powerful means of protection against the outside world. According to these notions, poking fun at schlemiels and pushy Jewish mothers is a way of creating group solidarity and deflecting possible outside criticisms.[64] Like male comics before them, when Jewish women comedians and writers use jokes that denigrate Jewish mothers they invert outsider ridicule. Making the stereotypes excessive through insult humor may thus actually explode them, revealing through exaggeration that despite the kernel of truth that may lurk within, the caricature is anachronistic and incorrect.[65]

The fact that female Jewish comedians, in particular, share the same sex as the targets of this insider humor has added significance. To succeed in stand-up, a particularly tough arena for women, they must often take on aggressive styles of humor that are staples of the comedy club circuit. "It's harder for women in this country," Judy Gold explains. "Stand-up comedy is not a feminine profession at all. . . . There's nothing more threatening to a man than a female comic."[66] The difficulty female comics face as performers is exacerbated by the misogyny, homophobia, and ethnic and racial stereotyping that have become regular features of the rapid-fire, slick, stand-up style. "The most apparently obvious way for a woman comic to cope with the club style and audiences," writes one critic, "is to behave as if she were male."[67]

When this happens, Jewish mother jokes can serve as identity markers, testifying to the performers' professional status as comedians as well as to the fact that they are proudly Jewish and female. The fact that female comics protest that they do not really hate their mothers is important; they acknowledge their mothers' overbearing characteristics yet declare their respect for them. Like the Borscht Belt comedians, their seemingly contemptuous mockery of the Jewish mother has a nostalgic edge, for in recalling their mothers' deep (if unwanted) concern, they draw a picture of family life that is close and caring and, in its way, functional and affectionate.[68]

Through their jokes, the new comedians remind us that Jewish mothers love their daughters so much that they can never separate from them. And they allow these daughters to reveal their own contradictory truths—that the mothers' insistent and often carping interference can not only be unwelcome all the time, but also can be hateful and hated. At the same time, it is a sign of the comfort and nurturance that the mothers continue to offer in their own way. And the comedian daughters, like the sons before them, seem to know it.

"We're all saying that our mothers care deeply for our health and well-being but they can sometimes go to extremes," says Wendy Liebman, 1997 winner of the Best Female Stand-Up Award. Although Liebman does Jewish mother jokes in her act ("Is there a doctor in the house? My mother wants me to marry you." "My mom was a ventriloquist and she always was throwing her voice. For ten years I thought the dog was telling me to kill my father." "My grandmother always said, 'Don't marry for money . . . divorce for money.'"), she says that neither her mother nor grandmother are "like this in real life *at all*." She admits she is "perpetuating a stereotype of the Jewish matriarch," though she is not exactly sure why. "Maybe I want to show how my mother and grandmother want to take care of me and this is how I know how to communicate that." Maybe, too, "the more annoying the comedian . . . the more annoying her mother." Liebman suggests that Jewish women comedians may resemble male African American comedians who truly love their mothers yet do "yo' mama" jokes. Perhaps, she says, "Jewish females are hostile towards their mothers on stage because it's the way we show our love . . . if the audience can laugh with me as I'm perpetuating a stereotype, maybe they'll listen to what else I have to say."[69]

For still other Jewish comedians, mothers remain comic material, but in different, and potentially stereotype-defying, ways. Cory Kahaney, a popular New York comedian who reverses stale caricatures in her show, *JAP: Jewish Princesses of Comedy*, honoring early Jewish woman comics, was inspired to do stand-up by her own Jewish mother's humorous impersonations and her family's regular trips to Grossinger's, where they loved the comedy acts. One of her signature routines pokes fun not at her mother, but at her own parenting of her teenage daughter, whom she raised as a single mother. For Kahaney, the humor in the life of the contemporary Jewish mother lies in her offspring's "attitude" and in her own lack of power. "The other day, she emptied the dishwasher, which is like an annual act," Kahaney says. "And she asks, 'Do I get a cell phone now?' And I said: 'What happens when you take out the garbage? Do you get a Mercedes?' "[70]

The routines of the wickedly funny Sarah Silverman, star, writer, and producer of *Jesus Is Magic*, a film documentary of her stand-up act, also testify to the brave new world of comedy in which Jewish women of the next generation are subverting cultural stereotypes. In Silverman's blunt comedy, there are no cultural taboos; she offers edgy jokes about minorities, AIDS, the Holocaust, Martin Luther King, 9–11, rape, and sexual abuse. With her stunning brunette good looks, Silverman combines a demure innocence with an appealing sexuality that allows her to say anything, no matter how extreme. Silverman acts as "approachable though deranged, a sort of twisted Gracie Allen," writes Dana Goodyear in a *New Yorker* profile. She "crosses boundaries that it would not occur to most people even to have. The more innocent and oblivious her delivery, the more outrageous her commentary becomes."[71] The discrepancy between Silverman's appearance and her matter-of-fact vulgarity has led critics to label her queen of "shock comedy," a new Lenny Bruce or Richard Pryor.[72]

Silverman makes the most of her Jewishness. Although she was fired from *Saturday Night Live* after only a year, the one time she was able to appear on its "Weekend Update," she gave a "personal news" report, with a picture from her sister Susan's wedding in the background, announcing that "the most important event of this past week was, of course, the wedding of my sister, Susan Silverman, to Yosef Abramowitz. It was a really neat wedding, too, you know, 'cause they took each other's last names and hyphenated it. So now my sister's name is Susan Silverman-Abramowitz. But they're thinking of shortening it to just 'Jews.' "[73] Silverman's family was not religious, but the cultural Judaism she imbibed growing up is fundamental to her act.

Like Roseanne Barr, Silverman had a grandmother who was a Holocaust survivor. But the Holocaust appears much more frontally in Silverman's routine than in it did in Roseanne's stand-up act; Silverman's is in fact dedicated to her beloved nana, Rose Silverman, who died in 2000. In the film, she quips that her grandmother was in Auschwitz, one of the "better camps," since she got a "vanity" ID tattoo there. But the bathos Silverman exhibits about her bubbe's death is combined with the comedian's politically incorrect signature humor. The joke that her ninety-six-year-old grandmother died after an anal rape and that an autopsy was being performed is a recurring theme in *Jesus Is Magic*. Silverman often talks about her grandmother in club and television appearances as well. "God, I miss her," she emotes. Then she quickly confides that boyfriend Jimmy Kimmel's testicles remind her of the smell of her dear nana's house.

"Cigarettes and brisket . . . Maybe that's how you know it's the one." Brisket, the Jewish mother's and grandmother's favorite dish, is a frequent reference in Silverman's comedy, no doubt because it marks Silverman as a traditional "nice" Jewish girl. But she combines this identity with subtle references to her wildness: perhaps, for example, the autopsy will turn up brisket in her grandmother's vaginal fluid. So important is brisket to a Jewish girl's identity (and to her sexuality), she seems to be saying, that if she were to write her own autobiography, Silverman would call it, *Traces of Brisket*.[74] Underneath her well-groomed innocence, she is a *vilde chaye* (wild animal). The combination of bawdiness, incongruity, and her defiance of social expectations, especially those that women ought to cherish, gives Silverman's humor its edginess.

Silverman's fond memories of her grandmother join spoofs about her mother, whom she says she takes after, since her mother was a performer, recording the local New Hampshire movie theater's answering message. Silverman's mother, Beth Ann, was in fact founding director of the theater at a small liberal-arts college, which she called the New Thalian Players, after the muse of comedy. Her mother observes that Sarah grew up watching television, but unlike Roseanne's family, which had been glued to TV comedians, Silverman's mother recalls that "we were a family that would talk back to the television. We would question everything. She learned that it was O.K. to make fun of what seems to be ridiculous."[75]

Silverman learned that lesson well. But in spite of the family's open-mindedness, like Gold and other contemporary feminist comics, Silverman came to fear that she was *becoming* her mother. This was not, however, because of her thespian talents: "So there I was licking jelly off my boyfriend . . . and I thought: Oh my God, I'm turning into my mother!" "It's so scary." In this single instant, Silverman calls upon the daughter's matrophobia (the fear of becoming one's mother) to subvert the stereotype of the frigid Jewish American princess by turning her into her opposite, the passionate but atypical sexually exotic Jewish mother. In another joke, she brings the two Jewish types together, recalling subliminally the Jewish mother's desire that her daughter marry well: "I was raped by a doctor," she says, "which is so bittersweet for a Jewish girl." Silverman jokes about marrying out and becoming a modern, intermarried Jewish mother. When asked how she and her Gentile boyfriend will explain their religious beliefs to future offspring, she responds: "Mother is one of the chosen people and Dad believes Jesus is magic."

Claiming her Jewish identity as a "nice" Jewish daughter who fondly recalls maternal role models as she mocks the stereotypes on which they are based helps Silverman find the cover that allows her to spew forth humor that is crude and transgressive. In the words of *New York Times* critic A. O. Scott, "Scatology! Baby killing! Masturbation!"[76] But her fresh take on being a Jewish daughter is part of a broader assault on identity politics. Silverman pokes fun not only at being Jewish, but also at being "white," moving back and forth between the two identities—she tells Dave Chappelle's jokes as a white woman, for example, and relates that her former mixed-race boyfriend objected to her compliment that he would have made an "expensive slave" because he has "self-esteem" issues.[77]

Some media critics see Silverman's ethnic and racial jokes as serious efforts to talk about how to negotiate mixed-race and multiethnic relationships, indeed how to live in a modern, multicultural society. Her flagrant use of stereotypes, with "deadpan irony," flaunts liberal pieties, as, for example, when she mocks her lust for a jewel made from deboning and grinding the spines of starving Ethiopian babies but insists that although this process probably exploits the "unions" that mine the babies' spines, "you have to pick your battles." By performing this kind of privileged whiteness, Silverman exposes issues of racism and ethnic stereotyping and challenges the listener to pay close attention.[78] Being a Jewish woman in comedy, a proud Jewish daughter and granddaughter, is part of the identity that allows her to stake a claim to taking humor seriously.

As Silverman's routine and those of other contemporary Jewish female comics hint, in this new millennium where the demography of Jewish motherhood is changing all the time, labels should no longer matter, and stereotypes of old-style Jewish mothers may well decline, because the cultural patterns on which they are based are becoming anachronistic. But there is little doubt that the pendulum between blaming Jewish mothers for their faults and praising them for what they have accomplished will continue to swing, because Jewish children will always measure their own achievements, and mark their identities, in ethnic and gendered terms. Even as they resist the legacies of their Jewish mothers, daughters will still hear their mothers' voices in their heads.[79]

As my own daughters inform me, mothers *are* inherently laughable, even as the terms of what is considered funny adapt to new possibilities. In the coming years, as the daughters of Jewish feminist mothers increasingly occupy the arenas of popular culture, we may experience yet another new twist in the narratives of Jewish mothers performed on the stage of American cultural life.

EPILOGUE

A SHORT WHILE AGO, when my older daughter, Lauren, a comedian, was performing at Don't Tell Mama's, a cabaret theater in midtown Manhattan, she spotted me in the audience and interrupted her prepared routine with a personal revelation. "I do have something to tell you, Mom," she blurted out. "I'm dating a non-Jew!"

This was just the beginning of what became a very funny stand-up routine in which my daughter had a lot to say about and to her Jewish mother, although her observations came from being the daughter of a feminist rather than the daughter of a typical Jewish mother. My daughter's narrative was that I had taught her to become a feminist without first teaching her how to be a girl. So she learned to fight misogyny whether on the camp or school sports field or in local politics but had no lessons in makeup, grooming, or the girly aspects of growing up. Being a "DJF"—daughter of a Jewish feminist—meant learning to fight the patriarchy, but not what to wear when you were doing it.

My daughters, Lauren and Rachel, and others like them, see a difference between the Jewish mother and the Jewish feminist mother. As Lauren jokes:

> A Jewish mother would call and say, "Honey, have you looked outside? It's snowing. You might want to put on a jacket. You know what, on second thought maybe a snowsuit; I'm gonna revise that, you're gonna need a shield. On third thought, don't go outside at all . . . *you could die!*"
>
> But a Jewish feminist mother would call and say, "Honey, have you looked outside? It's snowing. I hope you don't think that's a reason to stay inside and take

Courtesy of Associação Brasileira 'A Hebraica' de São Paulo, Brasil.

a break from fighting the patriarchy. Because the misogyny happens out there whether it's raining or sleeting or snowing or whatever. And what?! Are you going to wait for a man to shovel the snow? I don't think so. Let's get serious . . . and put on a coat.

In Lauren's telling of this story, the Jewish mother is no longer overprotective and wracked with anxiety about her offspring's safety and physical well-being. Rather she hopes that her daughter will boldly step up to the challenge of fighting against the forces that deny women and girls their rights. Nonetheless, as opposed to her boyfriend's mother—who my daughter says is simply glad to see him alive—her own feminist Jewish mother is full of advice, deeply involved in her daughters' lives, and ever present. Perhaps she is not a conventional Jewish mother, as my daughter astutely notes, but she might well represent yet another reinvention of Jewish mother traits chronicled in so many generations of performances, writings, and reports. My daughter's routine demonstrates anew the remarkable resiliency of this enduring cultural type.

As I watch my daughter onstage telling her stories about coming of age as a DJF, I am proud that even as she pokes fun at her mother and the childhood lessons she imbibed at home, she has in fact taken on the mantle of feminism. Her act ends with her acknowledgment that you can dress with pizzazz even as you march on the patriarchy, but it is a battle that must be engaged.

NOTES

Introduction

1. *An Evening with Mike Nichols and Elaine May*, original cast recording, Polygram Records, 1960.

2. Mike Nichols, in Abigail Pogrebin, ed., *Stars of David: Prominent Jewish Talk about Being Jewish* (New York: Broadway Press, 2005), 79–80.

3. See George Jessel, *"Hello, Momma"* (Cleveland, Ohio: World Publishing, 1946).

4. Of the many books of humor that include Jewish mother jokes, see, for example, William Novak and Moshe Waldoks, *The Big Book of Jewish Humor* (New York: Harper-Collins, 1981), and Henry D. Spalding, ed., *Encyclopedia of Jewish Humor: From Biblical Times to the Modern Age* (New York: Jonathan David Publishers, 1969). Novak and Waldoks's book, reprinted in a 25th anniversary edition in 2006, includes excerpts from *How to Be A Jewish Mother* and *Portnoy's Complaint*; Spalding's anthology includes boasting jokes about "my son, the medical student' and mothers who carp and criticize.

5. Charlotte Baum, Paula Hyman, and Sonya Michel, *The Jewish Woman in America* (New York: New American Library, 1976), 236–237.

6. Irving Howe, *World of Our Fathers* (New York: Harcourt Brace Jovanovich, 1976), 177.

7. On the JAP caricature, see Bernard Saper, "The JAP Joke Controversy: An Excruciating Psychosocial Analysis," in *Humor* 4 (1991): 223–239; Alan Dundes, "The J.A.P. and the J.A.M. in American Jokelore," *Journal of American Jokelore* 98 (1985): 456–475, reprinted as "The Jewish American Princess and the Jewish American Mother in American Jokelore," in Dundes, *Cracking Jokes: Studies of Sick Humor Cycles and Stereotypes* (Berkeley, Calif.: Ten Speed Press, 1987), 62–81; Esther Fuchs, "Humor and Sexism," in Avner Ziv, ed., *Jewish Humor* (Tel Aviv: Tel Aviv University/Papyrus, 1986), 111–122; Judith Stora-Sandor, "From Eve to the Jewish American Princess: The Comic Representation of Women in Jewish Literature," in Avner Ziv and Anat Zajdman, *Semites and Stereotypes: Characteristics of Jewish Humor*

(Westport, Conn.: Greenwood Press, 1993), 131–141; and Riv-Ellen Prell, *Fighting to Become Americans: Jews, Gender, and the Anxiety of Assimilation* (Boston: Beacon Press, 1999), especially chap. 6.

8. Paul Mazursky, *Show Me the Magic* (New York: Simon and Schuster, 1999), 79–80.

9. Philip Roth, interview with author, May 26, 1991.

10. Retirement party for Lawrence H. Fuchs, Brandeis University, May 1, 2002.

11. Lawrence J. Epstein, *The Haunted Smile: The Story of Jewish Comedians in America* (New York: Public Affairs, 2001), xiii.

12. Cited by Paul Mazursky, in Pogrebin, *Stars of David*, 362.

13. Ruth Landes and Mark Zborowski, "Hypotheses Concerning the Eastern European Jewish Family," *Psychiatry* 13, no. 4 (November 1950): 447–464; quotation reprinted in Norman Kiell, ed., *The Psychodynamics of American Jewish Life: An Anthology* (New York: Twayne Publishers, 1967), 31.

14. Gladys Weisberg Rothbell, "The Case of the Jewish Mother: A Study in Stereotyping," Ph.D. dissertation, State University of New York at Stony Brook, 1989, 679–80.

15. Christie Davies, "An Explanation of Jewish Jokes about Jewish Women," *Humor* 3 (1990): 363, 366, 375. Also see Theodore Reik, *Jewish Wit* (New York: Gamut Press, 1962), 82.

16. Dundes, "The Jewish American Princess and the Jewish American Mother in American Jokelore," 80–81.

17. Joseph Boskin and Joseph Dorinson, "Ethnic Humor: Subversion and Survival," *American Quarterly* 37, no. 1 (1985): 81; Joseph Boskin, *Humor and Social Change in Twentieth Century America* (Boston: Boston Public Library, 1979), 28.

18. Dundes, *Cracking Jokes*, 74; Alan King, *Alan King's Great Jewish Joke Book* (New York: Crown, 2002), 97. On Jewish humor, see William Novak and Moshe Waldoks, *The Big Book of Jewish Humor* (New York: HarperCollins, 1981).

19. Baum, Hyman, and Michel, *The Jewish Woman in America*, 251; Rachel Josefowitz Siegel, Ellen Cole, and Susan Steinberg-Oren, eds., *Jewish Mothers Tell Their Stories: Acts of Love and Courage* (New York: Haworth Press, 2000), 5.

20. Siegel, Cole, and Steinberg-Oren, *Jewish Mothers Tell Their Stories*, 4; Baum, Hyman, and Michel, *The Jewish Woman in America*, 242.

21. Paula Hyman, "Battling Stereotypes of the Jewish Mother," in Sharon Strassfeld and Kathy Green, eds., *The Jewish Family Book* (New York: Bantam Books, 1981), 15.

22. Paula E. Hyman, *Gender and Assimilation in Modern Jewish History: The Roles and Representation of Women* (Seattle: University of Washington Press, 1995), 189. On mother-blame, also see Molly Ladd-Taylor and Lauri Umansky, *"Bad" Mothers: The Politics of Blame in Twentieth-Century America* (New York: New York University Press, 1998), 6, 13, 18, 22; Paula Caplan, *Don't Blame Mother: Mending the Mother-Daughter Relationship* (New York: HarperCollins, 1989); Caplan, "Don't Blame Mother: Then and Now," in Andrea O'Reilly and Sharon Abbey, eds., *Mothers and Daughters: Connection, Empowerment and Transformation* (Lanham, Md.: Rowman and Littlefield, 2000), 237–245; and Ruth Feldstein, *Motherhood in Black and White: Race and Sex in American Liberalism, 1930–1965* (Ithaca, N.Y.: Cornell University Press, 2000).

23. Beverly Gray Bienstock, "The Changing Image of the American Jewish Mother," in Virginia Tufte and Barbara Myerhoff, eds., *Changing Images of the Family* (New Haven: Yale University Press, 1979), 174.

24. Martha Ravits, "The Jewish Mother: Comedy and Controversy in American Popular Culture," *MELUS* 25 (Spring 2000): 5–7. Ravits locates the construction of the stereotype in the 1960s; although I date its emergence earlier, I find Ravits's interpretation compelling and am grateful for its many insights.

25. Hyman, *Gender and Assimilation in Modern Jewish History*, 189.

26. Erika Duncan, "The Hungry Jewish Mother," in Susannah Heschel, ed., *On Being a Jewish Feminist* (New York: Schocken Books, 1983), 27.

27. Ann Douglas, *Terrible Honesty: Mongrel Manhattan in the 1920s* (New York: Noonday Press, 1995), chap. 6.

28. See, for example, Mari Jo Buhle, *Feminism and Its Discontents: A Century of Struggle with Psychoanalysis* (Cambridge: Harvard University Press, 1998), and Lisa Appignanesi and John Forrester, *Freud's Women* (New York: Basic Books, 1992).

29. Philip Wylie, *Generation of Vipers* (New York: Rinehart, 1942).

30. Among the extensive literature on mothers and daughters, see, for example, Adrienne Rich, *Of Woman Born: Motherhood as Experience and Institution* (New York: Norton, 1976); Judith Arcana, *Our Mothers' Daughters* (London: Woman's Press, 1979); Cathy N. Davidson and E. M. Broner, *The Lost Tradition: Mothers and Daughters in Literature* (New York: Frederick Ungar, 1980); Elizabeth Debold, Marie Wilson, and Idelisse Malave, *Mother Daughter Revolution: From Betrayal to Power* (Reading, Mass.: Addison-Wesley, 1993); O'Reilly and Abbey, *Mothers and Daughters*; Suzanna Danuta Walters, *Lives Together/Worlds Apart* (Berkeley: University of California Press,1992); Judith Shapiro, compiler, *Mothers through the Eyes of Women Writers: A Barnard College Collection* (Berkeley, Calif.: Conari Press, 2000); and Deborah Tannen, *Your're Wearing That?: Understanding Mothers and Daughters in Conversation* (New York: Random House, 2006).

31. On the many works about psychological separation between children and mothers, see Carol Gilligan, *The Birth of Pleasure* (New York: Alfred A. Knopf, 2002); Roni Cohen-Sandler and Michelle Silver, *"I'm Not Mad, I Just Hate You!"* (New York: Viking, 1999).

32. Alan M. Dershowitz, *Chutzpah* (Boston: Little, Brown, 1991), 247 n.

33. Steven Mintz, "How We All Became Jewish Mothers," *National Post* (Canada), Feb. 17, 2006, Council on Contemporary Families Archive, http://listserv.uh.edu/cgi-bin/wa?A2=indo602&L=ccf&T=o&P=798. On anxious parenting, see, for example, Peter N. Stearns, *Anxious Parenting: A History of Modern Childrearing in America* (New York: New York University Press, 2003), and Susan J. Douglas and Meredith W. Michaels, *The Mommy Myth: The Idealization of Motherhood and How It Has Undermined Women* (New York: Free Press, 2004).

34. E-mail communication to author from Tova Hartman, Dec. 9, 2002.

Chapter 1

1. See, for example, Paula E. Hyman, *Gender and Assimilation in Modern Jewish History* (Seattle: University of Washington Press, 1995), 27.

2. On the role of Jewish women in European society, see Marion A. Kaplan, *The Making of the Jewish Middle Class: Women, Family, and Identity in Imperial Germany* (New York: Oxford University Press, 1991); ChaeRan Y. Freeze, *Jewish Marriage and Divorce in Imperial Russia* (Hanover, N.H.: University of New England Press, 2002); and Iris Parush, *Reading Jewish Women: Marginality and Modernization in Nineteenth-Century Eastern European Jewish Society* (Hanover, N.H.: University of New England Press, 2004).

3. Edith B. Gelles, "Abigaill Levy Franks: The Story of a Jewish Woman in Early Eighteenth Century New York," unpublished paper. Also see Gelles, ed., *The Letters of Abigaill Levy Franks, 1733–1748* (New Haven: Yale University Press, 2004), and Eli Faber, *A Time for Planting: The First Migration, 1654–1820* (Baltimore: Johns Hopkins University Press, 1992).

4. On nineteenth-century patterns of Jewish assimilation, see Hasia R. Diner, *A Time for Gathering: The Second Migration, 1820–1880* (Baltimore: Johns Hopkins University Press, 1992).

5. Diane Lichtenstein, *Writing Their Nations: The Tradition of Nineteenth-Century American Jewish Women Writers* (Bloomington: Indiana University Press, 1992), 22–23. On American Jewish women in the nineteenth century, also see Karla Goldman, *Beyond the Synagogue Gallery: Finding a Place for Women in American Judaism* (Cambridge: Harvard University Press, 2000), and Dianne Ashton, *Rebecca Gratz: Women and Judaism in Antebellum America* (Detroit: Wayne State University Press, 1997).

6. Irving Howe, *World of Our Fathers* (New York: Harcourt Brace Jovanovich, 1976), 171. Of the many works that illuminate the experience of Eastern European immigrant women, see, for example, Joyce Antler, *The Journey Home: How Jewish Women Shaped Modern America* (New York: Schocken Books, 1997); Hasia R. Diner and Beryl Lieff Benderly, *Her Works Praise Her* (New York: Perseus, 2002); Susan A. Glenn, *Daughters of the Shtetl: Life and Labor in the Immigrant Generation* (Ithaca, N.Y.: Cornell University Press, 1990); Linda Gordon Kuzmack, *Woman's Cause: The Jewish Woman's Movement in England and the United States, 1881–1933* (Columbus: Ohio State University Press, 1990); Annalise Orleck, *Common Sense and a Little Fire: Women and Working-Class Politics in the United States, 1900–1965* (Chapel Hill: University of North Carolina Press, 1995); Faith Rogow, *Gone to Another Meeting: The National Council of Jewish Women, 1893–1993* (Tuscaloosa: University of Alabama Press, 1993); and Sydney Stahl Weinberg, *The World of Our Mothers: The Lives of Jewish Immigrant Women* (Chapel Hill: University of North Carolina Press, 1988). Also see Joyce Antler, Nina Schwartz, and Claire Uziel, "How Did the First Jewish Women's Movement Draw on Progressive Women's Activism and Jewish Traditions, 1893–1936?" *Women and Social Movements in the United States, 1600–2000*, www.binghamton.edu/womhist/jewishfem/doclist.htm.

7. Irena Klepfisz, "Introduction," in Frieda Forman, Ethel Raicus, Sarah Silberstein Swartz, and Margie Wolfe, eds., *Found Treasures: Stories By Yiddish Women Writers* (Toronto: Second Story Press, 1994), 36. Also see Sylvia Barack Fishman, *Follow My Footprints: Changing Images of Women in American Jewish Fiction* (Hanover, N.H.: University of New England Press, 1992), 16; David G. Roskies, *A Bridge of Longing: The Lost Art of Yiddish Storytelling* (Cambridge: Harvard University Press, 1995), 10.

8. Judith Stora-Sandor, "From Eve to the Jewish Princess: The Comic Representation of Women in Jewish Literature," in Avner Ziv and Anat Zajdman, eds., *Semites and Stereotypes: Characteristics of Jewish Humor* (Westport, Conn.: Greenwood Press, 1993), 135.

9. Louis Harap, *Creative Awakening: The Jewish Presence in Twentieth-Century American Literature, 1900–1940s* (Westport, Conn.: Greenwood Press, 1987), 1; 7.

10. Sophie Tucker uses the spelling "Yiddisha Mama"; I will use the more common spelling, "Yiddishe Mama."

11. Sophie Tucker, *Some of These Days* (New York: Doubleday, 1945), 224.

12. Ibid., 226.

13. Ibid., 234, 260.

14. Mark Slobin, *Tenement Songs: The Popular Music of the Jewish Immigrants* (Urbana: University of Illinois Press, 1996), 57–58.

15. Ibid., 124.

16. Tucker, *Some of These Days*, 260; Slobin, *Tenement Songs*, 205; Irv Saposnik, "Jolson, the Jazz Singer and the Jewish Mother: or How My Yiddishe Momme Became My Mammy," *Judaism* 43, no. 4 (Fall 1994): 432–442.

17. Song lyrics are from Slobin, *Tenement Songs*, 203–204.

18. Saposnik, "Jolson, the Jazz Singer and the Jewish Mother," 438–439. Also see Ted Merwin, *In Their Own Image: New York Jews in Jazz Age Popular Culture* (New Brunswick, N.J.: Rutgers University Press, 2006), 54–55.

19. This is adapted from Antler, *The Journey Home*, 146–147. Tucker appeared on *Person to Person* on April 15, 1955.

20. On Tucker as bawdy singer, see June Sochen, "Fanny Brice and Sophie Tucker: Blending the Particular with the Universal," in Sarah Blacher Cohen, ed., *From Hester Street to Hollywood* (Bloomington: Indiana University Press, 1986), 44–57, and Sochen, "From Sophie Tucker to Barbra Streisand: Jewish Women Entertainers as Reformers," in Joyce Antler, ed., *Talking Back: Images of Jewish Women in American Popular Culture* (Hanover, N.H.: University Press of New England, 1998), 68–84.

21. The play opened on Broadway on September 15, 1925, and ran for two years. For Jolson's Jewish background, see Michael Alexander, *Jazz Age Jews* (Princeton: Princeton University Press, 2001), 139–140, 167.

22. Lyrics from Susan Gubar, *Racechanges: White Skin, Black Face in American Culture* (New York: Oxford University Press, 1997), 68.

23. Slobin, *Tenement Songs*, 195.

24. Arthur Hertzberg finds the "silent, weeping" mother to be "archetypal." Arthur Hertzberg, *The Jews in America—Four Centuries of an Uneasy Encounter: A History* (New York: Simon and Schuster, 1989), 215.

25. Gubar, *Racechanges*, 69–72. The end of the film differs from that of the play, where Jack chooses to follow his father on the bimah. It is not at all certain that he will return to the stage.

26. Matthew F. Jacobson, *Whiteness of a Different Color* (Cambridge: Harvard University Press, 1998), 120. Michael Rogin's, *Blackface, White Noise: Jewish Immigrants in the Hollywood Melting Pot* (Berkeley: University of California Press, 1996), has had great influence; see 100. Also see John Strasbaugh, *Black Like You: Blackface, Whiteface, Insult and Imitation in American Popular Culture* (New York: Penguin, 2006); Alexander, *Jazz Age Jews*; and Gubar, *Racechanges*.

27. Alexander, *Jazz Age Jews*, 172–173.

28. Gubar, *Racechanges*, 70–73.

29. Jeffrey Melnick, *A Right to Sing the Blues: African Americans, Jews, and American Popular Song* (Cambridge: Harvard University Press, 1999), 107.

30. Merwin, *In Their Own Image*, 153.

31. See Andrea Most, *Making Americans: Jews and the Broadway Musical* (Cambridge: Harvard University Press, 2004), 23.

32. Rogin, *Blackface, White Noise*, 82, 100.

33. Saposnik, "Jolson, the Jazz Singer and the Jewish Mother," 440.

34. Tucker, *Some of These Days*, 35; Pamela Brown Lavitt, "First of the Red Hot Mamas: 'Coon Shouting' and the Jewish Ziegfeld Girl," in Joyce Antler, ed., "Performance and Jewish Cultural History," *American Jewish History* 87, no. 4 (Dec. 1999): 254.

35. Tucker, *Some of These Days*, 34–35, 40–41.

36. Lavitt, " 'Coon Shouting,' " 259.

37. Saposnik, "Jolson, the Jazz Singer and the Jewish Mother," 440.

38. John Cooper, *The Child in Jewish History* (Northvale, N.J.: Jason Aronson, 1996), 338; Glenn, *Daughters of the Shtetl*, 66–67.

39. Hertzberg, *Jews in America*, 196, 198; Lawrence H. Fuchs, *Beyond Patriarchy: Jewish Fathers and Families* (Hanover, N.H.: University of New England Press, 2000), 114.

40. Fuchs, *Beyond Patriarchy*, 109.

41. Cooper, *The Child in Jewish History*, 338.

42. Mary Antin, *The Promised Land* (Boston: Houghton Mifflin, 1912), 10, cited in Fuchs, *Beyond Patriarchy*, 118; see Fuchs, 118–119.

43. See J. Hoberman, in *Bridge of Light: Yiddish Film between Two Worlds* (Philadelphia: Temple University Press, 1995), 116; Hertzberg, *The Jews in America*, 198.

44. Cited in Cooper, *The Child in Jewish History*, 338.

45. Howe, *World of Our Fathers*, 174–177.

46. Ibid., 254, 174, 176–177.

47. Back jacket copy, Sholom Asch, *The Mother* (New York: Horace Liveright, 1930). Asch became a naturalized American citizen in 1920.

48. Kathie Friedman-Kasaba, *Memories of Migration: Gender, Ethnicity, and Work in the Lives of Jewish and Italian Women in New York, 1870–1924* (Albany: State University of New York Press, 1996), 92.

49. Alfred Kazin, *A Walker in the City* (New York: Harcourt, Brace, 1951), 172.

50. Friedman-Kasaba, *Memories of Migration*, 92; see Michael Gold, *Jews without Money* (New York: Horace Liveright, 1930).

51. Sam B. Girgus, *The New Covenant: Jewish Writers and the American Idea* (Chapel Hill: University of North Carolina Press, 1984), 66.

52. Ibid., 77.

53. Abraham Cahan, *The Rise of David Levinsky* (New York: Harper and Bros., 1917; Harper Torchbooks, 1960), 96–97. Citations are to the 1960 edition. Also see Girgus, *The New Covenant*, 85–91.

54. Janet Burstein, *Writing Mothers, Writing Daughters: Tracing the Maternal in Stories by American Jewish Women* (Champaign: University of Illinois Press, 1996), 27, 300–331, 38–39.

55. Anzia Yezierska, *Bread Givers* (New York: Persea Books, 1975), 126–127, 12.

56. Henry Roth, *Call It Sleep* (New York: Farrar, Straus and Giroux, 1991), 127.

57. Howe, *World of Our Fathers*, 176; also see Ruth R. Wisse, *The Modern Jewish Canon: A Journey Through Language and Culture* (New York: Free Press, 2000), 278.

58. S. P. Rivo, "Projected Images: Portraits of Jewish Women in Early American Film," in Antler, *Talking Back*, 42. Ted Merwin sees immigrant mothers less empowered in these films than does Rivo; see *In Their Own Image*, 153.

59. Rogin, *Blackface, White* Noise, 84.

60. Rivo, "Projected Images," 36–37.

61. Susan Koppelman, *The Stories of Fannie Hurst* (New York: The Feminist Press, 2004), xv, cited in Antler, *The Journey Home*, 153.

62. *Humoresque*, UCLA Film and Television Archive, Los Angeles, California.

63. Patricia Erens, *The Jew in American Cinema* (Bloomington: Indiana University Press, 1984), 78, 84–85; Rivo, "Projected Images," 36–37.

64. See Rivo, "Projected Images," 37–39. The film draws on several of Yezierska's short stories, including "The Lost Beautifulness," where the mother loses in court, and "Where Lovers Dream," in which the daughter is abandoned by her well-born lover because of her poverty. Yezierska's daughter called the film a "mishmash of opposing ideas" and recalled how her mother hated it. Louise Levitas Henriksen, *Anzia Yezierska: A Writer's Life* (New Brunswick, N.J.: Rutgers University Press, 1988), 166–168; Henriksen's interview with the author, Waltham, Mass., March 14, 1993.

65. Henriksen, *Anzia Yezierska*, 167.

66. At the conference "Developing Images: Representations of Jewish Women in American Culture," Brandeis University, March 14–16, 1993, where the film was screened, Henriksen appreciated the audience's positive response.

67. *His People*, a 1925 film directed by Edward Sloman, offers another portrait of a Jewish family in which Rosa Rosanova stars as a righteous mother. In a retelling of the patriarchal narrative of Isaac and Rebekah, two sons go in different directions. The good-hearted Sammy, who wants to be a boxer, is disowned by his father. Firstborn Morris, a spoiled, selfish lawyer, is his father's pet. The mother loves both sons equally but sees the good in Sammy that the father misses. See Erens, *The Jew in American Cinema*, 85–86.

68. Koppelman, "Introduction," *The Stories of Fannie Hurst*, xix.

69. Thanks to Andrea Most for her helpful comments.

70. See Erens, *The Jew in American Cinema*, 140–141.

71. Ibid., 132.

72. On the principles and administration of the Hollywood Production Code, see Thomas Doherty, *Pre-Code Hollywood: Sex, Immorality, and Insurrection in American Cinema, 1930–1934* (New York: Columbia University Press, 1999).

73. See, for example, Neil Gabler, *An Empire of Their Own: How the Jews Invented Hollywood* (New York: Crown, 1988); Steven Alan Cart, *Hollywood and Anti-Semitism: A Cultural History Up to World War II* (Cambridge: Cambridge University Press, 2001); and J. Hoberman and Jeffrey Shandler, *Entertaining America: Jews, Movies and Broadcasting* (Princeton: Princeton University Press, 2003).

74. William Wyler's *Counsellor-at-Law* (1933) concerns an upwardly mobile lawyer, George Simon (John Barrymore), who has made it, but not without some indiscretions along the way. Unlike the rich sons of the other movies, George's heart is in the right place and he helps those who cannot pay. His Gentile wife deserts him in his time of need, but his mother comes to his aid.

75. Katrina Irving, *Immigrant Mothers: Narratives of Race and Maternity, 1890–1925* (Urbana: University of Illinois Press, 2000), 85. Kellor's quote is from her 1916 article, "Straight America" (24), cited in Irving, ibid. For a comparison of social reformers' attitudes to immigrant and black mothers, see Irving, 17. Also see Friedman-Kasaba, *Memories of Migration*, 109–110.

76. Zelda F. Popkin, "Mother Love in Mean Streets," *The American Hebrew*, May 5, 1922, 700. Thanks to Ted Merwin for this reference.

77. Ibid.

78. B. Goldberg, "Fanny Hurst's 'Humoresque' at the Vanderbilt Theater," *Der Tog*, March 9, 1923, cited in Merwin, *In Their Own Image*, 90.

79. See, for example, Irving, *Immigrant Mothers*, 84–85.

80. Cooper, *The Child in Jewish History*, 343.

81. Jacob Kohn, *Modern Problems of Jewish Parents: A Study in Parental Attitudes* (New York: The Women's League of the United Synagogue of America, 1932), 119, cited in Cooper, *The Child in Jewish History*, 344.

82. Cooper, *The Child in Jewish History*, 343.

83. Ibid., 333–335.

84. Cited in ibid., 337.

85. Kazin, *A Walker in the City*, 32, cited in Hasia Diner, *Hungering for America: Italian, Irish and Jewish Foodways in the Age of Migration* (Cambridge: Harvard University Press, 2001), 193.

86. Diner, *Hungering for America*, 192–193, 213–214, 216, 219.

87. Ibid., 214.

88. Ruth Zuckoff, "Mothers Who Go to School with Their Children—That Is, In Spirit, At Least," *Forward*, Jan. 18, 1925.

89. Ibid.

90. Ibid.

91. Nathaniel Zalowitz, "Ungrateful Children of Sacrificing Parents: Many Parents Sacrifice Everything for Children Who Reward Them by Contempt—Are Jewish Children Less Grateful to Their Parents Than Any Other?" *Forward*, June 14, 1925.

92. Ibid.

93. Ibid.

94. Ibid. Also see Edith B. Coff, "*Yes*, A 'Greenhorn' Mother Is Also Entitled to Respect," Feb. 15, 1925; Joseph A. Miller, "What Do Children Owe Their Parents?" May 24, 1925;

Jacob F. Berenson, "Parents Have Duties Too, Says This Writer," June 21, 1925; L. Davidson, "What Parents and Children Owe Each Other," June 28, 1925, Foreword.

95. Cited in Cooper, *The Child in Jewish History*, 339.

96. George M. D. Wolfe, "A Study in Immigrant Attitudes and Problems, Based on an Analysis of Four Hundred Letters Printed in the 'Bintel Brief' of the 'Jewish Daily Forward,'" New York Public Library. Wolfe was an M.A. candidate at the Graduate School for Jewish Social Work in New York. Thanks to Stephen Brumberg for this reference. (Wolfe translates it as "bunch"; the more common translation is "bundle.")

97. Wolfe, "A Study in Immigrant Attitudes and Problems," 399.

98. Ibid., 425.

99. Ibid., 427.

100. Ibid., 281–287, 304–305.

101. Ibid., 120–121.

102. Ibid., xxxi (case no. 245).

103. Ibid., xlix (case no. 356).

104. Ibid., xxxi (case no. 247).

105. Ibid., xlii (case no. 311).

106. Ibid., xli (case no. 310).

107. Ibid., xxxiii (case no. 263).

108. Ibid., xxxii, xliii (case no. 249, 319).

109. Ibid., li (case no. 370).

110. Ibid., xxxviii (case no. 286).

111. Ibid., liii (case no. 378).

112. Ibid., xxxv (case no. 268).

113. In *Adapting to Abundance: Jewish Immigrants, Mass Consumption, and the Search for American Identity* (New York: Columbia University Press, 1990), Andrew Heinze argues that the skills of Jewish *balabostes* as consumers propelled Jews' adaptation to urban America; see chap. 6, 105–115.

114. See Clifford Odets, *Awake and Sing!* (1935), in Ellen Schiff, ed., *Awake and Singing: Seven Classic Plays from the American Jewish Repertoire* (New York: Mentor, 1995).

115. Beverly Gray Bienstock, "The Changing Image of the American Jewish Mother," in Virginia Tufte and Barbara Myerhoff, *Changing Images of the American Jewish Family* (New Haven: Yale University Press, 1979), 179–180.

116. Gerald Weales, *Clifford Odets, Playwright* (New York: Pegasus, 1971), 59–60.

117. Clifford Odets, *Awake and Sing!* 223–224, 279.

118. Ibid., 223–224, 283.

119. Schiff, *Awake and Singing*, 220–221. An example of this inflection is the mother's line, "By me is no jumping off a roof." See "I Got the Blues," Odets Papers, Box 4, Lincoln Center Library of the Performing Arts. I am grateful to Ellen Schiff for this reference.

120. Odets, *Awake and Sing!* 250, 269, 279.

121. Ibid., 240.

122. Robert Warshow, "Poet of the Middle Class: Clifford Odets Voices Its Conflicts and Frustrations," *Commentary* 1, no. 7 (May 1946): 17–22.

123. Ibid., 22.

124. Margaret Brenman-Gibson, *Clifford Odets, American Playwright: The Years from 1906 to 1940* (New York: Atheneum, 1981), 254.

125. Weales, *Clifford Odets, Playwright*, 19–20.

126. Odets's father described his wife as "selfish, unfaithful, cold, demanding." Others described her as saintly, "nunlike"; Brenman-Gibson, *Clifford Odets*, 23.

127. Ibid., 214.

128. Ibid., 215.

129. Clifford Odets, *The Time Is Ripe: The 1940 Journal of Clifford Odets* (New York: Grove Press, 1988), 236, 298, 293; also see 163–164, 239, 252.

130. Brenman-Gibson, *Clifford Odets, American Playwright*, 23.

131. Odets, *The Time Is Ripe*, 17–18.

Chapter 2

1. After 1931, the radio show aired nightly, for some years carried by both CBS and NBC. The show played live on television from 1949 to 1954 on CBS, then NBC, and for a few months in 1954 on the Dumont Network. A series of filmed episodes was syndicated on local stations from 1955 to 1956.

2. J. Hoberman, "The [Jewish] Mother of Us All," symposium on "The Legacy of the Goldbergs," American Historical Society and Yeshiva University, New York City, April 23, 2006, and personal communication to author, April 26, 2006.

3. On *The Goldbergs*, see Riv-Ellen Prell, *Fighting to Become Americans: Jews, Gender, and the Anxieties of Assimilation* (Boston: Beacon Press, 1999), 169–172; Vincent Brook, "The Americanization of Molly: How Mid-Fifties TV Homogenized *The Goldbergs* (and Got "Berg-larized" in the Process)," *Cinema Journal* 38, no. 4 (Summer 1999): 45–69, and Brook, *Something Ain't Kosher Here: The Rise of the "Jewish" Sitcom* (New Brunswick: Rutgers University Press, 2003), chaps. 2, 3, 5; Donald Weber, "Memory and Repression in Early Ethnic Television: The Example of Gertrude Berg and the Goldbergs," in Joel Foreman, ed., *The Other Fifties: Interrogating Midcentury American Icons* (Urbana: University of Illinois Press, 1997), 144–165; Weber, "The Jewish-American World of Gertrude Berg: The *Goldbergs* on Radio and Television, 1930–1950," in Joyce Antler, ed., *Talking Back: Images of Jewish Women in American Popular Culture* (Hanover, N.H.: University of New England Press, 1998), 85–102; Weber, "Taking Jewish American Popular Culture Seriously: The Yinglish Worlds of Gertrude Berg, Milton Berle, and Mickey Katz," *Jewish Social Studies* 5 (Fall 1998/Winter 1999): 124–153; Weber, *Haunted in the New World: Jewish American Culture from Cahan to the Goldbergs* (Bloomington: Indiana University Press, 2005), chap. 6; David Zurawik, *The Jews of Prime Time* (Hanover, N.H.: University of New England Press, 2003), chap. 1; George Lipsitz, "The Meaning of Memory: Family, Class, and Ethnicity in Early Network Television," in *Time Passages: Collective Memory and American Popular Culture* (Minneapolis: University of Minnesota Press, 1990), 39–75; and Joan Jacobs Brumberg, "Gertrude Edelstein Berg," in Barbara Sicherman and Carol Hurd Green, eds., *Notable American Women: The Modern Period*, vol. 4 (Cambridge: Harvard University Press, 1980), 73–74.

4. Aviva Kempner, in "From the Goldbergs to 2005: The Evolution of the Family Sitcom," Museum of Television and Radio New York Satellite Seminar, Nov. 16, 2005.

5. See Joyce Antler, *The Journey Home: How Jewish Women Shaped Modern America* (New York: Schocken Books, 1998), 233–240.

6. William A. H. Birnie, "Molly Goes Marching On," *The American Magazine*, Nov. 1941, 24, Gertrude Berg Papers, Special Collections Research Center, Syracuse University.

7. Glenn Delton Smith, Jr., " 'It's Your America': Gertrude Berg and American Broadcasting, 1929–1956," Ph.D. dissertation, University of Southern Mississippi, 2004, 131.

8. Ibid., 95; "Personalities: Gertrude Berg," *American Hebrew*, Oct. 8, 1943, 8, Berg Papers.

9. Ibid.

10. Cited in Weber, "The Jewish-American World of Gertrude Berg," 94.

11. Sulamith Ishi-Kishor, "Interesting People: Gertrude Berg," *The Jewish Tribune*, Oct. 10, 1930, 7, Berg Papers.

12. Morris Freedman, "The Real Molly Goldberg: Baalebosteh of the Air Waves," *Commentary* 21 (April 1956): 360.

13. Donald Weber, "Goldberg Variations: The Achievements of Gertrude Berg," in J. Hoberman and Jeffrey Shandler, *Entertaining America: Jews, Movies, and Broadcasting* (New York and Princeton: Jewish Museum of New York and Princeton University Press, 2003), 115–116. Edward R. Murrow uses "Mollypropisms," in his interview with Gertrude Berg on *Person to Person*, June 4, 1954, typescript, Berg Papers.

14. For an extended discussion of "Molly's Hat," see Joyce Antler, " 'Yesterday's Woman,' Today's Moral Guide: Molly Goldberg as Jewish Mother," in Jack Kugelmass, ed., *Key Texts in American Jewish Culture* (New Brunswick, N.J.: Rutgers University Press, 2003), 129–146.

15. Gertrude Berg, with Cherney Berg, *Molly and Me: The Memoirs of Gertrude Berg* (New York: McGraw Hill, 1961), 191; Gertrude Berg, "Foreword," *Who's Who in TV and Radio*, vol. 1, no. 1, 1951, 32–33, Berg Papers.

16. See, for example, Zurawik, *The Jews of Prime Time*, 26.

17. Cited in Smith, " 'It's Your America,' " 441, 453.

18. Ibid., 91.

19. See, for example, Charles Angoff, " 'The Goldbergs' and Jewish Humor," *Congress Weekly: A Review of Jewish Interests* 18 (March 5, 1951): 13.

20. Smith, " 'It's Your America,' " 1, 100.

21. For a comparison of Odets's characterization of the Jewish family, and Berg's, see Prell, *Fighting to Become Americans*, 135–139.

22. Gertrude Berg, "I Know What I Like," *The Theater*, April 1959, 17, 25, Berg Papers.

23. Berg, *Molly and Me*, 182.

24. Gertrude Berg, "The Real Story behind the 'House of Glass,' " Radio Mirror, [circa July 1935], Berg Papers.

25. Berg, *Molly and Me*, 194; David Morris, "Sketch Was Too Realistic: 'The Goldbergs' Originally Rejected Because It Was Too Lifelike," *New York Sun*, May 23, 1936, Berg Papers.

26. Berg, "I Know What I Like," 17; Berg, *Molly and Me*, 194; Morris, "Sketch Was Too Realistic."

27. Morris, "Sketch Was Too Realistic"; "It's Gotta Be Real for Molly!" *TV* Forecast, Dec. 30, 1950, 4; Birnie, "Molly Goes Marching On," 120; "Gertrude Berg Mother to Two Full 'Families,' " *Milwaukee Wisconsin Journal*, June 14, 1936, Berg Papers.

28. "Personalities: Gertrude Berg," *American Hebrew*, Oct. 8, 1943, 8, 14; Dan Senseney, "The Heart of the Goldbergs," *TV Radio Mirror*, August 1954, 40–43, 91–93; " 'It's Gotta Be Real for Molly!' " 14, and *TV Guide*, Dec. 2, 1950, Berg Papers.

29. Gertrude Berg, untitled clipping from *Home Stages*, n.d., Berg Papers.

30. Hank O'Hare, "Bouquets 'n Barbs," *TV Digest*, April 14, 1951, 14, Berg Papers.

31. Jack Cluett, "Radio," *Woman's Day*, Dec. 1949, Berg Papers.

32. Angoff, " 'The Goldbergs' and Jewish Humor," 12–13.

33. Morris Freedman, "The Real Molly Goldberg," 359–364; also see "It's Gotta Be Real for Molly!" and "Personalities: Gertrude Berg," 14.

34. Cited in Weber, *Haunted in the New World*, 134.

35. Ruth Gay, *Unfinished People: Eastern European Jews Encounter America* (New York: Norton, 1996), 220–221.

36. Neil M. Cowan and Ruth Schwartz Cowan, *Our Parents' Lives: Jewish Assimilation in Everyday Lives* (New Brunswick, N.J.: Rutgers University Press, 1996).

37. David Marc, *Demographic Vistas: Television in American Culture* (Philadelphia: University of Pennsylvania Press, 1984), 13; Ella Taylor, *Prime Time Families: Television Culture in Postwar America* (Berkeley: University of California Press, 1989), 27.

38. See Prell's discussion of Berg and Clifford Odets in *Fighting to Become Americans*, 134. Also see Joyce Antler, "A Bond of Sisterhood: Ethel Rosenberg, Molly Goldberg, and Radical Jewish Women of the 1950s," in Marjorie Garber and Rebecca L. Walkowitz, eds., *Secret Agents: The Rosenberg Case, McCarthyism and Fifties America* (New York: Routledge, 1995), 197–214.

39. Berg, *Molly and Me*, 191.

40. Birnie, "Molly Goes Marching On," 118.

41. Edward R. Murrow, *Person to Person*, June 4, 1954, excerpted in "From the Goldbergs to 2005," Museum of Television and Radio.

42. Berg, *Molly and Me*, 167.

43. David Marc, *Comic Visions: Television Comedy and American Culture* (Boston: Unwin Hyman, 1989), 51.

44. Zurawik, *The Jews of Prime Time*, 32–35.

45. Kempner, "From the Goldbergs to 2005."

46. Senseney, "The Heart of the Goldbergs."

47. Interview with Cherney and Dorothy Berg in Smith, " 'It's Your America,' " 402.

48. Gilbert Seldes, "The Great Gertrude," *Saturday Review*, June 5, 1956, 26.

49. This account is based on Glenn Smith's interviews with Berg's two children; Harriet Schwartz, interviewed Aug. 17, 1998, and Cherney Berg, interviewed Oct. 10, 1998. Harriet and Cherney disagreed about the time of Dinah's death, with Cherney placing it between 1940 and 1945 and Harriet earlier; Smith, " 'It's Your America,' " 40, 53–54, 399, 411.

50. Smith, " 'It's Your America,' " 410–411.

51. Senseney, "The Heart of the Goldbergs."

52. Ibid.

53. "The Rent Strike," Sept. 5, 1949. *Goldberg* episodes may be screened at the Museum of Radio and Television in New York and Los Angeles, at the National Jewish Archive of Broadcasting at the Jewish Museum in New York, and at the Radio and Television Archive at the University of California at Los Angeles (UCLA).

54. Donald Weber, "Popular Culture and Middle-Class Imagination: The Figure of Gertrude Berg in Radio and Television, 1930–1962," 1993, unpublished paper, 36.

55. Dena Reed, "Are You a Good Listener?" *True Confessions*, Jan. 1951, 10–11, Berg Papers.

56. *The Goldbergs*, April 3, 1950.

57. "The Rent Strike."

58. *The Goldbergs*, Oct. 22, 1943, Yom Kippur show, no. 1585, Berg Papers.

59. "Dreams," March 3, 1955.

60. "The Boyfriends," Feb. 23, 1955, Berg Papers.

61. "Rosie the Actress," 1955 (nd).

62. "The Girl Scouts," March 15, 1956.

63. "Molly, a Member of the Jury," July 14, 1955; Charles Angoff, "The Goldbergs," *The Reconstructionist*, Dec. 24, 1954, 19–22.

64. Syndicated through the Seven Arts Syndicate, the column, which appeared as "Mamatalks," appeared in Jewish newspapers in Boston; Philadelphia; Syracuse; Washington, D.C.; Atlantic City; Albany; Dallas; Chicago; Pittsburgh; Omaha; and Des Moines. The first column, published October 19, 1934, in the *Boston Advocate* and other syndicate papers, noted that "If Mama were listened to more carefully," many of the misunderstandings in the contemporary world would disappear; Berg Papers.

65. Gertrude Berg, "Privacy," "Mamatalks," Jan. 4, 1935, Berg Papers.

66. Seven Arts Syndicate clipping, n.d, Berg Papers.

67. Cited in Nancy Pottisham Weiss, "Mother, the Invention of Necessity: Dr. Benjamin Spock's *Baby and Child Care*," in N. Ray Hiner and Joseph M. Hawes, eds., *Growing Up in America: Children in Historical Perspective* (Urbana: University of Illinois Press, 1985), 290.

68. Berg, "Mamatalks," Dec. 7, 1934, Berg Papers.

69. Berg, "Mamatalks," April 5, 1935, Berg Papers.

70. Berg, "Mamatalks," Nov. 9, 1934, Berg Papers.

71. See, for example, Sharon Hays, *The Cultural Contradictions of Motherhood* (New Haven: Yale University Press, 1996), 46, 49.

72. Weiss, "Mother, the Invention of Necessity," 292–294; also see Ann Hulbert, *Raising America: Experts, Parents, and a Century of Advice about Children* (New York: Alfred A. Knopf, 2003), chap. 8.

73. "*Mamatalks* No. 1," Jan. 22, 1936, Berg Papers (all references to *Mamatalks* episodes in the following notes are from the Berg Papers).

74. *Mamatalks* No. 2, Jan. 29, 1936.

75. *Mamatalks* No. 1.

76. *Mamatalks* No. 7, March 4, 1936.

77. *Mamatalks* No. 15, May 13, 1936.

78. *Mamatalks* No. 12, April 22, 1936.

79. Ibid.

80. *Mamatalks* No. 10, March 25, 1936.

81. *Mamatalks* No. 8, March 11, 1936. The principles that Berg espoused on the *Mamatalks* shows are similar to those championed by Sidonie Gruenberg, executive director of the Child Study Association of America. On Gruenberg, see Roberta Lyn Wollons, "Educating Mothers: Sidonie Matsner Gruenberg and the Child Study Association of America, 1881–1929," Ph.D. dissertation, University of Chicago, 1983.

82. *Mamatalks*, circa 1945, Berg Papers.

83. "Rosie's Composition," October 10, 1949, University of California at Los Angeles Film Archive. All quotes excerpted in the following paragraphs are from this episode.

84. Joan Kapp Philips, "'Every Day a Mother's Day': TV's Molly Goldberg Says It's Time for Mom to Assert Herself in Family Affairs," *TV Family*, Dec. 11, 1951, Berg Papers.

85. Berg also wrote the script for "Mind Over Momma," a 1955 *Elgin Hour* drama, about "a well-meaning but over-possessive mother"; "Mind Over Momma," *Elgin Hour*, May 31, 1955, *New York Herald Tribune TV and Radio Magazine*, Berg Papers.

86. Gertrude Berg (alias Molly Goldberg), "I Like Living in a Small Community," *TV and Radio*, Oct. 9–15, 1955, 14–15, Berg Papers.

87. "For the Ladies," *TV Guide*, April 8, 1950, 20, Berg Papers.

88. *The Goldbergs*, "Sammy's Wedding," May 11, 1954. UCLA Film and Television Archive.

89. This description of *The House of Glass* is based on Samantha Goldstein, "For the Amusement of the Guests: How Gertrude Berg Brought the Catskills to Radio and TV," Catskills Institute Conference, Monticello, New York, Aug. 26, 2005, 202–204. Gertrude Berg, "Realism in Radio," *Radio Rays*, n.d.; and Berg, "The Real Story behind the House of Glass," 22–24.

90. On this episode, see Weber, *Haunted in the New World*, 150–151.

91. "Reach for the Moon," Dec. 15, 1955; Brook, "The Americanization of Molly," 50.

92. "The Milk Farm," 1955, Berg Papers.

93. Betty Friedan, *The Feminine Mystique* (New York: Norton, 1963).

94. "Dreams," March 3, 1955.

95. Brook, "The Americanization of Molly," 61. On the ideological contradictions of

the Goldbergs' move to the suburbs, see Marla Brettschneider, "Arrested Assimilation: The Goldbergs in the Suburbs," paper presented at the The Legacy of the Goldbergs Conference, Center for Jewish History, New York City, April 23, 2006.

96. Hal Himmelstein, *Television Myth and the American Mind* (New York: Praeger, 1984), 84–97; Marc, *Comic Visions*, 65; Darrell Y. Hamamoto, *Nervous Laughter: Television Situation Comedy and Liberal Democratic Ideology* (New York: Praeger, 1989), 24–25. For a discussion of television's role as mediator between changing consumer roles and family life, see Lipsitz, "The Meaning of Memory," 39–75.

97. Vincent Brook argues that the 1955–56 *Goldbergs* was essentially a new show since the Goldbergs lost their ethnic, working-class characteristics. In the move away from "women-centered sitcoms" to "male-dominated/children-centered 'domestic melodramas,'" Brook believes that Molly was "decentered"; Brook, *Something Ain't Kosher Here*, 35. Riv-Ellen Prell sees Jake, not Molly, as "decentered" and marginalized, his masculinity "uprooted"; *Fighting to Become Americans*, 170–171. David Marc describes the suburban *Goldbergs* as one of the vanishing "urban ethnicoms"; *Comic Visions*, 53.

98. The influence of *The Goldbergs* on *I Remember Mama* is recalled in Rosemary Rice, Dick Van Patten, and Robin Morgan, *I Remember Mama* Symposium, Museum of Radio and Television, Los Angeles, Dec. 17, 1985. George Lipsitz writes that the success of a radio performance of *I Remember Mama* led to the television version in 1949–50; "Why Remember Mama? The Changing Face of a Woman's Narrative," in Joanne Morreale, ed., *Critiquing the Sitcom: A Reader* (Syracuse, N.Y.: Syracuse University Press, 2003), 16. Judith E. Smith, *Visions of Belonging: Family Stories, Popular Culture, and Postwar Democracy, 1940–1960* (New York: Columbia University Press, 2004), sees a difference between *Mama* and *The Goldbergs'* "vaudeville style ethnic humor" (99).

99. Cited by Smith, "'It's Your America,'" 3. On the Loeb episode, also see Zurawik, *The Jews of Prime Time*, 42–45; Thomas Doherty, *Cold War, Cool Medium: Television, McCarthyism, and American Culture* (New York: Columbia University Press, 2003), 41–48.

100. Zurawik, *The Jews of Prime Time*, 26.

101. Nina C. Leibman, *Living Room Lectures: The Fifties, Family in Film and Television* (Austin: University of Texas Press, 1995), 197.

102. Lipsitz, "Why Remember Mama?" 10.

103. On the importance of ethnic memory as a part of *The Goldbergs'* appeal, see Weber, "Memory and Repression in Early Ethnic Television." On the show's appeal to contemporary Americans, see Francine Klagsbrun, "'The Goldbergs'—Stereotypes Loved by Americans," *New York Times*, August 8, 1988; Brook, "The Americanization of Molly," 52.

104. Molly describes herself as a "yesterday woman" in the 1949 episode, "Molly's Hat"; see Antler, "'Yesterday's Woman,'" 140–143.

105. Zurawik, *The Jews of Prime Time*, 26.

Chapter 3

1. Philip Wylie, *Generation of Vipers* (New York: Rinehart, 1942).

2. Jennifer Terry, "'Momism' and the Making of Treasonous Homosexuals," in Molly Ladd-Taylor and Lauri Umansky, *"Bad Mothers": The Politics of Blame in Twentieth-Century America* (New York: New York University Press, 1998), 176.

3. Rebecca Jo Plant, "The Repeal of Mother Love: Momism, and the Reconstruction of Motherhood in Philip Wylie's America," Ph.D. dissertation, Johns Hopkins University, 2002, 12, 21, 84, 116.

4. Ibid., 126.

5. Mark Zborowski and Elizabeth Herzog, *Life Is with People: The Jewish Little-Town of*

Eastern Europe (New York: International Universities Press, 1952). The subtitle was changed to "The Culture of the Shtetl" when Schocken issued the first paperback edition in 1962.

6. Barbara Kirshenblatt-Gimblett, "Introduction," in Mark Zborowski and Elizabeth Herzog, *Life Is with People: The Culture of the Shtetl* (1952; repr., New York: Schocken Books, 1995), xxxi. All citations following are from the 1995 edition.

7. Kirshenblatt-Gimblett, "Introduction," ix, xxix.

8. Ibid., xxix, 293–294; minutes of the Jewish Group Meeting, Aug. 11, 1949, Margaret Mead Papers, Library of Congress, Washington, D.C. (Minutes of the Jewish Group Meetings are to be found in the Mead Papers, G50.)

9. Dolores Janiewski and Lois W. Banner, "Introduction," in Janiewski and Banner, eds., *Reading Benedict, Reading Mead: Feminism, Race, and Imperial Visions* (Baltimore: Johns Hopkins University Press, 2004), viii.

10. Kirshenblatt-Gimblett, "Introduction," xxxi. Examples of the many references to *LIWP* include John Cooper, *The Child in Jewish History* (Northvale, N.J.: Jason Aronson, 1996), 262; Alan Dundes, "The J. A. P. and the J. A. M. in American Jokelore," *Journal of American Folklore* 98, no. 390 (Oct.–Dec. 1985): 456–475; Deborah S. Bernstein, ed., *Pioneers and Homemakers: Jewish Women in Pre-State Israel* (New York: State University of New York Press, 1992), 2; Lawrence H. Fuchs, *Beyond Patriarchy: Jewish Fathers and Families* (Hanover, N.H.: University of New England Press, 2000), 91, 95, 100; Nathan Glazer, "Ethnic Groups and Education: Towards the Tolerance of Difference," *Journal of Negro Education* 38, no. 3 (Summer 1969): 187–195; Joel Martin Halpern and David A. Kideckel, "Anthropology of Eastern Europe," *Annual Review of Anthropology* 12: 377–402; Barbara Myerhoff, *Number Our Days* (New York: Dutton, 1978), 292; Benjamin Schlesinger, "The Jewish Family in Retrospect," in Schlesinger, *The Jewish Family: A Survey and Annotated Bibliography* (Toronto: University of Toronto Press, 1971), 14.

11. On Mead and Benedict's war work, see Lois W. Banner, "Margaret Mead," in Susan Ware, ed., *Notable American Women: A Biographical Dictionary* (Cambridge: Harvard University Press, 2004), 440, and Lois Banner, *Intertwined Lives: Margaret Mead, Ruth Benedict, and Their Circle* (New York: Alfred A. Knopf, 2003), 411–432: Mary Catherine Bateson, *With a Daughter's Eye: A Memoir of Margaret Mead and Gregory Bateson* (New York: William Morrow, 1984), 230; Mead, "Foreword," in Zborowski and Herzog, *Life Is with People*, 14.

12. Margaret Mead, *An Anthropologist at Work: The Writings of Ruth Benedict* (1959; repr., Westport, Conn.: Greenwood Press, 1977); Margaret Mead, *Ruth Benedict* (New York: Columbia University Press, 1974), 57–61. See Margaret Mead and Rhoda Métraux, eds., *The Study of Culture at a Distance* (Chicago: University of Chicago Press, 1953), 97. Mead served as executive secretary of the National Research Council's Committee on Food Habits from 1942 to 1945.

13. Mead, *Ruth Benedict*, 57–59; Judith Schachter Modell, *Ruth Benedict: Patterns of a Life* (Philadelphia: University of Pennsylvania Press, 1983), 268–271; Banner, *Intertwined Lives*, 415–419. Also see Christopher Shannon, "'A World Made Safe for Difference': Ruth Benedict's *The Chrysanthemum and the Sword*," in Janiewski and Banner, *Reading Benedict, Reading Mead*, 74.

14. See Modell, *Ruth Benedict*, 287–288; Margaret M. Caffrey, *Ruth Benedict: Stranger in This Land* (Austin: University of Texas Press, 1989), 326; Shannon, "'A World Made Safe for Difference,'" 70–85; Nanako Fukui, "The Lady of the Chrysanthemum: Ruth Benedict and the Origins of *The Chrysanthemum and the Sword*," in Janiewski and Banner, *Reading Benedict, Reading Mead*, 115–125; Douglas Lummis, "Ruth Benedict's Obituary for Japanese Culture," in Janiewski and Banner, *Reading Benedict, Reading Mead*, 126–140; and Pauline Kent, "Misconceived Configurations of Ruth Benedict: The Debate in Japan over *The*

Chrysanthemum and the Sword," 179–190, in Janiewski and Banner, *Reading Benedict, Reading Mead.*

15. Mead, *Ruth Benedict,* 68.

16. The RCC sought to contrast behaviors among Great Russian, Czech, and Polish cultures, all stemming from the same area of Europe and sharing in "past and contemporary relationships"; Syria was included because few Middle Eastern countries had been subject to the national-character-based anthropological approach and because many Middle Eastern nationals in the United States were from Syria. Chinese culture—based on research with the "Cantonese" enclave in New York's Chinatown—was the largest research group and required the longest period of research. Margaret Mead, "Research in Contemporary Cultures," in Harold Guetzkow, ed., *Groups, Leadership and Men: Research in Human Relations* (Pittsburgh: Carnegie Press, 1951), 106, 109–115. The group's representation in New York City was also an important selection criterion; General Seminar Notes, Sept. 18, 1947, Mead Papers.

17. Mead, *Ruth Benedict,* 59. Mead's first interest in studying Eastern European Jewish culture came from a conversation with Erich Fromm; see Mead, "Foreword," 13–14.

18. Kirshenblatt-Gimblett, "Introduction," xxvii.

19. Mead, "Foreword," 16. Mead told the RCC team that she and Benedict developed the plan for studying Jewish culture cross-nationally in 1943; Jewish Group Meeting Minutes, Sept. 15, 1949, Mead Papers. Also see Ruth Benedict, "Suggested Guide for a Field Study of Jewish Americans," G51, Mead Papers.

20. Mead, *Ruth Benedict,* 70. Because Columbia University did not provide space for the project, research groups met in the homes of members and other borrowed spaces all over the city. In its final years, the project acquired office space in an old, condemned building at the Columbia University Medical School.

21. On the relationship between Mead and Benedict, see Banner, *Intertwined Lives.* Also see Hilary Lapsley, *Margaret Mead and Ruth Benedict: The Kinship of Women* (Amherst: University of Massachusetts Press, 1999).

22. Mead and Métraux, *The Study of Culture at a Distance,* 100; Research in Contemporary Cultures, Sixth General Seminar; Dec. 4, 1947, G13, Mead Papers.

23. Mead, "Discussion of Benedict's 'Child Rearing in Certain European Countries,'" Columbia University in Contemporary Cultures Research Materials, Cross Cultural documents nos. 1–8, G31, Mead Papers. Mead, *Ruth Benedict,* 71; Mead and Métraux, *The Study of Culture at a Distance,* 99.

24. Caffrey, *Ruth Benedict,* 343; Mead, *An Anthropologist at Work,* 435; Mead, "Research in Contemporary Cultures," 107.

25. Kirshenblatt-Gimblett, "Introduction," xxxi; Report of General Seminar, Sept. 18, 1947, Mead Papers.

26. Mead and Métraux, *The Study of Culture at a Distance,* 95, n. 1; Margaret Mead, "The Postwar Years: The Gathered Threads," in *An Anthropologist at Work: The Writings of Ruth Benedict,* 434–435; Caffrey, *Ruth Benedict,* 343–345.

27. The Jewish Research Group collected 307 documents and held 32 seminars; Mead, "Suggested Project on Jewish Culture."

28. Mead and Métraux, *The Study of Culture at a Distance*; Ruth Landes and Mark Zborowski, "Hypotheses Concerning the Eastern European Jewish Family," *Psychiatry* 13, no. 4 (November 1950): 447–464, reprinted in Norman Kiell, ed., *The Psychodynamics of American Jewish Life: An Anthology* (New York: Twayne Publishers, 1967), 23–55; Martha Wolfenstein, "Two Types of Jewish Mothers," in Margaret Mead and Wolfenstein, eds., *Childhood in Contemporary Cultures* (Chicago: University of Chicago Press, 1955), 424–440.

29. Mead, "Foreword," 16.

30. Sally Cole, *Ruth Landes: A Life in Anthropology* (Lincoln: University of Nebraska Press, 2003), 32. Landes, the daughter of Joseph Schlossberg, cofounder of the American Clothing Workers of America, took an early interest in African American cultural life. After graduating from New York University, Landes studied Harlem storefront churches for her master's thesis, published forty years after the research was undertaken; see Geyla Frank, "Jews, Multiculturalism, and Boasian Anthropology," *American Anthropologist* 99 (1997): 731–745, and Cole, "Ruth Landes and the Early Ethnography of Race and Gender," in R. Behar and D. A. Gordon, eds., *Women Writing Culture*, 166–185. A member of the Department of Scientific Research of the American Jewish Committee, Landes joined the RCC team toward the end of the project (Mead, "Foreword," 17).

31. Dolores E. Janiewski, "Woven Lives, Raveled Texts: Benedict, Mead, and Representational Doubleness," in Janiewski and Banner, *Reading Benedict, Reading Mead*, 14–15.

32. See Kirshenblatt-Gimblett, "Introduction," xxviii–xxxi, for a full discussion of the American Jewish Committee's role in the publication of the book.

33. Ibid., xxxvi. See S. Anthill Fineberg to Area Directors and Executive Assistants, American Jewish Committee, April 22, 1958, for a discussion of the charges against Zborowski and the AJC's reaction; RG 347, AJC Records, Gen-10, 73 Box 211, File: Mass Media, Books, "Life Is with People," Archives of the YIVO Institute for Jewish Research.

34. Kirshenblatt-Gimblett, "Introduction," xxxvi.

35. Ibid., xxx.

36. Ibid., ix–xlviii, xxxi, xxxvi–xxxviii. Kirshenblatt-Gimblett notes that the concept of the shtetl was "hypothetical . . . synthetic"; it emerged as a product of the convergence of challenges and ideologies (xxxiiii–xxxiv). See Jewish Group Meeting notes, Dec. 2, 1947, for a discussion of the shtetl pattern.

37. Kirshenblatt-Gimblett suggests it might have provided a "safe haven, a cover" ("Introduction," xxxvii).

38. Ibid., xiv; personal communication to author from Barbara Kirshenblatt-Gimblett, July 16, 2006.

39. Wolfenstein's article was reprinted in Marshall Sklare, ed., *The Jews: Social Patterns of an American Group* (New York: Free Press, 1958), 520–534. It was cited as evidence of Jewish family patterns by numerous social scientists; for example, Andrew Greeley, "A Model for Ethnic Political Socialization," *American Journal of Political Science* 19, no. 2 (May 1975): 196; Dundes calls it a "brilliant essay" ("The J.A.P. and the J.A.M. in American Jokelore," 475). The team interviewed an additional ten people born in the United States.

40. Aug. 11, 1949, and Sept. 30, 1949, Mead Papers.

41. Jewish Group Meeting, Sept. 30, 1949, Mead Papers.

42. Zborowski and Herzog, *Life Is with People*, 293.

43. Ibid., 294.

44. Ibid., 293.

45. Ibid., 291, 303.

46. Cole, *Ruth Landes*, 247.

47. Landes and Zborowski, "Hypotheses," 46; 49; 52, n. 29.

48. Ibid., 30.

49. Landes and Zborowski, "Hypotheses," 29, 33; Zborowski and Herzog, *Life Is with People*, 132–133, 297.

50. Cole, *Ruth Landes*, 225, 247. Cole writes: "While Margaret Mead generalized the 'ethos' of a harmonious cultural whole, Edward Sapir theorized 'general culture,' Ruth Benedict identified 'patterns,' and Melville Herskovits looked for 'survivals,' Landes asked questions about internal diversity—especially about diversity based on social positions determined by race, class, gender, and sexuality. . . . Her focus on differentiation, and her

delight in the contradictions she observed in the dynamics of culture frustrated many of her contemporaries" (247). Landes may have been influenced by Gregory Bateson's use of "ethos." Mary Catherine Bateson explains that what Benedict called "pattern," Gregory Bateson labeled "ethos"—the "pervasiveness and congruity of style within a system that make any culture more than a list of traits and institutions"; Bateson, *With a Daughter's Eye*, 73.

51. Cited in Cole, *Ruth Landes*, 31.

52. Landes and Zborowski, "Hypotheses," 30.

53. Zborowski and Herzog, *Life Is with People*, 295–296.

54. Landes and Zborowski, "Hypotheses," 31.

55. Ibid., 33, 36.

56. Ibid., 24.

57. Benedict, "Suggested Guide for a Field Study of Jewish Americans," in Ruth Benedict Papers, Research Materials, G51, Mead Papers.

58. Margaret Mead, "Research in Contemporary Culture," Memo 1, Nov. 15, 1950, G16, Mead Papers.

59. Wolfenstein, "Two Types of Jewish Mothers," 438.

60. Ibid., 436.

61. Ibid., 430.

62. Ibid., 438.

63. Ibid., 438.

64. Jewish Group Meeting, Aug. 11, 1949 and Sept. 30, 1949, Mead Papers.

65. Jewish Group Meeting, Sept. 30, 1949, Mead Papers.

66. Ibid.

67. Ibid.

68. Zborowski and Herzog, *Life Is with People*, 297.

69. Ibid., 335.

70. Ibid., 296.

71. Ibid., Jewish Group Meeting, Dec. 2, 1947; Mead Papers.

72. Landes and Zborowski, "Hypotheses," 30.

73. Jewish Group Meeting, Aug. 3, 1949, Mead Papers.

74. Landes and Zborowski, "Hypotheses," 27.

75. Theodore Bienenstok, "Father-Mother-Son Relationship," Dec. 13, 1947, G13, Mead Papers; Landes and Zborowski, "Hypotheses," 32–34.

76. Landes and Zborowski, "Hypotheses," 35–37.

77. Ibid., 36–37.

78. Jewish Group Meeting, Aug. 11, 1949, Mead Papers.

79. Zborowski and Herzog, *Life Is with People*, 348, 330; Jewish Group Meeting, Aug. 3, 1949, Mead Papers.

80. Lawrence J. Friedman, *Identity's Architect: A Biography of Erik H. Erikson* (New York: Scribner, 1999), 135–139, 165.

81. Erik H. Erikson, *Childhood and Society* (New York: Norton, 1950), 355; Friedman, *Identity's Architect*, 171.

82. Erikson, *Childhood and Society*, 288.

83. Ibid., 288–291.

84. These were "Free associations" by Erikson on the "basis of Jewish cultural material presented to him orally by Ruth Benedict, March 4, 1948. Taken down by Margaret Mead as he spoke"; "E. H. Erichson [*sic*]: Free Associations," G51, Mead Papers.

85. Ibid.

86. Ibid.

87. Report on Erik H. Erikson's Lecture, March 5, 1948, to Twelfth General Seminar, Research in Contemporary Cultures, Margaret Mead Presiding, Mead Papers; also see Jewish Group Meeting, March 2, 1948, Mead Papers.

88. Friedman, *Identity's Architect*, 42, 431–433; Sue Erikson Bloland, *In the Shadow of Fame: A Memoir by the Daughter of Erik H. Erikson* (New York: Viking, 2005), 53, 137–38.

89. Friedman, *Identity's Architect*, 298. Freud's relationship to his mother was not dissimilar. According to Ann Douglas, because Freud found it much harder to separate from his powerful Jewish mother than his father ("I am the mother," was Amalia Freud's simple introduction to her son's colleagues), the entire corpus of his work contained a "hidden matricidal scenario." Freud was in his early seventies when Amalia Freud, in her nineties, died; Douglas, *Terrible Honesty: Mongrel Manhattan in the 1920s* (New York: Farrar, Straus, and Giroux, 1995), 236–237.

90. Jewish Group Meeting, Aug. 11, 1949, Mead Papers.

91. Ibid.; Wolfenstein, "Two Types of Jewish Mothers," 436; Martha Wolfenstein, "Notes for Hypotheses on Moral Training," to All Child Study Field Workers, May 25, 1949, G20, Mead Papers.

92. Wolfenstein, "Notes for Hypotheses on Moral Training," 8, Mead Papers.

93. Jewish Group Meeting, Aug. 11, 1949, Mead Papers.

94. Margaret Mead, "Theoretical Setting—1954," in Mead and Wolfenstein, *Childhood in Contemporary Cultures*, 6.

95. Jewish Group Meeting, Aug. 11, 1949, Sept. 30, 1949, Mead Papers.

96. "Quarreling," May 3, 1948, Columbia University Research in Contemporary Cultures, Cross-Cultural Documents, Mead Papers.

97. Jewish Group Meeting, Aug. 11, 1949, Mead Papers.

98. Ruth Benedict, "Child Rearing in Certain European Countries," Paper Read Before Psychiatric Society, April 14, 1948, Mead Papers. The paper was presented at the 1948 meeting of the American Orthopsychiatric Association and was published in Mead, *An Anthropologist at Work*, 449–458.

99. Mead, "Discussion of Benedict's 'Child Rearing in Certain European Countries,'" Mead Papers.

100. Jewish Group Meeting, Sept. 30, 1949, Mead Papers. According to Mead's daughter, anthropologist Mary Catherine Bateson, Mead's wide circle of Jewish acquaintances influenced her sense of the "unconditional" nature of Jewish mothers' love; in addition, two younger sisters were married to Jewish men—cartoonist William Steig and novelist and Yiddish translator Leo Rosten, whom Mead consulted about the project; author's interview with Mary Catherine Bateson, Sept. 28, 2005.

101. Zborowski and Herzog, *Life Is with People*, 293.

102. Natalie Joffe, "Tickling Points in Accepted Cultural Phrasing," paper read to General Seminar, February 9, 1950, G14, Mead Papers.

103. Jewish Group Meeting, Aug. 3, 1949, Mead Papers.

104. Ibid.

105. J. Hoberman, *Bridge of Light: Yiddish Film between Two Worlds* (Philadelphia: Temple University Press, 1991), 213.

106. Jewish Group Meeting, Aug. 3, 1949, Mead Papers. *A Brivele der Mamen* was rereleased in 1949 as *The Eternal Song*.

107. Third General Seminar, Oct. 16, 1947, Mead Papers.

108. John Weakland, "Feature Films as Cultural Documents," in Paul Hockings, ed., *Principles of Visual Anthropology* (The Hague: Mouton, 1975). 233.

109. Clifford Geertz, *The Interpretation of Cultures* (New York: Basic Books, 1975), 14.

110. Hoberman, *Bridge of Light*, 9–11.

111. Ibid., 205–206.

112. Ibid., 333.

113. Landes and Zborowoski, "Hypotheses," 30–31.

114. Hoberman, *Bridge of Light*, 290.

115. Ibid., 291.

116. Landes and Zborowoski, "Hypotheses," 31–32, 46.

117. Margaret Mead, "National Character," in A. L. Kroeber, ed., *Anthropology Today: An Encyclopedic Inventory* (Chicago: University of Chicago Press, 1953), 659.

118. Zborowoski and Herzog, *Life Is with People*, 294.

119. Kirshenblatt-Gimblett, "Introduction," xiii.

120. Ibid., xvi–xvii.

121. Landes and Zborowski, "Hypotheses," 24.

122. Naomi Chaitman, "Summary of Some Points on Jewish Child Study," Feb. 1949; Chaitman, "Moral Ideas of East European Jewish Parents and Children," Jan. 12, 1950, G19–20, Mead Papers.

123. Chaitman, "Moral Ideas of East European Jewish Parents and Children."

124. Ibid.

125. By the end of the 1950s, the cultural relativism of the "culture and personality" school had lost ground to the cultural evolutionists; Caffrey, *Ruth Benedict*, 334–336, 342.

126. Mead addresses the "caricature statement" about swaddling in her essay, "National Character," 644–645. Also see Margaret Mead, "The Swaddling Hypothesis: Its Reception," *American Anthropologist* 56, no. 3 (June 1954): 395–409. Caffrey suggests that the emotional tone of the criticisms of the RCC was a "sure sign" that the real issues with the project were not being addressed (*Ruth Benedict*, 342–343).

127. Modell, *Ruth Benedict*, 289; Caffrey, *Ruth Benedict*, 335–336; Micaele di Leonardo, *Exotics at Home: Anthropologies, Others, American Modernity* (1998; paperback repr., Chicago: University of Chicago Press, 2000), 210–214. Di Leonardo describes the criticism to Mead's *Male and Female* (1949) as similarly based on her failure to consider institutional structures and relationships and her overuse of Freudian perspectives.

128. Jenna Joselit, *The Wonders of America* (New York: Hill and Wang, 1994), 70 (italics in original).

Chapter 4

1. Edward Shapiro, *A Time for Healing: American Jewry since World War II* (Baltimore: Johns Hopkins University Press, 1992), 157.

2. Herman Wouk, *Marjorie Morningstar* (Boston: Little Brown, 1955), 172.

3. Ibid.

4. Cited in Jonathan Sarna, *American Judaism: A History* (New Haven: Yale University Press, 2004), 282.

5. Seymour Levantman, "From Shtetl to Suburb," in Peter I. Rose, ed., *The Ghetto and Beyond: Essays on Jewish Life in America* (New York: Random House, 1969), 33–56.

6. Albert I. Gordon, *Jews in Suburbia* (Boston: Beacon Press, 1959), 59.

7. Karen Brodkin, *How Jews Became White Folks and What That Says about Race in America* (New Brunswick, N.J.: Rutgers University Press, 1998), 161. Brodkin's account draws on Riv-Ellen Prell, *Fighting to Become Americans: Assimilation and the Trouble between Jewish Women and Jewish Men* (Boston: Beacon Press, 2000), and Paula E. Hyman, *Gender and Assimilation in Modern Jewish History* (Seattle: University of Washington Press, 1995).

8. Brodkin, *How Jews Became White Folks*, 161–162.

9. Marshall Sklare and Joseph Greenblum, *Jewish Identity on the Suburban Frontier: A Study of Group Survival in the Open Society* (1967; repr., Chicago: University of Chicago Press, 1979), 256.

10. Gordon, *Jews in Suburbia*. For other works on the suburbs and second-generation Jews' experience, see Judith R. Kramer and Seymour Levantman, *Children of the Gilded Ghetto* (New Haven: Yale University Press, 1961).

11. Oscar Handlin, "Introduction," in Gordon, *Jews in Suburbia*, ix.

12. Gordon, *Jews in Suburbia*, 59.

13. Ibid., 60.

14. Ibid., 61.

15. Ibid., 63.

16. Ibid., 78.

17. Ibid.

18. Ibid., 78–79.

19. Ibid., 63–64.

20. Sklare and Greenblum, *Jewish Identity on the Suburban Frontier*, 256.

21. Ibid., 257–258.

22. See Miriam Isaacs, in collaboration with Trude Weiss Rosmarin, *What Every Jewish Woman Should Know* (New York: The Jewish Book Club, 1941).

23. See Joellyn Wallen Zollman, "Shopping for a Future: A History of the American Synagogue Gift Shop," Ph.D. dissertation, Brandeis University, 2002, and Jenna Weissman Joselit, *The Wonders of America: Reinventing Jewish Culture, 1880–1950* (New York: Hill and Wang, 1994), chap. 4.

24. Isaacs, *What Every Jewish Woman Should Know*, 31.

25. Ibid., 10–11.

26. Shapiro, *A Time for Healing*, 152.

27. James A. Sleeper, "Introduction," in James A. Sleeper and Alan L. Mintz, eds., *The New Jews* (New York: Vintage, 1971), 3–23, cited in Shapiro, *A Time for Healing*, 153.

28. Aleisa Fishman, "Consuming Is Believing: Jewish Women Building Community in Suburbia, 1946–1960," presented at the 2004 Biennial Scholars' Conference on American Jewish History, Washington, D.C., June 7, 2004.

29. Gladys Rothbell, "The Jewish Mother: Social Construction of a Popular Image," in Steven M. Cohen and Paula E. Hyman, eds., *The Jewish Family: Myths and Reality* (New York: Holmes and Meier, 1986), 120–122.

30. John Cooper, *The Child in Jewish History* (Northvale, N.J.: Jason Aronson, 1996), 344–346.

31. Wouk, *Marjorie Morningstar*, 564.

32. See, for example, Arthur Knight, "*SR* Goes to the Movies: Shirley, Who Needs Her?" *Saturday Review*, vol. 41, April 26, 1958, 25.

33. Herman Wouk, "My Search for Marjorie," *The American Weekly*, May 11, 1958, 8.

34. Wouk, *Marjorie Morningstar*, 196, 550, 207.

35. Ibid., 197, 199.

36. Ibid., 14.

37. Ibid., 191–192, 551.

38. Ibid., 561.

39. Phil Brown, ed., *In the Catskills: A Century of the Jewish Experience in "The Mountains"* (New York: Columbia University Press, 2002), 13. Also see Brown, *Catskill Culture: A Mountain Rat's Memories of the Great Jewish Resort Area* (Philadelphia: Temple University Press, 1998); Irwin Richman, *Borscht Belt Bungalows: Memories of Catskill Summers* (Philadelphia: Temple University Press, 1998); Stefan Kanfer, *A Summer World: The Attempt to Build a Jew-*

ish Eden in the Catskills, from the Days of the Ghetto to the Rise and Decline of the Borscht Belt (New York: Farrar Straus Giroux, 1989); and Myrna Katz Frommer and Harvey Frommer, *It Happened in the Catskills: An Oral History in the Words of Busboys, Bellhops, Guests, Proprietors, Comedians, Agents, and Others Who Lived It* (New York: Harcourt Brace Jovanovich, 1991), 147–154.

40. Morris Freedman, "Grossinger's Green Pastures" (II. "For Everything, A Season") *Commentary*, Aug. 1954, 154.

41. Lawrence J. Epstein, *The Haunted Smile: The Story of Jewish Comedians in America* (New York: Public Affairs, 2001), 112. For an account of Danny Kaye and the author's father in the Catskills, see Joyce Antler, "The Doctor and the Comedian," in Ilana Abramovitch and Sean Galvin, eds., *Jews of Brooklyn* (Hanover: University of New England Press, 2002), 318–321.

42. Kanfer, *A Summer World*, 220–221.

43. Brown, *In the Catskills*, 12.

44. Esther Romeyn and Jack Kugelmass, *Let There Be Laughter: Jewish Humor in America* (Chicago: Spertus Press, 1997), 49–50. The phrase "de-Semitization of American culture" is quoted from Henry Popkin (49).

45. Ibid., 56–57.

46. Ibid., 57.

47. Freedman, "Grossinger's Green Pastures," 149.

48. Romeyn and Kugelmass, *Let There Be Laughter*, 57.

49. On the rise of Jewish mother jokes in this period see Rothbell, "The Jewish Mother," 120–122.

50. Brown, *In the Catskills*, 15.

51. Frommer and Frommer, *It Happened in the Catskills*, 45.

52. Samantha Hope Goldstein, "'Don't Mind Me, I'll Just Sit Here In the Dark,': Illuminating the Role of Women in Catskills Performative Culture," Ph.D. dissertation, University of California, San Diego, 2005, 69, 131–139; Rachel Kranson, "Staging the Ideal Jewish Community: Women Hotel Owners in the Catskills, 1950–1970," Catskills Institute Conference, Monticello, New York, August 26, 2005. Brown, *In the Catskills*, 68. Also see Esterita "Cissie" Blumberg, *Remember the Catskills: Tales by a Recovering Hotelkeeper* (Fleischmanns, N.Y.: Purple Mountain Press, 1996).

53. Frommer and Frommer, *It Happened in the Catskills*, 47.

54. Ibid., 49, 52.

55. Kranson, "Staging the Ideal Jewish Community."

56. Morris Freedman, "Grossinger's Green Pastures," *Commentary*, July 1954, 56.

57. Ibid.

58. Frommer and Frommer, *It Happened in the Catskills*, 45. (The reminiscence is from Tania Grossinger, Karla's daughter. Karla married one of the Grossingers.)

59. Freedman, "Grossinger's Greener Pastures," 152.

60. Freedman, "Grossinger's Green Pastures," 61, and "Grossinger's Greener Pastures," 153.

61. Freedman, "Grossinger's Green Pastures," 61.

62. Ibid., 62.

63. Kanfer, *A Summer World*, 221.

64. Cited in Prell, *Fighting to Become Americans*, 147.

65. Ibid.

66. Henny Youngman, *Take My Wife, Please!* (Secaucus, N.J.: Citadel Press, 1998), 26.

67. Joan Rivers, in Jewish Women's Archive Productions, LLC, *Making Trouble*, 2006.

68. Prell, *Fighting to Become Americans*, 148–150.

69. Alan King, *Alan King's Great Jewish Joke Book* (New York: Crown Publishers, 2002), 97–98.

70. Goldstein, " 'Don't Mind Me, I'll Just Sit Here in the Dark,' " 20, 36–37.

71. Prell, *Fighting to Become Americans*, 150.

72. Romeyn and Kugelmass, *Let There Be Laughter*, 58.

73. Samuel S. Janus, "The Great Jewish-American Comedians' Identity Crisis," *American Journal of Psychoanalysis* 40, no. 3 (Sept. 1980): 259–265, cited in Gladys Weisberg Rothbell, "The Case of the Jewish Mother: A Study in Stereotyping," Ph.D. dissertation, State University of New York at Stony Brook, 1989, 610–615.

74. Kanfer, *A Summer World*, 223.

75. Ruth Gay, *Unfinished People: Eastern European Jews Encounter America* (New York: Norton, 1996), 221.

76. Kanfer, *A Summer World*, 228.

77. Mark Shechner, "DEAR MR. EINSTEIN: Jewish Comedy and the Contradictions of Culture," in Sarah Blacher Cohen, ed., *Jewish Wry: Essays on Jewish Humor* (Bloomington: Indiana University Press, 1987; Detroit: Wayne State University Press, 1990), 141–157. Citations are to the 1990 edition.

78. Shechner, "DEAR MR. EINSTEIN," 144.

79. Freedman, "The Green Pastures of Grossinger's," 58.

80. Freedman, "Grossinger's Greener Pastures," 153–154.

81. Ibid., 154.

82. Harold Jaediker Taub, *Waldorf in the Catskills: The Grossinger Legend* (New York: Sterling, 1952), 226.

83. Ibid., 227.

84. Molly Goldberg and Myra Waldo, *The Molly Goldberg Cookbook* (Garden City, N.Y.: Doubleday, 1955); the author is not Gertrude Berg, but her character. Also see the "Revised and Enlarged Edition" of *The New Settlement Cookbook*, originally compiled by Mrs. Simon Kander (New York: Simon and Schuster, 1954), released the year before. Also see Sara Kasdan, *Love and Knishes: How to Cook Like a Jewish Mother* (Greenwich, Conn.: Fawcett, 1956).

85. Harry Gersh, "Mama's Cooking: Minority Report," *Commentary*, Oct. 1947, 367, cited in Jenna Joselit, *The Wonders of America*, 183.

86. Irvin Nussbaum, "In Defense of Mama," letters from readers, in *Commentary*, Dec. 1947, 586–587, cited in Joselit, *The Wonders of America*, 322–323.

87. Kranson, "Staging the Ideal Jewish Community."

88. Susan Marks, *Finding Betty Crocker* (New York: Simon and Schuster, 2000), 116.

89. Barry Lewis, "Jennie G. Still Means Quality," *Middletown (NY) Times Herald Record*, August 8, 2002; Rachel Kranson, "Cold Beet Borscht en Glasse: Dining in the Jewish Catskills," unpublished paper.

90. Lewis, "Jennie G. Still Means Quality."

91. Suzan Herskowitz (Stephens City, Va.), customer review, Amazon.com, Oct. 15, 2005.

92. Paul Grossinger, "Introduction," in Jennie Grossinger, *The Art of Jewish Cooking* (New York: Random House, 1965), ix.

93. Grossinger, *The Art of Jewish Cooking*, viii, cited in Kranson, "Cold Beet Borscht en Glasse." I am grateful to Rachel Kranson for this interpretation of *The Art of Jewish Cooking*.

94. Vincent Brook, "The Americanization of Molly: How Mid-Fifties TV Homogenized *The Goldbergs* (and Got "Berg-larized" in the Process)," *Cinema Journal* 38, no. 4 (Summer 1999): 52. According to Nach Waxman, who operates a book-search service, Jennie Grossinger's *The Art of Jewish Cooking* is the most-wanted cookbook title—"an example of people who want to keep a flame, or a flavor, alive" (Julia Moskin, "Kitchen Classics, In the Eye of the Beholder," *New York Times*, Nov. 1, 2006).

95. Kanfer, *A Summer World*, 221.

96. Goldstein, "'Don't Mind Me, I'll Just Sit Here in the Dark.'"

Chapter 5

1. Sallie Gordon to Jennie Loitman Barron, April 21, 1959, Jennie Loitman Barron Papers, Schlesinger Library, Radcliffe Institute, Cambridge, Mass.

2. Letter from Rabbi Solomon B. Freehof, Rodef Shalom Temple, Pittsburgh, n.d., Barron Papers.

3. A. L. Sachar to Mrs. William Walsh, March 19, 1959, Barron Papers.

4. "Judge Barron Shares New Honors with Family," *Boston Traveler*, Feb. 5, 1959; *Washington Post and Times-Herald*, May 6, 1959, Barron Papers.

5. "Judicial Solemnity, Aimless Chatter with Young All Part of Nanny's Day," *Evening Bulletin*, Dec. 8, 1954, Barron Papers.

6. Author's interview with Joy Rachlin, Brookline, Mass., Jan. 30, 2002.

7. Jennie Loitman Barron, "Jury Service for Women," 1925, Barron Papers.

8. "Judge Is Mother of the Year," *Washington Post and Times-Herald*, May 6, 1959, Barron Papers.

9. Virginia Bohlin, "A Home Small Enough for Two—And Big Enough for Forty: The Traveler Visits Judge Jennie Loitman Barron," *Boston Traveler*, Feb. 10, 1959, Barron Papers.

10. Jennie Loitman Barron to "Darling Joysie," July 13, 1950, Barron Papers.

11. Rachlin interview.

12. "Judicial Solemnity, Aimless Chatter with Young All Part of Nanny's Day."

13. Discussion with Roland Gittelsohn, Jan. 19, 1958, Barron Papers.

14. Notes on "Judge and Mother," Barron Papers.

15. Discussion with Roland Gittelsohn.

16. See Joyce Antler, *The Journey Home: How Jewish Women Shaped Modern America* (New York: Schocken Books, 1997), 105.

17. On maternalism, see Seth Koven and Sonya Michel, eds., *Mothers of a New World: Politics and the Origins of Welfare States* (New York: Routledge, 1994); and Lynn Y. Weiner, "Maternalism as a Paradigm, Defining the Issues," *Journal of Women's History* 5 (Fall 1993): 96–131. On Hadassah's work, see Mary McCune, *"The Whole Wide World, Without Limits": International Relief, Gender Politics, and American Jewish Women, 1893–1930* (Detroit: Wayne State University Press, 2005), and Erica B. Simmons, *Hadassah and the Zionist Project* (Lanham, Md.: Rowman and Littlefield, 2006). On the National Council of Jewish Women, see Faith Rogow, *Gone to Another Meeting: The National Council of Jewish Women, 1893–1993* (Tuscaloosa: University of Alabama Press, 1993). Also see Antler, *The Journey Home*, esp. chap. 4.

18. Rabbi Philip Goodman, "Habanoth Manual: A Guide for Jewish Girls Clubs," Women's Branch of the Union of Orthodox Jewish Women's Congregations of America, n.d. Also see "That's What Yiddish Mamas Are!" Hachocdesh, Women's Branch UOJCA, no. 581, 1979, American Jewish Historical Society.

19. Jenna Weissman Joselit, *The Wonders of America: Reinventing Jewish Culture, 1880–1950* (New York: Hill and Wang, 1994), 73–75.

20. On the Emma Lazarus Federation, see Joyce Antler, "Between Culture and Politics: The Emma Lazarus Federation of Jewish Women's Clubs and the Promulgation of Women's History, 1944–1989," in Linda K. Kerber, Alice Kessler-Harris, and Kathryn K. Sklar, eds., *U.S. History as Women's History* (Chapel Hill: University of North Carolina Press, 1995), 267–295.

21. Judith Arcana, *Grace Paley's Life Stories: A Literary Biography* (Urbana, Ill.: University

of Chicago Press, 1993), 150; Arcana, "Truth in Mothering: Grace Paley," in Brenda O. Daly and Maureen T. Reddy, *Narrating Mothers: Theorizing Maternal Subjectivities* (Knoxville: University of Tennessee Press, 1991), 200. The novel's full title is *Yonnondio: From the Thirties* (New York: Delacorte Press, 1974).

22. Arcana, *Grace Paley's Life Stories*, 14–15.

23. Ibid., 23.

24. On Paley, see Dena Mandel, "Keeping Up with Faith: Grace Paley's Sturdy American Jewess," *Studies in American Jewish Literature* 3 (1983): 85–98; and Minako Baba, "Faith Darwin as Writer-Heroine: A Study of Grace Paley's Short Stories," *Studies in American Jewish Literature* 7 (Spring 1988): 40–55.

25. Neal D. Isaacs, *Grace Paley: A Study of the Short Fiction* (Boston: G. K. Hall, 1990), 113.

26. Ibid., 119–120, 136, 113.

27. Adapted from Antler, *The Journey Home*, 312.

28. Arcana, *Grace Paley's Life Stories*, 63–64.

29. Ibid., 150.

30. Arcana, "Truth in Mothering," 199.

31. Oliver B. Pollack, "Tillie Olsen," in Paula E. Hyman and Deborah Dash Moore, *Jewish Women in America: An Historical Encyclopedia* (New York: Routledge, 1997), 1003.

32. See Deborah Rosenfelt, "From the Thirties: Tillie Olsen and the Radical Tradition," in Judith Newton and Deborah Rosenfelt, eds., *Feminist Criticism and Social Change: Sex, Class and Race in Literature and Culture* (New York: Methuen, 1985), 220.

33. Rosenfelt, "From the Thirties," 224.

34. Tillie Olsen, "I Stand Here Ironing," reprinted in Joyce Antler, ed., *America and I: Short Stories by American Jewish Women Writers* (Boston: Beacon Press, 1990), 160, 164.

35. Adapted from Antler, "Introduction," *America and I*, 12–13; Tillie Olsen, *Tell Me a Riddle* (New York: Delacorte Press/Seymour Lawrence, 1979).

36. Cited in Constance Coiner, *Better Red: The Writing and Resistance of Tillie Olsen and Meridel Le Sueur* (New York: Oxford University Press, 1995), 142.

37. Ibid., 143.

38. Grace Paley, *The Little Disturbances of Man* (New York: Doubleday, 1959).

39. Sandy Pinsker, *The Comedy That "Hoits": An Essay on the Fiction of Philip Roth* (Columbia: University of Missouri Press, 1975), 4.

40. Daniel Walden, "Goodbye Columbus, Hello Portnoy—and Beyond: The Ordeal of Philip Roth," *Studies in American Jewish Literature* 3, no. 2 (Winter 1977–78): 3.

41. See Murray Baumgarten and Barbara Gottfried, *Understanding Philip Roth* (Columbia: University of South Carolina Press, 1990), 21–51.

42. Ibid., 23.

43. Philip Roth, *Goodbye, Columbus* (Boston: Houghton Mifflin, 1959), 5–6, 43, 76.

44. Ibid., 64–65.

45. Ibid., 87–88.

46. See Alan Cooper, *Philip Roth and the Jews* (Albany: State University of New York Press, 1996), 42–50; Riv-Ellen Prell, *Fighting to Become Americans: Assimilation and the Trouble between Jewish Women and Jewish Men* (Boston: Beacon Press, 2000), 225–227.

47. On Jewish mothers in the 1960s, see Martha Ravits, "The Jewish Mother: Comedy and Controversy in American Popular Culture," *MELUS* 25, no 1 (Spring 2000): 3–16, and Beverly Gray Bienstock, "The Changing Image of the American Jewish Mother," in Virginia Tufte and Barbara Myerhoff, *Changing Images of the American Jewish Family* (New Haven: Yale University Press, 1979), 184–189. Also see Charlotte Baum, Paula Hyman, and Sonya Michel, *The Jewish Woman in America* (New York: New American Library, 1977), 236–238, 248–251.

48. See, for example, Melvin J. Friedman, "Jewish Mothers and Sons: The Expense of *Chutzpah,*" in Irving Malin, ed., *Contemporary American-Jewish Literature: Critical Essays* (Bloomington: Indiana University Press, 1973), 160.

49. Bienstock, "The Changing Image of the American Jewish Mother," 184.

50. Gerald Nachman, *Seriously Funny: The Rebel Comedians of the 1950s and 1960s* (New York: Pantheon, 2003), 321.

51. Bruce Jay Friedman, *A Mother's Kisses* (New York: Simon and Schuster, 1964), 93, 91, 280, 57.

52. Ibid., 91, 165.

53. Ibid., 225.

54. Ibid., 181.

55. Ibid., 196.

56. Ibid., 286.

57. Among the commentators who cite these works as primary sources for the "composite picture" evoked by the words "Jewish mother" are Baum, Hyman, and Michel, *The Jewish Woman in America,* 237.

58. The publication data is from Fred Bernstein, *The Jewish Mothers' Hall of Fame* (Garden City, N.Y.: Doubleday, 1986), 8.

59. Josh Greenfield, "Portnoy's Complaint," *New York Times Sunday Book Review,* Feb. 23, 1969; Mordecai H. Levine, "Philip Roth and American Judaism," *CLA Journal* 14 (December 1970): 166.

60. Dan Greenburg, *How to Be a Jewish Mother: A Very Lovely Training Manual* (Los Angeles: Price, Stern, Sloan, 1964).

61. Ibid., 13.

62. Ibid., 61.

63. Ibid., 62.

64. Ibid., 16.

65. Ibid., 16; also cited in Prell, *Fighting to Become Americans,* 149.

66. Ibid., jacket flap.

67. Bernstein, *The Jewish Mothers' Hall of Fame,* 10–11. Greenburg has gone on to write a successful series of children's book in the voice of his son, Zack, which presents "Grandmother Leah" as a regular character. In *Zack Files 24: My Grandma, Major League Slugger* (New York: Grosset and Dunlap, 2001), Grandma Leah is a four-foot-ten-inch-tall eighty-year-old who insists on feeding her grandson. "When Grandma Leah wants you to eat, you might as well eat, because you're going to do it anyway."

68. Judy Klemesrud, "Some Mothers Wonder What Portnoy Had to Complain About," *New York Times,* March 31, 1969.

69. See Melvin Friedman, "Jewish Mothers and Sons," 167, and Prell, *Fighting to Become Americans,* 149.

70. Philip Roth, "On the Great American Novel," in *Reading Myself and Others* (New York: Farrar, Straus and Giroux, 1975), 81; also cited in Alan Cooper, *Philip Roth and the Jews,* 100.

71. Philip Roth, "Document Dated July 27, 1969," in *Reading Myself and Others,* 31.

72. Walden, "Goodbye Columbus, Hello Portnoy—and Beyond," 10.

73. Roth, "Document Dated July 27, 1969," 26.

74. *Fresh Air,* Sept. 27, 2005, transcript of Terry Gross interview with Philip Roth. Roth spoke similarly to Charles McGrath in his article, "Why Is This Man Smiling?" *New York Times,* Sept. 4, 2005: "Everybody knew about masturbation. What they were really offended by was the depiction of this level of brutality in a Jewish family."

75. Gross, interview with Philip Roth.

76. Roth, "In Response to Those Who Have Asked Me: 'How Did You Come to Write That Book, Anyway?'" in *Reading Myself and Others*, 37.

77. Ibid., 39.

78. Gross, interview with Philip Roth.

79. Ibid.

80. Philip Roth, *Portnoy's Complaint* (New York: Vintage Books, 1997) 146; cited in Baum, Hyman, and Michel, *The Jewish Woman in America*, 250.

81. Ibid., 12, 44.

82. Ibid., 95.

83. Ibid., 11–12, 87.

84. Ibid., 15, 34–37.

85. Ibid., 15, 34–37.

86. Ibid., 40.

87. Ibid., 112.

88. Shortly after the publication of *Portnoy's Complaint*, Charlotte Baum and Sonya Michel discovered they had the same "angry reaction" to Roth's attack on Jewish motherhood. As Baum recalled, "Hadn't these women been severely maligned—and hadn't she been, too?" With Paula Hyman, Baum and Michel determined to write a history to correct this and other "myths" about Jewish women. The result was *The Jewish Woman in America*, the first history of American Jewish women, published in 1976; Baum, Hyman, and Michel, *The Jewish Woman in America*, x–xiii; Marya Mannes, "A Dissent," *Saturday Review* 22 (Feb. 1969): 39.

89. Cooper, *Philip Roth and the Jews*, 116, 106, 110.

90. Gross, interview with Philip Roth.

91. Philip Roth, *Patrimony: A True Story* (New York: Simon and Schuster, 1991), 36–38.

92. Sanford Pinsker, "Philip Roth," in Daniel Walden, ed., *Dictionary of Literary Biography*, vol 28, *Twentieth-Century American-Jewish Fiction Writers* (Detroit, Mich.: Gale Research, 1984), 270.

93. Ravits, "The Jewish Mother," 8, 11–12, 15–17; Prell, *Fighting to Become Americans*, 210, 222.

94. Cited in Baum, Hyman, and Michel, *The Jewish Woman in America*, 243.

95. Ravits, "The Jewish Mother," 17.

96. Roth, *Portnoy's Complaint*, 93.

97. Klemesrud, "Some Mothers Wonder What Portnoy Had to Complain About."

98. This point is made by Ruth Wisse, *Some Serious Thoughts about Jewish Humor*, Leo Baeck Memorial Lecture 45 (New York: Leo Baeck Institute, 2001), 17–18; Roth, *Portnoy's Complaint*, 111.

99. Zena Smith Blau, "In Defense of the Jewish Mother," *Midstream* 13 (Feb. 1967): 43.

100. On Jewish educational achievement and family values, see Sydney Stahl Weinberg, *The World of Our Mothers: The Lives of Jewish Immigrant Women* (Chapel Hill: University of North Carolina Press, 1988), 241–243; Joel Perlmann, *Ethnic Differences, Schooling and Social Structure among the Irish, Italians, Jews and Blacks in an American City, 1880–1935* (Cambridge: Cambridge University Press, 1988); Stephan F. Brumberg, *Going to America, Going to School: The Jewish Immigrant Public School Encounter in Turn-of-the-Century New York City* (New York: Praeger, 1986); Barry Chiswick, "The Earnings and Human Capital of American Jews," *Journal of Human Resources* 18 (1983): 313–336; Chiswick, "Labor Supply and Investment in Child Quality: A Study of Jewish and Non-Jewish Women," *Review of Economics and Statistics* 47 (November 1986): 4, and Chiswick, "Labor Supply and Investment in Child Quality: A Study of Jewish and Non-Jewish Women: A Reply," *Review of Economics and Statistics* 74 (1992): 726–727.

101. Blau, "In Defense of the Jewish Mother," 49.

102. Ibid., 48.

103. Alexander Grinstein, "Profile of a 'Doll'—A Female Character Type," in Norman Kiell, ed., *The Psychodynamics of American Jewish Life* (New York: Twayne Publishers, 1967), 84–85.

104. Pauline Bart, "Portnoy's Mother's Complaint," *TransAction* 8, nos. 1 and 2 (Nov.–Dec. 1970): 69–74, also appeared as "Depression in Middle-Aged Women," in Vivian Gornick and Barbara K. Moran, eds., *Women in Sexist Society* (New York: Basic Books, 1971), 105–115.

105. "Pauline Bart: Outrageous Feminist," *Off Our Backs*, Dec. 1998; Bart, "Portnoy's Mother's Complaint," 74.

Chapter 6

1. Debra L. Shultz, *Going South: Jewish Women in the Civil Rights Movement* (New York: New York University Press, 2001), 15.

2. Ibid., 16; italics in original.

3. Adrienne Rich, *Of Woman Born: Motherhood as Experience and Institution* (New York: Norton, 1976), 226.

4. Grace Paley, "Other Mothers," *Feminist Studies* 4 (June 1978): 166–169.

5. See, for example, Wini Breines, *Young, White and Miserable: Growing Up Female in the Fifties* (Boston: Beacon, 1992), 78.

6. Material on Betty Friedan and Bella Abzug is adapted from the account in Joyce Antler, *The Journey Home: How Jewish Women Shape Modern America* (New York: Schocken Books, 1997), 262, 267–278.

7. Gloria Steinem "Bella Abzug," *Ms.*, Jan./Feb. 1996, 63.

8. Author's interview with Bella Abzug, March 31, 1995.

9. For a discussion of divergent views of motherhood that includes white (Jewish) and black feminists, see M. Rivka Polatnick, "Diversity in Women's Liberation Ideology: How a Black and a White Group of the 1960s Viewed Motherhood," *Signs* 21 (1996): 679–706.

10. Breines, *Young, White and Miserable*, 82–83.

11. Ruth Rosen, *The World Split Open: How the Modern Women's Movement Changed America* (New York: Penguin, 2001), 43, 45.

12. Ibid., 45–46.

13. Anne Roiphe, *Fruitful: Living the Contradictions: A Memoir of Modern Motherhood* (New York: Penguin Books, 1997), 18–19.

14. Cited in Gladys Weisberg Rothbell, "The Case of the Jewish Mother: A Study in Stereotyping," Ph.D. dissertation, State University of New York at Stony Brook, 1989, 863.

15. Alix Kates Shulman, *A Good Enough Daughter: A Memoir* (New York: Schocken Books, 1999), 190.

16. Interview with Shulman, cited in Polatnick, "Diversity in Women's Liberation Ideology: How a Black and a White Group of the 1960s Viewed Motherhood," 691; Rosen, *The World Split Open*, 234.

17. Rosen, *The World Split Open*, 234–235.

18. Ibid., 230.

19. Phyllis Chesler, "Jewish Mother and Son: The Feminist Version," in Rachel Josefowitz Siegel, Ellen Cole, and Susan Steinberg-Oren, eds., *Jewish Mothers Tell Their Stories: Acts of Love and Courage* (New York: The Haworth Press, 2000), 96–97; Rosen, *The World Split Open*, 39.

20. Lauri Umansky believes Firestone's critique of motherhood surpassed "that of

virtually all other early feminists"; Umansky, *Motherhood Reconceived: Feminism and the Legacy of the Sixties* (New York: New York University Press, 1996), 32.

21. Rosen, *The World Split Open*, 134–135.

22. Jo Freeman edited the newsletter; for an account of the Westside group, see Jennifer Scanlon, "Jo Freeman," in Scanlon, ed., *Significant Contemporary American Feminists* (Westport, Conn: Greenwood Press, 1999), 104–110.

23. Shulamith Firestone, *The Dialectic of Sex: The Case for Feminist Revolution* (New York: Morrow Quill Paperbacks, 1970), 270.

24. Ibid., 270–271.

25. Ibid., 270.

26. Ibid., 273–274.

27. Rabbi Tirzah Firestone, *With Roots in Heaven: One Woman's Passionate Journey into the Heart of Her Faith* (New York: Plume Books, 1999), 36, 64, 72, 77.

28. Ann Snitow, "Motherhood—Reclaiming the Demon Texts," *Ms.* May/June 1991, 34–37.

29. Ibid.

30. Marianne Hirsch, *The Mother/Daughter Plot: Narrative, Psychoanalysis, Feminism* (Bloomington: Indiana University Press, 1999), 164.

31. Ibid.; Sharon Abbey and Andrea O'Reilly, eds., *Redefining Motherhood: Changing Identities and Patterns* (Toronto: Second Story Press, 1998), 75–77.

32. Umansky, *Motherhood Reconceived*, 117–118; also see Myra Marx Ferree and Beth B. Hess, *Controversy and Coalition: The New Feminist Movement* (Boston: Twayne Publishers, 1985); Robin Morgan, *The World of a Woman: Feminist Dispatches, 1968–1992* (New York: Norton, 1992), 50–51.

33. Robin Morgan, ed., *Sisterhood Is Powerful: An Anthology of Writings from the Women's Liberation Movement* (New York: Vintage Books, 1970), 1.

34. Umansky, *Motherhood Reconceived*, 117.

35. Robin Morgan, *Saturday's Child: A Memoir* (New York: Norton, 2001), 157, 165.

36. Ibid., 133.

37. Ibid., 134, 17.

38. Ibid., 130.

39. Ibid., 140, 192.

40. Ibid., 14.

41. Ibid., 134.

42. Letter written to herself, Sept. 12, 1962, in Robin Morgan, *Going Too Far: The Personal Chronicle of a Feminist* (New York: Random House, 1977), 25.

43. Morgan, *Saturday's Child*, 134.

44. Ibid., 17.

45. *Morgan, Going Too Far*, 158–159.

46. Ibid., 159.

47. *Ms.* chat, www.msmagazine.com/chat/chat_robinmorgan04232003, accessed July 27, 2003 (no longer available online).

48. Jane Alpert, *Growing Up Underground* (New York: Citadel Press, 1990), 310.

49. Ibid., 298.

50. Ibid., 345.

51. Ibid., 346.

52. Jane Alpert, "Mother Right: A New Feminist Theory," *Ms.*, August 1973, 91.

53. Ibid., 92–94.

54. Alpert, *Growing Up Underground*, 33–34.

55. Ibid., 334, 350.

56. Ibid., 346; Umansky, *Motherhood Reconceived*, 119.

57. Alix Kates Shulman, "A Mother's Story," in Christina Looper Baker and Christina Baker Kline, eds., *The Conversation Begins: Mothers and Daughters Talk about Living Feminism* (New York: Bantam, 1996), 90–91.

58. Ibid., 91–92.

59. Shulman, *A Good Enough Daughter*, 90–101, 187, 192.

60. The *Oxford Companion to Women's Writing in the United States* calls it "the first important novel to emerge from the women's liberation movement" (805; New York: Oxford University Press, 1995).

61. Alix Kates Shulman, *Burning Questions* (New York: Thunder's Mouth Press, 1990), 143.

62. Baker and Kline, *The Conversation Begins*, 94.

63. Shulman, *A Good Enough Daughter*, 191–192, 160.

64. Janet Burstein writes about both authors in *Writing Mothers, Writing Daughters: Tracing the Maternal in Stories by American Jewish Women* (Urbana: University of Illinois Press, 1996), 106–109.

65. Umansky, *Motherhood Reconceived*, 135; Burstein, *Writing Mothers, Writing Daughters*, 106–109.

66. Jane Lazarre, *The Mother Knot* (New York: McGraw-Hill, 1976), 28.

67. Lazarre, *The Mother Knot*, 10. On daughters' loss of mothers, see Lynn Davidman, *Motherloss* (Berkeley: University of California Press, 2000), and Hope Edelman, *Motherless Mothers: How Mother Loss Shapes the Parents We Become* (New York: HarperCollins, 2006).

68. Lazarre, *The Mother Knot*, 10.

69. www.phyllis-chesler.com/review-w-child.html (accessed July 18, 2005).

70. Chesler, "Jewish Mother and Son," 92–93.

71. Ibid., 93–94.

72. Rich, *Of Woman Born*, 237; also see Natalie M. Rosinsky, "Mothers and Daughters: Another Minority Group," in Cathy N. Davidson and E. M. Broner, *The Lost Tradition: Mothers and Daughters in Literature* (New York: Frederick Ungar, 1980), 280.

73. Rich, *Of Woman Born*, 226.

74. Umansky, *Motherhood Reconceived*, 123–124.

75. Dorothy Dinnerstein, *The Mermaid and the Minotaur: Sexual Arrangements and Human Malaise* (New York: Harper and Row, 1976), xii, 161; Jane Lazarre, review of "'The Mermaid and the Minotaur: Sexual Arrangements and Human Malaise' by Dorothy Dinnerstein," *Ms.*, July 1977, 38–43.

76. Nancy Chodorow, *The Reproduction of Mothering: Psychoanalysis and the Sociology of Gender* (Berkeley: University of California Press, 1978), 209. On Dinnerstein and Chodorow and the tradition of object relations, see Mari Jo Buhle, *Feminism and Its Discontents: A Century of Struggle with Psychoanalysis* (Cambridge: Harvard University Press, 1998), 254–259; Umansky, *Motherhood Reconceived*, 138–146.

77. Among other examinations of motherhood written by Jewish women in the period 1976–1980 are Nancy Friday, *My Mother/Myself: The Daughter's Search for Identity* (New York: Delacorte Press, 1977); Judith Arcana, *Our Mother's Daughters* (Berkeley: Shameless Hussy Press, 1979); and Sara Ruddick, "Maternal Thinking," *Feminist Studies* 6, no. 2 (Summer 1980): 342–367.

78. Susan Gubar, "Eating the Bread of Affliction: Judaism and Feminism," in *Critical Condition: Feminism at the Turn of the Century* (New York: Columbia University Press, 2000), 89.

79. Ibid., 83, 79.

80. Rich, *Of Woman Born*, 238.

81. Ibid., 201, 237–238.

82. Ibid., 237–238, 224–225.

83. Betty Friedan, "Women and Jews: The Quest for Selfhood," *Congress Monthly* 52 (February/March 1985): 9.

84. Martha Ravits, "The Jewish Mother: Comedy and Controversy in American Popular Culture," *MELUS* 25, no. 1 (Spring 2000): 18.

Chapter 7

1. David Marc, "Roseanne," in J. Hoberman and Jeffrey Shandler, *Entertaining America: Jews, Movies, and Broadcasting* (New York and Princeton: Jewish Museum and Princeton University Press, 2003), 199.

2. On Jewish mothers and daughters in 1970s fiction, see Janet Burstein, *Writing Mothers, Writing Daughters: Tracing the Maternal in Stories by American Jewish Women* (Urbana: University of Illinois Press, 1996), especially chap. 4.

3. Riv-Ellen Prell, *Fighting to Become Americans: Assimilation and the Trouble between Jewish Women and Jewish Men* (Boston: Beacon Press, 2000), 178–179.

4. Pogrebin, in the *Northern California Jewish Bulletin*, July 26, 1991, cited by Prell, *Fighting to Become Americans*, 296, n. 11. For the protest against JAP images, see Sherry Chayat " 'JAP'-Baiting on Campus," *Lilith* 17 (Fall 1987): 6–7; Susan Schnur, "When a JAP Is Not a Yuppie: Blazes of Truth," *Lilith* 17 (1987): 10–11, cited in Prell, *Fighting to Become Americans*, 296, nn. 7, 3.

5. Lester D. Friedman, *The Jewish Image in American Film* (Secaucus, N.J.: Citadel Press, 1987), 192.

6. Ibid.; Patricia Erens, *The Jew in American Cinema* (Bloomington: Indiana University Press, 1984), 304.

7. Erens, *The Jew in American Cinema*, 304.

8. Ibid., 307.

9. Friedman, *The Jewish Image in American Film*, 193–196. Also see Erens, *The Jew in American Cinema*, 321.

10. Joe Brown, "New York Stories," *Washington Post*, March 3, 1989.

11. Martha A. Ravits, "The Jewish Mother: Comedy and Controversy in American Popular Culture," *MELUS* 25 (Spring 2000): 23.

12. This point is made by Martha Ravits, for whom *Oedipus Wrecks* is an example of the way in which "the male view of the Jewish mother is complicated by the conjunction of homophobia and matrophobia" (ibid., 22–25).

13. David Plotz, "Domestic Goddess Dethroned," *Slate*, May 18, 1997 (www.slate.msn.com; accessed Aug. 12, 2004).

14. Roseanne Barr, *Roseanne: My Life as a Woman* (New York: Harper and Row, 1989), 163, 197.

15. Ibid., 163.

16. Plotz, "Domestic Goddess Dethroned."

17. Ibid.; Eric Deggans, "Moms with Attitude," *St. Petersburg Times*, May 9, 2002; Andrew Billen, "A Post-Modern Finale to Roseanne,"*New Statesman*, June 20, 1997, 40–41.

18. Naomi Pfeferman, "Roseanne Makes Nice in Reality TV," *Jewish Journal of Greater Los Angeles*, July 25, 2003.

19. Barr, *My Life as a Woman*, xiii.

20. Ibid., 9.

21. Ibid., 4, 9.

22. Ibid., 10.

23. Ibid.

24. Ibid., 32.

25. Ibid., 33–34.

26. Ibid., 32, 35.

27. Ibid., 58–59.

28. Ibid., 15–16.

29. Ibid., 18–19.

30. Ibid., 8.

31. Ibid., 111.

32. Ibid., 173.

33. Ibid., 178.

34. Ibid., 176.

35. Ibid., 173, 180.

36. Geraldine 207; Barr, *My Sister Roseanne: The True Story of Roseanne Barr Arnold* (Secaucus, N.J.: Birch Lane Press, 1994), 104, 110, 113, 129.

37. Barr, *My Life as a Woman*, xvii, xx, xxii.

38. Ibid., 65–66.

39. Ibid., 163–164.

40. Ibid.

41. Ibid., 197, Barr, *My Sister Roseanne*, 128–129.

42. Kathleen Rowe Karlyn, "Unruly Woman as Domestic Goddess," in Joanne Morreale, ed., *Critiquing the Sitcom* (Syracuse, N.Y.: Syracuse University Press, 2003), 260; also see Patricia Mellencamp, *High Anxiety: Catastrophe, Scandal, Age and Comedy* (Bloomington: Indiana University Press, 1992), 338–350.

43. Marc, "Roseanne," 200.

44. Jon Caramanica, "The Domestic Goddess at the Height of Her Power," *New York Times*, Sept. 25, 2005; Billen, "A Post-Modern Finale to Roseanne."

45. Rhoda Zuk, "Entertaining Feminism: *Roseanne* and Roseanne Arnold," *Studies in Popular Culture* 21.1 (October 1998): 43

46. Hal Himmelstein, *Television Myth and the American Mind* (Westport, Conn.: Praeger, 1984), 135; Marc, "Roseanne," 200.

47. Zuk, "Entertaining Feminism," 41. Also see Karlyn, "Unruly Woman as Domestic Goddess."

48. Zuk, "Entertaining Feminism," 51.

49. Barr, *My Life as a Woman*, 195.

50. Ibid., 180.

51. Marc, "Roseanne," 199.

52. A few years before the demise of the show, Roseanne joined the Kabbalah Centre in Los Angeles, to which she credits a vibrant spiritual transformation; yet her much publicized break with her family (on the grounds that her parents allegedly sexually abused her as a child, which they deny) diluted her connection to her Jewish background for many years. On the show, Roseanne learns that her father was Jewish after his death.

53. In "The Domestic Goddess at the Height of Her Power," Caramanica writes that Roseanne's "greatest asset is her gravitational pull, a force that enchants while holding things, and people, at a comfortable distance. It is the power of a whole planet, pulling everything around it inexorably into its orbit."

54. Maureen Rubin, professor of journalism at California State University, Northridge, cited in Joseph Hanania, "Playing Princesses, Punishers and Prudes," *New York Times*, March 7, 1999.

55. John J. O'Connor, "This Jewish Mom Dominates TV, Too," *New York Times*, Oct. 14, 1993.

56. The discussion of Jewish mothers in television draws on Joyce Antler, "Not 'Too Jewish' for Prime Time," in Neal Gabler, Frank Rich, and Joyce Antler, *Television's Changing Image of American Jews* (New York and Los Angeles: The American Jewish Committee and the Norman Lear Center, 2000), 50–67.

57. Lois K. Solomon, "Farewell, Fleischman: As Rob Morrow Departs 'Northern Exposure,' TV's Jewish Landscape is Diminished," *Baltimore Jewish Times*, Feb. 3, 1995, 44.

58. Michael Elkin, "Mother's Daze: What to Get Mrs. Constanza of 'Seinfeld' for Sunday? How About a New Son!" *Jewish Exponent*, May 8, 1997, ix.

59. Nora Lee Mandel, "Media Watch: What the World Sees in 'The Nanny,'" *Lilith* 32, no. 4 (Dec. 31, 1996): 40; Robin Cembalest, "Big Hair, Short Skirts—and High Culture," *Forward*, Feb. 14, 1997.

60. Harry Medved, "The Invisible Minority: Jewish Images on the Tube," *Jewish Family and Life!* www.jewishfamily.com (accessed Nov. 9, 1998).

61. Another non-Jewish "Jewish mother" type on recent television is the character Marie Barone in the award-winning sitcom *Everyone Loves Raymond* (1996–2005). This naggingly intrusive Italian mother is played by Doris Roberts, who won four Emmys for the role. Typically Jewish-identified, the Jewish-born Roberts played Jewish mothers in such film and television productions as *The Heartbreak Kid*, *Hester Street*, and *The Diary of Anne Frank*; in the recent film *Keeping Up with the Steins*, Roberts played a sympathetic Jewish grandmother. Her portrait of a loving but extremely overbearing mother in *Raymond* transfers some of the typical traits associated with Jewish mothers to a related, but more neutrally presented, ethnic group.

62. Ephron has said that her mother was "basically the only working mother in Beverly Hills"; Peter Biskin, "The World According to Nora," *Premiere*, March 1992, 23.

63. Robert Ebert, review of *The Mirror Has Two Faces*, *Chicago Sun-Times*, Nov. 15, 1996.

64. Thanks to Rachel Werner for her helpful comments.

65. For a different view, see Gail Dines, "Invisible in Hollywood: Jewish Women," *Boston Globe*, Jan. 16, 2006.

66. In *Keeping the Faith* (2000), another romantic comedy that presents a Jewish son in a relationship with a Gentile woman, the Jewish mother, played by Anne Bancroft, initially rejects her rabbi son's romantic choice but realizes her mistake after suffering a stroke. "It's hard to see your son as a man," she says.

Chapter 8

1. Janet Burstein, "Restorying Jewish Mothers," in Andrea O'Reilly and Sharon Abbey, *Mothers and Daughters: Connection, Empowerment and Transformation* (Lanham, Md.: Rowman and Littlefield, 2000), 39, 41. Also see Janet Burstein, *Writing Mothers, Writing Daughters: Tracing the Maternal in Stories by American Jewish Women* (Urbana: University of Illinois Press, 1996), and Burstein, *Telling the Little Secrets: American Jewish Writing since the 1980s* (Madison: University of Wisconsin Press, 2006).

2. Wendy Wasserstein, *Making Trouble*, JWA Productions, 2006. On Wasserstein's relationship to her own mother, see "My Mother, Then and Now," in *Bachelor Girls* (New York: Vintage, 1991), 17–22.

3. Helen Epstein, *Children of the Holocaust: Conservations with Sons and Daughters of Survivors* (New York: Penguin, 1979), 9–14, 208, 217, 220.

4. Helen Epstein, *Where She Came From: A Daughter's Search for Her Mother's History* (New York: Plume, 1997), 10.

5. Ibid., 11.

6. Vivian Gornick, *Fierce Attachments: A Memoir* (New York: Simon and Schuster, 1987); Kim Chernin, *In My Mother's House: A Daughter's Story* (1983; repr. New York: Harper-Collins, 1994).

7. Melvin Jules Bukiet, ed., *Nothing Makes You Free: Writings by Descendants of Jewish Holocaust Survivors* (New York: Norton, 2002), 14.

8. Eva Hoffman, *After Such Knowledge: Memory, History, and the Legacy of the Holocaust* (New York: Public Affairs, 2004), 6.

9. Fern Schumer Chapman, *Motherland Beyond the Holocaust: A Mother-Daughter Journey to Reclaim the Past* (New York: Viking Penguin, 2000; New York: Penguin Paperback, 2001), 7. Citation is from the 2001 edition.

10. Cited in Dinitia Smith, "An Artistic Quest: For the Holocaust 'Second Generation,'" *New York Times*, Dec. 23, 1997.

11. Epstein, *Children of the Holocaust*, 18.

12. Hoffman, *After Such Knowledge*, 62.

13. For an insightful analysis of Epstein's journey in *Where She Came From*, see Burstein, *Telling the Little Secrets*, 45–46.

14. Chapman, *Motherland*, 31, 20.

15. Ibid., 20, 21, 147.

16. Ibid., 186. Also see Irena Klepfisz, "Bashert," in *A Few Words in the Mother Tongue: Poems Selected and New* (Portland, Ore.: Eighth Mountain Press, 1990).

17. New York Public Library, "Letters to Sala: A Young Woman's Life in Nazi Labor Camps"; Ann Kirschner, *Sala's Gift: My Mother's Holocaust Story* (New York: Free Press, 2006); author's interview with Ann Kirschner, April 30, 2006; Gail Beckerman, "Fifty Years Later, a World of Holocaust Memories is Exposed," *Jerusalem Post*, April 13, 2006.

18. Gerda Lerner, *Fireweed: A Political Autobiography* (Philadelphia: Temple University Press, 2002), 146; author's interview with Gerda Lerner, March 31, 2004.

19. Lerner, *Fireweed*, 145.

20. Gerda Lerner, "Ili Kronstein: An Artist's Life," in *Die Welt der Ili Kronstein/The World of Ili Kronstein, Werke, 1938–1943*, edited by Werner Hanak, on behalf of the Jewish Museum of Vienna (Vienna: Jewish Museum of Vienna, 2000). For studies of the female Holocaust experience in fiction, see S. Lillian Kremer, *Women's Holocaust Writing: Memory and Imagination* (Lincoln: University of Nebraska Press, 2001) and Sara B. Horowitz, "Women in Holocaust Literature," in Dalia Offer and Lenore J. Weitzman, *Women in the Holocaust* (New Haven: Yale University Press, 1998), 364–377.

21. Chernin, *In My Mother's House*, 12.

22. Ibid.

23. Gornick, *Fierce Attachments*, 193, 196.

24. Chernin, *In My Mother's House*, 16.

25. Ibid., 184.

26. Janet Burstein, "Restorying Jewish Mothers," 37–45, and Burstein, *Writing Mothers, Writing Daughters*, 165, 168–174; Chernin, *In My Mother's House*, 291.

27. Gornick, *Fierce Attachments*, 17, 24.

28. Ibid., 6, 193, 198–200, 204.

29. Vivian Gornick, "A Memoirist Defends Her Words," Aug. 12, 2003, http://dir.salon.com/story/books/feature/2003/08/12/memoir_writing/index.html.

30. Kim Chernin, "In the House of the Flame Bearers," *TIKKUN* 2, no. 3 (Aug. 1987): 55.

31. Ibid., 58.

32. Letty Cottin Pogrebin, *Deborah, Golda, and Me: Being Female and Jewish in America* (New York: Crown, 1991), 150.

33. Ibid., 27.

34. Joy Horowitz, *Tessie and Pearlie: A Granddaughter's Story* (New York: Scribner's, 1996), 260.

35. Ibid., 253, 254.

36. Ibid., 257.

37. Ibid., 272.

38. Ibid., 260.

39. Elizabeth Ehrlich, *Miriam's Kitchen: A Memoir* (New York: Viking, 1997), xi, xii.

40. Ibid., 5.

41. Ibid., xii.

42. Ibid.

43. Ibid., xii–xiii.

44. E. M. Broner, *Her Mothers* (New York: Holt, Rinehart and Winston, 1975; Bloomington: Indiana University Press, 1985), 63, 125, 164–165, 168. Citations are to the 1985 edition.

45. Ibid., 116; interview with the author, Sept. 21, 2000. Broner's short story collection, *Ghost Stories* (New York: Global City Press, 1995), explains the relationship between a woman and her dying mother. Also see Broner, "The Book of Genesis and Its Relativity in Our Life Today," E. M. Broner Papers, Robert D. Farber University Archives and Special Collections Department, Brandeis University.

46. A sample of this writing, including short stories, poems, and essays, appeared in Faye Moskowitz's 1994 anthology, *Her Face in the Mirror: Jewish Women on Mothers and Daughters* (Boston: Beacon Press, 1994).

47. Andrew Furman, "Anne Roiphe's Ambivalence: A Jewish Feminist Looks at Israel," *MELUS* 21, no. 2 (Summer 1996): 137. Furman relates that the *Ms.* reviewer labeled *Lovingkindness* a "feminist nightmare." Anne Roiphe, *Lovingkindness* (New York: Summit, 1987).

48. Allegra Goodman, *Kaaterskill Falls* (New York: Dial Press, 1998); see Ranen Omer-Sherman "Tradition and Desire in Allegra Goodman's Kaaterskill Falls," *MELUS* 29 (Summer 2004): 273–274, 285. For fiction about contemporary Orthodox mothers and daughters, also see Tova Mirvis, *The Outside World* (New York: Alfred A. Knopf, 2004); Mirvis, *The Ladies' Auxiliary* (New York: Norton, 1999); and Pearl Abraham, *The Romance Reader* (New York: Riverhead, 1995). Acknowledging her Sephardic roots taught Gloria Kirchheimer "what it is to have a maternal language"; Kirchheimer, "Food for Love," in Melanie Kaye/Kantrowitz and Irena Klepfisz, *The Tribe of Dina: A Jewish Women's Anthology* (Montpelier, Vt.: Sinister Wisdom Books, 1986), 59–63, originally published in *Schmate* (Dec. 1983); and Kirchheimer *Goodbye, Evil Eye: Stories* (New York: Holmes and Meier, 2000).

49. Rebecca Goldstein, *Mazel* (New York: Viking, 1995), 334.

50. Rosellen Brown, *Half a Heart* (New York: Farrar, Straus and Giroux, 2000); Marge Piercy, *Three Women* (New York: William Morrow, 1999); Letty Cottin Pogrebin, *Three Daughters* (New York: Farrar, Straus and Giroux, 2002), 240, 340.

51. Erica Jong, "My Mother, My Daughter, and Me," in Judith Shapiro, ed., *Mothers through the Eyes of Women Writers* (Berkeley, Calif.: Conari Press, 1998), 148–149. Also see Molly Jong-Fast, "Tell Me about Your Mother," in Ruth Andrew Ellenson, ed., *The Modern Jewish Girl's Guide to Guilt*, (New York: Dutton, 2005), 25.

52. Burstein, *Telling the Little Secrets*, 87, 153.

53. Gerda Lerner, *The Majority Finds Its Past* (New York: Oxford University Press, 1975).

54. Sydney Stahl Weinberg, *The World of Our Mothers: The Lives of Jewish Immigrant Women* (New York: Schocken, 1988), 144–148.

55. Susan Glenn, *Daughters of the Shtetl: Life and Labor in the Immigrant Generation* (New York: Cornell University Press, 1990), 239–240, 242, 208.

56. Ruth Jacknow Markowitz, *My Daughter, the Teacher: Jewish Teachers in the New York City Schools* (New Brunswick, N.J.: Rutgers University Press, 1993), 12–13.

57. Judith Plaskow, *Standing Again at Sinai: Judaism from a Feminist Perspective* (New York: HarperCollins, 1991), 43, 9, 27.

58. These books include Ellen Frankel, *The Five Books of Miriam: A Woman's Commentary on the Torah* (Philadelphia: Jewish Publication Society, 1996); Norma Rosen, *Biblical Women Unbound: Counter-Tales* (Philadelphia: Jewish Publication Society, 1996); Naomi Mara Hyman, *Biblical Women in the Midrash: A Sourcebook* (Northvale, N.J.: Jason Aronson, 1997); Rachel Adler, *Engendering Judaism: An Inclusive Theology and Ethics* (Philadelphia: Jewish Publication Society, 1998); E. M. Broner, *Bringing Home the Light: A Jewish Woman's Handbook of Rituals* (San Francisco: Council Oak Books, 1999); Elyse Goldstein, *The Women's Torah Commentary: New Insights from Women Rabbis on the Fifty-Four Weekly Torah Portions* (Woodstock, Vt.: Jewish Lights Publishing, 2000).

59. Sylvia Barak Fishman, *Follow My Footprints: Changing Images of Women in American Jewish Fiction* (Hanover, N.H.: University Press of New England, 1992), 3.

60. Anita Diamant, *The Red Tent* (New York: A Wyatt Book for St. Martin's Press, 1997).

61. Jeanette Friedman, "Gail Reimer, Preserving History," *Lifestyles*, vol. 30, no. 178 (pre-Spring 2002), 34.

62. Ibid.

63. Ibid.

64. Ibid. Henrietta Szold, Bella Abzug, and E. M. Broner are among the many Jewish women who described the deprivation they felt because they could not say kaddish for loved ones.

65. Judith A. Kates and Gail Twersky Reimer, *Reading Ruth: Contemporary Women Reclaim a Sacred Story* (New York: Ballantine, 1994).

66. Gail Twersky Reimer and Judith A. Kates, *Beginning Anew: A Woman's Companion to the High Holy Days* (New York: Simon and Schuster, 1997).

67. For information about the Jewish Women's Archive, see jwa.org.

68. Art Spiegelman, *Maus: A Survivor's Tale: My Father Bleeds History* (New York: Pantheon Books, 1991); also see, for example, Clancy Sigal, *A Woman of Uncertain Character: The Amorous and Radical Adventures of My Mother Jennie (Who Always Wanted to Be a Respectable Jewish Mom) by Her Bastard Son* (New York: Carroll and Graf, 2006); Thomas Cottle, *When the Music Stopped: Discovering My Mother* (Albany, N.Y.: State University of New York Press, 2004).

Chapter 9

1. Sara Ruddick, *Maternal Thinking: Toward a Politic of Peace* (New York: Ballantine, 1989), 40, cited in Andrea O'Reilly and Sharon Abbey, eds., *Mothers and Daughters: Connection, Empowerment, and Transformation* (Lanham, Md.: Rowman and Littlefield, 2000), 4–5.

2. This research used the World of Our Mothers Study of Jewish and Italian Immigrant Women data set (made accessible in 2001, original paper records and audiotapes). These data were collected by Rose Laub Coser and are available through the Henry A. Murray Research Archive of the Institute for Quantitative Social Science at Harvard University, Cambridge,

Massachusetts (producer and distributor). All quotations are from the Jewish sample of this study. The study's lengthy interview schedule included sections on immigration, marriage, language, home life, food, children, family size and sexuality, home economy, entrepreneurship, work outside the home, health, education, welfare, religion, politics, philanthropy, and popular culture. The interviewers included sociologists Rose Coser, Kath Dahlman, and Gladys Rothbell and historian Laura Anker.

3. Joyce Antler, 2003 Jewish Mothers Survey, Brandeis University National Women's Committee, Broward County, Florida. I am grateful to Amy Sales, Jacqueline Boone James, and Janet Zollinger Giele for their assistance in designing this survey.

4. There are few studies that connect parental attitudes and culture with Jewish children's achievements. For a debate about Jewish mothers' work patterns and possible effect on children's education, see Barry R. Chiswick, "Labor Supply and Investment in Child Quality: A Study of Jewish and Non-Jewish Women," *Review of Economics and Statistics* 68, no. 4 (Nov. 1986): 700–703; Byron G. Spencer, "Labor Supply and Investment in Child Quality: A Study of Jewish and Non-Jewish Women: A Comment," *Review of Economics and Statistics* 74, no. 4 (Nov. 1992): 721–725; and Chiswick's "Reply," in *Review of Economics and Statistics* 74, no. 4 (Nov. 1992): 726–727.

5. Rose Laub Coser, Laura S. Anker, and Andrew J. Perrin, *Women of Courage: Jewish and Italian Immigrant Women in New York* (Westport, Conn.: Greenwood Press, 1999), 10. Coser wrote the four chapters on immigrant women and families (Andrew Perrin edited them after her death); the concluding three chapters on women and work were written by Laura Anker.

6. Coser, World of Our Mothers Study, Henry A. Murray Research Archive.

7. Jayne K. Guberman, ed., *In Our Own Voices: A Guide to Conducting Life History Interviews with American Jewish Women* (Brookline, Mass.: Jewish Women's Archive, 2005).

8. Founded in 1948, the same year as Brandeis University, the Brandeis University National Women's Committee (BUNWC) is a volunteer organization that provides financial support for Brandeis and its libraries. With eighty-three chapters and some forty-two thousand members nationwide, it is the largest friends-of-a-library group in the world. Key features include study group courses created for members by Brandeis faculty and annual national faculty lecture tours to participating chapters.

9. For a sense of how mothering experiences affected self-evaluations in later life, see Jacquelyn Boone James and Nicole Zarrett, "Ego Identity in the Lives of Older Women," unpublished paper based on interviews with the original Coser respondents, Henry A. Murray Research Center, Radcliffe Institute, 1999.

10. Coser, Anker, and Perrin, *Women of Courage*, 8.

11. Ibid., 8.

12. Rose Coser, "Mother Love: Myth and Reality," *Contemporary Sociology* 11, no. 6 (Nov. 1982): 694–696. Thanks to Eugene Sheppard for this reference.

13. Coser, Anker, and Perrin, *Women of Courage*, 9.

14. Ibid., 8.

15. Quotations without endnote references are taken from coded interview and survey responses in Coser, World of Our Mothers Study, Henry A. Murray Research Archive.

16. Coser, Anker, and Perrin, *Women of Courage*, 96, 111, 129.

17. Ibid., 43.

18. Ibid.

19. While there were many similarities between the Jewish and Italian mothers in the study, several important differences were cited: Jews maintained "centrifugal" family structures, adopting to new surroundings by "orienting out of the family, aiming to assimilate to

mainstream culture"; Italians were more "centripetal," forming more insular groups and attempting to maintain a more thoroughly Italian culture (ibid., 4, 40, 43, 46).

20. For selected interview material from the *Weaving Women's Words* interviews, see "Baltimore Stories" and "Seattle Stories," *Weaving Women's Words*, jwa.org, and Guberman, *In Our Own Voices*.

21. Twenty-nine women, almost half of the sample, said that they were raised in Orthodox families. Twelve had left Orthodoxy as adults, but eleven of these women remained affiliated to some synagogue. Twelve women were raised Reform and five unaffiliated. The remaining three were raised in Conservative synagogues. Only one woman not raised Orthodox became Orthodox as an adult.

22. Dorothy Muscatel, *Weaving Women's Words*, "Seattle Stories."

23. Hanna Weinberg, *Weaving Women's Words*, "Baltimore Stories."

24. Elsie Miller Legum, Bernice Rind, *Weaving Women's Words*, "Baltimore Stories."

25. Shirley G. Bridge, *Weaving Women's Words*, "Seattle Stories."

26. Frieda Sondland, Tillie De Leon, *Weaving Women's Words*, "Seattle Stories."

27. Louise Azoze, *Weaving Women's Words*, "Seattle Stories."

28. Elsie Miller Legum, *Weaving Women's Words*, "Baltimore Stories"; Jane Shapiro, Amelie Rothchild, *Weaving Women's Words*, "Seattle Stories."

29. Clementine Kaufman, Laura Zabin, *Weaving Women's Words*, "Baltimore Stories."

30. Louise Azoze, *Weaving Women's Words*, "Seattle Stories."

31. All data is from Antler, 2003 Jewish Mothers Survey.

32. On the role of parents as educators, see Seymour Sarason, *And What do You Mean by Learning?* (Portsmouth, N.H.: Heinemann, 2004), 43, 53.

Chapter 10

1. *Fresh Air*, Sept. 27, 2005, transcript of Terry Gross interview with Philip Roth.

2. On joke cycles as cultural signals, see Joseph Boskin, *Rebellious Laughter: People's Humor in American Culture* (Syracuse, N.Y.: Syracuse University Press, 1997), 202.

3. Karla Goldman, "Preserve the Shards of the Shattered Glass Ceiling," *Forward*, July 7, 2006; Penny Leifer, "Who Are the Women Who Changed the Movement?" *Women's League Outlook Magazine*, www.wlcj.org/outlook_articles/women_change_movement.html, July 20, 2006; Mindy Avra Portnoy, *Ima on the Bima: My Mommy Is a Rabbi* (Rockville, Md.: Kar-Ben Copies, 1986).

4. Rabbi Judy Chessin, "Celebrate Mother's Day the Jewish Way," *Jewish Federation of Greater Dayton News*, May 2006 (www.jewishdayton.org); italics added.

5. Steve Kroft, "The Echo Boomers," cbsnews.com, Dec. 26, 2004, www.cbsnews.com /stories/2004/10/01/60minutes/printable646890.shtml.

6. Sharon Hays, *The Cultural Contradictions of Motherhood* (New Haven: Yale University Press, 1996), x, 10; also see Susan J. Douglas and Meredith W. Michaels, *The Mommy Myth: The Idealization of Motherhood and How it Has Undermined Women* (New York: Free Press, 2004), and Janna Malamud Smith, *A Potent Spell: Mother Love and the Power of Fear* (Boston: Houghton Mifflin, 2003).

7. See Peter N. Stearns, *Anxious Parents: A History of Modern Childrearing in America* (New York: New York University Press, 2003), and Ann Hulbert, *Raising America: Experts, Parents and a Century of Advice about Children* (New York: Alfred Knopf, 2003).

8. Dr. Mel Levine of the University of North Carolina at Chapel Hill, cited in Kroft, "The Echo Boomers"; Steven Mintz, "How We All Became Jewish Mothers," *National Post*

(Canada), Feb. 17, 2006, http://listserv.uh.edu/cgi-bin/wa?A2=ind0602&L=ccf&T=0&P =798 (accessed Nov. 29, 2005).

9. Cited in David Hochman, "Mommy (and Me)," *New York Times*, Jan. 30, 2005.

10. Emily Bazelon, "So the Torah Is a Parenting Guide?" *New York Times Sunday Magazine*, Oct. 1, 2006, 64.

11. www.greatertalent.com/biography.php?id=229; Aron Hirt-Manheimer, "'The Present Parent': A Conversation with Dr. Wendy Mogel about What Parents Can Do to Truly Be There for Their Children," *Reform Judaism* (Summer 2004): 49–50, 71; Wendy Mogel, *The Blessings of a Skinned Knee: Using Jewish Teachings to Raise Self-Reliant Children* (New York: Penguin Books, 2001), 34–35; Bazelon, "So the Torah Is a Parenting Guide?" 65.

12. Mogel, *The Blessings of a Skinned Knee*, 20–34; Bazelon, "So the Torah Is a Parenting Guide?"

13. Egon Mayer, Barry Kosmin, and Ariela Keysar, American Jewish Identity Survey, 2001, Center for Jewish Studies, Graduate Center of the City University of New York.

14. Chaim I. Waxman, *Jewish Baby Boomers: A Communal Perspective* (Albany: State University of New York Press, 2001), 153, 106.

15. Diane Tobin, Gary A. Tobin, and Scott Rubin, *In Every Tongue: The Racial and Ethnic Diversity of the Jewish People* (San Francisco: Institute for Jewish and Community Research, 2005), 21–23. Danielle Hass, "Opening Up the Jewish Gene Pool," *Jerusalem Report*, Sept. 6, 2004, 25, gives a lower estimate, suggesting that 10 percent of American Jewry today may be nonwhite, compared to slightly more than 5 percent in 1990. Also see Ira Rifkin, "Out of Egypt," *Jerusalem Report*, Jan. 23, 2006, 28–29.

16. Patricia Lin, "Patricia Yu Chava Esther Lin Bat Avraham," *Reform Judaism*, Spring 2004, 53–56, 62. Also see Merri Rosenberg, "Jewish Moms, Chinese Daughters," *Lilith*, Spring 2006, 24–27, 33.

17. Angela Warnick Buchdahl, "Kimchee on the Seder Plate," *Reform Judaism*, Spring 2004, 63.

18. Aron Hirt-Manheimer, "Focus: Jewish Diversity. Signs," *Reform Judaism*, Spring 2004, 63–64, 66.

19. Conversation with Jamaica Kincaid, Brandeis University, Oct. 5, 2006.

20. Jane Lazarre, *Beyond the Whiteness of Whiteness: Memoir of a White Mother of Black Sons* (Durham, N.C.: Duke University Press, 1996), 66–70.

21. Katya Gibel Azoulay, *Black, Jewish, and Interracial: It's Not the Color of Your Skin, but the Race of Your Kin, and Other Myths of Identity* (Durham, N.C.: Duke University Press, 1997) 113, 153–155. Also see Rebecca Walker, *Black, White and Jewish: Autobiography of a Shifting Self* (New York: Riverhead Books, 2001).

22. James McBride, *The Color of Water: A Black Man's Tribute to His White Mother* (New York: Riverhead Books, 1997), 87, 92.

23. Keren R. McGinity, "Still Jewish: A History of Women and Intermarriage in America," Ph.D. dissertation, Brown University, 2005. On contemporary intermarriage, see also Sylvia Barack Fishman, *Double or Nothing: Jewish Families and Mixed Marriage* (Hanover, N.H.: University of New England Press, 2004), 85–87, 70.

24. McGinity, "Still Jewish," 266, 270; Laurie Gwen Shapiro, "Oy Christmas Tree, Oy Christmas Tree," in Ruth Andrew Ellenson, ed., *The Modern Jewish Girl's Guide to Guilt* (New York: Dutton, 2005), 228.

25. McGinity, "Still Jewish," 290.

26. Ibid., 291, 308.

27. Hass, "Opening Up the Jewish Gene Pool," 25.

28. See Melissa Fay Greene, "The Orphan Ranger," *The New Yorker*, July 17, 2002,

38–45; "Healing Hands," *People*, November 12, 2001, 131–132, 134. On adoption, also see Barbara Katz Rothman, *Weaving a Family: Untangling Race and Adoption* (Boston: Beacon Press, 2005); and Marla Brettschneider, "All Points Bulleting: Jewish Dykes Adopting Children," in David Shneer and Caryn Aviv, *Queer Jews* (New York: Routledge, 2002), 239.

29. Author's interview with Dr. Jane Aronson, New York City, July 20, 2003.

30. See Jan Balakian, "Wendy Wasserstein," in Paula E. Hyman and Deborah Dash Moore, eds., *Jewish Women in America: An Historical Encyclopedia*, vol. 2, (New York: Routledge, 1997), 1456–1459. In Wasserstein's *Heidi Chronicles*, art historian Heidi Holland adopts a daughter as a single parent, and she is hopeful that her daughter will grow up to fulfill the goals of the feminist movement.

31. Naomi Pfefferman, "Being a Woman in Wasserstein's World," *The Jewish Journal of Greater Los Angeles*, Sept. 19, 2003, http://www.jewishjournal.com/home/searchview.php?id =11053 (accessed June 30, 2004).

32. Ibid.

33. Ibid.

34. Author's interview with Kate Bornstein, Oct. 6, 2006; Kate Bornstein, "Her Son/Daughter: A Mother's Funeral, A Familiar Stranger Makes an Appearance," *New York Times Sunday Magazine*, Feb. 7, 1997.

35. Jacob Berkman, "Chicken Soup or Kimchi?" *New Jersey Jewish Standard*, May 11, 2006.

36. See John Lahr, "Screwballs and Oddballs," *The New Yorker*, April 5, 2004, 78.

37. Ibid.

38. Kenneth Jones, "Don't Put Your Mother on the Stage: Playwright's 'Mom' Disrupts New Play," *Playbill*, Mar. 30, 2004; www.playbill.com/features/article/85244.html.

39. Philip Roth, *The Plot Against America* (Boston: Houghton Mifflin, 2004), 64.

40. Ibid., 191.

41. Ibid., 340.

42. Ibid., 40. See Philip Roth, *Patrimony : A True Story* (New York: Simon and Schuster, 1991), 36–38.

43. Roth, *The Plot Against America*, 190.

44. Ibid., 193–194.

45. Ibid., 328.

46. Ibid., 333.

47. Ibid., 220.

48. Ibid., 256.

49. Ibid., 257.

50. Cited by Martin Denton, Review of *700 Sundays*, nytheatre.com review, Dec. 8, 2004, http://www.nytheatre.com/nytheatre/archweb/arch2005_01.htm#5 (accessed Nov. 23, 2006). Also see Matthew Murray's review of the show in *Talking Broadway's "Broadway Reviews,"* Dec. 5, 2004.

51. Soriya Daniels, "Billy Crystal Pens Book," http://www.jewishaz.com/jewishnews/040625/billy.shtml; Paul Fischer, "Cranky Critic Star Talk," http://www.crankycritic.com/qa/pf_articles/billycrystal.html.

52. *So Laugh a Little*, Jewish Women's Archive DVD, Copacabana, New York City, March 14, 2005.

53. Amy Borkowsky, *Amy's Answering Machine: Messages from Mom* (New York: Pocket Books–Simon and Schuster, 2001), 7–8, 17, 33, 42.

54. Ibid., 8–9.

55. Lori Gottlieb describes a similar caricature: Having spent her entire life trying to

detach from her mother whom she describes as a PMD, a "Person of Mass Destruction," Gottlieb buys a phone with caller ID to screen out her mother's constant calls. But even caller ID proves futile when faced with this "loving but lethal mother" who was not "mean-spirited. She's just, well, Jewish. Which means she loves me more than life itself, but nothing I do is good enough, even though I'm perfect"; see Gottlieb, "My Private Caller," in Ellenson, *The Modern Jewish Girl's Guide to Guilt,* 102, 106, 109.

56. Gold, *So Laugh a Little.* The autobiography joke is from Judy Brown, *She's So Funny* (Kansas City, Mo.: Andrews McMeel, 2004), 99.

57. Gold, *So Laugh a Little.*

58. Tripp Whetsell, "Mom-Zilla," *New York Post,* Oct. 8, 2006.

59. Author's interview with Judy Gold, April 16, 2006.

60. Dan Pine, "Good as Gold: Popular Comic Headlines Her Second Kung Pao Kosher Gig," http://www.jewishf.com/, Dec. 3, 2004 (accessed July 19, 2005; website no longer available).

61. Ron Kaplan, "Good as Gold: New Jersey Funny Lady Returns to Her Roots," *New Jersey Jewish News,* May 26, 2005, 26.

62. Winnie McCroy, "A Little Bit Meshugah: Judy Gold Gets Serious about Jewish Motherhood," *Cabaret,* Feb. 2–8, 2006.

63. Marjorie Ingall, "The East Village Mamele: 'Funny Ladies,'" *Forward,* March 25, 2005. Debra Nussbaum Cohen, writing in *Jewish Women Magazine* ("Funny Girls," Spring 2004), takes it a step further: "[Y]ou gotta love Gold for saying the things that we all think, but dare not utter, about our own mothers" (16; www.jwmag.org/articles/10Spring04/p16.asp). Gold's show, *25 Questions for a Jewish Mother,* was nominated for a Drama Desk Award in 2006 for solo performance. A book based on the show, co-authored by Kate Moira Ryan, is dorthcoming from Hyperion in 2007.

64. See, for example, Boskin, *Rebellious Laughter,* 44. Also see Sarah Blacher Cohen, ed., *Jewish Wry: Essays on Jewish Humor* (Detroit: Wayne State University Press, 1987); Nancy Walker, "Toward Solidarity: Women's Humor and Group Identity," in June Sochen, ed., *Women's Comic Visions* (Detroit: Wayne State University Press, 1991), 58.

65. See Joanne R. Gilbert, *Performing Marginality: Humor, Gender, and Cultural Critique* (Detroit: Wayne State University Press, 2004), 58.

66. Cohen, "Funny Girls," 16.

67. Frances Gray, *Women and Laughter* (Charlottesville: University Press of Virginia, 1994), 135–136.

68. A. Greenberg (1972), cited by Mahadev Apte, *Humor and Laughter* (Ithaca, N.Y.: Cornell University Press, 1985), 149.

69. Wendy Liebman's e-mail communication to author, Aug. 11, 2005.

70. Ronnie Cohen, "Chef-Turned-Comic Will Dish Up Laughs at Kung Pao," www.jweekly.com/oldjewishsf/www/bko21213/et36b.shtml.

71. Dana Goodyear, "Quiet Depravity: The Demure Outrages of a Standup Comic," *New Yorker,* Oct. 24, 2005, 51.

72. Michael Rechtshaffen, "Sarah Silverman: Jesus is Magic," *The Hollywood Reporter.com,* Nov. 11, 2005, www.hollywoodreporter.com/hr/search/article_display.jsp?vnu_content_id=1001477918. Also see J. Hoberman, "Sarah Silverman: 'Jesus Is Magic,'" *Village Voice,* Nov. 8, 2005.

73. Sarah Silverman, cited in Goodyear, "Quiet Depravity," 53.

74. *Jimmy Kimmel Show,* Nov. 10, 2005.

75. Goodyear, "Quiet Depravity," 52.

76. A. O. Scott, "A Comic in Search of the Discomfort Zone," *New York Times,* Nov. 11, 2005.

77. Cited in Henry Jenkins, "Awkward Conversations about Uncomfortable Laughter," www.flowtv.org, vol. 3, no. 5, http://jot.communication.utexas.edu/flow/?jot=view&id=1239.

78. Ibid. Shulman's oldest sister, Susan, a rabbi, is the mother of four children, one of them adopted from Ethiopia.

79. See Perri Klass and Sheila Solomon Klass, *Every Mother Is a Daughter: The Never-Ending Quest for Success, Inner Peace, and a Really Clean Kitchen (Recipes and Knitting Patterns Included)* (New York: Ballantine Books, 2006), and Deborah Tannen, *You're Wearing That? Understanding Mothers and Daughters in Conversation* (New York: Random House, 2006).

ARCHIVAL SOURCES

American Jewish Archives, Cincinnati, Ohio, Sophie Tucker Papers

American Jewish Historical Society, New York, Papers of the Union of Orthodox Jewish Congregations of America

Robert D. Farber University Archives & Special Collections Department, Brandeis University, Waltham, Massachusetts, E.M. Broner Papers

Harvard University Institute for Quantitative Social Science, Henry A. Murray Research Archive, Rose Laub Coser Papers

Jewish Museum, New York, National Jewish Archive of Broadcasting

Jewish Women's Archive, Brookline, Massachusetts, Weaving Women's Words Oral History Project

Library of Congress, Manuscript Division, Washington, D.C., Margaret Mead Papers, Sidonie and Benjamin Gruenberg Papers

Museum of Television and Radio, New York and Los Angeles, Audio, Films/Videos/Moving Image Collections

National Center for Jewish Film, Brandeis University, Rutenberg and Everett Yiddish Film Library

New York Public Library of the Performing Arts, Billy Rose Theater Collection, Clifford Odets Papers

Schlesinger Library, Radcliffe Institute, Harvard University, Jennie Loitman Barron Papers

Syracuse University, Special Collections Research Center, Gertrude Berg Papers

UCLA Film & Television Archive, Los Angeles, California, Television and Motion Picture Collections.

INDEX